CW00708446

SL

LOW

S

PACE

SLOW SPACE

Edited by Michael Bell and Sze Tsung Leong

The Monacelli Press

First published in the United States of America in 1998 by
The Monacelli Press, Inc.
10 East 92nd Street, New York, New York 10128.

Copyright © 1998 The Monacelli Press, Inc., and The Future Project

All rights reserved under International and Pan-American Copyright
Conventions. No part of this book may be reproduced or utilized in
any form or by any means, electronic or mechanical, including pho-
tocopying, recording, or by any information storage and retrieval
system, without permission in writing from the publisher. Inquiries
should be sent to The Monacelli Press, Inc.

Library of Congress Cataloging-in-Publication Data
Slow space / edited by Michael Bell and Sze Tsung Leong.
   p. cm.
Includes bibliographical references.
ISBN 1-885254-73-3
1. Cities and towns. 2. Sociology, Urban. I. Bell, Michael (Michael J.).
II. Leong, Sze Tsung.
HT151.S49 1998
307.76—dc21   98-4583

Printed and bound in Singapore

The Future Project board: Michael Bell, Sze Tsung Leong, and
Stanley Saitowitz
Design: Sze Tsung Leong
Cover design: Rebeca Méndez

We gratefully acknowledge the generous support of the Graham
Foundation for Advanced Studies in the Fine Arts and the LEF
Foundation.

Institutional support: Rice University School of Architecture and the
Department of Architecture, University of California at Berkeley.

Special thanks: Andrea E. Monfried, Steven Sears, Jen Bilik, Lars
Lerup, Sanford Kwinter, Chui Hua Chung, Marina Drummer, Byron
Kuth, Norman Bryson, Roger Montgomery, Gary Brown, Ina Evans,
Sheila Dickie, Rain Simar, Doris Anderson, Elaine Sebring, Mason
Wickham, Ruben Suare, David Marini, Peony Quan, and Kelly Ishida.

That the configuration of the contemporary city has transcended the realm of idealized geometry is by now an obvious fact—yet surprisingly, one largely unheeded by an architectural and urban practice which still clings to the removed, visual techniques of formal composition. Far from the canonical and "official" urban models that still grip most of the discipline's imagination, cities such as Houston, characterized simultaneously by the fluid instabilities of accelerated and self-regulating economies and by the inertia of their material residue, have become the paradigm of late-twentieth-century urbanism. These cities are created by default rather than intention, left in the wake of increasingly shifting and invisible forces such as demographic segmentation, marketing and consumer analysis, or the uncompromising movements of post–World War II capital. What remains is an increasingly unfamiliar urban landscape, one that is dissipated, entropic, and saturated with the effluent detritus of amorphous spaces.

Slow Space was formed in and by these spaces—the vacancies that, by having become the unintended archetype of contemporary urbanism, coerce an evolution of conventional visuality and inhabitation. The comprehension of an urban condition rendered through processes—machinic, regulatory, managerial— thus resides in the temporal. Alongside a spectrum of coexisting yet often incommensurate urban dimensions—the near instantaneity of financial transactions; the clandestine deployment of power; the daily cycles of events, occupation, and use; the periodic shifts in urban densities; the anomie of the residual no-man's-land—are a set of parallel velocities: the slow alchemies of the architectural; the even slower movement of matter, now as permeated by economics and finance as by finite mechanics; and the viscous emergence of latent histories as sites to be reinhabited. These durations, imbricated with the variable flows of the metropolis, form the medium for the twenty-three essays and projects that make up *Slow Space*. This book represents an attempt to make time material, and an effort to find an architecture and a practice that engages and catalytically reconfigures the spaces and processes of the contemporary city.

CONTENTS

347 Years: Slow Space Michael Bell and Sze Tsung Leong 14

Doublespace Lars Lerup 26

Still Architecture Álvaro Siza with text by Peter Testa 44

Quasi-Infinities and the Waning of Space Robert Smithson 70

Having Heard Mathematics: The Topologies of Boxing Michael Bell 78

Community Property: Enter the Architect, or, The Politics of Form Dana Cuff 120

Unlawful Desire Durham Crout 146

The Unconstructed Subject of the Contemporary City Albert Pope 160

Readings of the Attenuated Landscape Sze Tsung Leong 186

Knee Play Mark Wamble 220

Croton Aqueduct Study RAAUm group 236

Artists' Space Installation Greg Lynn / **The Parsing Eye** Mark Wamble 254

Gaining a Free Relation to Technology Hubert L. Dreyfus 272

We Play until Death Shuts the Door Elizabeth Burns Gamard 284

The Rapture Adi Shamir Zion 318

Hadrian's Villa Robert Mangurian and Mary-Ann Ray 334

Yuan Yung-Ho Chang 346

Mill Race Park Structures Stanley Saitowitz 360

Museum of Contemporary Art, Helsinki Steven Holl / **Over Dilation, Over Soul** Michael Bell 384

Latent Parallelepipeds Farès el-Dahdah 408

Burn Karen Bermann, Jeanine Centuori, and Julieanna Preston 426

Gestation Rebeca Méndez 436

Nothing but Flowers: Against Public Space Aaron Betsky 456

347 YEARS: SLOW SPACE

Michael Bell and Sze Tsung Leong

1993: Islands of Extreme Wealth. The latent topologies of contemporary urban configurations coalesced momentarily when, in a January 1993 interview, Noam Chomsky was asked whether he agreed with political economist Gar Alperovitz's characterization of America as "in for a long, painful era of unresolved economic decay." In reply, Chomsky suggests that first the terms need to be more precisely defined: "If we mean the geographical area of the United States, I'm sure that's right . . . there has been decline and there will continue to be decline." The United States, says Chomsky, is "developing characteristics of the third world."[1] Because American corporations are trading entities virtually unrelated to the cartography of national borders and have increasingly been since the close of World War II, however, Chomsky qualifies his prediction. In a global economy, "U.S. corporate share in production was probably increasing," though the distribution of profits was increasingly pooled in investors' hands. The current mode of economic globalization that is changing the shape of class structure and its relation to space in contemporary American—and world—cities, according to Chomsky, has been abetted by two major factors: the dominance of commerce as the principal force around which governmental authority is structured, and the dismantling of the Bretton Woods system, which was originally established in 1944 to create the International Monetary Fund (IMF) and regulate international currencies. In 1971, the Nixon administration dismantled portions of the Bretton Woods treaties that secured international trade to a gold standard. The resulting economic deregulation allowed international trade to occur against fluctuating currencies, exacerbating the already deterritorialized, or disconnected, relations between capital production and geography. The global dispersal of labor and industrial production, argues Chomsky, "extends the Third World model to industrialized countries. In the Third World, there's a two-tiered society—a sector of extreme wealth and privilege, and a sector of huge misery and despair."[2] This scenario is physically manifested as the juxtaposition of islands of concentrated wealth and distended, empty zones of urban blight and anomie, an incommensurate arrangement now typical in American cities. This condition offers at least two new dimensions for urban and architectural design: it suggests that the figure and ground of a contemporary city can be studied not as form, but instead as an economic entity that involves an increasingly stratified and immobile class structure; and it suggests that the liquidity of capital, having long ceased correlating itself to cartographic delineations, effectively unhinges a major portion of urban analysis from geometric description, architecture's historic dimension of authority.

1762: The Body Politic. The advanced form of the city and its role as civil protectorate—the body politic—was described in Jean-Jacques Rousseau's *The Social Contract* as that "public person, so formed by the union of all other persons." As it is commonly represented in America's political history, civic identity is imagined as an "act of association" in which each person places in common "his person, and all his power," an alliance represented by a social contract guided "under the supreme direction of the general will."[3] This alliance is premised on the recognition that human beings have reached some crisis with nature—a point at which a person's individual strength is insufficient to provide protection from the unpredictable and uncontrollable "attacks he is subject to"—and is imagined as an association "produced in

concurrence" as a means of preservation, through civic reassurances, against the forces of an uncertain and predatory nature. According to Rousseau, however, this association entails both sacrifice and the possibility of abuse: the rewards of the collective are accepted only because they override or compensate the "natural" freedoms the individual has sacrificed. Citizenship in this "indivisible" association further entails the person's acceptance of his or her role as a subject, in that he or she is subjected to the laws of the collective: "Whoever refuses to obey the general will, shall be compelled to do so by the whole body. This means nothing less than that he will be forced to be free."[4]

Seen as a mode of organization, a city thus formed is arithmetic in calculation—composed of an additive assemblage of persons—but, as proven by the historical development of economic and industrial technologies, exponential in effect.[5] Configured as such, the city fosters the general thesis that capitalist production garners authority in the surplus it creates while sustaining a collective that believes urban forces are arithmetically or geographically configured.

1651: War/Border Crossings. Slow Space situates itself on the agitated cusp of two intervals. It derives from the strife generated along the economically conflated border of the first and third worlds—the contemporary topology of a city as described by Noam Chomsky. It is the alienation of a city that has historically seen itself as a territorial entity of people and place even as it operates as an abstract and nongeographic economic entity. It is the ambient heat that accompanies thwarted attempts at border migrations from the third world to the first, and it is the catalytic reaction—the friction—of the first world's residence in the third. This habitation on the edge of borders and between doctrines challenges every traditional paradigm of urban form: material and matter no longer result from gravity or iconographic form but instead from capital, and subjects and space are no longer constructed from the subject-centered conceits of ocular perspective but instead from syntactic code. *Slow Space* is an attempt to *see* what is by now a dissipated, entropic city in which the physical and geometric reassurances of civil society have all but dissolved, an attempt to see the association and arrangement of modes of power that by now constitute surreptitiously predatory systems quite unlike the protective associations as imagined by Rousseau. As described in 1651 by Thomas Hobbes in *Leviathan,* war is not only the state of arms but those states that precede and follow actual battle; war is the strife on either side of confrontations, a disequilibrium in the requirements of the political, economic, and human domains. If we suscribe to Hobbes's definition of war as that state in which a greater "one" does not provide for the peaceful coexistence of the many, *Slow Space* describes war.[6] In our case, the greater "one" is not a theological deity, nor is it nature, but instead the city as a matrix of legal, economic, and technological powers.

1830: Instrumentalization. In the scenario of the contemporary city, such a war state is not progressive, but rather is protracted by an apparatus producing what Guy Debord terms a "static monotony" of artificial economic and cognitive relationships.[7] The apparatus of this protraction was inadvertently confirmed by German physiologist Johannes Müller's optical research, as articulated by Jonathan Crary in his 1988 essay "Modernizing Vision." According to Crary, Müller discovered that "the nerves of the different senses were physiologically distinct," a discovery that "asserted quite simply—and this is what marks its epistemological scandal—that a uniform cause (e.g. electricity) would generate different sensations from one kind of nerve to another. Electricity applied to the optic nerve produces the experience of light, applied to the skin the sensation of touch."[8] Crary also presents Müller's converse findings—that different inputs to the same nerve do not produce different sensations—revealing a fundamentally arbitrary relation between stimulus and sensory reception. The body thus possesses an inborn ability to misperceive, unable to register semantic input and, essentially, intent; in other words, this is an observing subject "for whom sensations are interchangeable." Müller's research effectively eradicated the possibility of a stable and ingrained ground of referentiality, threatened any coherent system of meaning, and provided an autonomous base upon which "new instrumental techniques" could "construct for an observer a new *real* world."[9]

Rousseau's treatise on the city and human freedom examined the possibilities for abuse through corporeal subjugation to law, and here those possibilities are accelerated to indicate the by now routine subjugation of human consciousness to unanchored and abstracted stimuli. For a constituency that, even today, persists in formulating its ideals of "city," "state," and "identity" within the corporeal realm of a protective body politic via codes of monocularity and centered subjectivity descended from the Renaissance, the instrumentalization of visual subjectivity suggests a prolongation of a Hobbesian war. The "static monotony" of constructed—and by now *naturalized*—commodity relations has transformed class differences into the managerial requirements of market classifications. In other words, the engineering of what constitutes "reality" through instrumentalization and normalization allows the collective to believe it is a body politic—a people—though the same mechanisms would have been considered a mode of tyranny in Rousseau's or Hobbes's time. This engineering offers, in the form of nihilism, the possibility of a subject whose strife is unanchored from its source and whose grief loses the metaphorically semantic weight it acquired from gravity. In Crary's terms, "Müller's theory was potentially so nihilistic that it is no wonder that . . . [those] who accepted its empirical premises were impelled to invent theories of cognition and signification which concealed its uncompromising cultural implications."[10]

1971: Deep Structure. In the early 1970s, Noam Chomsky's research in linguistics provided the foundations for an essay by Peter Eisenman entitled "From Object to Relationship II: Casa Giuliani-Frigerio," which introduced the term "deep structure" to architectural criticism.[11] In the context of Chomsky's work, the term points to the underlying rules and relationships that constitute a grammar through which infinite syntactic transformations may be generated. Even though "the deep structure of a syntactic description determines its semantic interpretation," there may not necessarily be any similarities between the two—what is in fact revealed is a system that manifests sharp incongruencies between its visible, surface structure and its deep structure of underlying relations.[12]

Deep structure for Eisenman is, in one dimension, a means toward an architectural autonomy based on a syntax of formal transformations; more importantly, however, the concept of deep structure reveals an invisible structure of "conceptual relationships which are not sensually perceived . . . attributes which accrue to relationships between objects, rather than to the physical presence of the objects themselves."[13] In 1998, one wonders if Chomsky would characterize the differential yet intertwined velocities of urban infrastructures that underlie the contemporary global city—to wit, the instantaneity of capital, the mobile grids of market classifications, the surreptitious deployment of surveillance and managerial regulation, the periodic shifts in demographic configurations—as essentially a mode of deep structure. This economic domain is a subjectless and mostly invisible geometry of dexterous morphological skill whose surface need not, and indeed does not, look like its base system of rules. It seems to be a form of predatory nature not unlike the *nature* whose threats Rousseau claimed instigated the crisis that compelled people to enter into reconfigured modes of association.

The link between deep structure and autonomy in Eisenman's work was partly intended to lead to an authorless architecture, but must ultimately be understood as pointing to the possibility of a *presubjective* space, revealing a system of rules that otherwise would remain on a less-than-conscious level. In this sense much of *Slow Space* is also presubjective: a transformed subject enmeshed in the ecologies of urban assemblages seems to be immanent in each essay or project. At the core of *Slow Space*'s analytical trajectory is an inevitable critique of technology's ultimate goal—the maximization of an ever narrowing profit margin through efficiency, accelerated productivity, and soft management. These priorities lead to the tedious normalization of subjects and most of space, ultimately resulting in a hyper-engineered and surreptitiously coercive urban form.

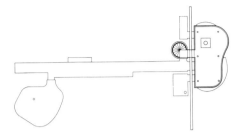

John Hejduk, Bye House, 1973.

1998: Durations. Within an architectural practice whose legal and contractual involvement with the city seems to lead to the finitude of building form, the productive aim of *Slow Space* is to be found in the latent—and perhaps unexpected—possibilities of autonomy. Such possibilities are revealed in the architectural investigations exemplified by John Hejduk's Bye House, a project which, even in its autonomy, allowed potentials of time through matter itself. Though conceived as an autonomous object, the Bye House paradoxically instigates *affects* beyond its apparent finitude. Hejduk has accomplished this via the geological durations accessed by the density and opacity of matter, the inanimate animations produced by its spatial and topological compressions, and the enlisting of time as tectonic material.[14] In a sense, these reconfigurations of the abstract realms of the nonocular into building material offer the possibility of accessing infrastructures that might otherwise remain hidden. These reconfigurations further establish the coda for an architecture that might be seen enzymatically to reconfigure the spaces of the city and the domains of the subject, and to establish a mode of materiality as a potential gap even within the commodification and instrumentalization of movement, material, and time in the metropolis—an architectural provision of authentic experience. Architecture is here sped up beyond its commonly purified domain to create subjective, spatial, and programmatic affects within the multivalent velocities and milieus of the contemporary city.

Slow Space thus delineates two simultaneous trajectories. The first is an analysis of a contemporary city whose infrastructures—in the broader sense of the word, encompassing realms such as capital movement, managerial systems, and the deployments of power—

remain on a less-than-conscious and mostly invisible level. Insofar as the configuration of the city no longer operates on a visual level, architecture that is premised on the compositional is doomed to ineffectuality. The second trajectory runs in opposition to the fast realm of vision and capital and asserts the *reconfigurative* potential of architecture. This reconfiguration imagines architecture as a particular temporality whose boundaries with the multivalent forces of the city are not absolute, nor negational, nor entirely absent, but instead are differentiated, as Gilles Deleuze and Félix Guattari would have it, by the gradients "between slowness and speed."[15] *Slow Space* is thus intended to serve as evidence of a model at once metabolic and thermodynamic, recognizing the inherent duration of the architectural and its role as catalyst within the larger milieus of the contemporary city.

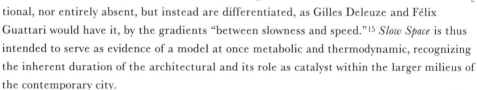

Notes

1. Noam Chomsky, "The New Global Economy," interview by David Barsamian, in *The Prosperous Few and the Restless Many* (Berkeley: Odonian Press, 1993), 8.

2. Chomsky, 6.

3. Jean-Jacques Rousseau, *The Social Contract and Discourses* (1762), trans. G. D. H. Cole (London: J. M. Dent and Sons, 1973), 175.

4. Rousseau, 177.

5. "Ten workers in an assembly line can fabricate forty-eight thousand pins in one day." If they had worked independently, "certainly could not each one of them make twenty." Adam Smith, *An Inquiry into the Nature and Causes of the Wealth of Nations* (1789), ed. Edwin Cannan (New York: Random House, 1937), 5.

6. Thomas Hobbes, *Leviathan, or, The Matter, Forme, and Power of a Commonwealth, Ecclesiasticall and Civil* (1651), ed. Michael Oackeshott (Oxford: Basil Blackwell, 1928), 136.

7. Guy Debord, *The Society of the Spectacle,* trans. Donald Nicholson-Smith (New York: Zone Books, 1994), 120.

8. Jonathan Crary, "Modernizing Vision," in *Vision and Visuality,* ed. Hal Foster (Seattle: Bay Press, 1988), 39.

9. Crary, 40.

10. Crary, 40.

11. Peter Eisenman, "From Object to Relationship II: Casa Giuliani-Frigerio," published in *Perspecta* 13/14 (1971): 36–65. Eisenman's analysis of Giuseppe Terragni's Casa Giuliani-Frigerio, in Como, portrays a "conceptual ambiguity" developed "from the use of two opposing conceptions of space. The first considered space as subtractive, or cut away from a solid . . . The second . . . considers space as additive." Eisenman's essay depicts both concepts as simultaneously at work in the Casa Giuliani-Frigerio. The analysis seeks to reveal the potential of "abstract relationships" as conceivably independent of actual ones, and proposes that the search for an architectural syntax—in this text loosely referred to as the presumed goal of autonomy—is likely to be found in the ambiguity between these conceptual and actual relationships. Eisenman's essay ultimately seems to reveal Terragni's architecture to be a Bergsonian *third duration*, one that encapsulates the expansion and contraction of its two types of space. Also on Eisenman's relation to duration and matter, see Sanford Kwinter, "The Genius of Matter: Eisenman's Cincinnati Project," in *Peter Eisenman and Frank Gehry* (New York: Rizzoli, 1991).

12. Noam Chomsky, *Syntactic Structures* (The Hague: Mouton and Co., 1965), 16. Quoted in Eisenman, 39.

13. Eisenman, 39.

14. According to Hejduk, the wall is imagined as the present, while the circulatory elements—ramp, passageway, stair—are imagined as the past, and the living spaces as the future: "The new space was that space which was the quickest, the most fleeting, the most compressed, the shortest distance, the present. It was meant to heighten the fact that we are continuously going in and out of the past and future, cyclical. We never stop to contemplate the present for we cannot; it passes too quickly . . . In a way, ironically, this house had to do with the 'idea' of the present . . . it was leading and condensing to a point. It had to do with time." John Hejduk, *Mask of Medusa* (New York: Rizzoli, 1985), 59.

15. Gilles Deleuze and Félix Guattari, *A Thousand Plateaus*, trans. Brian Massumi (Minneapolis: University of Minnesota Press, 1987), 254.

DOUBLESPACE

Lars Lerup

1. The Straying Gaze

> The very idea of carving an armored car out of stone smacks of a certain psychological acceleration, of the sculptor being a bit ahead of his time. As far as I know, this is the only monument to a man on an armored car that exists in the world. In this respect alone, it is a symbol of a new society. The old society used to be presented by men on horseback. —Joseph Brodsky, describing a statue of Lenin standing on top of an armored car, in front of former Leningrad's Finland Station. From "A Guide to a Renamed City," in *Less Than One: Selected Essays*.

The wanderer's eyes stray from the center—from Lenin's statue to the armored car. It may be curiosity, shame, boredom, even a kind of laziness that makes the gaze waver and shift its focus to the margin. Like a hand before the eyes, this is a view that favors the horizon over the center.

At this margin, fused here at Finland Station, is both Lenin's vehicle and the customary base. The traditional equestrian has been replaced by a pedestrian, standing on an armored car. The car, and its implied motion, in turn replaces the fixity of the customary base, the miniature version of the same base that sets up the tripartite facade of the classical Renaissance palazzo, versions of which hover not far from here. By implication, the anthropomorphic trace slips across the margins from horse to armored car, from old to new society, from lofty equestrian hero to man-of-the-street,[1] from nobility to working class, from statue to palazzo. Georges Bataille would link the palazzo's monumentality and expression of authority to the prison, an edifice inherently susceptible to attack by the storming mob of the street—the stone masons, the bronze casters, the grooms, and the crews of the armored cars—as was the fate of the Bastille. Let us follow the *dérive* (drift) of the straying gaze. Radically peripatetic, let's move from city to city, from revolution to revolution, and past the mob and the petrified armored car that left its base in the dust (and recently its rider too). Let's trade Leningrad and Paris for Rome, and Lenin and his revolution for Trajan and his column, or better for his son Hadrian and his Pantheon. Here too, the foundations will shift.

The straying gaze needs its centers as parasites require hosts. At Pantheon we can establish at least three, apart from the perspective of strict architectural history that forms the basis for the entire discussion.[2] The first is drawn by Michel Serres and his stones momentarily at rest in the foundations of Rome; the second by Michel Foucault and his all-seeing eye that forces those confined to the building's interior to confess; and the third by Denis Hollier's interpretation of Georges Bataille whose man in the piazza is squashed by the sheer monumentality of the building.

The perspectives are not entirely comparable, but serve as strategic positions in this text. Serres's is both historical and poetic and serves as the foundation for the main argument here. The two others are recto and verso of the same coin, fixed points of the stage on which the primary plot of this text is acted out. Foucault and Hollier will set the rules for the action, while Serres will assist in the escape. As "the peasant gives the land a landscape,"[3] these nuclei of steady gazes will help to construct a set of positions in and around the ancient monument, positions that curve, shape, and delimit our conceptual geography. The faint outline of a space appears between them—a lacuna—a lunar lake that in its solid darkness is hard-pressed to reveal its secrets.

2. Stones at Rest

Geometry has to make itself stone before the word can make itself flesh . . . The object apprehended by Galileo required two worlds, or rather two spaces and one time. The incandescent space of geometry and the dark world of opaque mass. Nothing is so easy as to understand the first—it is there only to understand and be understood; nothing is so easy to hear as the word—it is there to be heard; but nothing so obscure as the second—nothing so difficult to conceive as the body, flesh or stone, nothing so hard to hear as the sound that escapes from it; nothing is so difficult as to know how it receives and envelops light. —Michel Serres, *Rome: The Book of Foundations*

2.1. Geometry versus Stone. Geometrically speaking (which historians have done well), Pantheon is a sphere, a miniature universe, a heaven on earth—a mental structure to be kept in one's head for memory's sake, precise, clear, and there to be heard. On the other hand, behind its immediate surface Pantheon is dark, thick, and formidable in its ambiguity. Pantheon as material, as stone, as the other space, or even specifically as bricks, rocks, mortar, and Roman concrete, will not break its silence. To apprehend it briefly via the anthropometric trace as towering and wide, a giant black skull, Pantheon fills one end of a small piazza. It is considered, with the sculpture of Trajan on its priapic column, to be one of the two most spectacular Roman monuments. How and why they have survived is ambiguous at best:

Barbarians demolish buildings in order to bring the stone back to its function as projectile: wisdom builds in order to immobilize stone to appease hatred, to protect. Why do you think we have walls, towns, and temples, when we could sleep under the stars and prostrate ourselves before the horizon? We have only built to settle stones, which could otherwise fly continually in our midst.

The builder's plans barely count: the architectonic ideal exists only for representation—the point is that projectiles come to rest.[4]

Rome as represented by Pantheon is a quarry of weapons, dormant, petrified, and opaque. As such, Pantheon is a perfect symbol of Rome, because it is as if this lowbrow city had escaped all of the academic contemplation that is associated with the city: "Science never appeared in Rome, nor did geometry or logic: never anything but politics."[5] Imported for the convenience of politics (and warfare), the geometry of the half-circle that haunts the outer cupola and inner room (and our giant black skull) was for the Romans only a way to get to the projectiles—to the object—and this suits us fine. The difference between the geometry of the ideal sphere that lingers in Pantheon and the bordering outer geometry of the ideal Roman city—the checkerboard of the encampment—is just a line. The built difference between the spherical interior of the inner space of the temple, the outer skull, and the twisting fabric of the street is a gap filled by the opaque mass of material. That suits us fine too, because it is into this darkness that we will eventually stray.

2.2. Gray versus Black. As our first position, this fabric of stone must be held right here, because even as an arsenal of projectiles it becomes too metaphoric: the rocks and bricks will probably never fly again. Pantheon's weakness as an assembly of projectiles is already too theoretical. In fact, *all referentiality must be held back* in order for us to retain Pantheon's status as an opaque black mass. It may well be that we should refer to it as *gray* mass, recalling Foucault's speculation on painting:

> It is in vain that we say what we see; what we see never resides in what we say. And it is in vain that we attempt to show, by the use of images, metaphors, or similes, what we are saying; the space where they achieve their splendor is not that deployed by our eyes . . . But if one wishes to keep the relation of language to vision open, if one wishes to treat their incompatibility as a starting-point for speech instead of as an obstacle to be avoided, so as to stay as close as possible to both, then one must erase these proper names and preserve the infinity of the task. It is perhaps through the medium of this gray, anonymous language, always over-meticulous and repetitive because too broad, that the painting may, little by little, release its illuminations.[6]

Simply put, here the monument is a pile of rocks, stacked to be sure, and seen from too close a remove to reveal their horizon. And the light is bleak—just after daybreak. For now the insights are kept oblique. Here at degree zero, the wanderer's eyes remain in chiaroscuro.

3. The Eye in the Center

3.1. Insideoutside. It rained the day the wanderer first came to realize Pantheon's ambiguous status as "inside." A group of children danced in a circle, their faces upturned to catch the rain that in a fine mist fell from the great oculus in the sky. They were outside inside. Now the spherical interior wall becomes a facade. This may have been the ultimate intention of Nolli's map of Rome that includes in the rendition of the city with its streets and piazzas the interiors of the monuments, while the rest of the city with its dwellings and its work spaces is drawn as opaque and impenetrable. It is the bright light of the public world and the darkness of the private—Hannah Arendt's Greek Polis. The purpose of this duality was "to render accessible to a multitude of men the inspection of a small number of objects: this was the problem to which the architecture of temples, theatres and circuses responded."[7] When the wanderer joins his fellow tourists with their guides, maps, and incessant picture-taking, however, it is the opposite pole that comes to mind: "to procure for a small number of people, or even for a single individual, the instantaneous view of a great multitude."[8] Thus it is Foucault's reading of Bentham's Panopticon that comes to mind— architecture as a prison in which all space is controlled interior space. In fact, public space has disappeared in favor of social space. Although Pantheon is of antiquity and therefore, according to Foucault, rendered to serve the spectacle, the spectacle has also disappeared. The architectural skull is left behind, but the world has changed, and radically. As Foucault writes, "We are much less Greek than we believe. We are neither in the amphitheatre, nor on the stage, but in the panoptic machine, invested by its effects of power, which we bring ourselves since we are part of its mechanism."[9]

3.2. Surveillance. Bentham's Panopticon in its idealized form consists of two concentric spaces with "an annular building" at the periphery and a tower at the center. The tower is fitted with windows, as are the cells in the peripheral part of the building. The guards occupying the tower have the prisoners in full view. The building is thus fully transparent, but once the guards cannot be seen by the prisoners the "architectural apparatus" can sustain "the power relation independent of the person who exercises it, in short, that the inmates [are] caught up in a power situation of which they are themselves the bearers."[10]

Pantheon, caught in this Panoptic gaze, thus transforms the body of the emperor into light. The great oculus, rain or shine, throws light—diffuse (when overcast) or focused and columnar (when sunny)—across the space. Focused, the searchlight wanders across the warped surfaces. As in a theater set, the cells are rendered in trompe l'oeil from niches and coffers. Since the light never occupies the center, not even at the height of summer, there is no way to confuse oneself with the geometrical axis of the oculus and the center of the floor plan—the star, or the Celtic diagram, as Serres would describe it. The wanderer remains displaced, while the light is searching for him. If the wanderer is Hadrian, is this column of light Trajan? It must be so, since the light fathers the space.

Panoptically speaking, Pantheon is post-Panoptic. The central tower in which anyone may come and exercise "the functions of surveillance" has been removed and replaced by the giant searchlight, the reminder of the father. From Foucault's perspective, the wanderer is here "alone" with his fellow tourists under the auspices of generalized surveillance. The incessant urge to photograph; the urge to listen to the platitudes of tour guides; the obsessive reading of packaged history in guidebooks: all neglect to "use" the building, or even just look at it, in the way children once did. Touching is prohibited.

This is the manifestation of "the new physics of power . . . which has its maximum intensity not in the person of the king, but in the bodies that can be individualized by these relations"[11] in the generalized function of tourist behavior. This disciplinary mechanism becomes even more apparent when the column of light is diffused and it rains.

3.3. The Hollow. There is an escape. Although the departure must be sanctioned by authorities, the wanderer can momentarily steal away from the crowd: the spherical wall, with its interior facade overlooking the space we know as Pantheon, is partially hollow. In fact, it can be occupied.

The disciplinary subject of the great space has a double that, through the crevices, may observe the doppelgänger's attempt to avoid the light. The Panoptic theater has been turned inside out. The observer has become the observed. Yet, as we shall see later, this observer has no power, unless being close to the formal meaning of the monument endows this marginal subject with a certain wisdom.

4. The Face of Power

Bataille's prison derives from an ostentatious, spectacular architecture, an architecture to be seen; whereas Foucault's prison is the embodiment of an architecture that sees, observes, and spies, a vigilant architecture. Bataille's architecture—convex, frontal, extrovert—an architecture that is externally imposing, shares practically no element with that of Foucault, with its insinuating concavity that surrounds, frames, contains, and confines for therapeutic or disciplinary ends. Both are equally effective, but one works because it draws attention to itself and the other because it does not. One represses (imposes silence); the other expresses (makes one talk).

—Denis Hollier, Against Architecture: The Writings of Georges Bataille

4.1. The Skull. The forest of the giant portico's columns rushes by; released, the wanderer stumbles out in the blinding light of the piazza. Turning around, he faces the outer monument for the second time.

"Convex, frontal, extrovert": the skull of Pantheon, with its grin of columns, dominates his space. He stands in silence. Drifting, his gaze wanders to the bent horizon of the skull; the space between it and its jagged but rectilinear surround forms a blue shape, a lake between two worlds—one domestic, snug, and warm, the other imposing, broad, and stifling.

The wanderer's eyes oscillate from the majestic portico to the bent side elevations that, in their sober mural economy, curve themselves and, with the stepped cupola, create an infinite bow to the sky. Tensile and taut, Pantheon bulges like a sail whose ragged, pock-marked, and petrified surface anchors it to the geology below.

Auguste Rodin spoke of "l'exaggeration des formes," in which the exaggeration exploded from within the stone to rush toward the surface. This allowed Rodin to amplify a torso or limb such that the rest of the body would be rendered unnecessary. The fragment became the whole. The giant skull of Hadrian bulges with an explosive inner power that despite the wear of time, the loss of meaning, its status as tourist trap, and clouds of sulfuric acid, still exaggerates.

4.2. Domination & Transgression. States Bataille, "Thus great monuments are erected like dikes, opposing the logic and majesty of authority against all disturbing elements: it is in the form of the cathedral or palace that Church or State speaks to the multitudes and imposes silence upon them."[12] As Hollier suggests, Bataille sees architecture not just as an image of social order, but as instrumental in imposing the order: "From being a simple symbol it has become master."[13] There is an anthropomorphic sleight of hand at work here—the monument becomes a sentry, a human form. This is of particular interest, because the order Pantheon imposes on our wanderer—now Bataille's subject—is all there is. The skull is empty; its brain is gone.

Pantheon is what Italian architectural theorist Aldo Rossi calls "a pathological permanence": it is a museum of itself.[14] Bataille may approve of this pathology, and see it as an internal transgression, as the improbable putrefaction of the already petrified. For Bataille, argues Hollier, architecture is but the skeleton, the structure of human form: "Architecture retains of man only what death has no hold on."[15] Pantheon is, because of its internal demise—the collapse of its center—no longer reproducible. Once pollution has done its devastating job, there will be no more Pantheons.

Consequently, once the wanderer gets beyond the imposing skull, Pantheon reveals a truth: it is a corpse. The imposing power that it emanates is empty, symbolic. The intention of the rendering of Bataille's position, however, is to keep the subject imprisoned at the origin of his fixed gaze. Pantheon is "grouping servile multitudes" and, in its shadow, "imposing admiration and astonishment, order and constraint."[16] "Architecture," writes Hollier, "does not express the soul of societies but rather smothers it."[17] It is this suffocating dimension of architecture that will eventually fuel our wanderer's trespass.

In Bataille's view, architecture is then a complex villain even if it is static and stubbornly consistent. Standing somewhere between monkeys, men, and mathematics, architecture as an armature of domination is hard to tackle precisely because it is so easily confused with our own body. When we attack architecture, we attack man.

"If the prison is the generic form of architecture this is primarily because man's own form is his first prison," Hollier writes. In Bataille's view, intones Hollier, "the only way to escape "the architectural chain gang is to escape his form, to lose his head."[18]

Pantheon seems again to reveal a certain internal weakness, a second transgression. Hadrian has managed the impossible: he escapes the prison by leaving his skull behind (to paraphrase Bataille). The writing on the pediment of the portico (visible from the wanderer's position in the piazza), "Agrippa built this," may then be Hadrian's last joke: leaving his skull with the incorrect address.[19] With Pantheon severed from its body, untraceable, both the father standing on his column and his decapitated son fade away.

5. The Doublespace

5.1. Lacuna. Three positions—the opaque mass of the built substance and two prisons (one concave, the other convex)—are all cradled in the official history of the monument. As conceptual dominions, however, they do not fully map out Pantheon. Much like the lines in a value-engineer's graph, they leave a problem space, an uncharted territory—a lacuna (and potentially others that I cannot see). In the starkness of the real, this is particularly obvious: even a novice knows that when he passes from one prison to the other there is a gap.

Our wanderer first encounters the gap when he rushes through the portico, moving between the two prisons. This is a prime example of Benjamin's "distracted perception."[20]

The wanderer does not see the forest of columns, not just for the columns but for the pull of the space beyond, be it the outside or the inside. If he stops, the lacuna with the immense stillness of a petrified forest will immerse him. The architectural figure of the portico is here invisible. What is offered is only the insisting physical presence of the repetition of shaped and stacked stone disks, the lowered light, the sudden cool, the draft between inside and outside across his face and bared wrists.

Once inside, the second encounter comes when the wanderer's eyes drift from the candles and saints to linger in the niches, imprints that begin to hint at the actual nature of the wall. At first solid and continuous, the wall as seen with the invasion of the indentations becomes porous, permeable, and partially transparent. In fact, the entire structure is made apparent with the eight huge pylons that form the footprint of the immense half-sphere above. The formerly continuous wall is now made up of what Goethe, in speaking of Palladian villas, called the "contradiction" between surface and column. This contradiction stalls, if briefly, the onslaught of representation—of speech—to expose the writing of the wall. The wanderer has his third and ultimate encounter with the gap when he discovers that the wall between the pylons is hollow and, as previously mentioned, occupiable.

5.2. *Intra Muros.* Hollier refers repeatedly to a "gap" when he compares Foucault and Bataille, and also when he compares the slaughterhouse and the museum. These gaps are both conceptual and actual distances between loci. It is their status as voids that is significant, however, because the subtle and insidious connection between the loci is intramural. It is genetically inscribed. Bataille's view of the slaughterhouse and the museum has resonance in Pantheon too. As Serres describes, much blood was spilled, even among brothers, during the foundation of Rome. Some of it was certainly spilled in and around the foundations of Pantheon, and now it is a museum. Hollier writes, "The slaughterhouses are the negative pole, the generator of repulsion, the centrifuge . . . Museums, the pole of attraction, are centripetal. But within the heart of one the other is hidden."[21] Quoting Bataille, Hollier concludes: "The origin of the modern museum would thus be linked to the development of the guillotine."[22] Consequently, the actual distance between the slaughterhouse on the periphery of the city and the museum at the center is essential in maintaining their difference because of their similarity. This similarity is a symmetry without likeness. As prisons, the exterior and interior Pantheons are also symmetries without likeness, but as unified built substance their story is more complex.

The Pantheon-as-skull is a telling emblem of the veritable slaughterhouse that lies at the foundation of Serres's Rome. The gap in Pantheon's wall is neither sheer distance nor is it a vacuum; like a catacomb it is the secret refuge between the two surrounds and form, but blood has seeped in here as well. The inner gap is the mold of the two outsides—it is a space of transformation.

The void between Bataille's slaughterhouse and museum remains a simple geometrical distance: like that between day and night, or like the single shadow cast by a single light. Our gap is much more complex: the built in-between is not completely independent of outside or inside. A built distance, the gap is a quasi-space, a space in between wall and space.

The status of Serres's pile of rocks in reference to our gap is more obscure than that of the prisons. The built material—the bricks, the rocks, and the Roman concrete in Pantheon's case—make up, to borrow Aldo Rossi's term, the *fabricca*,[23] but since there is a physical gap in this *fabricca* it is not just solid material: the gap is a space, however narrow, made up of enclosed air surrounded by material. The tear in the descriptive-conceptual tissue is thus in Pantheon both a gap and a place, but more importantly, it is a locus of transit, like a tunnel between two worlds. An atmosphere prevails here: the compressed air of the interior's interior, light from both inside and outside transformed by the double wall to mix new light that in turn does not light very well, and sound that reverberates rather than communicates. This locus, like a peripheral other, repeats and doubles both the outer and inner monument, but lies outside the focus of what Norman Bryson calls "the menacing gaze."[24]

5.3. Le Regard. The genealogy of the disturbed and disturbing gaze in modern French thinking is a large and complex subject, and indeed is an essential ingredient of both Foucault's and Bataille's conceptions of their prisons. Bryson's essay "The Gaze in the Expanded Field," attempts to investigate "where the modern subject resides." This is important for architecture because the architect always assumes a subject, more or less consciously, for a building—the architect's homunculus. In turn, the building as institution produces a subject—Foucault's and Bataille's subject—that may not necessarily coincide with the assumed subject. Third, the building may also have its own subject that, like a phantom, resides in the building's very material, what we could call a formal subject—Serres's and architecture's subject. Modern life presumably, much like gravity, attempts to spin all subjects away from their natural center, which produces an additional decentered subject. The attempt below is to bring the decentered subject to momentary rest within the locus of the formal subject.

Discussing Jean-Paul Sartre and Jacques Lacan, Bryson argues that despite those philosophers' desire to decenter the subject, the "line of thinking remains held within a conceptual enclosure where vision is still theorized from the standpoint of a subject placed at the center of the world."[25] This can also be said of Foucault and Bataille vis-à-vis architecture as a prison. Rather than following Bryson's path to complete decenteredness or "nothingness" in the "expanded field" of Eastern philosophy, however, we shall enter into the gap.

5.4. The Double Wall. If we again imagine the wanderer, now climbing stairs inside the wall of Pantheon, we can assume that it is quite dark, and that kinesthetic sensations join with vision to aid his advancement.[26] If he ascends clockwise through the wall, its bulging convexity will be sensed by his right hand—a microcosmic "same" in Bataille's view, though the rough and gently curving surface must be more akin to a giant vessel than to a prison. The left hand will touch and feel the outer surface, the concave other. Unless our climber is claustrophobic, again it is not "surveillance" that must come to mind but materiality on the one hand and body on the other.

Here in the gap of the wall, the two outer gazes are tamed, disrupted, and displaced by the inner calm of the wall. This inner world has momentarily blinded all menacing gazes. The subject has been taken out of his obsessive self-enclosure to become one with the building's own enclosure. He has been truly decentered, moved out of the spectacle of the gaze of either prison. He has not been dumped in the darkness of Serres's pile of rocks, however, but into a narrow slot of faint light that leads him to the top of the world. He has also been returned to his body. But this is not an "untroubled place of acrobatic grace and perceptual accord between subject-world and object-world,"[27] nor is it the place for Jacques Derrida's "spaced out" subject, who in some delirious state avoids all attempts by architecture to produce its subject. This is only a momentary escape, a place of readjustment, reflection, and distance—architecture's catacomb. This gap is a perspective other than that of the prison. It is another position, another place—possibly the only one in Pantheon with a certain conceptual stillness. At least for the moment.

The gap is a place away from the insisting shadows of the various menacing figures, a place whose weight and value is in its material and its lack of reflective visual distance. A subject is produced here, but it is architecture's subject rather than the institution's or the critic's. Although this place may have a certain conceptual vacuity, its status is slippery and so is its subject.

5.5. Architecture. In *The Life of Forms in Art,* Henri Focillon gives us an important clue from whence we might project this subject. Like Foucault, Focillon believes that architecture produces a subject and, in fact, he maintains that entire styles do, en bloc:

Gothic art as a landscape, created a France and a French humanity that no one could foresee: outlines of the horizon, silhouettes of cities—a poetry, in short, that arose from Gothic art, and not from geology or from Capetian institutions.[28]

Focillon's work offers a very different take on architecture's role. There is no menacing gaze, but not because his is the view of an apolitical art historian; rather, a different status is given to form itself, and to its production. He writes: "Form has a meaning—but it is a meaning entirely its own, a personal and specific value that must not be confused with the attributes we impose on it."[29] Meanings such as those that Foucault and Bataille associate with architecture come and go. Interpretations are both "unstable and insecure. As old meanings are broken down and obliterated, new meanings attach themselves to form."[30]

The form of Pantheon remains the same, however, and so does its own "personal and specific value." The narrow path that loops through the wall of Pantheon is as close as we can come to the actual construction of the monument. In the innards, the arduous task of making such an immense structure reveals itself, unadorned—pedantically, as it were. Inside out, the microcosm of the two outer monuments—the inner cave and the outer skull—appears at the end of the body at its fingertips rather than at the end of a panoramic and "disturbed" gaze. Inside the wall, this reversal of inside and outside brings this interspace close to the status of a mold, like the mold from which sprung the bronze statue of Lenin at the outset, or the pink rubbery mold that the dentist takes of a patient's teeth. Mysteriously separate, peripheral, and humble, molds are yet the font from whence the object arises. As a mold, the inner world of Pantheon is real, gritty, and even dusty when it unashamedly reveals itself to our wanderer's touch. Form's "extraordinary vigor" (Rodin's exaggeration) stems from this inner gap, but form cannot be found here, since it has already exploded to the outer surfaces. It is the calm after the storm, but what about the explosion itself, or its traces?

5.6. Flung Ink. In Norman Bryson's example of the achievement of "nothingness," he uses an example of a fifteenth-century Ch'an painting by Jiun depicting the calligraphic sign for "man." In a flung-ink painting, the sign is done with great speed, such that the common stability and secure flow achieved by the deliberately careful movement of the skilled hand is abandoned to the speed of the gesture. This speed, combined with the effect of gravity, allows the ink to break its own surface viscosity. The result is a liquidity and independence of line that threatens the sign's function as exclusively a vehicle of meaning by forcing the sign into a double status: it is instead both form and figure, each with its independent claim to meaning.[31]

Similarly, the incidental and unkempt intimacy of the interspace (when juxtaposed with the precision and representability of the interior space and the unified power of the sign of the monument on the outside) produces the space from which the architectural subject can be molded. This subject is a formal consciousness. The very act of making and constructing dominates this subject. Inside the wall, the outer form as reflected and the inner form as likewise reflected are secondary to their own construction. The entire architectural algorithm is exposed, not just its answers or its figures. In contradistinction, the great interior space is made for an idealized observer whose interest is the meaning (a facsimile of the universe) rather than the factuality of the building, the *fabricca*. The interspace—the mold of both outside and inside—like a gene holds the inscription of the architectural act itself. (Like a bicycle's inner tube, it supports the apparent stability and strength of the outer tire). I shall call this inner, interspace the "doublespace."

The doublespace is produced, if not with the willfulness of the Ch'an painter, at least outside the view of the *Commendatore*.[32] He couldn't care less what happens here as long as the building stands up. Consequently, we can be sure that the Roman concrete was flung here with great gusto and speed. Like the broken line of the sign for "man" in the painting described above, the doublespace defies conventional geometrical definition; only fractal geometry would do.

5.7. Time-Out. The privileged importance given to this insignificant cavity in Pantheon's wall has a Modernist history. When Le Corbusier made the distinction between structure and surface in his walls, the walls were also given a new interiority. This formal manifestation of internal differences led the Italian architect Guiseppe Terragni to separate entire systems of columns and walls in order to produce zones of in-betweens in which various activities could be assigned. Each such zone was given its own physical vocabulary, clearly distinguished from the rest of the building. The beginning of this internal decomposition has, as the case of Pantheon proves, been falsely associated with Le Corbusier. To be sure, Pantheon is not the origin either.

The importance of this territory within the architectural body lies not only in its formal possibilities, but also in its formal significance. Differences in architecture are often driven by functional distinctions, but here they are driven by the nature of the form itself. This work is being done on the very vehicle of Focillon's formal meaning.

Architecture, as understood by Bataille and Foucault, "is the expression of every society's being." Hollier writes:

Architecture represents a religion that it brings alive, a political power that it manifests, an event that it commemorates, etc. Architecture, before any other qualifications, is identical to the space of representation; it always represents something other than itself from the moment it becomes distinguished from mere building.[33]

The rewriting of Pantheon attempts to claim an additional territory for architecture in the gap between architecture as representation and architecture as mere building. Simply put, architecture for Hollier and others is a form of speech, while by now it is also a form of writing, in Derrida's sense of the word, where the traditional priority of the immediacy of speech over the physicality of writing is reversed. The doublespace, the interspace, the time-out space is the other side of the coin of architecture, like "the hinge" as the common term for "articulation & difference" in *Of Grammatology*.[34] The articulation of the doublespace is the difference. This space is not dominated by the fixed gaze, but by the straying gaze, and because the stage is dimly lit, the weaker senses are allowed their much deserved handicap. (Vision has dominated architecture, as speech has writing). If this is the acknowledgment of a certain autonomy of architecture, then, to paraphrase Norman Mailer, "architecture's empty skull may have found its brain."

6. The New Map: 1998

The "acknowledgment of a certain autonomy" could be understood as an attempt to return to an earlier and more dogmatic time, but it is in fact the opposite in more than one way. The tactic used to escape the state and its disciplinary mechanisms belongs in the still obscure realm of what Machiavelli called *virtù* or, more generally, "the thinking of the public square." In Pantheon the wanderer, emerging from the mass in the piazza in front, escapes momentarily into the chiaroscuro of the doublespace, and there seamlessly joins, out of sight, with this space that thanks to its relative autonomy becomes the other in a Dionysian union.

Specifically, what is the threat to the bond between the architectural object and its other—the architect and, alas, the man in the street? The threat may no longer be Serres's mob demolishing Pantheon, chasing away its devotees with the building material as projectiles; nor is the threat Foucault's disciplinary power grid; nor even Bataille's hegemony of the state that forces architecture to be mere representation. Because on the one hand, Serres' proposition is surpassed by far more efficient ways of arming the mob, and on the other hand, the "paranoias" of Foucault and Bataille are rendered finite and limited because their extent has been severed by the momentary autonomy—by the double-space— "the gap in the garment," as Barthes wrote in another context.[35] And perhaps more fundamentally, discipline and state are limited by their affiliation to *either* the interior or the exterior realm, which is particularly ineffective in a world in which there is no longer an easy distinction between the two—even Nolli would have difficulties drawing the map.

The threat is now far more sinister, since the three previous threats still had some blind spots in which the subject could work and hide and remain in his reverie while the object was overlooked. The threat is more violent and more random in its specific attacks, but it is also more pervasive in that it is all-enclosing. Tentatively such a culprit is best illustrated by the pollution that is slowly attacking Pantheon's beautiful horizon (and city dwellers, aficionados, and members of the mob alike). Pollution of course solicits yawns in some quarters and hysterical fervor in others, so we must delve beyond pollution's common culprits—the automobile, the factory, and belching cows—to the market system, and to its harshest expression—the ubiquitous bottom line—drawn now not only across Reagan's Former Free World but even across Albania and the biggest market of all, China. The curious nature of the bottom line is that it pops out of all the pores of the city, leaking from the very gaps that gave us respite.

To face this ultimate challenge the subject, with all his senses reconstituted in the double space, must, vis-à-vis his desired object, add strategy to his tactics and stray as it were from his position in the public square. He must add a measure of speed. Fumbling in the darkness of the doublespace will not do. He must take the other position of Machiavelli's Prince, now far above the square in the castle. Our subject may conceptually have to move as fast as capital but also so fast that he appears to stand still, allowing the subject to synthesize with Focillon's animated object, without losing their respective autonomies. This ultimate comingling sweeps up the stones with the paranoias, racing along surfaces, cutting out beyond the building, thrusting the subject—mind and all his newly won senses—into the vast complex of the City.

Out of this frenzied drift the vague contours of a new map emerge.[36] Its constituent parts are momentary coalitions between subjects and objects rather than the neat separations between the actors and the fixed receptacles and channels of the past. The new coalitions collide seemingly at random. At best the events leave traces, imprints, compressions, dents, flecks, flickers, and flows, all evading the marks of common cartography yet taking shape. Partially invisible to the naked eye, not unlike toxic clouds, these new shapes have come to invade the subject—now a metropolitan subject—to give the architectural object a new status and the architect a new role.

Notes

1. It should be noted that Lenin had but "scorn for the life of the masses." Michel Maffesoli, *The Time of the Tribes: The Decline of Individualism in Mass Society* (London: Sage Publications, 1996), 154.

2. William MacDonald, *The Pantheon: Design, Meaning, and Progress* (Cambridge, Mass.: Harvard University Press, 1976).

3. Michel Serres, *Rome: The Book of Foundations,* trans. Felicia McCarren (Stanford: Stanford University Press, 1991), 62.

4. Serres, 64.

5. Serres, 64.

6. Michel Foucault, *The Order of Things: An Archaeology of the Human Sciences* (New York: Random House, 1970), 9–10.

7. Michel Foucault, *Discipline and Punish: The Birth of the Prison* (New York: Random House, 1979), 216.

8. Foucault, *Discipline and Punish,* 216.

9. Foucault, *Discipline and Punish,* 217.

10. Foucault, *Discipline and Punish,* 201.

11. Foucault, *Discipline and Punish,* 208.

12. Georges Bataille, quoted in Denis Hollier, *Against Architecture: The Writings of Georges Bataille* (Cambridge, Mass.: MIT Press, 1989), 47.

13. Hollier, 47.

14. Aldo Rossi, *The Architecture of the City* (Cambridge, Mass.: MIT Press, 1982), 60.

15. Hollier, 55.

16. Bataille, quoted in Hollier, 53.

17. Hollier, 47.

18. Hollier, xii.

19. The Latin inscription aside, historians seem to agree that the most likely architect is Hadrian.

20. Walter Benjamin, *Illuminations: Essays and Reflections,* ed. Hannah Arendt, trans. Harry Zohn (New York: Schocken Books, 1969), 239–241.

21. Hollier, xiii.

22. Hollier, xiii.

23. Aldo Rossi, *The Architecture of the City* (Cambridge, Mass.: MIT Press, 1984), 18. Rossi defines *fabricca* as "building" in the old Latin and Renaissance sense of man's construction as it continues over time. The Milanese still call their cathedral "la fabricca del dom," and understand by this expression both the difficulty of the church's construction and the idea of a building whose process goes on over time.

24. Norman Bryson, "The Gaze in the Expanded Field," in *Vision and Visuality*, ed. Hal Foster. (Seattle: Bay Press, 1988), 87.

25. Bryson, 87.

26. The point about imagination should be stressed here, since I have yet to visit the gap. This is not entirely due to lack of opportunity, but rather in order to keep the gap imaginary for as long as possible. A visit will eventually be necessary because, I have been told, gazing down through the oculus is one of the great architectural experiences.

27. Bryson, p. 110.

28. Henri Focillon, *The Life of Forms in Art* (New York: Zone Books, 1989), 61.

29. Focillon, 35.

30. Focillon, 36.

31. Bryson, 103.

32. Hollier, xi.

33. Hollier, 32–33.

34. Jacques Derrida, *Of Grammatology,* trans. Gayatri Chakravorty Spivak (Baltimore: Johns Hopkins University Press, 1976).

35. Roland Barthes, *The Pleasure of the Text*, trans. Richard Millert (New York: Hill & Wang, 1975), 9.

36. See my article "Stim & Dross: Rethinking the Metropolis," in *Assemblage* 25 (1995), which attempts to further outline this new map.

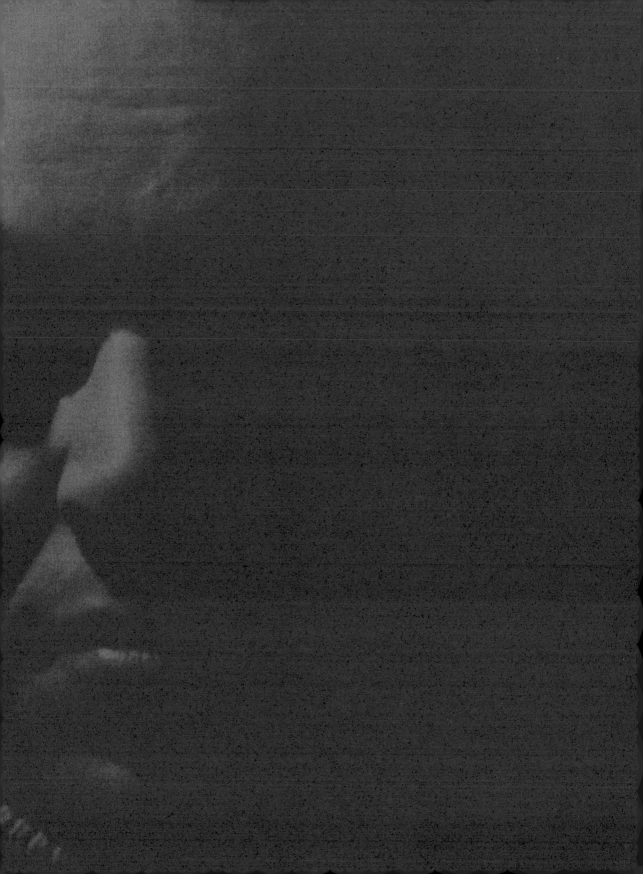

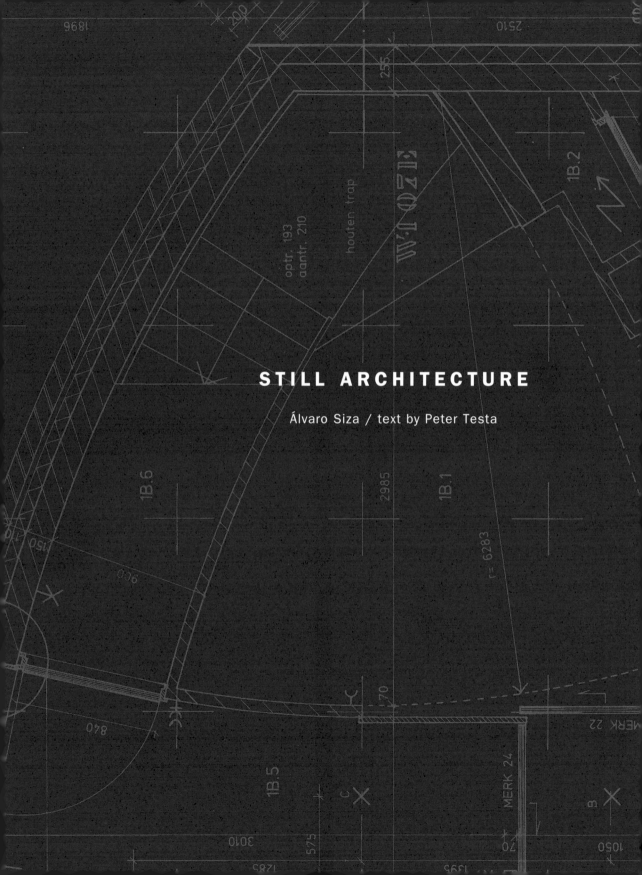

STILL ARCHITECTURE

Álvaro Siza / text by Peter Testa

In a dialectic at a standstill, the Two Houses in Van der Venne Park provide an immediate indication of the multiple versions of relationship involved in Álvaro Siza's architecture. The work derives its definition from patterns of interchange, combining anabolic synthesis and catabolic entropy to effect an urban dynamic of its own. Within this topological model of space, components of the context are interlinked like cybernetic circuits of interaction. Siza employs double description to create a species of information not produced from a single viewpoint.

SIZA / TESTA

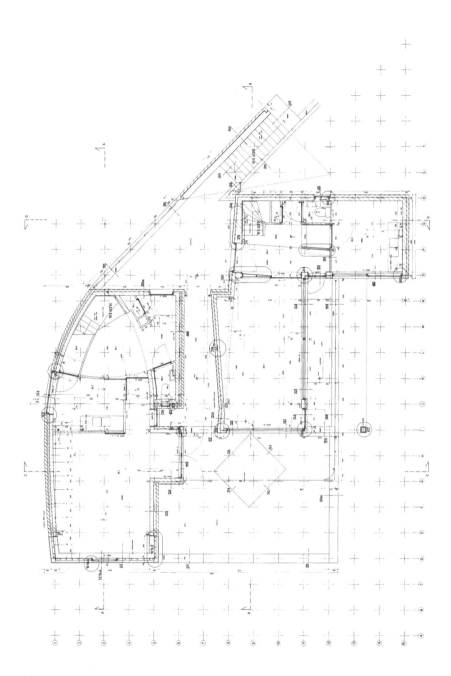

The **Ocean Swimming Pool at Leça da Palmeira**, completed over thirty years ago, is an eidetic image of Siza's recent production. Coherent with modern science, the work remains independent from modernist instrumental interpretations of nature because the natural is neither invaded by technique nor imbued with nostalgic naturalism. The physical universe precedes and envelops the phenomenal (human). Architecture acts as an intermediate world, a syncline between mind and nature. Without conventional openings, the work creates an androgynous zone between inside and outside. Landscape, architecture, and the environment continually exchange places. This work challenges the Cartesian paradigm, suggesting that the human relationship with space and nature include sensible as well as intelligible aspects and that these two categories exist side by side in contemporary society. Siza does not exhume from nature a hidden foundation for architecture, but sets into motion a thinking process that reveals the body as a great intelligence. He articulates new concepts of body, self, and nature, challenging with his transformations dualism of mind and nature as well as unity of self.

In contradistinction to the topographic sensibility at Leça da Palmeira, the Borges & Irmão Bank at Vila do Conde establishes continuities and discontinuities at various scales that form a postcubist model of topological space. Within the interior, Siza develops a physics of sensation that stresses the liminal qualities of both experience and sensory thresholds. The labyrinthine character of the bank brings into question the understanding of the building as an object and also reflects Siza's interpretation of the multiple temporal perspectives that combine to constitute the psychological reality of the city.

Siza explores the mysterious way in which experience combines with materials. Reinforced concrete is rendered simultaneously light, tensile, and massive. Glass is alternately transparent, reflective, opaque, and fluid. Marble is both geomorphic and polished. At various scales, the elements of building have an almost independent raison d'être, yet may be seen to be contained by their function within the form as a whole. Siza exposes the modern idiom to a new set of issues as the architecture continuously passes and repasses from the continuous to the discontinuous. This is an organicism that does not totalize in a demand for unity.

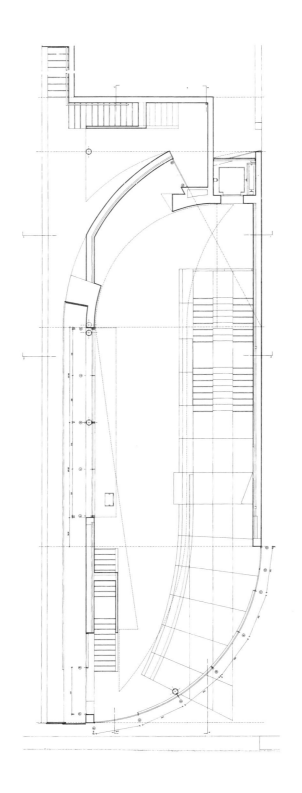

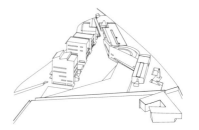

In the 1990's, the morphogenic processes operating in Siza's architecture are extended to include a rethinking of contemporary institutions, as evident in the Faculty of Architecture at Oporto and the Teachers' Training College at Sétubal. Within peripheral sites characterized not only by the absence of social space but also by the erosion of physical space, Siza destratifies consolidated institutions. The Faculty of Architecture is an allegory of Siza's syncretic design process. Restructuring and reanimating architectural knowledge, he retraces an institutional schema on a new provisional ground. This chimeric architecture emerges out of a radical transcription of the courtyard form, a unicellular model that progressively is seen to consist of several kinds of cells in various states of symbiosis. Built from multiple interacting selves, the architecture's range and power are a result of Siza's combinatorial capacity, by which the whole spontaneously becomes more than the sum of its parts. As the collective is reinvented within a posturban diffuseness, lacking centers to function as social and political arenas, this sensate genealogy of forms produces a new architecture. Neither a symbol of the insular city of antiquity nor the ideal open city, the Faculty of Architecture transcends self-sufficiency to support urban life and its transformations.

With its continuous courtyards and orthogonal structure, the Teachers' Training College
at Sétubal suggests the antithesis of the Faculty of Architecture at Oporto. Upon closer
examination, however, remarkable filial relations are evident in the two projects. Marked
by syndesis and asynchrony, these works achieve a momentary equilibrium among all of
the program's constitutive elements without relying on an absolute system. The lived
complexity at Sétubal is experienced as a series of counterposed architectural elements
coalescing to form a wide range of social spaces within the open landscape. Structural
and sensible elements are treated as components of equal importance. This dichotomy is
a constant source of tension that is most visible in the contrast between organic and
ridged elemental structures. The commitment to simplicity and economy in the nature of
a school is turned to cultural advantage in the planning grid, which is used as an anti-
natural object. Yet because the architectural elements are equal to the plan, Siza's
unique synecdochic approach breaks the hierarchy of control. Complexity is found in the
overlap of spatial fields, and the design establishes an unstable balance between all
these polymorphous elements. The homologous relations between parts provide an adequate metaphor for the multiple complexities represented by the work, wherein architectural elements are related by adjacency, parallelism, and complementarity. It is by
means of such anomalous yet structured relationships that Siza constructs the topological spaces of his architecture, working through fragmentation to a nonunitary whole.

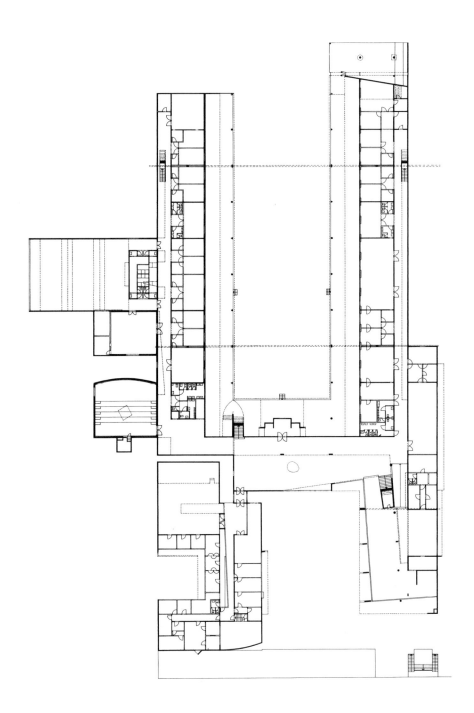

The Center of Contemporary Art at Santiago de Compostela synthesizes many of the themes and techniques developed in Siza's previous work and fully represents his unique capacity to build new topological models of urban and architectural space. In contrast to Oporto and Sétubal, Santiago de Compostela remains a remarkably continuous city, with the new museum interpreted as a point of transition between the stone city and the Galician landscape. Siza has added to the patrimony of Santiago de Compostela a work with the same effect as natural objects, the same spatiality, and the same relations to other things and to humans.

Schismatic relations between ground, volume, and surface establish a complex series of spatial inversions that open the galleries to the city and landscape. Two linear bars of building are overlaid, a double description that develops collaterally to produce a multidirectional spatial field. Movement is organized nonaxially, recapitulating patterns particular to this city where squares are entered tangentially. The spatial sequences combine the successive and simultaneous within an interior more luminous than the outside world, creating an intensification of nature at the core of the building. The descensional quality of Siza's reflection is most apparent at the end of the sequence on the stone roof terrace; one ascends only as high as the earth. No longer horizontal or vertical, Siza's groundless architecture represents a gliding vector of force with its own coordinates.

SIZA / TESTA

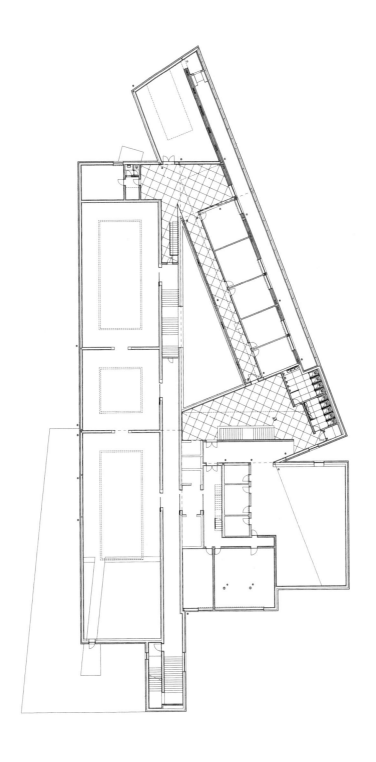

The **Metal Furniture Production Building for Vitra** composes the powers and velocities of architecture. Built, assembled, and kinetic elements syncopate human and machine. Separated from the ground and sky by steel channels, the enclosing skin of red brick suspends space. Prefabricated steel roof trusses supported on concrete columns form a rhythmic skeleton illuminated by vaulted roof lights. Within the factory shed, two free-standing constructions are inserted: a house-like building of concrete block with a segmented roof, serving the workers on the factory floor; and a round steel platform enclosed in glass and raised on columns that shelters both automated controls and offices overlooking the production space. These organic assemblies induce a tremor within a fully engineered world, creating between nature and artifice zones of imperceptibility.

Álvaro Siza's architecture combines the speed of
Every work proceeds on an indeterminate course, a
mining that interprets the world as becoming and
metamorphic capacity results in an architecture
that the visible represents only infinitesimal know-
architecture has a hidden strength, an infinitude

lightning and geological time.

processus infinitum, an active deter-

as life. This transformational and

with animate qualities. Conscious

ledge of an invisible universe, Siza's

beyond apparent stillness.

QUASI-INFINITIES AND THE WANING OF SPACE

Robert Smithson

Originally published in *Arts Magazine*, November 1966.

10. Ad Reinhardt installation, Dwan Gallery, Los Angeles, 1963.

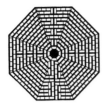

1. The Amiens Labyrinth, France

2. Built for Fabricus at the University of Padua

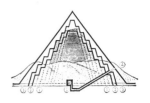

3. The Pyramid of Meidum

Around four blocks of print I shall postulate four ultramundane margins that shall contain indeterminate information as well as reproduced reproductions. The first obstacle shall be a labyrinth,[1] through which the mind will pass in an instant, thus eliminating the spatial problem. The next encounter is an abysmal anatomy theatre.[2] Quickly the mind will pass over this dizzying height. Here the pages of time are paper thin, even when it comes to a pyramid.[3] The center of this pyramid is everywhere and nowhere. From this center one may see the Tower of Babel,[4] Kepler's universe,[5] or a building by the architect Ledoux.[6] To formulate a general theory of this inconceivable system would not solve its symmetrical perplexities. Ready to trap the mind is one of an infinite number of "cities of the future."[7] Inutile codes[8] and extravagant experiments[9] adumbrate the "absolute abstraction."[10] One becomes aware of what T. E. Hume called "the fringe . . . the cold walks . . . that lead nowhere."

In Ad Reinhardt's "Twelve Rules for a New Academy" we find the statement: "The present is the future of the past, and the past of the future." The dim surface sections within the confines of Reinhardt's standard (60" x 60") "paintings" disclose faint squares of time. Time, as a colorless intersection, is absorbed almost imperceptibly into one's consciousness. Each painting is at once both memory and forgetfulness, a paradox of darkening time. The lines of his grids are

4. The Tower of Babel

5. Kepler's model of the universe

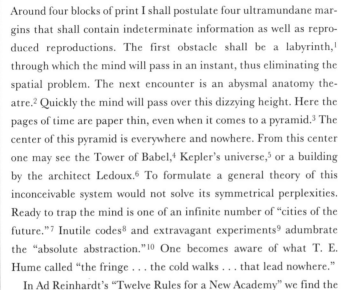

6. Claude-Nicolas Ledoux (1736–1806)

Without a time sense, consciousness is difficult to visualize.
— J. G. Ballard, *The Overloaded Man*

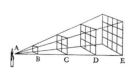

9. From Edgar Allan Poe's *Eureka*

8a. Dan Graham, *Discrete Scheme Without Memory*

8b. Non-code based on Ramon Lull's *The Ars Magna*

7. "City of the Future"

Although inanimate things remain
our most tangible evidence that
the old human past really existed, the
conventional metaphors used to
describe this visible past are mainly
biological.
—George Kubler,
The Shape of Time: Remarks on the
History of Things

nowhere

,

 barely visible; they waver between the future and the past.

George Kubler, like Ad Reinhardt, seems concerned with "weak signals" from "the void." Beginnings and endings are projected into the present as hazy planes of "actuality." In *The Shape of Time: Remarks on the History of Things*, Kubler says, "Actuality is . . . the interchronic pause when nothing is happening. It is the void between events." Reinhardt seems obsessed with this "void," so much that he has attempted to give it a concrete shape—a shape that evades shape. Here one finds no allusion to "duration," but an interval without any suggestion of "life or death." This is a coherent portion of a hidden infinity. The future crisscrosses the past as an unobtainable present. Time vanishes into a perpetual sameness.

Most notions of time (progress, evolution, avant-garde) are put in terms of biology. Analogies are drawn between organic biology and technology; the nervous system is extended into electronics, and the muscular system is extended into mechanics. The workings of biology and technology belong not in the domain of art, but to the "useful" time of organic (active) duration, which is unconscious and mortal. Art mirrors the "actuality" that Kubler and Reinhardt are exploring. What is actual is apart from the continuous "actions" between birth and death. Action is not the motive of a Reinhardt painting. Whenever "action" does persist, it is unavailable or useless. In art,

nowhere.

.

.

,

,

).

;

the pleasure
  nowhere.
    let him go to sleep

John Cage, *Silence*
(Cambridge: MIT Press, 1966)

Dr. J. Bronowski, among others, has
pointed out that mathematics,
which most of us see as the most factual of all sciences, constitutes
the most colossal metaphor imaginable, and must be judged, aesthetically as well as intellectually, in
terms of the success of this metaphor.
—Norbert Weiner,
The Human Use of Human Beings

17. The Guggenheim Museum is perhaps Frank Lloyd Wright's
      most visceral achievement. No building is more organic
      than this inverse digestive tract. The ambulatories are
      metaphorical intestines. It is a concrete stomach.

11. Any art that originates with a will to expression is not abstract, but representational. Space is represented. Critics who interpret art in terms of space, such as Clement Greenberg, see the history of art as a reduction of three-dimensional illusionistic space to "the same order of space as our bodies." Greenberg equates "space" with "our bodies" and interprets this reduction as abstract. (Clement Greenberg, *Abstract, Representational and So Forth*). This anthropomorphizing of space is aesthetically a "pathetic fallacy" and is in no way abstract.

action is always becoming inertia, but this inertia has no ground to settle on except the mind, which is as empty as actual time.

THE ANATOMY OF EXPRESSIONISM[11]

The study of anatomy since the Renaissance led to a notion of art in terms of biology.[12] Although anatomy is rarely taught in our art schools, the metaphors of anatomical and biological science linger in the minds of some of our most abstract artists. In the paintings of both Willem de Kooning[13] and Jackson Pollock,[14] one may find traces of the biological metaphor,[15] or what Lawrence Alloway called "biomorphism."[16] In architecture, most notably in the theories of Frank Lloyd Wright, the biological metaphor prevails.[17] Wright's idea of "the organic" had a powerful influence on both architects and artists. This in turn produced a nostalgia for the rural or rustic community or the pastoral setting, and as a result brought into aesthetics an anti-urban attitude. Wright's view of the city as a "cancer" or "social disease" persists today in the minds of some of the most "formal" artists and critics. Abstract expressionism revealed this visceral condition, without any awareness of the role of the biological metaphor. Art is still for the most part thought to be "creative" or, in Alloway's words, "phases of seeding, sprouting, growing, loving, fighting, decaying, rebirth." The science of biology in this case,

12. Plate probably drawn for Spigelius, 1627

13. Willem de Kooning

16. Lawrence Alloway, "The Biomorphic Forties," *Art Forum*, September 1965.

15. The biological metaphor is at the bottom of all "formalist" criticism. There is nothing abstract about de Kooning or Pollock. To locate them in a formalist system is simply a critical mutation based on a misunderstanding of metaphor— namely, the biological extended into the spatial.

14. Jackson Pollock

18. The truncated ideas in Burroughs's *Nova Express* (New York: Grove Press, 1964) disclose in part the "heat death" of the biological metaphor, "the insect brain of Minraud enclosed in a crystal." Marie Luise von Franz in *Time and Synchronicity in Analytic Psychology* states: "Physicists studying cybernetics have observed that what we call consciousness seems to consist of an intrapsychic flux or train of ideas, which flows 'parallel to' (or is even possibly explicable by) the 'arrow' of time. While M. S. Watanabe convincingly argues that this sense of time is a fact sui generis, others like Grunbaum tend to believe that entropy is the cause of time in man." J. T. Fraser, ed., *The Voices of Time* (New York: George Braziller, 1966), 218.

In principle, nothingness remains inaccessible to science.
—Martin Heidegger,
An Introduction to Metaphysics

The unity of Nature is an extremely artificial and fragile bridge, a garden net.
—T. E. Hulme, *Cinders*

It came to him with a great shock that not one of the robots had ever seen a living thing. Not a bug, a worm, a leaf. They did not know what flesh was. Only the doctors knew that, and none of them could readily understand what was meant by the words "organic matter."
—Michael Shaara, *Orphans of the Void*

becomes "biological-fiction" and the problem of anatomy dissolves into an "organic mass." If this is so, then abstract expressionism was a disintegration of "figure painting," or a decomposition of anthropomorphism. Impressionistic modes of art also suffer from this biological syndrome.

Kubler suggests that metaphors drawn from physical science rather than biological science would be more suitable for describing the condition of art. Since the nineteenth century, biological science has infused in most people's minds an unconscious faith in "creative evolution." An intelligible dissatisfaction with this faith is very much in evidence in the work of certain artists.

THE VANISHING ORGANISM

The biological metaphor has its origin in the temporal order, yet certain artists have "detemporalized" certain organic properties, transforming them into solid objects that contain "ideas of time." This attitude toward art is more Egyptian than Greek, static rather than dynamic. Or it is what William S. Burroughs calls "the thermodynamic pain and energy bank"[18]—a condition of time that originates inside isolated objects rather than outside. Artists as different as Alberto Giacometti and Ruth Vollmer to Eva Hesse and Lucas Samaras disclose this tendency.

24a. For further edification concerning obelisks see *A Short History of the Egyptian Obelisk* by W. R. Cooper (London: Samuel Bagster and Sons, 1877). "The first mention of the obelisk, or Tekhen, occurs in connection with the pyramid: and both are alike designated sacred monuments on the funereal stele of the early empire, and also were undeniably devoted to the worship of the sun; occasionally the obelisk was represented as surmounting a pyramid, a position which it has never actually been found to occupy."

24b. Charles E. Moldenke, *The New York Obelisk—Cleopatra's Needle* (New York: Anson D. F. Randolph, 1891). "We know of the Obelisk of Karnak, erected by Queen Hatasu, that the apex of its pyramidion was covered with 'pure gold.'"

24c. E. A. Wallis Budge, *Cleopatra's Needles and Other Egyptian Obelisks* (London: Religious Tract Society, 1926). Regarding obelisks in Rome: "The brass globe which had been fixed on the top of the obelisk when Caligula set it up was removed; it was empty, though many believed that it would be found to contain valuable objects."

19. Alberto Giacometti, *The Palace at Four A.M.,* 1932–33.

Giacometti's early work *The Palace at Four A.M.*[19] is enigmatically and explicitly about time. But, one could hardly say that this "time structure" reveals any suggestion of organic vitality. Its balance is fragile, precarious, and drained of all notions of energy, yet it has a primordial grandeur.[20] It takes one's mind to the very origins of time—to the fundamental memory. Giacometti's art and thought conveys an entropic view of the world. "It's hard for me to shut up," says Giacometti to James Lord. "It's the delirium that comes from the possibility of really accomplishing anything."[21]

There are parallels in the art of Ruth Vollmer to that of Giacometti. For instance, she made skeletal geometric structures before she started making her bronze "spheres," and like Giacometti she considers those early works "dead ends." But there is no denying that these works belong in the same class as Giacometti's, for they evoke both the presence and absence of time. Her *Obelisk*[22] is similar in mood to *The Palace at Four A.M.* One thinks of Pascal's "fearful sphere" lost in an Egyptian past, or in the words of Plotinus the Stoa, "shadows in a shadow."[23] Matter in *Obelisk*[24] opposes and forecloses all activity—its future is missing.

The art of Eva Hesse is vertiginous and wonderfully dismal.[25] Trellises are mummified, nets contain desiccated lumps, wires extend from tightly wrapped frameworks—a cosmic dereliction is

20. The following is part of a manuscript that describes *The Palace at Four A.M.* It was dictated by Giacometti to André Breton for publication in the magazine *Minotaure* (nos. 3-4, 1933) and was later translated by Ruth Vollmer into English (see the magazine *Transformation*, published by Wittenborn). "The object has taken form little by little; by the end of summer 1932 it clarified slowly for me, the various parts taking their exact form and their exact place in the ensemble. Come autumn it had attained such reality that its execution in space did not take more than one day." He also goes on to say, "The days and nights had the same color, as if everything happened just before daybreak."

21. James Lord, *A Giacometti Portrait,* (New York: Museum of Modern Art, 1965).

24d. Gustave Flaubert, *Salambo* (Berkeley: Berkeley Medallion, 1966). Describes obelisks in Byrsa as "poised on their points like inverted torches."

23. Quoted from *Enneads,* in *Concepts of Mass in Classical and Modern Physics* by Max Jammer (Cambridge, Mass.: Harvard University Press, 1961), 31. Jammer states that "Proclus, the other great exponent of Neoplatonism in the East, accepts Plotinus's doctrine, but with one important modification: the passivity or inertia of matter follows from its extension." The decline of the categories of "painting" and "sculpture" seem to be the result of this problem of spatial extension from matter. Space becomes an illusion on matter.

22. Ruth Vollmer, *Obelisk,* 1962

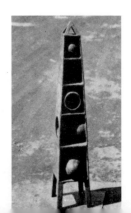

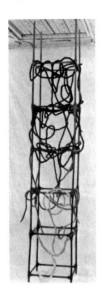

25a. Eva Hesse, *Laocoön*, 1965

25b. Pergamen(?) *Laocoön*

25c. In Hesse's *Laocoön*, based on the sculpture by Pergamen(?), second century B.C., we discover an absence of "pathos" and a deliberate avoidance of the anthropomorphic. Instead one is aware only of the vestigial and devitalized "snakes" looping through a lattice constructed with cloth-bound joints. Everything "classical" and "romantic" is mitigated and undermined. The baroque aesthetic of the original *Laocoön* with its flowing lines—soft and fluid—is transformed into a dry, skeletal tower that goes nowhere.

the general effect. Coils go on and on; some are cracked open, only to reveal an empty center. Such "things" seem destined for a funerary chamber that excludes all mention of the living and the dead. Her art brings to mind the obsessions of the pharaohs, but in this case the anthropomorphic measure is absent. Nothing is incarnated into nothing. Human decay is nowhere in evidence.

The isolated systems Lucas Samaras[26] has devised irradiate a malignant splendor. Clusters of pins cover vile organs of an untraceable origin. His objects are infused with menace and melancholy. A lingering narcissism[27] may be found in some of his "treasures." He has made "models" of tombs and monuments that combine the "times" of ancient Egypt with most disposable futures of science fiction.[28]

TIME AND HISTORY AS OBJECTS

At the turn of the century, a group of colorful artists banded together in order to get a jump on the bourgeois notion of progress. This bohemian brand of progress gradually developed into what is sometimes called the avant-garde. Both of these notions of duration are no longer absolute modes of "time" for artists. The avant-garde, like progress, is based on an ideological consciousness of time. Time as ideology has produced many uncertain "art histories" with the help of the mass media. Art histories may be measured in time by books

The individual is the seat of a constant process of decantation, decantation from the vessel containing the fluid of future time, sluggish, pale and monochrome, to the vessel containing the fluid of past time, agitated and multi-colored by the phenomena of its hours.
—Samuel Beckett, *Proust*

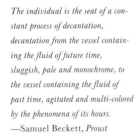

30a. Donald Judd has been interested in "progressions" and "regressions" as "solid objects." He has based certain works on "inverse natural numbers." Some of these may be found in *Summation of Series* by L. B. W. Jolley (New York: Dover Publications, 1961).

30b. Donald Judd, *Untitled*, 1965

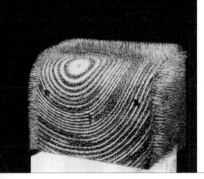

26. Lucas Samaras, *Untitled*, 1963

27. Self-love, self-observation, self-examination, and self-awareness result in an isolated mind. This kind of mind would tend to produce a fictitious "reality" detached from organic nature. *Monsieur Teste* by Paul Valery offers perhaps the greatest elucidation of narcissism: "He watches himself, he maneuvers, he is unwilling to be maneuvered. He knows only two values, two categories, those of consciousness reduced to its acts: the possible and the impossible. In this strange head, where philosophy has little credit, where language is always on trial, there is scarcely a thought that is not accompanied by a feeling that it is tentative."

(years), by magazines (months), by newspapers (weeks and days), by radio and television (days and hours), and at the gallery proper—*instants!* Time is brought to a condition that breaks down into "abstract objects."[29] The isolated time of the avant-garde has produced its own unavailable history or entropy.

Consider the avant-garde as Achilles and progress as the Tortoise in a race that would follow Zeno's paradox of "infinite regress."[30] This non-Aristotelian logic defies the formal deductive system and says that "movement is impossible." Let us paraphrase Jorge Luis Borges's description in *Avatars of the Tortoise* of that paradox: The avant-garde goes ten times faster than progress, and gives progress a head start of ten meters. The avant-garde goes those ten meters, progress goes one; the avant-garde completes that meter, progress goes a decimeter; the avant-garde goes that decimeter, progress goes a centimeter; the avant-garde goes that centimeter, progress, a millimeter; the avant-garde, the millimeter, progress a tenth of a millimeter; and so on to infinity without progress ever being overtaken by the avant-garde. The problem may be reduced to this series:

$$10 + 1 + 1/10 + 1/100 + 1/1000 + 1/10,000 + :::$$

29. *Abstraction and Empathy* by Wilhelm Worringer (London: Routledge and Kegan Paul, 1953), translated from the 1908 *Abstraktion und Einfuhlung*, elucidates this idea: "In so far, therefore, as a sensuous object is still dependent upon space, it is unable to appear to us in its closed material individuality," and "Space is therefore the major enemy of all striving after abstraction."

28. In *13 French Science-Fiction Stories,* edited by Damon Knight (New York: Simon and Shuster, 1961), is a story by Charles Henneberg called Moonfishers. "The Interplanetarians were landing in these sands. They were of many kinds. Much later, the Pharoah Psammetichus III noted: 'They fell from the sky like the fruits of a fig-tree that is shaken; they were the color of copper and sulphur, and some had eyes.'"

HAVING HEARD MATHEMATICS:
THE TOPOLOGIES OF BOXING

Michael Bell

Giuseppe Terragni. Casa Rustici, 1933–35. Milan, Italy.

Introduction

In his essay "The Gaze in the Expanded Field," Norman Bryson ascertains a subject persecuted at the center of both Jean-Paul Sartre's and Jacques Lacan's accounts of the gaze.[1] Bryson's critique asserts that both Sartre and Lacan retain a conceptual frame that posits a subject as the origin of space even as they reveal that this sovereignty is menaced by the presence of other origins. In Sartre's case this competing origin is another viewing subject, while in Lacan's scenario the subject is challenged by the opaque presence of other inanimate entities, things that "look back."

To illustrate Sartre's theorizing of the gaze, Bryson relies upon a composition by Raphael, *Marriage of the Virgin* (1504), in which he claims that Raphael has annihilated the viewing "subject as center" at the very instance when this subject has taken up the composition's offered station point. The vanishing point of Raphael's composition is portrayed as inextricably bound to the viewpoint; it leads the viewing eye toward what Bryson calls the "drain" or "black hole of otherness placed at the horizontal horizon."[2] Bryson's analysis of the painting reveals an implacable decentering: Raphael's architectural space is one that evades the sovereign occupation of a viewing subject at the crucible of this subject's attempts to occupy the apex of the pictorial field.

Bryson's characterization of the mechanics of this subjectless space bears quite literal similarities to both Frank Stella's critique of Piet Mondrian's *Broadway Boogie Woogie* (1942–43) in his book *Working Space* and to Robert Slutzky's self-defined initiatives in the series of fifteen paintings he completed between 1981 and 1984.[3] The pictorial device that Bryson refers to as a drain or black hole—the vertical white rectangle that composes the door within Raphael's architecture—has a correlative counterpart in both Stella's and Slutzky's pictorial explications. Stella also attributes to the device similar subject-annihilating tendencies: "It is here that Mondrian rattles the bones of human configuration for the last time; it is here that the white rectangle steps out of the background landscape into its own space,"[4] wrote Stella in the transcription of the Charles Eliot Norton Lectures he delivered at Harvard University in 1983 and 1984. Stella's depicts two techniques by which Mondrian transformed the reliance of pictorial space upon perspective, especially perspective's regulation of a frontal and positioned subject. Stella claims that the colored bars of Mondrian's late paintings span rather than divide the surface of the compositions and in doing so allow for the emergence of a truly modern pictorial space, a space of abstraction that does not rely on perspective's horizon line or a relative station point. Of the paintings *Victory Boogie Woogie* (1943–44) and *New York City* (1941–42), Stella states that Mondrian had given rise to a background source of light whose progressive emanation allows it to be understood as foreground. Within this foregrounded yet formless atmosphere, lies the enunciation of a space secured by Mondrian's "hot blooded structure" and "live-wire armatures," a space capable of providing a freely directionless extensivity of shape and duration. Though Stella does not offer this

Hoffman Genus 1: A minimal and embedded topological surface is boundaryless and non–self-intersecting. Described in finite terms, a minimal surface is capable of infinite extension without self-intersection.

DOUBLE DIHEDRAL HOUSE

DAVID LYMAN HOUSE AND GALLERY, 1992–93

In the essay "Mimicry and Legendary Psychasthenia," Roger Callois proposes that it is an organism's ability to distinguish itself from space that allows it to form a coherent concept of self—of personality.[1] That distinction between the self and space, however, is not easily defined. The Double Dihedral House consists of a house and art gallery situated opposite each other on four acres desert in Santa Fe, New Mexico. A cruciform volume is framed and unframed in the two structures; the house and gallery are each constituted in reference to their paired *other* structure. In the house, the roof and floor are cut away to reveal the interior. A subject's gaze traverses the desert floor, piercing both building volumes—the gaze's vectoral speed pauses momentarily to seek each surface before falling further in syncopation through subsequent layers. Eventually, the gaze is focused not on the building or the frame but on the unanchored space beyond. Under such circumstances the originative quality of perspectival space fails to provide the footing upon which to survey the Cartesian field. This failure also subsequently undermines the subject as the origin of space. Says Callois: "We are allowed to know, as we should, that nature is everywhere the same . . . then the body separates itself from thought, the individual breaks the boundary of his skin and occupies the other side of his senses. He tries to look at himself from any point whatever in space. He feels himself becoming space, dark space where things cannot be put."

1. Roger Callois, "Mimicry and Legendary Psychasthenia," in *October: The First Decade* (Cambridge, Mass: MIT Press), 70.

possibility, it seems that Mondrian's white rectangle places itself behind and around its frontal subject.

Within the same few years in which Stella delivered his Norton Lectures, Robert Slutzky prepared a series of fifteen paintings also dominated by a centralized and usually white square, what Slutzky calls an oculus. The paintings were presented at the Modernism Gallery in San Francisco in 1984 and subsequently were published in a monograph that includes an essay entitled "Color/Structure/Painting" that Slutzky cowrote with Joan Ockman. Slutzky and Ockman referred to this centralized square as the "counter eye in the canvas," an oculus that confronts "the artist and spectator alike." Bryson calls attention to this dynamic with Sartre, whose account of his solitary dominion over a park setting is undermined by the arrival of another person. Bryson cites this scenario in identifying a menaced and decentered subject within Sartre's conception of the gaze. Upon realizing he is not alone, Sartre finds himself occupying a tangential relationship to an other. His vision converges on this other, where he is not and where he cannot be. Slutzky and Ockman ascribe to these fifteen canvases a bit of both Sartre's animate other and Lacan's inanimate things that "look back." Though they do not ascribe to this "counter eye" the explicit existential aspects of Sartre's tangential subject, Slutzky and Ockman by interpolation instigate a transformation of vision's role in the positioning of the self as both origin of and object within a provisional field. In fact, it is the enframed field that these paintings slowly but surely reconfigure in an increasingly willful compositional process. As the oculus confronts the artist, the artist responds, and one epistemological crisis is undone by another: Slutzky and Ockman state that this oculus turns "space inside-out," and "like a torus-glove" it makes "figure and field ambiguously one." There is no doubt that these plastic mechanics ultimately remain dialectical despite the spatial ambiguity they portend and Slutzky betrays no need to deny the canvas as an originary surface. Like Sartre and Lacan, Slutzky and Ockman still seem to posit their subject, at least momentarily, as the origin of the visual field. Though perhaps his subject/painter is menaced as well, Slutzky's oculus offers an intuitive vantage and grasp of the inferable, a chance to seize and then occupy the composition's topologically transformed space.[5] In this way the dialectic transparency of Slutzky's techniques constitutes an unconcealment of the enframing device and of the mechanisms of representation. The oculus offers the opportunity to intuit the unframed duration of events. In providing the fixity and frontality that is both learned and reflexively anticipated, Slutzky also provides a comprehension of time as form—this work is representational, even perhaps a model, but it also operates enzymat-

The Double Dihedral House uses the oculus as a device to syncopate both vision and the perspectival field in a way that might spill their framed contents and alter their static basins. In these projects vision has a syncopated vector that threatens the stability of ocular distance. The relationship of perceiving subject and perceived object is here turned inside out, the hegemony of perspective's constructed subject and its fixed basin is overcome.

Right: Shock-wave pattern from a projectile at near-sonic speed.

Piet Mondrian, *Broadway Boogie Woogie*,
1942–43. Collection: The Museum of Modern Art.

Robert Slutzky, *Untitled C*, 1983.

ically in use, or more accurately, under duress. Here it ceases to be a model and becomes a lived experience. Slutzky's paintings offer the opportunity to relinquish form but they also suggest, perhaps fetishistically, that we decline the opportunity. This retaining of distance between viewing subject and perceived world allows for a critical vantage that is ultimately difficult to consider menaced. Slutzky and Ockman may here be understood to provide a pictorial impetus, a visual inducement, that forecloses on a final and catastrophic transformation of the pictorial field itself and with it the fixing of a discrete subject and an object. This transformation takes vision irrecoverably past the plastic limits of its learned Cartesian basin and in doing so moves the locus of our cognition onto a dispersed and unfolded field. In this sense Slutzky's work also asks viewers to annihilate their own visual origins and having done so to enter a space of extensivity, a space of uncharted and unanchored movements. To Bryson this type of expanded field results in an alleviation of the conceptual frame retained by Sartre and Lacan. Drawing from the philosophies of Kitaro Nishida and Keiji Nishitani, Bryson notes that it appears as the frame is "withdrawn." The subject/object dialectic that has been reified within modern practices dissolves in this expansion and the subject no longer posits itself against that which it is not.[6] In this manner the subject is able to reposition itself as a "being that exists through the existence of everything else in the universal field."[7]

Robert Slutzky's techniques operate within a structure of formalist mechanics; while color and shape modulate depth and Cartesian geometries provide a willful author's heuristic structure, Slutzky pushes each of these dimensions to their extremes, to their plastic limits. The painter speaks of blues that are not quite blue (as Josef Albers might have) and squares that are not quite square. Without this pushing of limits there would be good reason to believe that these techniques are no longer capable of serving as a critical apparatus. The topology of Slutzky's desired transfiguration of pictorial figure and ground presents the means for a significant critical reappraisal and transformation of Cartesian perspective's dominion in the description and regulation of a contemporary and increasingly visual subject. The pervasiveness of new and still predominantly visual computer interfaces are reason enough to continue to consider the ocular an important project, but these are clearly only the most blatant and erotically taunting conscriptions of cognitive vision that constitute daily life.

Slutzky, like Mondrian, seems to have been rattling "the bones of human configuration for the last time." He speaks of unanchoring our contemplative eyes for distant journeys and faraway places, loci of our memories rebirthed." Slutzky's paintings allow for the intuiting rather than the modeling of such a space. As such, these paintings must be understood to be critical; they offer the preservation of an immanence within the represented that could sustain the migratory and lateral passages and cycles of an expanded and authentic life. Bryson's essay concludes with the suggestion that the "real discovery" of his critique of the gaze is that "things we took to be private, secluded, and inward," such as "perception, art, the perception *of* art in a museum, are created socially. What is at stake is the discovery of a politics of vision."[8]

Double Dihedral House: A house without an interior. An approximate formal model or precedent: The bottle with no inside. This model of a Klein Bottle belongs to topologist Albert Tucker of Princeton University. Nobody will ever actually see an actual Klein Bottle because it exists only in the topologist's imagination. A true Klein Bottle passes through itself without the existence of a hole, which is a physical impossibility.

Within the dissipative and unbounded spaces of such contemporary urban cities as Houston, the idea of a withdrawn or expanded frame seems in some sense ironic.[9] On the plateau of late capitalism's vacated version of the "city,"[10] vision is alternatively vast and instrumental. What Martin Heidegger termed the "malice of rage"—an increasing tendency towards nihilism that is endemic to a reification of vision within modernism today—has an odd and complex resonance in the dissolute spaces of sprawling American cities such as Houston. Here the blankness of the white rectangle already predominates both in the vertical and horizontal planes, yet it rarely emerges in clear distinction and it hardly defines a landscape of its own, at least not a sublime landscape. In these cities, television's conscription of vision reigns over the fabrication of a cognitive and social citizen, yet the horizon—the real horizon—of this flat and immense city is literally a 360° circle, and its enveloping topology ultimately vanquishes any attempt to demarcate either a station point or origin. Malice is unable to find clear footing, and rage, when it does occur, seems unable to articulate its province and is thus unable to sustain prerogatives. The material, labor, and shape of space in these cities, almost exclusively orchestrated within the quadratic equations of capital investment, leave the eye/the subject/the citizen in the devastated scenario of trying to cohere the formed remnants and entropic by-products of a process of clandestine financial machinations. When an expected perspective does occur in the contemporary city it hardly constitutes a hegemonic device but rather a perceived relief. We know what it is and we probably even realize that it is artificially contrived. On one hand, vision is confiscated by the devices of the media, and on the other it is presented with a vacancy of such shapeless expanse that it is overwhelmed. Either scenario seems to lead toward a constituent humiliation. The white rectangle, Mondrian's sublime device of metropolitan criticism and of negative dwelling,[11] here offers an ironic and suffered respite.

"We are still in the *city*," states Cacciari in *The Dialectics of the Negative and the Metropolis*, "as long as we are in the presence of use values alone, or in the presence of the simple production of the commodity, or if the two instances stand next to each other in a nondialectical relation." We inhabit the metropolis "when production assumes its own social rationale, when it determines the modes of consumption and succeeds in making them function toward the renewal of the cycle." Houston, and indeed most of America's so-called metropolises, demands a renewed characterization of these terms, for one could argue that the distended space of these post-metropolitan cities is nondialectical even as it has succeeded in establishing modes of consumption that are essentially self-sustaining. The blankness of space in these cities seems also to engender a self-sustaining virus, a metabolic mechanism whose undermining presence is assured by managed capital's seeming inability to cohere plastic space. This blankness, a result of capital's desperate need to maximize the vectoral coefficients of production, nonetheless, poses its own dialectic traps of rather primitive geometric origin: efficiency of transportation relies on geometric parameters in the production and assembly of contemporary building

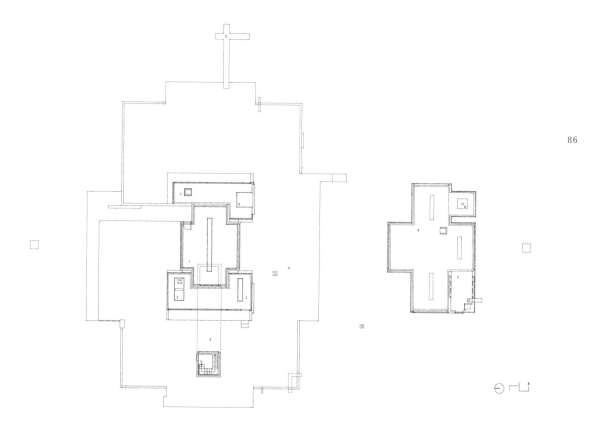

Site: La Cienega, New Mexico.

materials to such an extent that contemporary building techniques are almost incapable of producing truly plastic form or space. Efficiency in the production, sale, and transportation of materials also requires a clandestine, or at least hidden, method of dealing with gravity as it pertains to building design, material configuration, and ultimately to human weight and presence. The discrete nature of architectural practice within these post-metropolitan processes ironically might be understood to offer at least two alternatives both derived from an engagement of the limits of architecture's professional involvement in urban machinations of finance. The first alternative lies in the "rattling of the bones of human configuration for the last time," in occupying Slutzky's inside-out space. The nihilistic attributes of blankness recede in the expanded field.[12] Having occupied this space a second alternative emerges based in the activity of a "being that exists through the existence of everything else."[13] If this rattling is incomplete, if a vestige of a frame remains, it seems possible to work within, rather than model, the shapes and the processes of the contemporary city itself. In some sense Slutzky's oculus provides the sequel to the texts he wrote with Colin Rowe; the habitation of these spaces might be considered not as the mathematics of, but instead, the topology of the post-metropolitan city. It is a topology that must be lived rather than represented. The means of procurement of this lived space, however, must in some way remain visible if such a space is to endow its subject with critical authority.

Giuseppe Terragni: Vision and Duration

The following section presents an analysis of two buildings designed by Giuseppe Terragni in collaboration with Pietro Lingeri during the early 1930s. These two projects, Casa Rustici (1933–35) and Palazzo Littorio, Scheme A (1934), are characterized by an overt preoccupation with a classicized and monumental frontality. Both projects, however, also offer the potential of a transformed visual field, a field whose edges at times seem alternately expanded and eradicated. The essay's primary interest is the Palazzo Littorio, specifically the photoelastic/finite element analysis phase of this project; however, the issues of perspectivalism that this project involves itself in are related also to both Casa Rustici and Casa Giuliani-Frigerio (1939–40). Underlying this analysis is the assumption that Palazzo Littorio exemplifies a phase of design in which Terragni and Lingeri effectively unanchored form from vision and in doing so clarified the spatial potential of material and matter itself; in other words, they bring to a cognitive level an ideal of material duration as a replacement for perspectival relativity. Peter Eisenman's analysis of Casa Giuliani-Frigerio will later be brought to bear on the conception of an unframed and nondialectical, yet still plastic conception of architectural space, a space that has antecedents in the canonical works of de Stijl architecture and painting.[14]

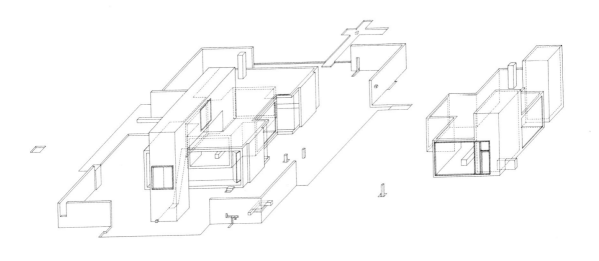

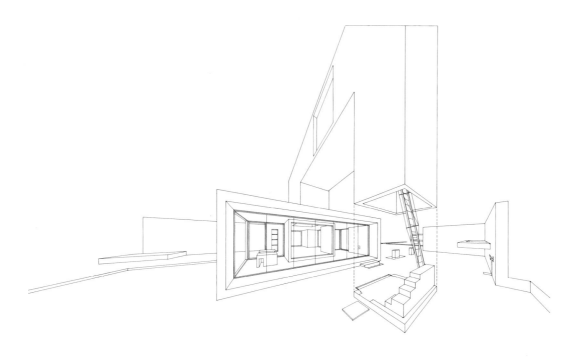

SLOW SPACE

Eyes in the Heat

The design of Palazzo Littorio was abetted by a series of photoelastic stress analysis experiments that were to predict the distribution of stress and strain forces in the surface of the building's cantilevered wall. These experiments were perfected within a general refinement of the principles and mechanics of camera and lens techniques, as well as the chemistry of the photographic process itself. Palazzo Littorio's program, in essence a speaking platform for Mussolini, was to be sustained by the spectacle of the massive cantilever allowed by these experiments. The *space* of this instrument of political authority was derived from the literally deep and frontalized choreography of a political audience, yet it was also a space of shallow depth developed within the camera and lens techniques of photoelastic processes. These techniques effectively flattened the actual perspectival depth of the project within the thermodynamics of photographic chemical processes. Palazzo Littorio's perceptual and literal frontality relates it vividly to the string of six apartment houses that Terragni designed with Lingeri in Milan, also during the early 1930s. The perspectival principles of these works culminate in Casa Rustici, a project that, like Palazzo Littorio, vigorously establishes a planar modulation of depth as it simultaneously threatens its compositional stability.

The frontal arrangement of space in Casa Rustici operates in a manner similar to both Mondrian's work as described by Frank Stella and Robert Slutzky's ocular paintings. Terragni and Lingeri overdilate the viewing eye; the architects invite the viewing subject to take up the apex of the offered space as they withdraw its authority. The proportion and rhythm of openings in the facade of Casa Rustici set up a syncopation within the parameters of a field established by the overt frame surrounding the primary facade of the building. Readings of apparently recessive or progressive planar depths are modulated peripherally and centrally in unexpected ways that ultimately undermine the eye's ability to cohere the classicized formal characteristics of the composition. Terragni and Lingeri focus the eye not

on the form of the building but on the central space between the two primary masses that house the apartment units. Like Mondrian's bars that Stella claims span rather than divide, the balconies of the Casa Rustici seem to span the voided center of the building. In doing so they give rise to a complex space, a space that cannot be read as positive or negative, recessive or progressive, or even as plastic in any traditional sense of the word. It is a space more akin to a vacuum than to a simple absence. The horizontal expanse of the facade establishes a distinct peripheral datum; against this datum it is

Giuseppe Terragni. Casa Rustici, 1933–35. Milan, Italy.

BELL

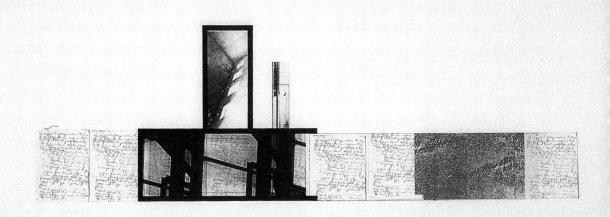

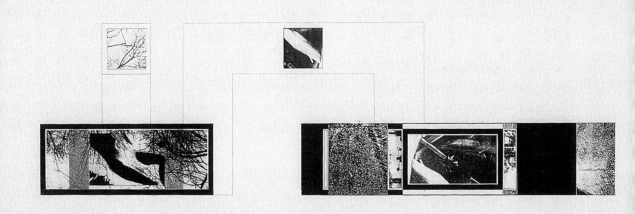

possible to read flanking window bays as progressive surfaces against a center that appears to be recessive. Yet the readings can be reversed; the light that Stella understood to emanate from the background of Mondrian's composition here forces the eye to relinquish its reliance on any expected background or foreground arrangement of space, thus mandating an abdication of enframement or plastic figuration. The peripheral surface's windows, stacked five floors high, appear oversized as well, an attribute consistent to both Loos and Terragni, as well as to contemporary work by Álvaro Siza and Frank Gehry. While they retain a vestige of the oculus, the window's expansiveness undermines the progressive reading of the surface; the eye falls deep into them, unable to grasp the distanced ocular frame. These wall surfaces are also at once progressive and recessive; against the outer edge of the facade's frame they appear to have receded, yet against the vectoral direction and speed of a frontal-ized vision they appear progressive. The oculus/window in these surfaces offers the depth-seeking eye a chance to move deeper into space,while offering nothing to look at. Recalling Lacan, it also seems here that nothing looks back either. Space seems to replace the other.

The proportion of the windows in the facade of Casa Rustici, however, is sufficient to cause a kind of peripheral delay or momentary pause. We are asked to consider the nature of the oculus and the *represented* before relinquishing either. This delay, if understood within a model of ballistics, instigates a degree of turbulence: ballistics tests have shown that when a bullet passes through a plane of Plexiglas, it causes a turbulence that is roughly coplanar with the surface of the glass but derived from the direction, velocity, and shape of the bullet. As the bullet continues its slowed and damaged trajectory, this turbulence models a topology that in effect resolves and describes the catastrophic col-laboration of the vectoral and planar dimensions of the experiment's two components. If the geome-tries of vision were equated with those that describe the movement of the bullet and given a conical form, the topology of the turbulence could be understood to seek the orthogonal building form. As the balcony/bridges span the white-hot void of the building's court, a subjectless court with a glass floor, the eye's ability to hold on to the form of the building and composition must ultimately be intuited rather than represented. The mechanics of the eye are thwarted in this struggle; the eye falls deep into the central space, its speed and directionality damaged by the interaction with the facade, but it is continuous nonetheless. The result is an awareness of the architectural form, presumably of human life, that extends beyond the relativity of the frontal view and of the station point. Terragni and Lingeri triangulate the anticipated bipartite relationship of subject and object within a durational field—the Casa Rustici denies both subject or object as origin, positing each as a durational entity within an expanded field.

Giuseppe Terragni. Casa Rustici, 1933–35. Milan, Italy.

What might happen in a space inside out? With the improvisational nature of his work John Cassavetes "entrusted his actors not just to portray characters but to become them, often to the extent of reacting to one another spontaneously and improvising dialogue." At this point Cassavetes, camera on his shoulder, began to improvise as well. Who was directing whom at this point? Where did the dialogue begin—what does the scene include or preclude? Try to establish the hierarchy in a scene from the film "Faces" that involves Cassavetes moving—the arced tangent of his shoulder and the geometry of his contorted body as it twists to catch an evolutionary script that has suddenly changed direction as Gena Rowlands and John Marley unfold into their characters. My point is not to offer film theory as an antecedent to architectural design, or even to offer improvisation as a method of architectural design, but to suggest that the apparent hegemony of the visual, and the Cartesian dialectics of observer and observed, is in some way ingeniously overcome when one pushes its techniques to their limits. This overcoming of elastic limits might stand in for a lineage of architectural attempts at the authorless: the unanticipated, the autonomous . . . the unbounded, the inbetween, the formless. But what isn't released in this dialectic of intuited limits is the plastic and more importantly the still discrete nature of architectural practice. The point at which a certain level of strife pushes something past the final point of stability is offered within the parameters of the finite. While one could hope that the truly new would emerge at this point, one could presumably at least count on the unpredicted.

Palazzo Littorio: Buckling and Immanence

The photoelastic stress analysis diagrams that accompany the design presented by Terragni and Lingeri for the 1934 Palazzo Littorio competition have garnered little attention and even less interpretation despite the fact that they have been published widely.[15] They appear in the Zanichelli monograph on Terragni, in the book *Surface and Symbol* by Thomas Schumacher, and I am sure that Peter Eisenman will address them in some format in his forthcoming book on Terragni. The reproduction of these images has consistently seemed dutiful rather than enlightening. This claim, however, sets aside Manfredo Tafuri's essay, "Giuseppe Terragni: Subject and Mask." Because Tafuri's explication does not examine the intrinsic properties of the photoelastic processes,[16] he is forced to reconcile their significance in the design of Palazzo Littorio within the linguistic prerogatives of his own research. Tafuri seemed unable to synthesize his linguistic research and his sometimes startling structural/mechanical insights. For example, while Tafuri recognizes that the apparent wall composing the primary facade is actually a "boxlike structure" rather than a wall—a fact that completely changes not only the mechanics of its cantilever but also its ability to "speak," in Tafuri's lexicon—the author still admits that he is unsure of the reason why the isostatic lines of the photoelastic process are represented on the surface of this facade.[17] Tafuri's analysis focuses on the belief that Terragni has reduced these "forces" to an arabesque, to a dissolution of an "apodictic word." The following analysis of Palazzo Littorio instead attempts to situate more completely Terragni and Lingeri's ambitions within the techniques of the photoelastic process itself. In doing so it reveals the building's fabrications of power and political authority, as they are manifested in the realms of optics, perspectivalism, lens and camera mechanisms, chemistry and photo processes, and ultimately in constituent subjectivity.

Photoelastic Stress Analysis

Photoelasticity was "the method of experimental stress analysis" during the 1930s.[18] As a form of finite element analysis the photoelastic process revealed an observable relationship between optical patterns generated within a transparent material and the distribution of stresses that migrate through the material under loading.[19] The behavior of the material under stress is witnessed in the patterns generated as a polarized light passes through the assembled model. The polarization produces a light whose waves vibrate within a single plane; as a control device, the polarization allows for the discretization of an otherwise infinite number of wave axes. In certain materials, the refraction of this polarized light coincides with the material's primary stress points. Changes in the "velocity of the transmission of light" as it passes through these materials reveal the pattern of stress distribution as it occurs in the model.[20] Since the model stands in for an actual material, the value of these results must be extrapolated in order to be of use. Given the scale of the cantilever that Terragni and Lingeri proposed in Scheme A of what would eventually total three design submissions, it is not surprising

Giuseppe Terragni and Pietro Lingeri. The Palazzo Littorio, Scheme A, 1934. Rome, Italy.

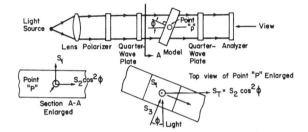

Fringe pattern in disk containing a central hole. Load applied at the top and bottom center. Patterns emerge as a result of polarization of light-wave vibrations; the waves vibrate at different magnitudes depending on the stress in the material they pass through or refract from.

Stress concentration factor determined by photoelasticity.

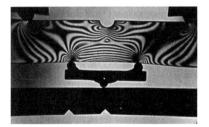

that they chose to perform some stress tests in the form of finite element analysis. But why would Terragni and Lingeri choose to implement the stress patterns culled from the photoelastic studies as a primary element in the final design proposal? In the case of Palazzo Littorio, the isostatic lines that depicted the evaluation of stresses in the photoelastic model were to be traced into the building's facade by steel support cables.

The facade of the proposed speaking platform from which Mussolini was to address an audience revealed the tracings of the stresses generated at the two massive trusses that were to support the cantilevered wall.[21] What is referred to here as a wall appears to be actually a curved diaphragm structure that operates as a thin-walled beam: in the perspective drawing that depicts the structure from above and in plan, two wall surfaces seem to compose a structure that synthetically acts as a hollow beam. As such, the suspension of this conflation between curved structural plate and box beam would have behaved very differently under loading than a single plate or wall surface would have. It is not clear if the photoelastic analysis was performed using a diaphragm model that accurately depicted the complexity of the proposed cantilever, nor is it clear if the modeled surface employed in analysis conformed to the curvature of the actual building design. In either case, neglecting these attributes would have rendered the test results inaccurate and the resulting construction almost invariably catastrophic.

The trusses that were to support a significant portion of this surface's weight, seen in the perspective illustration from above, would not have been visible to a viewer at ground level.[22] Their support of the eighty-meter-long porphyry wall occurred at two points that straddled the removed section of construction cut out to accommodate the balcony. The cut-out section effectively creates two almost independent surfaces that reconnect under the balcony; each in effect is supported at one point, but their joining also causes them to act as continuous structure. This places a great strain on the sur-

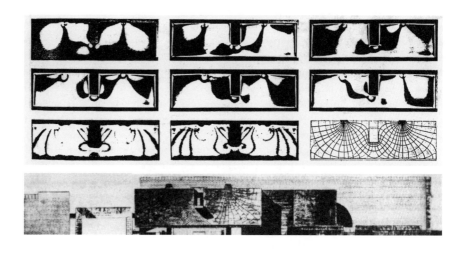

Photoelastic studies of Palazzo Littorio.

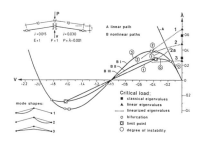

Hans Hofmann, *Ecstasy*, 1947.

Hans Hofmann, *Yellow Table on Yellow Background*, 1936.

Critical linear and nonlinear conditions of stability in a discretized analysis of structural mechanics.

"Push responds to pull"—Hans Hofmann used the phrase so often "that it became nearly synonymous with his style of painting." The spatial milieu of a Hofmann painting is one of complex geometries cohering active and reactive forces; in Hofmann's realm a pictorial push into space is answered by a rebounding pull back out. Of course these pushes and pulls were achieved not with the weight of gravity but with the weights of color, shape, and line—all activated by the velocity of vision and played out within the basin of the frame's and the picture's finite surface. Hofmann's paintings are "plastic," meaning that their space is active—even viscous and alluvial—they "animate" the initially "neutral" picture surface.

The trajectory of Hans Hofmann's spatial evolution seems to have moved in a staccato rhythm; innovations led to innovations but he also often returned to his foundations. One of his preoccupations was Matisse's structure of flat space. In works such as *Yellow Table on Yellow Background*, Hofmann tilts space forward to such a degree that it threatens to spill out of its frame. The paint is viscous and thick and applied with an aggressive stroke, but if this virtual pictorial spill were to become real it would certainly lose this thickness. *Yellow Table on Yellow Background* is a subjectless work: no human figure is present, and one wonders where a figure could be placed and how some form of a volumetric body might try to inhabit this space.

But what if push didn't answer pull? What if space wasn't plastic or viscous? What if space were more of an energy sink, having a dissipative quality—its basin involved in an expansive entropic creep rather than a shoring up contraction. Hofmann's thesis demands a rebuttal as Slutzky's and Le Corbusier's "thickened space" demands thinned space. That the antithesis of each argument has an asymptotic relation to the space we occupy in the modern "city" should be a reason to be alarmed: space in the contemporary city of finance must surely be aplastic. What viscous pulls shore us up and react to our pushes?

The antithesis to the stability of Hofmann's dialectic push-pull relation does in fact emerge in Hofmann's own work: *Ecstasy* (1947) so fully labors its flat canvas surface that push seems to implode the picture frame's geometry while pull threatens to spill its contents onto the gallery floor. The opposing forces' ability to counter each other is here lost as each seems to have well exceeded its elastic limits: push and pull threaten a new independence that in turn threatens the works' stability when each is stretched beyond its capacity to rebound.

faces that surround the cut-out. Given the slight curvature of the suspended wall surface, the pointal support of the trusses would have instigated rotational moments in not one but two axes, and each of these moments would threaten the ability of the structure to achieve or maintain equilibrium. The first rotational moment would have been parallel to the surface of the composition, and it would induce a membranic stress across the surface of the wall; the second rotational moment would have been instigated by the slight curvature of the wall surface and its axis would have been perpendicular to this surface. Both rotations would have critically altered the degree to which the photoelastic analysis, if performed on a flat surface, could predict the behavior of these surfaces and their beam configuration under loading. If the construction was indeed that of thin-walled beam, how and when it would fail would be very different from that of a singular plane. The design of the building, however, appears to anticipate the complexity of forces at play and it seems intuitively to both induce and counteract them. The diaphragm construction of the building's facade appears to be intended to provide the depth needed to counter these oblique loading conditions. While the shallow curvature of the plan exacerbated the capabilities of the cantilevered composition to maintain equilibrium, it also appears to provide the structural depth and ballast required to resist buckling and structural failure. The potential that the wall surface would buckle under its own loading would have been more complex at the central balcony, where a section of wall is removed. Terragni and Lingeri seemed willing to both allow for structural depth and curvature, and the concurrent deep pictorial depth and frontality that abetted the project's political requirements, while effectively trying to maintain a primarily surface or shallow distribution of stresses along the surface. The result is a construction that has qualities of both depth and surface, yet it is a composition that refuses the hierarchical dimension of either axial vector. This lack of hierarchy has confounded succinct readings of Terragni's political resolve.

If a slight adjustment were made in the calibration of surface curvature to wall thickness, wall height, vertical support, or material chemical stability, it is clear that the project could suffer a dramatic structural collapse. Terragni and Lingeri appear to have set the project on the verge of material and formal failure: in other words, it seems that they have found a combination of formal and material properties that reveal a threat to the stability of the status quo while allowing for its ultimate and highly dramatic sustenance. In this light the complexity of Terragni's political beliefs might find some clarity. Perhaps more significant, this project reveals the status of the dialectical imperatives that define its plastic and mechanical prerogatives, and so provides a critique of its own means and those of its patronage. This is something that contemporary conscriptions of the visual do not seem to provide. The polarization of the light source in the testing process delimits the plane about which the light waves vibrate, and relies upon the discretization of axial dimensions that were otherwise potentially infinite. Understood within the cultural and political regime for which this project was designed, this delimiting of mechanical and physical cycles allows for the dialectical confinement of what would

A house and studio on the edge of downtown Houston, Texas.

Ad Reinhardt, says Robert Smithson, is obsessed by what George Kubler called "the space between events"—"the interchronic pause when nothing is happening"—

"actuality."

Reinhardt tries to give shape to this interchronic "moment"; to do so he has to develop what Smithson calls "shapes that evade shape."

If market capitalism is an encompassing "shape . . . a fetishized passion" (Guattari) of infinite dexterity, that to an intolerable degree constitutes contemporary life, what "shape-evading shapes" need to be instigated in the usually finite basins of architecture?

In the thin city of capital—the city we have been building for at least thirty years—it seems that architecture must administer and cohere the vacant topologies of economic/urban time.

We need shape-evading buildings faster than money, whose slow material duration is undetected by the market.

A building that could induce fantastic topologies of matter, space, and time would provide a kind of stealth, capital-evading reflex to a modern "psychasthenic" citizen engulfed by the machinic.

Two architectural durations

duration 1. Matter/Movement: held in a taxis of torsional equipoise, topologies of membranic stress migrate spontaneously through and across a rigid Cartesian basin of plate glass and flat iron.

duration 2. Subjects/Movement: nomadic promenades among material durations: an aplastic basin.

have been infinite within nature. In essence, this delimiting *is* the architecture of Palazzo Littorio: an artificial contrivance and model of nature's duration, a frontalized and at least partially classicized architectural design whose structural mechanics instigate a pseudo migratory set of forces that mimic the duration of organic life. Within the discrete basin of modern engineering techniques, this dialectical device becomes a mechanical and translational model of what Guy Debord refers to as the "social appropriation of time." It is an edifice that both conceals and reveals "the power that built itself up on the basis of the penury of the society of cyclical time." Palazzo Littorio is "the power . . . of the class which organized social labor" and confiscated "the limited surplus value to be extracted" from it.[23] The Palazzo Littorio is a model of temporal surplus as disequilibrium. The surfaces upon which this power is inscribed instigate and resolve their own structural instabilities; while the relation of forces in the two cantilevers is binary, the origin of the instability appears to be migratory and floating. The resultant equilibrium is one that feigns surplus in a perpetual motion. Within the quantitative techniques of finite element analysis and the discretization of structural mechanics and optic properties of light, Terragni and Lingeri have assembled a model of structural immanence—a model that succeeds the dialectics of its own contrivance. Surely equilibrium is the necessary final state, but in choosing to represent the residual and latent forces—the surplus energies—at work in the creation of this spectacle, Terragni and Lingeri have created a critique of metropolitan dialectics and in doing so of metropolitan subjectivity. This wall, an expansive painting of sorts, delivers to Mussolini the pictorial gaze of an audience whose subjectivity it both conscripts and ironically also may sever.[24] In transforming the perspectival depth of a viewing subject into the thermodynamic modeling of light as material strain within photography, Terragni and Lingeri effectively have flattened the menacing distance that segregates subject and object. In other words, it is possible to read this pictorial field as both expanded *and* tragically foreclosed.

In his essay "Scopic Regimes of Modernity" Martin Jay describes the distinction between "artificial" and "synthetic perspective": artificial perspective places a flat and planar mirror to nature and therefore produces a flattened representation of it; synthetic perspective employs a concave mirror and, even though the concave surface still produces an ultimately homogeneous representation of nature, provides a multiplicity of potential vantage points.[25] The concave surface adds attributes of the infinite to the finite in its dissolution of the single station point. Synthetic perspective allowed work to be "successfully viewed from more than the imagined apex of the beholder's visual pyramid."[26] The facade of Palazzo Littorio, literally a concave surface that was to embrace a delivered and frontal audience,[27] in this light espouses the homogeneity of Cartesian perspective, yet could also be said to model the autonomy of the individual within a spectacle of synthetic perspective. While such a suggestion is plausible given Terragni's affiliations with the Fascist party, any attempt in design to eventually transpose Terragni's mechanics to contemporary sites within contemporary regimes is

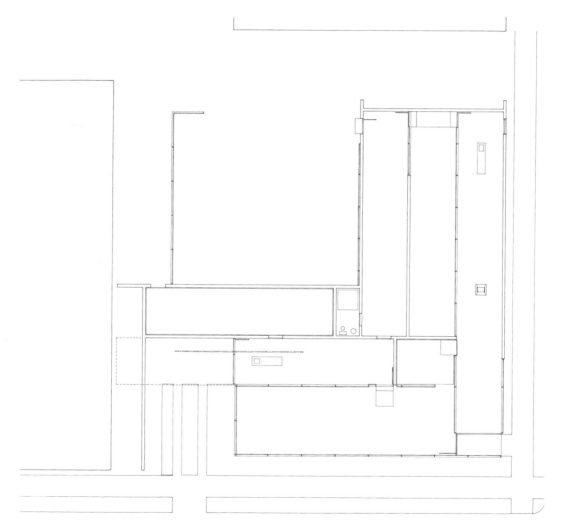

SLOW SPACE

haunted by an unresolved doubt. Jay clarifies this doubt in a reference to the camera obscura and the "gleeful conclusion" by Friedrich Nietzsche that "if everyone had his or her own camera obscura with a distinctly different peephole . . . then no transcendental world view would be possible." The monocularity of both the process by which Terragni and Lingeri attempted to deliver an audience to Mussolini and by which they employed the processes of photoelastic analysis relied upon the discretization of vision within an evolved photographic process, a single peephole in effect, that mimicked the quantitative and monocular geometries of Cartesian perspective. The photoelastic process could even be said to have transformed attributes of visuality into the chemical process of photography itself: the photographic surface *is* the hegemonic confiscation and dissolution of human vision—vision and figuration here become thermodynamic in a chemically "expanded" field. Is the curvature of Palazzo Littorio's facade a form of synthetic perspective, and if so, was Terragni interested in providing an individual *and* a transcendent worldview? If this is a correct reading of Terragni's intentions, does this "synthetic" subjectivity provide both the transcendent omniscience of its party's patronage in a monolithic form as it also provides the individuality of the single person? Given the ultimate homogeneity of synthetic perspective's structure and its ultimate failure to provide a truly unlimited number of vantage points or to relinquish enframing itself, is Palazzo Littorio an intimation of the impossibility of both transcendence and the monolithic?

The chemistry and optical mechanics of the photoelastic processes were perfected during the 1930s as Terragni and Lingeri completed the design of their project.[28] The implementation of this experimental technique in the design of Palazzo Littorio appears to be an isolated incident employed only once in Terragni's career. Terragni did, however, design and build other projects in which this technique would have been useful, if not necessary.[29] The manner in which and for whom the Palazzo Littorio project was produced is in this sense a unique instance in the history of architecture and optical experimentation.[30] The scion of Palazzo Littorio's patronage is undeniable; the photographic and lens techniques employed in the building's design at the very least aggressively attempted a resituating of an optic subject within a delivered mass audience. The paradigms of Cartesian perspectivalism, the monocularity of camera and lens mechanics, the discovery and manipulation of light waves, and the thermodynamics of the photographic process are employed in the design of Palazzo Littorio in a way that marks this project as one of the most advanced and complex attempts in the history of architecture to inculcate space and political authority.

In the case of Palazzo Littorio, it is clear that Mussolini becomes the metaphoric force that prevents both the collapse of the party and, figuratively, the collapse of the architectural apparatus itself. Thomas Schumacher speculates that Terragni's lacing of porphyry, an Egyptian stone available from only a single quarry, with steel was an appropriate image for the omnipotence of Fascist ambitions. It is hard to argue with this thematically, but Terragni's recurring willingness to retain an extravagant degree

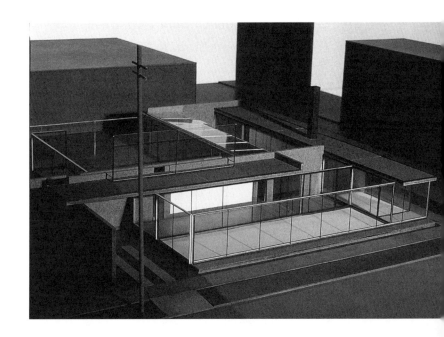

of both the figural and symbolic, and his willingness to *almost* allow the represented within the severity of his abstracting techniques require that we speculate further about the significance of this work in a context beyond those of either state ambitions or an architect's symbolization of those ambitions.

The mechanical and translational techniques that Terragni employed in his incantation of Mussolini's authority were also employed by Terragni in different programs toward completely other ends. The seeming portability of these techniques gives validity to a strictly formal analysis, even given the circumstances of this architect's patrons. While it could be argued that all of Terragni's works were completed within the margins of Fascism, it is difficult not to see these spatial interests as perhaps more endemic to Terragni himself. It is difficult to evaluate fully the pictorial mechanics of Terragni and Lingeri's collaborative works; these projects offer an architecture of dialectic pictorial means that expresses both the omniscience of authority, but also the negation of its discrete means. On a contemporary site, however, the techniques by which these projects orchestrate space offer in the catastrophe of their ocular engagement an ironic and unexpected experience. The widening of the visual field and overdilating of the eye afford access to a mode of time as duration. As such these techniques have value in the comprehension of the dissolute spaces of the late American metropolis.

The Centripetal and the Centrifugal: Dutch Matter

Peter Eisenman's research and analysis of Terragni's Casa Giuliani-Frigerio, published in the essay "From Object to Relationship II," more than twenty five-years ago, offer a model of Terragni's plastic mechanics that has yet to be fully assimilated into a larger critique of Terragni's enduring relevance. Casa Giuliani-Frigerio was completed in 1940, and in many ways the attributes that Eisenman reveals in this building indicate a conception of space that Terragni could not have imagined within the visual dialectics of either Palazzo Littorio's structure or Casa Rustici's perspectivalism. Only by passing through these stages and by unanchoring the visual from the formal could Terragni conceive of space in the manner that Eisenman presents. According to Eisenman, Casa Giuliani-Frigerio is involved in the simultaneous development of two types of space: the first considers space as subtractive, or cut away from a solid; the second considers space as additive "and understood to operate in the layering of planes." The key to Eisenman's explication is that these two techniques not only operate simultaneously, but that this simultaneity reveals an ambiguity in how the project exists "plastically." Eisenman's analysis portrays a "conceptual ambiguity" developed "from the use of two opposing conceptions of space"—the centripetal subtracting of space from an existing volume or mass, and the centrifugal layering of planes in a cumulative and additive process. The analysis seeks to reveal the potential of "abstract relationships" as conceivably independent of actual ones, and proposes that

When a brittle material such as glass is tempered it is reheated after formation and allowed to cool naturally. This tempering results in a material that can withstand severe forces perpendicular to its surface, but that
can easily be fractured by a slight tap on its edge. Tempered glass is stressed along its outermost surfaces.

Like concrete and steel, twentieth-century advances in the production of glass are the result of breakthroughs
in material science and chemical engineering. Material, perhaps the most fundamental ingredient of building
form, has properties of time and structure also intrinsic to building form. The Houston project isolates the relationship of matter and form: how matter acts under stress and strain and specifically under shear. Here glass
and concrete plates are arranged as a house of cards—reliant not merely on the structure of formal relationships, but, more importantly, on the structure of matter itself and on the structure of time in matter.

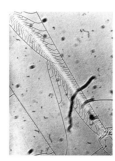 

Material topologies: Matter's internal geometries. "The strength of
brittle solids such as glass is dramatically reduced by surface dam-
age. Even slight contact can cause serious abrasion. This is a photograph of a crack caused by a slight accidental contact on the
surface of Pyrex glass. Magnification 700x."

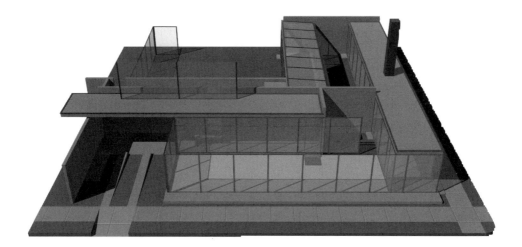

the search for an architectural syntax is likely to be found in the ambiguity between these conceptual and actual relationships. Eisenman's analysis ultimately tends toward a resolution of the questions of transformation and hermeneutics that preoccupy his own practice of architecture, but they might also be understood to reveal Terragni's architecture as a kind of Bergsonian duration, a type of third form that encapsulates the expansion and contraction of two types of space.[31] This offers a nonrepresented and nondialectic conception of matter, a conception of space that I would argue is the conception of "autonomy" that Eisenman's House X sought.[32] In his analysis of Terragni's Casa Giuliani-Frigerio, Eisenman moves the subject's cognition from the relative and the represented to the intuited and the conceptual, and in doing so places both the subject and the object within a *third* duration that allows the autonomy of each participant. While Casa Giuliani-Frigerio makes use of techniques endemic to pictorial space, such as frontality and depth, it does so in a multivalent manner that offers no real hierarchical viewpoint. It is perhaps the closest Terragni ever came to eradicating the vestige of per- spectivalism from his work. Even if we set Terragni aside, Eisenman's interpretation of space in this manner offers a mode of spatial comprehension in its own right. Eisenman has often stated that he *invented* Terragni, meaning that his own readings of Terragni were driven by his own concerns; given this context, it seems that Eisenman's findings are and should be transpositional—we should be able to use them in other contexts or within other regimes.

Eisenman's analysis has been criticized for isolating the formal aspects of Terragni's architecture both from the political milieu in which the works were generated and from the theological complexity of Terragni's own Catholicism. Eisenman has resisted this criticism, and in some ways this is unfortu- nate because the revelations of his analysis can be understood as a mechanism of broader critique of subjectivity as it is drawn within the machinic authority of metropolitan processes. The dialectic rela- tionship of centrifugal and centripetal forces that Eisenman's analysis disables are, in scenarios of contemporary urbanism, manifest almost exclusively by the demands of speculative capital. To para- phrase Guy Debord, the "dictatorship of the automobile, the pilot product of the first stage of com- modity abundance, has left its mark on the landscape in the dominance of freeways that bypass the old urban centers and promote even greater dispersal." The centrifugal satellite developments of Debord's scenario are themselves "subject to the irresistible centrifugal trend, and when, as partial reconstructions of the city, they in turn become overtaxed secondary centers, they are likewise cast aside." Within the machinations of a self-sustaining consumptive economy, the dissolution of the city is inevitable.[33] Eisenman's model of an ambiguous hierarchy of centripetal and centrifugal tendencies could be understood in this light to offer the possibility of an objective yet nonplastic architectural engagement in this dissolution: it seems that Eisenman found in the Casa Giuliani-Frigerio a kind of nonplastic space, a mode of willful yet nonsubjective composition, a manner of building that refuses to participate in the deployment of authority. Eisenman and Tafuri situate the bulk of their theses with-

Giuseppe Terragni. Casa Giuliani Frigerio, 1939–40. Como, Italy.

So-called cold societies are societies that successfully slowed their participation in history down to the minimum, and maintained their conflicts with the natural and human environments, as well as internal conflicts, in constant equilibrium. —Guy Debord, *The Society of The Spectacle.*

in the mechanisms of language; it could be argued that in doing so they suppress the potential plastic attributes of the work they analyze but also suppress its usefulness for fabricating a conception of plasticity in contemporary architectural and urban space.

Eisenman's analysis of Terragni must be understood as related to attributes of de Stijl conceptions of the real. Theo Van Doesberg wrote that "intrinsic reality" was "dynamic movement" and that this movement was established in "abstract art by the exact determination of the structure of form and space."[34] The trajectory of Terragni's experimentation as it moved from Casa Rustici and Palazzo Littorio to Casa Giuliani-Frigerio involved a search for the real as well, though this search tended to posit the real as something that must be intuited. Terragni never fully relinquished the enframing device, but he progressively diminished its presence while retaining its critical potential.

Addendum: de Stijl and the City

The question of an expansion and contraction of the visual field originated in a statement by Theo Van Doesberg about the nature of the terms "centrifugal" and "centripetal." Van Doesberg at times failed to mention the centripetal force in his descriptions of de Stijl architecture. The centripetal force is the necessary origin of the so-called centrifugal force, which in reality is not a force at all, but the inertia of an object and its tendency to move in a straight rather than curved path. This research is presented here as an addendum. I should also note that the buildings of Terragni and Lingeri inspired the use of Slutzky and Ockman's, Bryson's, and Stella's critiques. Most of the above was refined and clarified in a series of fourteen architectural projects that I designed between 1986 and 1996. Some of these thoughts were recorded in an earlier paper and project titled "House Inside Out: Unloading the Neoplastic Frame." The following section provides the context for the research attributes of the two design projects presented on these pages.

In referring to the architecture of the de Stijl movement in the essay "Sixteen Points of a Plastic Architecture," Theo Van Doesberg proclaimed that the "new architecture" was to be centrifugal in massing—"it throws its volumes from a center pinion."[35] At first glance, Van Doesberg's statement seems essentially clear, and a collection of presumed centrifugal works of architecture, from Wright to Mies to Neutra, comes to mind: the Usonian Houses, the Brick Country House, and the Kaufman Desert House are all derivations of some "pinwheel" centrifugal planning paradigm. Mies's project, however, is ambiguous in this regard—or at least its famous plan drawing is. The walls of Mies's composition, drawn in charcoal, continue to the edges of the paper—it is not clear if the generative origin of Mies's plan originates at the center of the drawing's surface or at the periphery, nor is it clear how one should view the plastic qualities of the wall masses themselves if neither tendency predominates. Historically Mies's plan is considered to have an antecedent in Van Doesberg's painting *Rhythm of a*

Russian Dance, and a closer scrutiny of Van Doesberg's proclamation reveals that perhaps the architect and painter has erred in his classical—that is physical—use of the word *centrifugal*. Van Doesberg has at least taken the word out of its expected context, and it seems mistakenly severed it from its correlative and originating relation to a centripetal force. Mies, Wright, and Neutra aside, what follows is an attempt to clarify the potential of Van Doesberg's possible misuse of the word *centrifugal* as well as to speculate on the implications of what seems to be Van Doesberg's fortuitous lack of research into the analogy he has drawn from physics. Van Doesberg's mistaken use of the word *centrifugal* may have been intended and if it was the spatial implications of this use reveal a complexity in the spatial ideals not only of de Stijl architecture but also, if extrapolated, of contemporary sites or the white rectangle of contemporary cities.

A centrifugal force is a reactive force, and in the strictest sense of the word it is actually not a force at all. What we call a centrifugal force is actually the inertia of an object as it tries to move along a straight path while being held in a circular one by a correlative centripetal force. Physicists refer to a centripetal force as center-seeking—it is the force that holds an object in a circular motion. A centrifugal force is referred to as center-fleeing, but in actuality this is not a force per se. What we call a centrifugal force arises within the object's attempt to move along a straight path tangential to the circular acceleration of the object's movement. The magnitude of a centrifugal force is defined by the inertia of the object, by its tendency to stay in motion. One then wonders whether Van Doesberg was loosely using a metaphor drawn from another field of inquiry, or whether he actually meant that the spatial qualities of de Stijl architecture were defined outside this otherwise dialectical relationship of opposing "forces." It seems that the latter is closer to the truth because Van Doesberg's statement, in its continuity, refers to a plastic ideal that ultimately is ambiguous in its spatial character. In Van Doesberg's proclamation, the new architecture was to have "a more or less floating aspect," an aspect that "works against the gravitational forces of nature." If the reactive tendencies of centrifugal and centripetal forces were somehow loosened or alleviated in the above physical model, something close to this effect would be achieved. The canonical de Stijl architectural compositions of Van Doesberg and Van Eesteren were supposed to be read as "more or less floating" and ultimately as neither centripetal nor centrifugal. In his omission of the term centripetal was Van Doesberg trying to describe a centrifugal plastic quality unanchored by an opposing centripetal force—a centrifugal "force" without an originary point? If this is the case, the idealized plastic qualities of a de Stijl composition are to be

Centripetal and centrifugal acceleration: position and velocity vectors for a particle in uniform circular motion.

understood as existing outside the dialectics of the opposing forces of centripetal and centrifugal, but how can such a composition cohere? How do we characterize the forces that assure its compositional density yet do not operate in a dialectical manner? Depending on where one looks within the de Stijl oeuvre and to which practitioner one turns, vastly different ways of answering these questions arise.

Mondrian, for example, spoke of composition in the form of both "static balance" and "dynamic equilibrium." In this paradigm, static balance defined the unity of individual forms within a composition, while dynamic equilibrium unified these individual elements in opposition. In this context, Van Doesberg is perhaps again errant in his description of physical laws, but his intention is nonetheless clear and *could* be situated within the problem as stated by Mondrian. To the static balance of individual forms Mondrian applied the term "limitation"; I would apply *centripetal.* To the term *dynamic equilibrium* Mondrian attached the term "extension"; I would apply *centrifugal.* But Mondrian goes further and gives insight into Van Doesberg's use of *centrifugal* in other dimensions: "Ultimately dynamic equilibrium destroys static balance."[36] It seems possible to understand Van Doesberg's intentions in this context: the extension of a centrifugal force would destroy the delimiting centripetal force that defined both the static balance of the individual components and the static balance of the complete composition itself. If Van Doesberg could alleviate the centripetal force—or at least its originary qualities—in defining the plasticity of his composition yet still not relinquish the vitalizing qualities of centrifugal extension, he could ascribe to these compositions a state of independence, autonomy, and self-description that was neither entropic nor metaphysical. Van Doesberg's architectural masterworks were confined to his projects with Van Eesteren, and they were to a great extent not constructed. Practice would surely have challenged the "more or less floating" aspect of these compositions.

In his De Vonk Holiday Residence (1919), J. J. P. Oud seems to have masterfully incorporated the bulk of Van Doesberg's polemic and the added dimension of gravity as it defines weight and mass. Here Oud mastered not only the simultaneous dynamics of the centrifugal and the centripetal, but

**De Vonk Holiday
Residence,
J. J. P. Oud. 1919.**

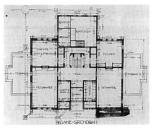

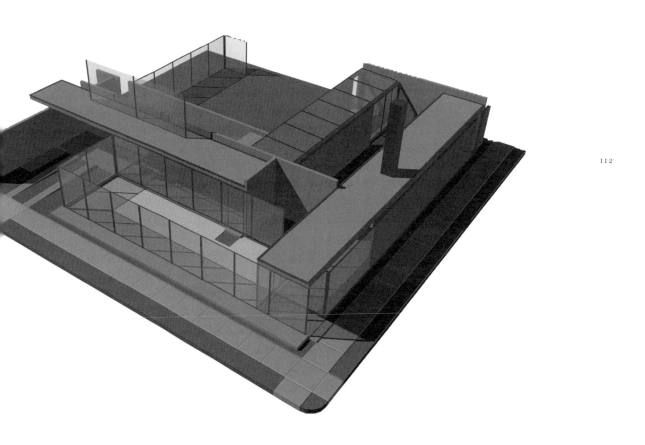

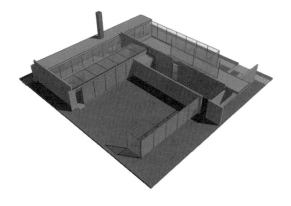

also added the tectonics and weight of material to the equation—something Van Doesberg's drawings were not required to reconcile. This is a building that seems to be at once additive and centrifugal in massing, yet subtractive and centripetal in volume. The masonry wall appears to be conceived of as hollowed out from inside—cored down to the severe thinness that reveals the tenuous stability of stacking bricks in a planar formation. Yet the building itself is also expansive in an admittedly tempered but de Stijl massing of its primary blocks. Oud's walls seem dangerously thin, and it is clear that the architect was interested in hewing them to a planar quality. The stair of the De Vonk residence sets in motion a complex reading of central and peripheral spatial mechanisms that further complicate this planar expansion of volume. The stair is flanked by two columns that carry the weight of the second floor above; these columns instigate a sense of weight that the stair seems to contravene as it tosses itself up through the opening in the floor. The stair seems to turn the space of the residence inside out—it is a topological device, a kind of horizontal oculus that threatens a rearrangement of the centripetal and centrifugal characteristics of the building's spaces. Oud, always a reluctant comrade of Van Doesberg, managed a feat of neoplastic space within the constraints of actual gravity and constituent material weight.

Though I do not believe the preceding assertions are something to prove or disprove critically, the omniscience and inevitability of dialectics in reference to the definition of a plastic work of art or architecture are revealed to be less conclusive than assumed. The questions are interesting to follow because they are rooted in the mechanics of physics, and to some degree it is possible to quantify our speculations. These questions are most interesting as they lead historically across a trajectory of architectures and architects of vastly different social and political situations. Frank Gehry's Hollywood Public Library would lend itself to this type of analysis. Peter Eisenman has spent a large part of his career looking for the mode of analysis that could reveal or produce this nondialectical ambiguity and one could argue that in fact he has achieved this if his work is viewed as a kind of Debord surplus—if we read the hermetic mechanics of its presumed autonomy as providing the surface upon which power may either be individually inscribed or withheld from politically fascist assertion. As such, architecture succeeds in what it manages to keep at bay. Given the degree to which the contemporary site of architecture is constructed by the invisible and the predatory, this should be a note of ironic strength. A Cartesian and almost nondialectical form of space and architecture could be understood ironically to provide a resistive critique of the dynamically mobile and exponentially trabeated orchestrations of labor and material in all modes of contemporary life. This form also provides both a critique of subjugation and a resourcing and aesthetic rejection of easily fabricated standard tectonic means. We shall live upon the inside-out surface of produced space.

Notes

1. Norman Bryson, "The Gaze in the Expanded Field," in *Vision and Visuality*, ed. Hal Foster (Seattle: Bay Press, 1988), 87–108.

2. Bryson, 89.

3. Robert Slutzky with Joan Ockman, "Color/Structure/Painting," in *Robert Slutzky: 15 Paintings, 1980–1984* (San Francisco: Modernism Gallery, 1984), unpaginated. Also contains essays by John Hejduk, Dore Ashton, and Alberto Sartoris.

4. Frank Stella, *Working Space: The Charles Eliot Norton Lectures* (Cambridge, Mass.: Harvard University Press, 1986), 82.

5. Robert Slutzky suggests that his paintings have topological qualities. They actually seem to intuit rather than model a particular type of topological form known as a minimal and embedded surface. A minimal and embedded topological surface is boundaryless and non-self-intersecting. Described in finite terms, a minimal surface is capable of infinite extension without self-intersection. Until recently only three such figures were known: the plane, the catenoid, and the helicoid. Others approximate the conditions described, such as the Menger Sponge and the Hypersphere. Their lack of boundary, framing datum, and segmentation disallows readings of space that seek distinctions or edges. Paraphrased from Ivars Peterson, *The Mathematical Tourist: Snapshots of Modern Mathematics* (New York: W. H. Freeman, 1988), 56–59.

6. For the sake of clarity I have attributed the concept of an "expanded" or "withdrawn" frame to Norman Bryson. Bryson is actually interpreting earlier work by Kitaro Nishida and Keiji Nishitani. Bryson situates the idea of an "expanded field" within his comparison of Sartre's, Lacan's, and Nishitani's theorizing of the gaze. Bryson, 96–98.

7. Bryson, 100.

8. Bryson, 108.

9. A characterization of space as thin or dissolute is related to a concept of thickened space as presented in another essay by Robert Slutzky, "Aqueous Humor." Slutzky portrayed what he called "a progressive and typically cubist thickening of space" in the late works of Le Corbusier, specifically in the buildings that employed the brise soleil. This thickening of space was generated largely by innovations in the vertical surface of Le Corbusier's buildings. "The cubist medium," says Slutzky, "is not one of ethereal clarities, but of dense, gelatinous ambiguities." Cubism, and in Slutzky's paradigm the architecture of Le Corbusier, "savors the water rather than the air." The cubist thickening of space that Slutzky depicts in these works of Le Corbusier is activated at the periphery of Le Corbusier's late buildings; here Le Corbusier instigates a turbulence that delaminates the otherwise unmitigated flow of space into and around a building mass and volume. At Chandigarh, the brise soleils of the Secretariat, the Palace of Justice, and the Assembly all activate a dramatic alluvial play of space that is perhaps the last great public manifestation of architecture within a vigorous and willful plastic sensibility. Le Corbusier's buildings are both the basin—"the container-like still life"—and the sieve; they operate as enzymatic perturbations in what would otherwise be a placid field. In a sense they both constitute the field and instigate a reformation of its plastic qualities, a dialectic process but one seemingly without origin.

Slutzky's reading of Le Corbusier's thickened space has a correlative antinomy in Rosalind Krauss's analysis of Man Ray's *Monument to De Sade* in the *October* essay "The Photographic Condition of Surrealism." Krauss suggests that the cruciform frame Man Ray has inscribed upon the surface of a photographic print provides a supportive reaction to the figure it contains. Krauss claims that the cruciform frame drawn on top of the Man Ray photograph shores up an otherwise dissipating body: "The structural reciprocity between frame and image, container and contained . . . The lighting of the buttocks and thighs of the subject is such that the physical density drains off the body as it moves from the center of the image, so that by the time one's gaze approaches the margins, flesh has become so generalized and flattened as to be assimilated into the printed page." But this assimilation is thwarted or held at bay: "Given this threat of dissipation of physical substance, the frame is experienced as shoring up the collapsing structure . . . and guaranteeing its density."

In the Krauss and Slutzky critiques, the relationship between the frame and that which it contains defines the plastic qualities of the works. The frame and subject are not independent, and in some way their relationship is organic because they are mutually interpolative; they posit each other in a spontaneously migrating reformation of supporter and supported. Man Ray loads the frame; on the verge of complete dissolution his subject is shored up before final disappearance yet this subject also assures the eventual stability of the frame as well. Le Corbusier's boxer, filtered through Slutzky's scenario, must be an aqueous being—a swimmer in a porous and viscous metropolitan match ring. The question that arises in this context is of unloading the frame—relieving the pressure or curtailing the interpolative dialectic relationship between frame and subject? In Krauss's scenario, would the anatomy completely dissipate if the frame were expanded or removed? And in Slutzky's case, would the "dense" space of cubism be possible without the transformative and dialectic mechanics that assured the virtuosity of their architect? There remains the prospect of a very interesting search into the qualities of an architectural, and ultimately urban, space of our time.

10. Massimo Cacciari, "The Dialectics of the Negative and the Metropolis," in *Architecture and Nihilism: On the Philosophy of Modern Architecture* (New Haven: Yale University Press, 1993), 7.

11. The reference to negative dwelling is derived from the term Kakania in Robert Musil's *The Man Without Qualities*. Kakania "was the most progressive State of all; it was the State that was by now acquiescing to its own existence. In it one was negatively free, constantly aware of the inadequate grounds for one's own existence and lapped by the great fantasy of all that had not happened, or at least had not irrevocably happened, as by the foam of the oceans from which mankind arose." Robert Musil, *The Man Without Qualities*, trans. Eithne Wilkins and Ernst Kaiser, (London: Picador, 1979), 34.

12. Bryson, 97. The term "blankness" is a reference to Nishitani; the actual term is *sunyata*. Bryson translates its intended meaning as "radical impermanence."

13. Bryson, 97.

14. Peter Eisenman, "From Object to Relationship II, Casa Giuliani-Frigerio: Giuseppe Terragni Casa Del Fascio," *Perspecta* 13/14, 36–65. On Eisenman's relation to Terragni also see Sanford Kwinter, "Challenge Match for the Information Age: Maxwell's Demons and Eisenman's Conventions," *Architecture and Urbanism* (September 1993): 146–149.

15. According to both the Zanichelli monograph and Manfredo Tafuri's *Modern Architecture,* Terragni's collaborators include A. Carminati, E. Saliva, L. Vietti, M. Nizzoli, and M. Sironi.

16. Manfredo Tafuri, "Giuseppe Terragni: Subject and Mask," trans. Diane Ghirardo, *Oppositions* (Winter 1977): 1–25.

17. Tafuri, 6. "Somehow those isostatic lines explain the form of the vertical incision, marking a weak point in the curved structure; nonetheless the reason for them is still not entirely clear."

18. R. C. Dove and Paul H. Adams, *Experimental Stress Analysis and Motion Measurement* (Columbus, Ohio: Charles E. Merrill, 1964), 288.

19. The question of photoelasticity is here bound up with issues of photography and to some extent a broader interest in overexposure or the overexposing of film. Moholy Nagy's film of the *Light-Space Modulator* is marked by an overexposing of film that results at times in a blank white screen. More recently, the photography of many of Bernard Tschumi's architectural models seems to present his buildings in some form of optic dissolve and at times blankness.

20. Paraphrased in part from R. C. Dove and Paul H. Adams, 288.

21. Thomas Schumacher, *Surface and Symbol: Giuseppe Terragni and the Architecture of Italian Rationalism.* (New York: Princeton Architectural Press, 1991), 183.

22. Schumacher, 183.

23. Guy Debord, *The Society of the Spectacle* (New York: Zone Books, 1994), 94.

24. Writes Jonathan Crary in his essay "Modernizing Vision," "the camera obscura defined an observer who was subjected to an inflexible set of positions and divisions." The spectacle of the camera obscura required an acquiescent subject; one who knew where to stand. Crary's observer "is a nominally free sovereign individual" standing in a "quasidomestic space separated from a public exterior world." Jonathan Crary, "Modernizing Vision," in *Vision and Visuality,* ed. Hal Foster (Seattle: Bay Press, 1988), 30–32.

25. Martin Jay, "Scopic Regimes of Modernity," in *Vision and Visuality,* 10–11.

26. Jay, 10.

27. Tafuri considered the curvature of the surface too shallow to effectively hold the space of the piazza.

28. Today this type of stress analysis is accomplished using computer modeling software and as such interacts differently with the eye's role in cognition. See "The Parsing Eye" by Mark Wamble in this volume.

29. A number of Terragni's projects appear to operate as thin-walled beams. The Novocomum in particular seems to operate as massive shell structure; its windows seem to remove material in a way that causes the building's shell to take on the properties of a box beam.

30. I refer to an assortment of situations that extend from the Greek manipulation of the stylobate to correct optic curvature to the architecture of the 1984 Los Angeles Olympics which was designed to interact with and to anticipate the television camera.

31. Gilles Deleuze describes a scenario of two fluxes contained within a third and quotes Henri Bergson: "Such is our first idea of simultaneity. We call simultaneous, then two external fluxes that occupy the same duration because they hold each other in the duration of the third, our own simultaneity of fluxes that brings us back to internal duration, to real duration." Gilles Deleuze, *Bergsonism* (New York: Zone Books, 1988), 80.

32. Though House X was the product of a process of de-composition, the project has plastic attributes that vividly relate it to Eisenman's work on Terragni. In the design of House X the decomposition procedures appear to give rise to an ambiguous hierarchy of centripetal and centrifugal tendencies. The grids that characterize much of the project appear at times to be recessive as well as projective, as do the building masses themselves. The project's spatial characteristics are largely those that Eisenman explicated in Terragni's Casa Giuliani-Frigerio. Eisenman's procedures also have direct relations to Slutzky's: Eisenman presents the vertebrate structure of House VI as the result of a transformation process that bisected two initial planes and then "turned them inside out." Peter Eisenman, *House X* (New York: Rizzoli, 1982), 88.

33. Debord, 124.

34. H. L. C. Jaffé, *de Stijl 1917–1931: The Dutch Contribution to Modern Art* (Cambridge, Mass. and London: Belknap Press, 1986), 109.

35. Theo Van Doesberg's "Sixteen Points of a Plastic Architecture" is referenced in Kenneth Frampton's *Modern Architecture: A Critical History* (London: Thames and Hudson, 1980), 145. "The new architecture is *anti-cubic,* that is to say, it does not try to freeze the different functional space cells in one closed cube. Rather, it throws the functional space cells (as well as the overhanging planes, balcony volumes, etc.) centrifugally from the core of the cube. And through this means, *height, width, depth, and time* (i.e. an imaginary four-dimensional entity) approaches a totally new plastic expression in open spaces. In this way architecture acquires a more or less floating aspect that, so to speak, works against the gravitational forces of nature."

36. Jaffé, 110.

Satellites and cars—preparing the infrastructural topologies of the megalopolis. Naval Research Labs electronics engineer William Bell supervises the loading of a communications satellite payload into a rented Ford Galaxy 500 at White Sands, New Mexico, 1968.

Overleaf: Houston, Aerial view, 1988.

COMMUNITY PROPERTY: ENTER THE ARCHITECT

OR, THE POLITICS OF FORM

Dana Cuff

The design of American cities today is as likely to take place in council chambers as in the offices of architects and planners. Through contentious development, increments of the city are planned as community activists expand their territory of perceived property rights. As a result of this growing political arena, the context for architectural work has changed so fundamentally that architects often express disdain for the hordes of community activists and special-interest lobbyists whose input muddles intentions, logistics, and schedules.[1]

After life and liberty, "the third absolute right . . . is that of property."[2] Fundamental to the American system of law and thought, property rights have come to profoundly affect the very nature of the city itself. Changes in the popular conception of real—as opposed to personal—property rights are largely responsible for community activism concerning development projects. An exploration of property-rights history and theory, as well as the political and philosophical roots of contentious development, provides an intellectual context to study the local politics of design and the currently evolving system of property relations. Despite the exasperation expressed by design professionals, property relations in urban development undertakings implicate both community opposition and the position of the architect. But contentious development also opens rare and profound opportunities for urban intervention that architects can utilize to create public realms, opportunities often hidden under animosity and impatience in the contentious planning process.

Political philosophy and the actual practice of present-day contentious development reverberate to unravel this subject. Emerging from the light each casts on the other is an image of these debates that bears more depth and texture than typically attributed to neighborhood activism. The simple idea of not-in-my-back-yard-ism (NIMBY) is a destructive force in urban planning and design because by definition it thwarts constructive action and asserts rights without commensurate responsibilities; urban debates of interest here are distinct from NIMBY's no-growth, no-change stances. Better characterized as negotiations, contentious developments are circumstances in which some change is recognized as desirable or inevitable; parties not only attempt to establish their property rights, but also ascertain property-related obligations on behalf of others. Through such negotiations, a cultural concept of environmental and community justice evolves.

In contentious developments, tireless citizen participation partially results from an expanded sense of ownership and an expanded set of property rights. Fundamental to these ideas is the American belief in the connection between work and property, articulated by John Locke in the seventeenth century: a person has claim over the land on which he or she labors. This Lockean notion of property, coupled with the historical understanding of land in postcolonial America, makes speculative development somewhat suspect, and simultaneously upholds the primacy of residents' rights over their neighborhood. Labor over a balance sheet does not count for much in the American mind, but where we mow, we expect authority.

Since the late 1960s, land-use regulation at all levels—federal, state, and local—has expanded dramatically, conscribing the liberties, duties, and rights associated with urban development.[3] Urban-development debates have contributed to that expansion, capitalized on those regulations, and, at the same time, defined a separate territory of political pressure by which development can be influenced. In addition, urban development is one of the only arenas in which notions of duty are coupled with notions of rights to formulate a concept of justice. In a country overly dominated by "rights talk" to the exclusion of concomitant responsibility, urban negotiations warrant scrutiny beyond their already important role in shaping not only contemporary development but also contemporary ideas of collectivity.[4]

Any contentious development documented in local newspapers concretely exemplifies these issues. In West Los Angeles, for example, a small group of residents occupies a narrow strip of land between the ocean and what has been called the largest planned urban development in the country. Because of their location, their concerns, along with those of other adjacent neighborhoods, have been taken seriously by Maguire Thomas Partners, developers of Playa Vista, who would otherwise be preoccupied with issues comparable in scale to their 1,087-acre undertaking. The thirty-two households of Vista del Mar have won sizable concessions: the underground installation of all utilities (at a cost of $5 million) and significant investment in the design and renovation of a neighborhood park.

In the popular view of community-developer negotiations, participants myopically protect their own interests vis-à-vis development, adversely affecting both regional planning and design quality. Community-developer negotiations generally suffer from the lack of parties that represent overarching concerns; instead, a fragmented environment of enclaves operates within a neglected, malfunctioning whole. Neighborhoods try to stop the homeless from occupying their streets by pushing them to other parts of the city; a building is designed to respond to local demands without regard for urban-design issues; environmental concerns are mollified by local solutions, such as parks, rather than the systemic solutions that sustainable development would demand. Because few constituencies advocate large-scale planning priorities, they are downplayed by voters who judge elected officials and in the advocacy-based process of hearings.

Although Vista del Mar's park and underground utilities are correctly termed developer concessions, in a more general sense they reflect the community's perception that Playa Vista is part of their neighborhood. The community has established expectations of developer responsibility toward adjacent residents. In exchange for ultimate benefits to the developer (profit) and to offset costs to the community (such as increased traffic congestion), residents effectively create a set of local obligations for the developer. Again in exchange for developer benefits, environmentalists created a second type of responsibility in lobbying successfully for restored wetlands at Playa Vista. The developer's duty to restore this environmental system is intended to have more global advantages, extending beyond the immediate vicinity and even to future generations. Thus both local and what I will call public responsibilities have been exacted and carried out.

Land and Property Rights in America

With land use the balance between private rights and public responsibilities is constantly restruck, although the latter are far more ambiguous than the former.[5] The dynamic between the two is apparent in development negotiations: both developers and community organizations claim their land rights, while communities, interest groups, planners, and politicians monitor public responsibilities. In a sense, most of these parties are manipulating property that, by legal and popular opinion, they do not own. While planners, politicians, and developers may have jurisdiction over property, an expanding crowd of others acts upon their perceived right to control property they do not legally own.[6]

The hard-line community activist stands in defiance of developers, who have a cowboy-like attitude toward their calling and detest the activists' "interference." Given the prevalence of neighborhood activism and its institutionalization via regulated review, the developer's frontier ethic is pure nostalgia. On the other side, communities are unable to arrest all development. The history of the frontier and theories of property rights offer insights into these conflicting positions and reveal many factors that contribute to the dynamic between private rights and public responsibilities of land.[7] A critical presentation of the frontier recognizes it as a construction by European settlers who brutally asserted their claims. It is this aggressive legacy of taking and laying claim, rather than one that Native American tradition might have spawned, that underlies contemporary development disputes.

In the settlers' United States, the ideal of private property has been one of complete freedom for the owner, as if once across the property boundaries the "law of the land" was one's own. No one could dictate what the owner on his or her land could do—and this seems to be a condition toward which every occupier, whether tenant farmer or apartment renter, has aspired. Historically, this ideal of autonomy has never been fully achieved, for communities, counties, and states have always exerted some pressure on individual landowners. Generally, individual property rights have been struck down when some public good takes priority.[8] Nevertheless the pioneer spirit, formed as settlers ventured into the wilderness, still figures prominently in the contemporary landowner's mind. Pioneers exhibited ingenuity, temerity, and a willingness to take risks—characteristics that may belong to present-day developers, but which also aptly describe the most involved community activists. The land pioneers settled on was not free and open for taking, of course, but was instead the site of much violence as it was wrested from the Native Americans, whose claims extended over many generations.[9] The westward expansion in America gave rise to several complicated components of current land-use debates: recognition that claim to land might involve usurpation; disregard for land as community property; the association of land with individual freedom, a Lockean ideal that ascribes natural ownership to those who apply their labor to the land; disregard for geographically specific resources; and general contempt for government restrictions on land.

A Wilderness for Speculation

In colonial America, land provided the principal economic base and, along with religion, the social order. Land ownership, with its prospects of independence and wealth, was a primary motivation for immigrating to the New World. Because land was plentiful and people few, attitudes toward the land and the system of land tenure developed accordingly. Although the colonies established a range of land tenures, according to historian Marion Clawson, the trend moved "toward giving the landowner greater rights to use his land as he saw fit, and toward reducing controls and restrictions over land use, whether the controls were from government or landlords. The idea of unrestricted land ownership, in sharp contrast to feudal land tenures, was widely held by the time of the Revolution."[10] The end of the Revolution witnessed extensive land speculation along with the agglomeration of new large holdings where Native Americans, farmers, and small landholders had once dominated. This fundamental shift from individuals with claims on the land they worked to a system driven by speculative finance sowed the seeds of controversy between resident-owners and all others with interest in the land. The settlers who had not given credence to Native American claims now ironically faced the threat of speculative interest, albeit less lethal, on their own property rights. Schisms developed between owner, laborer, resident, speculator, and state over whose rights to property were greater.

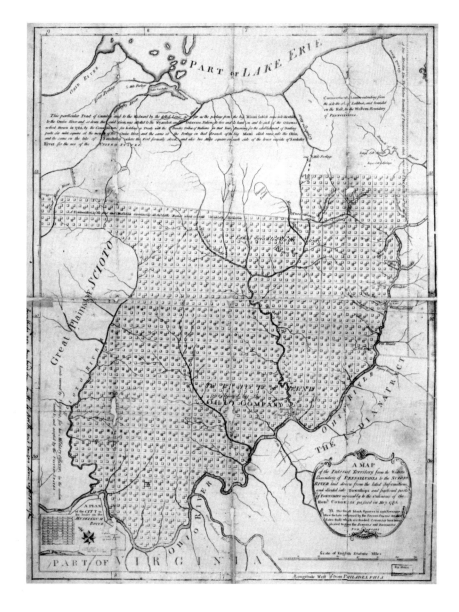

Manassah Cutler's Map of Ohio, ca. 1788, showing land divisions as mandated by Thomas Jefferson's Land Ordinance of 1785.

The Revolution had impoverished state and federal governments, and the speculative sale of large blocks of land became a way to replenish government treasuries. The long-term impact of this process was, however, not evaluated. States historian W. G. Bryant, "America got rid of feudalism at the price of handing over an altogether excessive part of the national patrimony to land grabbers, land jobbers, and profiteers. It was not an auspicious beginning."[11] The concept of land as public trust was challenged from the nation's earliest hour. With tremendous holdings of undeveloped territory (such as the Louisiana Purchase), state and federal governments appear to have given little thought to maintaining these lands. They were instead sold at unnecessarily low prices or were distributed in what has been called "the great giveaway" of land in the nineteenth century. This included, but was by no means limited to, the Homestead Act of 1862, under which between 1.5 and 2 million people acquired land.[12] Guided by the general ideal of the family farm, the reckless disposition of land fulfilled this model only modestly. The impact of the Homestead Act was limited, apparent in the fact that the population of the United States grew by 32 million during the same period in which fewer than 2 million people homesteaded land. Speculation by entrepreneurs was encouraged, often leaving the small farmer to resort to squatting without payment to anyone. In addition, natural resources were squandered as geographically unique ecologies were ignored.[13]

For large blocks to be parceled and sold to increase the national treasury, accurate land surveys were necessary to the uncontested disposition of property. Thomas Jefferson's Land Ordinance of 1785 resulted in the coordinated effort of townships and sections to lay a rigid grid over most of the United States west of the Mississippi.[14] The grid's advantages had little to do with local geography, ecology, or demography; instead, according to John W. Reps, it had everything to do with neat subdivision and subsequent speculation:

> The gridiron spread across the country as the natural tool of the land speculator. No other plan was so easy to survey, and no other system of planning yielded so many uniform lots, easy to describe in deeds or to sell from the auctioneer's block. Everywhere there was gold in the land if it could be bought, subdivided, and sold, even in the hills, if promoted by a skillful operator.[15]

The grid, molded over the hills of San Francisco just as it was laid flat across the Great Plains, became the accepted American standard. Into this nonhierarchical spatial system, communities organized themselves as best they could, making intersections or a stretch of Main Street—rather than central open spaces—the focus of the town. Most towns followed federal practice and placed all land on the market, relegating public areas to the spaces

Great Plains, aerial view.

in between. This settlement pattern reflected and reinforced the dominance of privatized property rights while subordinating the collective social order.

The end of the Revolution found most land in the continental United States under some entity's control, whether Native Americans with whom no treaty existed, a foreign government, a state, the federal government, or private individuals. With this shift grew a class of renegades who illegally occupied land belonging to others for various economic purposes such as trapping or farming. While this practice was first viewed as trespassing, it was not long before these illegitimate settlers' "crime of using or taking land not theirs was lightly regarded on a frontier where land was plentiful, and their disdain of government was often admired by more staid settlers."[16] The squatters manifested attitudes about land, ownership, and regulation that persist today. The links between land ownership and bravado, freedom, and independence are rooted in colonial America, setting a precedent from which contemporary developer ethics may have sprung.

Despite the dominance of privatization and individual freedom, there were also precedents for communal sentiment among settlers. Early colonial townships shared a strong sense of community, which was expressed in the subdivision of land. Villages were organized around a common green where livestock was penned, rather than dispersed according to rural patterns more typical of farming and agriculture. After collectively erecting a meeting hall on the common, settlers would build their houses around this center with fields stretching out behind.[17] It was also established that the larger public entity—town, county, or state—could take land for a greater public good as long as the individual landowner was appropriately compensated.[18] I suggest, however, that these communal ethics never melded with those of the pioneer, whose tough figure overshadowed the life of "townspeople." Instead, a charged duality between the frontiersman and the gentleman was established.[19]

The legacy of domination by the speculative objectives of autonomous and government-spurning pioneers, and of private land over public land, remains with us today in many—often opposing—guises. It has contributed to developers' belief in their own autonomy in relation to those enabling policies of cities that are now regularly challenged by communities. The historically privileged position of the private individual's right to property is also currently embodied in the homeowner's fight against any change that could threaten property values. At the same time, the modern-day townspeople may be those community activists who organize to achieve a higher quality of life for their neighborhood.

As long as agriculture was the basis of postcolonial society, wealth was equated with land, but with industrialization and a growing commercial base, wealth began to mean money in the nineteenth century.[20] Thus it became necessary for land to be easily converted into cash, requiring not only that land be subdivided into comparable lots as accomplished by the grid, but also that land be maintained in terms of use and future potential. It is not surprising, therefore, that zoning became the most common means of controlling development. While generally acknowledged to be clumsy tools, zoning regulations often embody the primary goal of preserving property values rather than forming a pleasant or rational urban structure.[21] Indeed, according to W. G. Bryant, "in North America, most people entertain the delusion that land is simply a particular sort of commodity."[22] While land can be bought and sold, it differs from other forms of property in that it can be transformed, be productive, and be a vehicle of expression, but it cannot be consumed or replaced. Most regulations nevertheless exist to protect land as commodity rather than resource.

Land and the dwelling or business that sits upon it remain both symbolically and concretely attached to wealth.[23] The size of landholdings has decreased dramatically since America's farming era: the United States has grown from a country of small farms into one of suburban lots, preserving the physical pattern of a detached dwelling surrounded by its own land.[24] The significance of this territorial display can be traced directly to frontier settlement, and manifests the subordination of public domain to private property. As in colonial America, however, when individuals banded into collective orders to confront adversity, contemporary neighborhoods organize to prevail against the disruption of the fabric of their everyday lives.

Theories of Property Rights

In debates about property rights, the conservative position seeks to produce a free-market situation for land with greater control for the individual landholder and reduced control for federal and state agencies.[25] In general, the conservative view favors local control. This position has been pitted against the so-called environmentalist position, which seeks to limit individual free choice regarding property in order to protect the greater good. Neighborhood activism has upset this simple dualism as individual landholders exert their property rights over those of other individuals to regulate land-use development in the interest of a greater good. Neighborhood activism inserts itself, in theory and practice, between environmentalists and individual-rights advocates.

Each individual engaged in a development dispute holds a personal and tacit theory of property-related rights and duties, believing that the latter apply only to others. When a community organization blocks the demolition of a derelict neighborhood school, purchased by a private developer who intends it for condominiums, both sides are claiming proprietary interests. The community feels a sense of ownership toward this once central public institution and its land; the owner has purchased the property with the right to transform it within existing regulatory constraints. As developers have discovered, entitlement is no longer sufficient to allow construction; even such imperfect entitlement has become difficult to invoke. The community may insist that the developer is obligated to mitigate the loss of this neighborhood resource.

Real property rights, as legal scholars, political theorists, and philosophers conceive them, contain the fuel for development disputes. Not only do these debates implicate one of the rights we consider most fundamental, the right to property, but so do they engage our ideas of justice, labor, and reward. If that were not enough, the disputes lack clarity because the very nature of land and the meaning of its ownership are disputed in legal theory.[26]

Ownership of private property has long been associated with work—a specific case of the fundamental connection between effort and reward. In the seventeenth century, with the pragmatic goal of undermining claims on property of royal absolutism, John Locke articulated a basis for property rights in "natural law" by which individuals would take something as their property, especially land, when they had applied their labor to it. In the second of his *Two Treatises of Government,* Locke stated:

> Though the Earth, and all inferior Creatures be common to all Men, yet every Man has a *Property* in his own *Person.* This no Body has any Right to but himself. The *Labour* of his Body, and the *Work*

of his Hands, we may say, are properly his. Whatsoever then he removes out of the State that Nature hath provided, and left it in, he hath mixed his *Labour* with, and joyned to it something that is his own, and thereby makes it his *Property*.[27]

When farmers till the soil, the labor they naturally own mixes with the land and thereby gives them claim to it. Indeed it was the rise of agriculture that necessitated fixed property for land.[28]

With regard to land, we have a unique interpretation of ownership that stems from the nature of landed property and from the history of land in America.[29] Unlike other forms of property, land is a palimpsest of the activities that take place on it. "The ownership of land, therefore, offers opportunities for self-expression and allegiance, not simply for marketing farm produce or the extraction of urban rents by the slum landlord," explains political theorist Alan Ryan.[30] This may be the reason that certain land-related rights are informally granted, depending upon tenure, or length and strength of connection, to that land. For example, the ownership of land that has belonged to a family of many generations is considered more sacred; such dynastic owners are perceived to have greater rights than those who have recently acquired land or those who rent. The severity of economic hardship during the Depression registered when the government auctioned farmlands taken from the hands of bankrupt families who had labored on them for generations. The Homestead Act, a direct descendant of Lockean natural law, intended to entitle land to those individuals who demonstrated through agricultural labor their worthiness to own and their commitment to maintain the land in a productive state. Today developers and even city officials suggest that local homeowners, more so than renters, are the vociferous stakeholders in contentious developments. Land has been long viewed as a central element of democracy and an accessible form of property for the hardworking, a principal component of the establishment of home and livelihood.[31]

In this sociohistorical light, the developer's position relative to land contradicts Lockean reasoning and popular belief. While developers mix their labor with the land, they generally do not do so as directly as the homeowner or even the contractor-builder. Instead, the developer's labor is one step removed from the property itself, concentrated upon gaining entitlements, putting together financing, and managing the process. To receive large financial gain for the sale of property with which one has so little direct connection seems unjustified within a labor theory of natural ownership—a theory that views land as distinct from other forms of property. According to the same principles, those individuals who own land with which they have mixed their labor—as even the most well-staffed homeowner will do—will feel particularly justified in exercising their rights while extracting the duties of others.

Industrialization in the capitalist state entrenched the relationship between work and property; compensation for workers on an assembly line, mixing their labor with a product they do not own, is income or other means to secure consumer goods. We say that a woman owns her Toyota not because she has labored to make the car, but because her labor provided the means to purchase it. Locke believed that the "Invention of Money" distorted the natural law of property. In this sense, Locke's second treatise on government provides the foundation of another challenge to the developer's property rights. Explaining that labor transforms into property that which was found in a natural state, Locke qualifies this principle as contingent upon the supply of land: "no Man but he can have a right to what that [labor] is once joyned to, at least where there is enough, and as good left in common for others."[32] Beyond scarcity and quality, Locke further elaborates that land apportionment is fair when measured by its direct usefulness to the laborer, this being distorted only by the "Invention of Money," which enlarged possessions beyond the basic needs of the possessor.[33] According to Locke's reasoning, prior to the valuation of money and scarcity, society's understanding of property rights could exist without the need of laws:

> Right and Conveniency went together; for as a Man had a Right to all he could imploy his Labour upon, so he had no temptation to labour for more than he could make use of. This left no room for Controversie about the Title, nor for Incroachment on the Right of others.[34]

The legitimate use of property is described in terms of sufficiency; in the natural state, we take only what we need from the environment, leaving as much and as good for others. In civilized society, those whose land use respects the sufficiency rule have claims that are perceived as more valid than the claims of those whose land use exceeds natural rights. Locke's romantic portrayal of property corresponds more closely to a tacit popular theory of property rights than to formal property law. Contentions over new developments arise when developers act in ways that distort the legitimate use of property. First, citizens see that land is scarce and believe that the quality of their community will deteriorate with further modification. In these terms, it seems no one can satisfy the sufficiency criterion of leaving as much and as good for others. Second, the developer's interest in the land extends beyond what is personally useful, and to monetary value. The developer thus creates the controversy about encroachment upon the rights of others—in other words, creates contentious development. Though many laws, of course, entitle developers to act as they do, these laws contradict the individual's tacit, Lockean theories of property.

In her broad discussion about the role of rights in American society, *Rights Talk: The Impoverishment of Political Discourse,* political theorist Mary Ann Glendon makes a number of astute observations about Locke and the ideal of property, comparing the American system to those of other countries. The idea that each one of us exists as our own property, she notes, is a unique, if not bizarre, formulation of ownership and selfhood. In Locke's conception, the rights that befall us by virtue of the fact that we own ourselves are not balanced by any sense of responsibility toward others. In the so-called natural state, we exist in relationships with others only in the abstract sense that we must leave enough and as good so that the next individuals can claim the land with their labor. It follows that the resident-owner, equated with the laborer, has primary property rights without perceiving any of her own duties. If any duties are identified, they are assigned to the nonlaboring owner-speculator, who in turn does not recognize her own duties, or those of anyone else, but only her property rights. Few developers, even in the public language of press relations, acknowledge their duties to the community. Instead, what they consider to be extractions they publicly identify as gifts; for example, restoration of wetlands is not the developer's duty because she has been granted the right to build thousands of new homes, but is rather a generous civic donation. Glendon observes that our limited language of duties, overshadowed by our rights-rich discourse, restricts the evolution of a more balanced social and legal system. Even neighborhood activists and preservationists frame what are easily considered responsibilities in the language of rights: the public has a right to restored wetlands. This formulation is unfortunate, since it makes it easier for the developer to assert rights that supersede counterclaims, deny the association of duties and rights, and claim generosity over duty. Glendon summarizes the uniquely American political discourse:

> American rights talk [exhibits] . . . a tendency to formulate important issues in terms of rights; a bent for stating rights claims in a stark, simple, and absolute fashion; an image of the rights-bearer as radically free, self-determining, and self-sufficient; and the absence of well-developed responsibility talk.[35]

In a Houston public-housing project threatened with redevelopment, residents tried to force the local authority to expend allocated rehabilitation funds while the authority requested federal permission to demolish the project and sell the land.[36] In this heated debate that has raged for the better part of a decade, both parties have attempted to establish priority over competing claims, to stop one party from impinging upon the rights of the other, and to establish the duties of the agency. It is fundamentally a debate about justice, characteristic of development disputes in general. This very core of urban disputes helps to explain why NIMBY-ism and community activism are such powerful forces.

According to eighteenth-century philosopher David Hume, justice and property rights evolve together.[37] Alan Ryan elaborates, "Were men to be spontaneously altruistic, or goods not at all scarce, property rights would have no point; there would be no need for rules to assign priority to some claims over others, and no need for authority to deter one man from invading another's rights."[38] In this light, contemporary development disputes are readily seen as struggles for justice or, better, as struggles to define what is just.

If justice and property rights arise in tandem, then injustice also arises. The birth of fixed ownership of land is often cited as the basis for class inequality and is, according to Jean-Jacques Rousseau, the basis for a government that favors the landed rich over the poor.[39] Claims on property privilege the homeowner and those who own the most or the most valuable land. Translated into present-day circumstances, regulations favor the owner over the renter; among owners, the developer's landholdings outweigh those of homeowners, forcing the latter to organize to be heard. Homeowner organizations have been highly successful, paradoxically, because home ownership has long been equated with democracy and a responsible citizenry.

Characteristics of Property Rights

Property rights are not singular and clear-cut, thus leaving much room for individual and circumstantial interpretation. A number of elements, drawn from the work of legal theorist Jeremy Waldron, frame the property-rights debate in urban development undertakings: dynamic systems of rights, multiple claims, common and collective property, scarcity, and conflicts between rights and duties.

Property rights must be considered as an evolving construction that changes over time from society to society. According to Waldron, "In each society the detailed incidents of ownership amount to a particular concrete conception of this abstract concept [of private property]."[40] The system of property rights with regard to land is ambiguous because land is both material, entailing resources such as minerals or arable soil, and spatial, an abstract location in three-dimensional space.[41] These distinctions are challenged by actions such as the transfer of development rights.[42] With such occurrences, the system of property rights related to land evolves. Waldron argues that property is best conceived as a system of rules governing property relations and not as incidents of private ownership. For example, a corporation is owned by a collection of shareholders who, according to a set of rules, have a degree of access to and control of the corporation. In modern economic life, continues Waldron, an individual's "wealth is constituted for the most part by his property relations," the preindustrial equation of wealth and land.[43]

Property relations extend to planners, architects, interest groups, and community members who do not privately own a particular conception of a site's future, but who control it because of existing rules of property relations: the architect owns access to and control of the design;[44] the neighborhood, via the public hearing process, has a right of review; planners utilize regulatory jurisdiction to set restrictions for development proposals, and so on. The ownership by these parties is defined by sets of property relations, established by social contract, law, common practice, and contention. Contentions establish practices and imply property relations in advance of the law. Through a sequence of local urban debates, communities, architects, and developers come to understand the limits of their authority over property, the extent of their obligations, and the lengths to which they must go in order to prevail. An informal series of precedents is established by contentions that set expectations for future situations. Thus contention is an effective mechanism for pushing property relations into new terrain and for establishing new concepts of justice.

Contemporary property relations have been fundamentally transformed by more complex and numerous claims on property, many of which are accepted rather than legally obligated. Several parties with rights over the same resource place multiple claims on a property. For example, multiple claims may be held by the landowner, the lender, the county, a regional body such as a coastal commission, a smaller region such as the community as designated by a specific plan, and the adjacent neighbors. Claims operate in multiple domains, such as planning and zoning or design review, each having its own compliance procedure. In urban developments, the chaos of competing claims acts as a perfect medium for contention as individuals and groups try to establish their own theory of rights. Neighborhood opposition to affordable housing, for example, will focus upon environmental protection, historic preservation, or federal regulation about distributive equity, when the primary issue is actually xenophobia or property values.[45]

Waldron distinguishes between three systems of property rights: private, collective, and common.[46] The predominance of any one system is a sociohistorical phenomenon of temporary balance and significance. While a system of private property has always dominated postcolonial America, I have explained that a notion of collective property was also prevalent in the early colonial period. Some of the present contentions over urban development are struggles to lower the status of private property in order to subordinate uses that detract from the collective social interest. For example, preservationists battle the destruction of historic property in the apparent interest of present and future generations. Similarly, the maintenance of parkland or undeveloped wilderness qualifies as a system of common property intended to benefit all members of society. Contemporary development contentions often pit the developer-owner's private property against the community's common property.[47]

In the context of scarce resources, common and collective systems of property are increasingly important, which explains the vehemence of development debates in big cities where land is scarce in relation to population density. Indeed, scarcity is a presupposition in all discussions about property and contentious development.[48] A development undertaking that would result in the loss of some resource constitutes grounds for community opposition. The loss of agricultural land or "rural atmosphere" in urbanizing areas, the loss of convenient parking and traffic-free streets, or the decline of natural habitats are all viewed as the creation of scarcity. Resources perceived as scarce are likely to become the most urgent topics of debate.

Existing with regard to property are clusters of associated liberties, rights, and duties, which are the foundations of ownership because they establish the social relations that define property.[49] A poorly developed sense of obligation in American law follows the popular perception of "the other's duties."[50] While one's own obligations remain muted, the duties of the other are readily articulated in development contentions. Community members and city councils, at times on opportunistic grounds, develop elaborate and predictable sets of duties for developers who seek the right to implement a project. Thus the most explicit changes in property relations pertain to duties. Under the guise of extractions, impact fees, and other forms of mitigation and compensation, developers are required to fulfill certain obligations to balance this gain with the impact and losses the developers' property may visit upon the community.

Typically, we think of ownership as a relationship between a person and a thing, but in legal terms the relationship is among persons. People, rather than land or houses, are presumed to have rights and obligations. As explained earlier, the assigned term "owner" does not imply much about ensuing rights and duties without reference to the more specific legal relations that differentiate the relations of mortgage holder, the general partner, the managing partner, the shareholder, or the lessor.

In the debate over rights and obligations, liberties are always given boundaries. In the urban development context, increased state, federal, and local regulation have placed greater restrictions on the liberties of individual property owners such that compliance procedures and community opposition exert greater control over those liberties. Duties extending to land

within some perceived jurisdiction, as toward individuals living near a project site, are negotiated simultaneously with rights. In the Playa Vista case, for example, wetlands restoration
and traffic mitigation were identified as essential duties of the developers if they were to
receive necessary approvals. The extent of these duties, however, has been the subject of
much heated controversy. Because the duties of property owners or anyone else are not clearly defined by American law, the owner's duties, now more than ever, are negotiated with
many diverse groups and on a case-by-case basis: experts such as traffic engineers; elected
officials; organizations representing some public good, such as environmental or historic
preservation; and individuals, such as adjacent homeowners, with an interest in the project.

Immanuel Kant made a distinction between two types of moral duties that imperatives
express. The first, called a hypothetical imperative, involves "rules of action only for those
who share the objectives they are intended to promote."[51] For example, if developers want
to build a shopping center, they ought to mitigate the traffic impact. This duty is relevant
because of the development plans, but the developers have no fundamental obligation to
mitigate traffic. The second type of duty, a moral imperative, is an unconditional, universally valid rule of action for all rational beings. I believe that communities often incorporate
moral imperatives into development disputes; for instance, one person should not defile the
home of another. Whether or not legal restrictions apply, a developer who blocks the light
of an adjacent property or inserts an incompatible land-use structure is considered to have
disobeyed a moral imperative. The architect is implicated simultaneously, since any design
solution translates moral duties, or their absence, into built form.

Implications of Contentious Development for Design

Contentious developments direct a focus on design. They challenge the self-determined
interest of developers and their self-serving design proposals with the moral imperative that
individual desires are secondary to public interest. The expanded sense of the residents'
Lockean rights and the developers' duties nurtures fertile soil for local, semipublic, urban,
and regional missions. Even in small-scale developments, a justice is forged by inserting
collective interests into once-private terrain. While assertions of rights and duties are raised
in discussion, the contenders rarely resolve contradictions among competing claims or
visualize the manifestation of those assertions. All this conflict fuels the architect's traditional motive to control the design, but another role simultaneously generated is that of the
visionary in a politicized public realm.

Where communities or special-interest groups unite to establish a developer's duties, they carve out new territory in development debates—a territory that supports the design and creation of a public realm. Ironically, the architect's task is designing a solution that the paying client does not want. The idea that the architect is duplicitous is not new; typically, however, the deception has not been justified by public interest but by architecture for its own sake. In her analysis of the contemporary architecture profession, sociologist Magali Larson states: "As a form of cultural production, modern architecture must simultaneously convince and deceive the client."[52] Architect Vittorio Gregotti tells her something similar in an interview: "The typical duplicity of the architect is precisely that of having in mind two different goals simultaneously—architecture as autonomous culture *and* the client."[53] Architects in contentious developments participate in this two-part deception by incorporating a second, amorphous "client," the public realm. I would argue that architects have an ethical and professional obligation to convince and, in many cases at least initially, deceive the client in this matter.

If the architect can help to create the opportunity for public work, it will initially be through planning mechanisms and later through acts of physical design. Design, in turn, will be a strategic act. To survive the corrosive process of contentious development, design proposals must exhibit certain characteristics. First, the skeleton of the proposal, both formal and conceptual, must be able to withstand incremental and individual demands without deteriorating the whole. As neighbors voice their concerns about noise, views, parking, preservation, or adjacencies, the underlying design structure can easily erode. Its resistance depends upon a recognition of more fundamental constraints as well as desires. Second, a design proposal appropriate for contentious development is made clear and explicit to laypeople, so that it can be easily represented to and understood by others. This procedure argues for conceptual simplicity both in rhetoric and form. The last directive to the architect of a contentious project contradicts the stereotype that the physical outcome is achieved through politicized development. In order to gain advocates, the design proposal for a contentious project needs to have a visionary quality. The proposal cannot be mediocre nor ambivalent, even if the most central contested terrain remains malleable.

If good design in contentious development has a strong underlying concept with a clear visionary quality and is founded on central political concerns, then it is not surprising that few development undertakings are well designed. Superior design is rarely found in current urban scenarios, least of all those involving the most cost-conscious of clients (developers), and the most argumentative processes. In the realm of contentious development, the architect's role has been complicated by new challenges, which can be seen as opportunities, that demand superior design. Consequently, the architect is elevated to a crucial position as the one who not only must synthesize order out of chaos, but who also must realize its physical manifestation.

Political philosophy and history justify this role for the architect. But if architecture as a profession is to survive, its visionary proposals should prioritize public interest over the local demands of contentious development.[54] An editorial by Tom Fisher in *Progressive Architecture* states the case similarly: "The profession of architecture was founded to guard the public, not just the public's health and safety through building and zoning codes, but the public realm and the public interest broadly defined."[55] In this process, the architect is neither neutral party nor mere mediator, but instead an advocate for what is often difficult to determine, the public good.

If architects are to assume stewardship of the public realm, many changes must take place within the profession.[56] These changes imply improving education about the environment, a standard that architecture schools have yet to achieve; and expanding the architect's political participation and advocacy of regional issues that typically have no constituents, two activities currently absent from our profession. Acting as a steward for the public good jeopardizes the architect's business relations, but if we do not assume this responsibility, our profession will be marginalized further in a society that already looks at architecture askance.

Notes

1. The other three elements that, from my own analysis, have significantly altered current conditions of architectural practice are recession, rapid changes in technology, and increasingly complex project-delivery systems.

2. Sir William Blackstone, *Commentaries on the Laws of England*, book I (1765), ed. John Frederick Archbold (London: M. and S. Brooke, Paternoster-Row, 1811). Although Blackstone was referring to rights "inherent in every Englishman," by some accounts, his *Commentaries* constituted the whole of American law before and after the American Revolution. See Daniel Boorstin, *The Mysterious Science of the Law* (Cambridge, Mass.: Harvard University Press, 1941).

3. See Ellen Frankel Paul, *Property Rights and Eminent Domain* (New Brunswick: Transaction Books, 1987). Paul, however, primarily identifies expansion on the state and federal levels.

4. See Mary Ann Glendon, *Rights Talk: The Impoverishment of Political Discourse* (New York: The Free Press, 1991).

5. See W. G. Bryant, *Land: Private Property, Public Control* (Montreal: Harvest House, 1972).

6. For example, architectural preservationists lobby effectively to force developers to redesign in historically appropriate manners. Those most persistent in such efforts are perceived to be "quacks" by more mainstream parties to the negotiations. I suggest such extremism rests on the preservationists' belief that their rights over someone else's private property are greater than society now acknowledges. They, in fact, may be visionary, if present trends in property relations continue to give communities even more say over environmental design. The complementary explanation would suggest that hard-line activists foresee the expansion of the developer's duties.

7. Glendon disagrees with the proposition that a frontier ethic has shaped our present view of property rights. Instead, she attributes greater influence to the history of law and its popular diffusion. See Glendon, *Rights Talk: The Impoverishment of Political Discourse*.

8. For example, in some colonial townships, citizens were required to build their houses within half a mile of a meeting house. More recently, the federal highway program, through eminent domain, has razed hundreds of neighborhoods in the name of the greater good. See

Marion Clawson, *Man and Land in the United States* (Lincoln: University of Nebraska Press, 1964), 36.

9. See Richard White and Patricia N. Limerick, *The Frontier in American Culture*, ed. J. R. Grossman (Berkeley: University of California Press, 1994).

10. Clawson, 37.

11. Bryant, 69–70.

12. See Bryant, *Land: Private Property, Public Control* and Henry Nash Smith, *Virgin Land; The American West as Symbol and Myth* (Cambridge, Mass.: Harvard University Press, 1950).

13. Bryant, 79–81. The Homestead Act of 1862 gave each individual a free quarter-section, or 160 acres, regardless of suitability for cultivation versus grazing, etc. This homogenous policy eventually led to the well known Dust Bowl conditions in Oklahoma.

14. See John W. Reps, *The Making of Urban America* (Princeton: Princeton University Press, 1965).

15. Reps, 302.

16. Clawson, 45.

17. See Reps, *The Making of Urban America* and J. B. Jackson, *Landscapes* (Amherst: Univ. of Massachusetts Press, 1970).

18. See Clawson, *Man and Land in the United States.*

19. Jackson, 19. Jackson adds that the village model disintegrated, as lots on the common were filled and villagers began speculating, selling their remote farmlands and wood lots to recent arrivals.

20. See Alan Ryan, *Property* (Milton Keynes: Open University Press, 1987).

21. For a concise discussion of exclusionary zoning and the NIMBY syndrome, see Philip Bettencourt, "'Not in My Back Yard: Removing Barriers to Affordable Housing," in *Advisory Commission on Regulatory Barriers to Affordable Housing, Report to President Bush and Secretary Kemp* (Washington: 1991).

22. Bryant, 9.

23. See Jan Cohn, *The Palace or the Poorhouse: The American House as a Cultural Symbol* (East Lansing: Michigan University Press, 1979).

24. On the other extreme, large land holders control even larger parcels—a dumbbell phenomenon.

25. According to conservative analyst Ellen Paul, federal and state power over land takes three forms: taxation, police power, and eminent domain.

26. See C. Reinold Noyes, *The Institution of Property* (New York: Longmans, Green, and Company, 1936).

27. John Locke, *Two Treatises of Government*, ed. Peter Laslett (Cambridge, England: Cambridge University Press: 1960), 305–306.

28. See Ryan, *Property*.

29. To read about land as a special type of non-consumable property, see the introduction to Alan Ryan, *Property and Political Theory* (Oxford: Basil Blackwell, 1984).

30. Ryan, 72.

31. See Cohn, *The Palace or the Poorhouse: The American House as a Cultural Symbol.*

32. Locke, 306.

33. Locke, 311.

34. Locke, 320.

35. Glendon, 107.

36. See Dana Cuff, "Beyond the Last Report: The Case of Public Housing in Houston," in *Places* (Winter 1985), 23–43.

37. David Hume, *A Treatise of Human Nature*, ed. L. A. Selby-Bigge (Oxford: Clarendon Press, 1888), III, ii.2.

38. Ryan, 96.

39. See Jean-Jacques Rousseau, "A Discourse on the Origin of Inequality," in *The Social Contract and Discourses*, trans. G. D. H. Cole (London: Dent Dutton, 1973).

40. Jeremy Waldron, *The Right to Private Property* (New York: Oxford University Press, 1988), 31.

41. Noyes, 395, and Waldron, 37.

42. For example, a transfer of air rights occurs when one owner is permitted to build higher than her property allows by purchasing the height allowance or building envelope of another piece of property. See Ronald Coase, "The Problems of Social Cost," in *Journal of Law and Economics* 2 (October, 1960) on the market realloca-tion of property rights.

43. Waldron, 37.

44. This happens by virtue of intellectual property rights. However, ownership in this sense has significant limita-tions, particularly in relation to the client-owner.

45. See Bernard Frieden, *The Environmental Protection Hustle* (Cambridge, Mass.: MIT Press, 1979).

46. Waldron, 38–41.

47. Sometimes community activists advocate individual interests, but this is by no means the only scenario.

48. See Waldron, *The Right to Private Property.*

49. Waldron, 27.

50. This is most shockingly apparent in our no-duty-to-res-cue rule, aptly described in Glendon, 78–89.

51. Allen D. Rosen, *Kant's Theory of Justice* (Ithaca: Cornell University Press, 1993), 52.

52. Magali Sarfatti Larson, *Behind the Postmodern Facade* (Berkeley: University of California Press, 1993), 147.

53. Larson, 147.

54. Survival is a real concern, given recent moves in Britain to remove the registration requirement for architects with the justification that architecture does not serve the public interest.

55. Thomas Fisher, "Systems of (Professional) Survival," in *Progressive Architecture* (December 1993), 7.

56. To cite a few of the diverse publications on architecture and the public interest: Jane Jacobs, *Systems of Survival* (New York: Random House, 1992); Stephen Carr, M. Francis, L. G. Rivlin, and A. M. Stone, *Public Space* (Cambridge, England: Cambridge University Press, 1992); Peter Katz, *The New Urbanism* (New York: McGraw-Hill, 1994); and Nathan Glazer and Mark Lilla, eds., *The Public Face of Architecture* (New York: The Free Press, 1987). My own work on public good in contentious developments and its manifestation as a public realm is contained in a chapter of the book I am presently writing.

The following books were not specifically cited in the text but were instrumental in preparing this essay: Brian Barry, *Theories of Justice* (Berkeley: University of California Press, 1989); Diane Favro, "Roman Solar Legislation," *Passive Solar Journal* 2:2 (1983): 90–98; Reiko Habe, "Public Design Control in American Communities" *Town Planning Review* 2 (1989): 195–219; Douglas R. Porter and Lindell L. Marsh, eds., *Development Agreements: Practice, Policy, and Prospects* (Washington, D.C.: The Urban Land Institute, 1989); Timothy J. Sullivan, *Resolving Development Disputes Through Negotiations* (New York: Plenum Press, 1984); and Jeremy Waldron, ed., *Theories of Rights* (New York: Oxford University Press, 1984).

UNLAWFUL DESIRE[1]

Durham Crout

The problem of the burial cult pushes ever more into the foreground these days, when there are very few Europeans remaining who have not lost a relative or friend in the mass genocide.

— Bruno Taut, 1917[2]

1. *Unlawful Desire* is the first part of an ongoing series of projects entitled *Hearing Aids*. "Hearing Aids: Unlawful Desire" began during a monthlong residency with Alice Aycock in the summer of 1989. This construction was further developed with the help Anarag Nema, Eddie Bello, Robin Roberts, Catie Shanks, Christine Tedesco, and Peter Przekop. When I first presented an early version of this work in November 1991 at the Public Domain conference in Atlanta, Georgia, I received many helpful insights from both Robert Cheatham and Harris Dimitropoulos. An expanded version was presented in April 1993 as part of Emerging Voices, a Princeton University Graham Foundation PhD Symposium. I would like to thank Mark Linder for the generous invitation to join in this symposium as well as those students who participated in the series. I am also grateful for valuable comments from Jack Reece, Andrew London, Beth Daniell and Karen Bermann. As always, I am greatly indebted to Jennifer Bloomer, Marco Frascari, and Robert Segrest. As a collective endeavor, however, this work is not concerned with the notion of "collective work" as a more appropriate or correct way of doing things. Instead, this collective endeavor is an attempt to get things done *now*. For a short discussion of this notion of collective work, see "Art and Activism: A Conversation between Douglas Crimp and Gregg Bordowitz, January 2, 1989," in *AIDS: The Artist's Response*, ed. Jan Zita Grover (Columbus: Ohio State University, 1989), 10.

2. Quoted in Iain Boyd Whyte, *Bruno Taut and the Architecture of Activism* (Cambridge: Cambridge University Press, 1982), 47. "Hearing Aids: Unlawful Desire" aspires to operate in the same vein as Charlotte's miraculous, terrific, radiant, humble, and egg-sacked writing for Wilbur. Or, as Pearl Cleage states, "I am writing to find solutions and pass them on. I am writing to find a language and pass it on. I am writing, writing for my life." See E. B. White, *Charlotte's Web* (New York: Harper, 1952); and Pearl Cleage, *Mad at Miles: A Black Woman's Guide to Truth* (Southfield: Cleage Group, 1990), 5. It is also a text as Paul Monette explains in *Borrowed Time: An AIDS Memoir* (New

York: Harcourt Brace Jovanovich, 1988), written "with a very blunt instrument, but groping at last toward leaving a record—'to say we have been here.'" In the installation piece *Let the Record Show*, the notion of "leaving a record" includes the documentation of individuals and their "persecutory, violent, homophobic statements [and/or silences] about AIDS." It is a documentation of the United States "government's abysmal failure to confront the [AIDS] crisis." This writing is the record of a similar architectural failure. For an analysis of *Let the Record Show*, see Douglas Crimp's introduction to *AIDS: Cultural Analysis/Cultural Activism* (Cambridge, Mass.: MIT Press, 1988); and Douglas Crimp and Adam Rolston, "AIDS Activist Graphics: A Demonstration," in *AIDS Demographics* (Seattle: Bay Press, 1990).

Unlawful Desire is dedicated to Jim Owens. Jim was a registered pediatric nurse, a caregiver, and a "wound dresser." See Walt Whitman, "The Wound-Dresser," in *The American Tradition in Literature*, ed. Sculley Bradley et al., (New York: Grosset and Dunlap, 1974), 31–33. The last stanza of this poem reads:

> Thus in silence in dream's projections,
> Returning, resuming, I tread my way through the hospitals,
> The hurt and wounded I pacify with soothing hand,
> I sit by the restless all the dark night, some are so young.
> Some suffer so much, I recall the experience sweet and sad,
> (many a soldier's loving arms about this neck have
>   cross'd and rested,
> Many a soldier's kiss dwells on these bearded lips.)

This work is also dedicated to all the members of my dead, dying, and dying-to-live family: Mark H., Damon L., Owen B., Doug C., Peter W., Paul P., Charlie Y., Tom T., Jim O., Jim W., Jeff C., Dan K., Charlie B., Keith K., Walt D., Jonathan L., Jack R., Jim Wh., Dan E., Porter C., Tom S., Rudy C., Teddy L., Rick C., Carl J., Jay M., Brian B., Kevin M., Craig O., Alan J., Brooks H., Nathan P., and (Steve, Kurt, Steven, John, Mark, and Amado). In May of 1990, I myself also tested positive for the HIV virus.

How is it that one person can be in the presence of another person in pain and not know it—not know it to the point where he himself inflicts it, and goes on inflicting it?

–Elaine Scarry, 1985[3]

The countless number of contemporary papers, books, buildings, and conferences that have addressed architecture's relationship to the body, to gender, and to sexuality have delicately and skillfully constructed a positively negative space within contemporary architectural thinking. Housed within these tightly constructed spaces is a series of bodies, genders, and sexualities that proper academic and professional architectural discourse must not touch.

Glimpses of these abject bodies, genders, and sexualities have, however, recently begun to emerge within contemporary architectural discourse—most notably in the work of Beatriz Colomina and Jennifer Bloomer.[4] Colomina begins the introduction to her collection of essays entitled *Sexuality and Space* (assembled from a 1991 symposium of the same name) with a brief discussion of the Princeton University housing policy with regard to sexual orientation.[5] She states that until March 1991, "sexuality [had been], at least officially, left at [Princeton's/the academy's] door."[6] Following Colomina, I believe it is important to always remember, however, that it was not "sexuality" that was left at the door (although academia has never been particularly hospitable to sex in any of its flavors), but, instead, very specific *categories* of sexuality.[7]

Significant references to these sexualities (lesbian, gay, bisexual, and transgendered) appear only twice in Colomina's book—in Patricia White's essay on lesbian sexuality and in Jennifer Bloomer's piece on homosexuality and bisexuality. This lack of exploration with regard to sexuality might suggest that the overriding issue of that book is in fact gender housed within an unspoken and critically unexamined, heterosexually determined matrix. I have suggested elsewhere that the seeming inability of architecture to interrogate the heterosexual/homosexual binary might be due to its resistance to consider gender and sexuality as separate, although intertwined, axes of analysis. Gayle Rubin states:

> I am now arguing that it is essential to separate gender and sexuality analytically to reflect more accurately their separate social existence . . . In the long run, feminism's critique of gender hierarchy must be incorporated into a radical theory of sex, and the critique of sexual oppression should enrich feminism. But an autonomous theory and politics specific to sexuality must be developed.[8]

Despite the incontestable importance of the *Sexuality and Space* text and symposium in opening vital discussions concerning architecture's relationship to bodies, genders, and sex-

3. Elaine Scarry, *The Body in Pain: The Making and Unmaking of the World* (New York: Oxford University Press, 1985), 12.

4. See Colomina's contributions to the *Queer Space* exhibit at the Storefront for Art and Architecture in May of 1994; and Bloomer's ANY conference entitled *Art and the Feminine* in November 1993. Aaron Betsky, Henry Urbach, and OLGAD have also begun to explore these bodies, genders, and sexualities with regard to both the profession and the discipline of architecture.

5. Colomina states that "in March 1991, after much debate, Princeton University approved a new policy giving domestic partners of gay and lesbian graduate students access to university housing, a right previously granted only to married students." See "Introduction," in *Sexuality and Space*, ed. Beatriz Colomina (New York: Princeton Architectural Press, 1992). The Sexuality and Space symposium was held at Princeton University's Betts Auditorium on March 10 and 11, 1990.

6. Colomina, "Introduction," in *Sexuality and Space*.

7. This should not be taken as a simple return to what might be called "identity politics" or, worse yet, political correctness. Judith Butler states:

> My own view is that it is imperative to assert identities at the same time that it is crucial to interrogate the exclusionary operations by which they are constituted. So what I'm calling for is not the surpassing of particularities, but rather a double movement: the insistence on identity and the subjection of identity-terms to a contestation in which the exclusionary procedures by which those identity-terms are produced are called into question. This seems to me to be the necessary and contingent place of identity within a radical democratic culture.

See Judith Butler's comments in the discussion portion of "The Identity in Question" symposium, in *October* 61, (Summer 1992), 108. With regard to the notion of sexual categories, Gayle Rubin says:

> Our categories are important. We cannot organize a social life, a political movement, or our individual identities and desires without them. The fact that categories invariably leak and can never contain all the relevant "existing things" does not render them useless, only limited. Categories like "woman," "butch," "lesbian," or "transsexual" are all imperfect, historical, temporary, and arbitrary. We use them, and they use us. We use them to construct meaningful lives, and they mold us into historically specific forms of personhood. Instead of fighting for immaculate classifications and impenetrable boundaries, let us strive to maintain a community that understands diversity as a gift, sees anomalies as precious, and treats all basic principles with a hefty dose of skepticism.

Gayle Rubin, "Of Catamites and Kings: Reflections on Butch, Gender, and Boundaries," in *The Persistent Desire: A Femme-Butch Reader*, ed. Joan Nestle (Boston: Alyson Publications, 1992), 477–478. *Unlawful Desire* attempts to employ a strategy of "fatigue/overload" with regard to individual identity formations/structures. This strategy is greatly indebted to Gregg Bordowitz's film *Fast Trip, Long Drop*.

8. Gayle Rubin, "Thinking Sex: Notes for a Radical Theory of the Politics of Sexuality," in *Pleasure and Danger: Exploring Female Sexuality*, ed. Carol S. Vance (London: Pandora Press, 1989), 308–309. For another discussion of this topic, see Eve Sedgwick, "Introduction: Axiomatic," in *Epistemology of the Closet* (Berkeley: University of California Press, 1990).

ualities, it is nonetheless difficult to reconcile those innovations with the omission of any discussion (or even mention) of HIV disease.[9] The only such mention in both book and symposium, ironically, falls in a marginal footnote to Bloomer's essay "D'Or."[10] Bloomer states, "the phenomenon of blaming the victim is surely familiar to anyone who, over the past five years, has read the reportage of the American press on AIDS."[11] In this footnote, Bloomer unfortunately collapses people living with HIV disease into the category of victim—a reduction that AIDS activists have been resisting since its original employment.[12] Bloomer claims that such a conflation had been going on for five years, starting in 1985 (the year of Rock Hudson's death due to complications from HIV disease, the first wake-up call for many heterosexuals to the AIDS crisis). By 1990, however when Bloomer was writing her essay, both the crisis and the collapsing of categories had been dangerously operating for not five years, but for ten. A discussion of AIDS and its relationship to space would seem to have been an important (if not unavoidable) addition to any conference or text framed, according to Colomina, as "an understanding of architecture as a system of representation."[13] According to Douglas Crimp, "AIDS intersects with and requires a critical rethinking of all of culture: of language and representation, of science and medicine, of health and illness, of sex and death, of public and private realms."[14] Simon Watney says, "AIDS is not only a medical crisis on an unparalleled scale, it involves a crisis of representation itself, a crisis over the entire framing of knowledge about the human body and its capacities for sexual pleasure."[15] With regard to such silences and omissions, architectural or otherwise represented here by *Sexuality and Space,* Crimp claims it is vital to understand that

> for anyone living daily with the AIDS crisis, ruthless interference with our bereavement is as ordinary an occurrence as reading the *New York Times*. The violence we encounter is relentless, the violence of silence and omission almost as impossible to endure as the violence of unleashed hatred and outright murder. Because this violence also desecrates the memories of our dead, we rise in anger to vindicate them. For many of us, mourning becomes militancy. The social and political barbarism we daily encounter requires no explanation whatsoever for our militancy. On the contrary, what may require an explanation, as Larry Kramer's plaint suggested, is the *quietism*.[16]

Within our own architectural context, "the violence of silence and omission" begs the question: does the continually avoided discussion of HIV/AIDS bodies, genders, and sexualities facilitate the construction of a proper architectural discourse? Why are these bodies considered distressing, threatening, intolerable, and dangerous with regard to even our most transgressive discussions about architecture?[17] The ongoing revival of the relationship

9. I have used *Sexuality and Space* to illustrate these points for three reasons: one, the stated agenda of both the text and the conference is often aligned with many of the same concerns outlined in much contemporary queer/AIDS work; two, the timing of the text and conference coincided with that moment when queer/AIDS work was emerging within many areas of inquiry; and three, it represents, by far, some of the most important work being done today in the realm of architectural studies as related to issues of sexuality and gender.

10. Jennifer Bloomer, "D'Or," in *Sexuality and Space*, 42.

11. Bloomer, "D'Or," 171.

12. See Jan Zita Grover, "AIDS: Keywords" and Max Navarre, "Fighting the Victim Label," both in *AIDS: Cultural Analysis/Cultural Activism*, ed. Douglas Crimp (Cambridge: MIT Press, 1988). The inability to hold such distinctions as that between "victim" and "people living with HIV disease" for example, has produced a conservative and, I believe, extremely damaging critical category called "victim art." See Arlene Croce, "Discussing the Undiscussable," in *The New Yorker*, December 26, 1994–January 2, 1995, 54–60.

13. Colomina, "Introduction."

14. Douglas Crimp, "AIDS: Cultural Analysis/Cultural Activism," in *AIDS: Cultural Analysis/Cultural Activism*, 15.

15. Simon Watney, *Policing Desire: Pornography, AIDS, and the Media* (Minneapolis: University of Minnesota Press, 1987), 9.

16. Douglas Crimp, "Mourning and Militancy," *October* 51, (Winter 1989), 10. Although "Unlawful Desire" is momentarily concerned with gay male HIV-positive bodies, these arguments are meant to pose questions with regard to all people with HIV disease. In "AIDS: Cultural Analysis/ Cultural Criticism," Douglas Crimp states:

> AIDS is a central issue for gay men, of course, but also for lesbians. AIDS is an issue for women generally, but especially for poor and minority women, for child-bearing women, for women working in the health care system. AIDS is an issue for drug users, for prisoners, for sex workers. At some point, even "ordinary" heterosexual men will have to learn that AIDS is an issue for them, and not simply because they might be susceptible to "contagion."

For a thoughtful discussion concerning the relationship AIDS has established between gay men and lesbians see Ruth L. Schwartz, "New Alliances, Strange Bedfellows: Lesbians, Gay Men, and AIDS," in *Sisters, Sexperts, Queers: Beyond the Lesbian Nation,"* ed. Arlene Stein (New York: Penguin Group, 1993). It is my hope that these new connections will ask gay men to examine more rigorously their own brands of misogyny and privilege. It is also my hope that the AIDS crisis will continue to ask gay men (a phrase that has come to mean *white* gay men) to examine and challenge our racism. See *Brother to Brother: New Writings by Black Gay Men,* edited by Essex Hemphill and conceived by Joseph Beam before his death due to complications from HIV disease. Catherine Saalfield and Ray Navarro state: "We recognize that every death related to HIV/AIDS complications is an act of racist, sexist, and homophobic violence." See Catherine Saalfield and Ray Navarro, "Shocking Pink Praxis: Race and Gender on the ACT UP Frontlines," in *inside/out: Lesbian Theories, Gay Theories*, ed. Diana Fuss (New York: Routledge, 1992). Also see Thomas Yingling, "AIDS in America: Postmodern Governance, Identity and Experience," in *inside/out: Lesbian Theories, Gay Theories*, 293–294; and Martha Fleming and Lyne Lapointe, "Animal Love: Miasme/Hyene et Valve," and Monika Gagnon and Tom Folland, "The Spectacular Ruse," both in *A Leap in the Dark: AIDS, Art, and Contemporary Cultures,* ed. Allan Klusacek and Ken Morrison (Montreal: Vehicule Press, 1992). Following Eve Sedgwick, I believe that "feminist analysis [is] considerably more developed than gay male or antihomophobic analysis at present—theoretically, politically, and institutionally." See Eve Sedgwick, "Introduction: Axiomatic," in *Epistemology of the Closet* (Berkeley: University of California Press, 1990). I also hold to Judith Butler's belief that

> an analysis which foregrounds one vector of power over another will doubtless become vulnerable to criticisms that it not only ignores or devalues the others, but that its own constructions depend on the exclusion of the others in order to proceed. On the other hand, any analysis which pretends to be able to encompass every vector of power runs the risk of a certain epistemological imperialism which consists in the presupposition that any given writer might fully stand for and explain the complexities of contemporary power. No author or text can offer such a reflection of the world, and those who claim to offer such pictures become suspect by virtue of that very claim.

See Judith Butler, *Bodies that Matter*, 18–19.

between architecture and the body has, among other things, led to the ambiguous celebration of certain modes of corporeality while disowning those considered improper. This exclusion necessarily marks as provisional whatever proper discourse architecture has established through such a revival. Elizabeth Grosz, following Sigmund Freud, claims that: "civilization is founded on the sacrifice or expulsion of [certain] polymorphous pleasures."[18] It is necessary to understand, however, that what has been expelled or sacrificed "can never be fully obliterated . . . [it] *hovers* [emphasis added] at the borders . . . [always] threatening apparent unities and stabilities with disruption and possible dissolution."[19]

It is nothing short of obscene that the architectural community, some fourteen years into this epidemic, remains, for the most part, silent.[20] The silence is simultaneously marked by an architecture that is (even after years of deconstruction) still adamant in its structural heteronormalcy.[21] Established through an apparent resistance to examining architecture's heterosexual/homosexual binary as rigorously and as brilliantly as the discipline has explored both gender oppression and the mind/body distinction, this structural security keeps architecture free from HIV disease, but open to accusations of heterosexism and homophobia. How is it that architecture can remain so silent when, in every imaginable direction, HIV-positive bodies, genders, and sexualities have been taken up as a political issue and everywhere constructed as a threat to what Simon Watney describes as the "apparently endlessly vulnerable values of hearth and home"?[22]

152

17. For a discussion of the ways in which both the discipline and profession of architecture construct themselves through exclusionary acts, see Catherine Ingraham, "The Faults of Architecture: Troping the Proper," in *Assemblage* 7 (October 1988): 8. Following Vitruvius, Ingraham states:

> Architecture defines its sphere of propriety as the fixing of what is, at any given moment, the authoritative interpretation of an event . . . The so-called principles of authoritative construction that constitute proper building are generated from just such accounts of cultural and political 'propriety.'

Critical silences with regard to HIV disease work to secure architecture's "proper" domain. Such stories often breach both "cultural and political [and architectural] 'propriety,'" while undoubtedly breaching *the* authoritative interpretation of the AIDS "event" established, and yet to be challenged, during the Reagan administration. According to Avital Ronell:

> Ever since the original Reagan ban on the word [AIDS] (however repressed or forgotten this initial "response" may be), a politics of containment and border patrol has dominated the way this culture looks at AIDS. On a level of far less consequence, AIDS has not yet acquired the status of an object worthy of scholarly [architectural] solicitude. Looking back, we can understand why there was such resistance . . . to admitting the epidemic into the rarefied atmosphere of academic inquiry; AIDS infected the academy, dissolving boundaries that traditionally set the disciplines off from one another, if only to secure their sense of self-knowledge . . . When it did come about, the study of AIDS encouraged the emergence of new marginal and "deviant" areas of inquiry in the humanities: gender studies, gay studies, queer theory, multicultural networks, mutant French theory, and even computer-based cyberpunk speculations.

See Avital Ronell, "A Note on the Failure of Man's Custodianship," in *Public* 8 (1993): 57–58. It is interesting to compare Ronell's observations about AIDS and academia with the 1986 editorial agenda of *Assemblage,* which some fourteen years into this epidemic and nine years in print, has yet to even mention the word—instituting a dangerous (albeit repressed or forgotten) repetition. See K. Michael Hays, "About Assemblage," in *Assemblage* 1, (October 1986): 4–5.

18. Elizabeth Grosz, "The Body of Signification," in *Abjection, Melancholia, and Love: The Work of Julia Kristeva,* ed. John Fletcher (New York: Routledge, 1990), 86. For a reading of HIV-positive bodies as "abject," see Simon Watney, *Policing Desire;* and Judith Williamson, "Every Virus Tells a Story: The Meanings of HIV and AIDS," in *Taking Liberties: AIDS and Cultural Politics,* ed. Erica Carter and Simon Watney (London: Serpent's Tail, 1989); and Judith Butler, *Gender Trouble: Feminism and the Subversion of Identity* (New York: Routledge, 1990).

19. Grosz, 87.

20. I am here reminded of B. Ruby Rich's statement that "to speak of sexuality and the body, and not also speak of AIDS, would be, well, obscene." Quoted in Douglas Crimp, "AIDS: Cultural Analysis/Cultural Activism," 14.

21. I do not want to collapse HIV disease with homosexuality, but the fact that they have already been collapsed is important to consider in examining the deadly persistence of this architectural silence. In "AIDS in America: Postmodern Governance, Identity, and Experience," Thomas Yingling states:

> Myths of identity have framed the interpretation of AIDS, and it remains a disease that attaches—rightly or wrongly—to identities: gay, IV-drug user, African, hemophiliac, infant, transfusion patient . . . Because AIDS has been read so persistently within a paradigm of group and/or individual identity, one of the continuing tasks facing those who respond to it has been to insist on it as a collective calamity . . . 'AIDS' as a signifier lodges in deep subliminal zones of memory, loss, and (im)possibility, *zones that in the end are among the most crucial sites on which disciplinarity is inscribed and therefore potentially disrupted* [emphasis added].

22. Watney, 15.

The very act of remembering begins to resemble a phobic state—feeding on every missed chance, stuck forever in the place without doors . . . My white-knuckle grip on happiness, hoarded against the gloating of my enemies, against the genocide by indifference that has buried alive a generation of my brothers.

—Paul Monette, 1992 [23]

1.   The drawings and constructions for "Unlawful Desire" are demonstrations that work to foreground the "negative" construction (through acts of silence and exclusion) of HIV positive bodies, genders, and sexualities in architecture, both professional and disciplinary, while simultaneously attempting an aggressive architectural reconfiguration and redeployment of these negative representations.[24] These drawings and constructions are intended to ignite the constructive unfolding of what might be referred to as *"queer spaces"* and *"queer identities."* [25]

2.   This work deploys such spatial configurations within a variety of sites: within the critical texts of the discipline, pedagogical positions, buildings, and city fabrics.[26] This work is specifically concerned with the emergence of such spatial possibilities in Atlanta, Georgia.

3.   These drawings and constructions operate under the intention of fighting HIV disease, AIDS phobia, and homophobia in the southeastern United States—a region where, according to the Centers for Disease Control "AIDS is increasing faster than in any other [region] of the country. While the number of AIDS cases increased 5% nationwide in 1990–1991, it increased 10% in the South." [27]

23. Paul Monette, *Becoming a Man: Half a Life Story* (New York: Harcourt Brace Jovanovich, 1992), 172. Thomas Yingling states,

> Plague will not do for this analysis because it seems to belong to a lifeworld 'of indeterminate horizons from which phenomena arise' rather than to the deliberate annihilation of vast numbers of people . . . the point for us is that AIDS shares more, finally, with genocide than with plague.

See Thomas Yingling, "AIDS in America," 306. Or, as Douglas Crimp states, one must decide "whether the crisis is . . . a natural, accidental catastrophe—a disease syndrome that has simply struck at random at this time and in this place—or . . . a result of gross negligence or mendacity—an epidemic that was allowed to happen." See "Mourning and Militancy," 6.

24. Crimp argues for "the necessity of reinscribing our subjectivity—that is, gay-male (or lesbian, or black, or Latin) subjectivity—in the work that we do on the crisis." See "Art and Activism," 10. Along with this notion of reinscription, "representations of AIDS have to [also] be X-rayed for their fantasmatic logic." See Leo Bersani, "Is the Rectum a Grave?" in *AIDS: Cultural Activism/Cultural Criticism,* 210.

25. For the sake of clarity, I refer to homosexual identity as a construction that designates a "perverse negative of heterosexuality." It is a medical term that has served to pathologize homosexuality while naturalizing and dehistoricizing heterosexuality. Simon Watney states that heterosexuality is "understood as a 'natural' domain of unassailable, rigidly gendered characteristics organized around the prime purpose of sexual reproduction and the 'protection' of asexual children." See Simon Watney, "School's Out," in *inside/out: Lesbian Theories, Gay Theories,* ed. Diana Fuss (New York: Routledge 1991), 395. I understand gay identity as a move away from homosexual pathology to signify the "recognition and acknowledgement of all forms of consensual erotic and sexual behavior." See Simon Watney, "The Possibilities of Permutation: Pleasure, Proliferation, and the Politics of Gay Identity in the Age of AIDS," in *Fluid Exchanges: Artists and Critics in the AIDS Crisis,* ed. James Miller (Toronto: University of Toronto Press, 1992), 330–332. Queer identity I take to "point out a wide field of normalization." It combines "resistance on the broad social range of the *normal* with more specific resistance on the terrain of phobia, queer bashing on the one hand, or of pleasure on the other." See Michael Warner, "Introduction: Fear of a Queer Planet," in *Social Text* 9, no. 29 (1991). The assertion of queer identity also includes an interrogation of the exclusionary operations by which the assertion of any identity, queer or otherwise, is even possible. I also take queer identity to be inseparable from the crisis of gay identity that has been brought about by HIV disease. It is important to note that within queer politics itself, crossings (and, perhaps, recrossings) must continually occur. According to Judith Butler, "Queer politics" has often

> appeal[ed] to a younger generation who want to resist the more institutionalized and reformist politics sometimes signified by "lesbian and gay"; in some contexts, sometimes the same, it has marked a predominantly white movement that has not fully addressed the way in which "queer" plays—or fails to play—within nonwhite communities; and whereas in some instances it has mobilized a lesbian activism, in others the term represents a false unity of women and men. Indeed, it may be that the critique of the term will initiate a resurgence of both feminist and antiracist mobilization within lesbian and gay politics or open up new possibilities for coalitional alliances.

See Judith Butler, *Bodies that Matter: On the Discursive Limits of "Sex"* (New York: Routledge, 1993), 228–229. It is important to here employ a critique of the term *queer* with regard to HIV disease, as some have argued that the term has been used to distance the lesbian, gay, and bisexual communities from AIDS. Queer politics must continually be opened and reopened to include concerns such as sexism, racism, and AIDS phobia, which it might be excluding in its ongoing construction. See Lee Edelman, "The Mirror and the Tank: AIDS, Subjectivity, and the Rhetoric of Activism," in *Writing AIDS: Gay Literature, Language, and Analysis*, ed. Timothy F. Murphy and Suzanne Poirier (New York: Columbia University Press, 1993). With regard to film, see Penny Florence, "We Are Here but Are We Queer?: Lesbian Filmaking versus Queer Cinema Conference, London, 12 March, 1994," in *Screen,* no. 3, (Autumn 1994).

26. This is not to say that such spatial configurations, although constantly threatened with erasure, are not already figured within these sites. This deployment and redeployment might, in many ways, follow the "six collective aims" laid out for "activism criticism" by James Miller, "Criticism as Activism," in *Fluid Exchanges: Artists and Critics in the AIDS Crisis,* ed. James Miller (Toronto: University of Toronto Press, 1992).

27. James T. Sears, "Adding 'Them' to 'Us': The South as the New Battleground for Gay Rights," in *Empathy: An Interdisciplinary Journal for Persons Working to End Oppression on the Basis of Sexual Identities* 3, no. 2, (1992–1993).

4.   These drawings and constructions encourage the production of knowledge about HIV disease, help to articulate this knowledge, help to codify concrete and specific issues, and work as an organizing tool that compresses information, political positions, and architectural concerns.[28] This work asserts the belief that architecture has the power to help save lives, and holds a significant place within the cultural practices that have actively participated in the struggle against HIV disease.

5.   These drawings and constructions appropriate the "style" of what has become known as "Decon."[29] This appropriation is carried out not because we see this style as representing deconstruction as a system of thought (discussions of architectural style are not even appropriate here) but because in 1989 (when we began this project) it was the most seductive architectural imagery and language in circulation within the Atlanta architectural community. With this reinscription (this subversive repetition),[30] we hoped to get the attention of those people interested in and/or desiring such images. We simultaneously attempted to open up these images and their producers to discussions about the relationship between architecture and the concerns of lesbians, gays, bisexuals, transgendered people, and those living with HIV disease. Or, as Gregg Bordowitz states:

> How are we going to develop more effective means of representation "for us," for the people who are affected by AIDS, unless we use the available forms? That means employing cliché forms. What we can try to do is to alter them and make them signify for us, so that what we come up with is something radically different than what is presented to us. It's radically different because it's "us" making meaning about our situation and not just waiting for an invitation from "culture," which someone else has always defined.[31]

6.   These drawings and constructions are not meant to establish the specificity of homosexuality against heterosexuality. Instead, this work is an attempt to turn homophobic constructions against the frame that stabilizes and secures heterosexuality as both originary and natural.[32] This work also wants to remain carefully aware that AIDS and Queer activism, although connected, are often separate endeavors.[33] This work wants to also take into account the new trend toward "the *professionalization* of gayness and the institutionalization of AIDS," a problematic situation. We want to be engaged both carefully and critically as lesbians, gays, bisexuals, and transgendered people who have long been the "*objects* of 'knowledge,' constructed *in* theory" and rarely the producers of it.[34]

7.   These drawings and constructions are drawn with blood and tears. They are attempts to overcome both disciplinary and governmental inaction with regard to HIV disease, to allow for mourning as a collective possibility, and to retain pleasure in our gay, lesbian, bisexual, and transgendered sexualities as well as *continuing* to construct our sexualities as communal experiences.[35]

28. Crimp, "AIDS Activist Graphics: A Demonstration," p.20.

29. See Douglas Crimp's discussion of Mapplethorpe's appropriation of style in his essay "Appropriating Appropriation," and his reconsideration of these original insights in "Photographs at the End of Modernism," both in Crimp, *On the Museum's Ruins* (Cambridge: MIT Press, 1993).

30. Judith Butler states:

> All signification takes place within the orbit of the compulsion to repeat . . . If the rules governing signification not only restrict, but enable the assertion of alternative domains of cultural intelligibility . . . then it is only within the practices of repetitive signifying that a subversion of identity becomes possible . . . There is only a taking up of the tools where they lie, where the very "taking up" is enabled by the tool lying there . . . The critical task is, rather, to locate strategies of subversive repetition enabled by those constructions, to affirm the local possibilities of intervention through participating in precisely those practices of repetition that constitute identity and, therefore, present the immanent possibility of contesting them.

See *Gender Trouble: Feminism and the Subversion of Identity* (New York: Routledge, 1990). Also see Howard Singerman, "Seeing Sherrie Levine," in *October* 67 (Winter 1994); and James Meyer, *What Happened to the Institutional Critique?* (New York: American Fine Arts Co., 1993).

31. Douglas Crimp in "Art and Activism," 9. This strategy is, in many ways, similar to those strategies employed by the Situationists—in particular their notion of *detournement*.

See Saalfield and Navarro, "Shocking Pink Praxis," 363; and David Deitcher, "Grand Fury," in *Conversations in Postmodern Art and Culture*, ed. Russell Ferguson (Cambridge: MIT Press, 1990), 196–208.

32. Judith Butler, "Imitation and Gender Insubordination," in *inside/out: Lesbian Theories, Gay Theories,* ed. Diana Fuss (New York: Routledge, 1992), 17.

33. For a critique of the construction of the AIDS activist, see Lee Edelman, "The Mirror and the Tank: 'AIDS,' Subjectivity, and the Rhetoric of Activism," in *Writing AIDS: Gay Literature, Language, and Analysis,* ed. Timothy F. Murphy and Suzanne Poirier (New York: Columbia University Press, 1993).

34. Bad Object-Choices, "Introduction," in *How do I Look?: Queer Film and Video* (Seattle: Bay Press, 1991), 12. With regard to the *Queer Space* exhibition at the Storefront for Art and Architecture, Herbert Muschamp states: "This agenda raises the issue of exploitation. Are these theorists using an academic discipline to support an embattled minority, or are they using that minority's struggle to prop up Derrida?" Herbert Muschamp, "Designing a framework for Diversity," *New York Times*, Sunday, June 19, 1994, 34.

35. See Douglas Crimp in "Art and Activism," 10. Saalfield and Navarro state that "AIDS activists must encourage responsibility in sexual relations while perpetually testing the limits of that pleasure." See Saalfield and Navarro, "Shocking Pink Praxis," 357. For a further development of these themes, see "Hearing Aids Part II: Wasting Architecture," in *Lusitania*, no. 7 (1994).

How are we going to develop more effective means of representation "for us," for the people who are affected by AIDS, unless we use the available forms? That means employing cliché forms. What we can try to do is to alter them and make them signify for us, so that what we come up with is something radically different than what is presented to us. It's radically different because it's "us" making meaning about our situation and not just waiting for an invitation from "culture," which someone else has always defined.

— Gregg Bordowitz

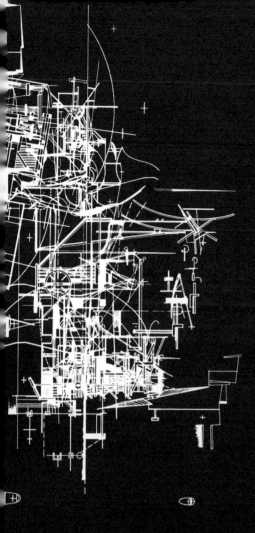

I'd been there a few minutes, setting up command, when Roger began to moan. It was the saddest, hollowest sound I've ever heard, and loud, like the trumpet note of a wounded animal. It had no shape to it, nothing like a word, and he repeated it over and over, every few seconds. . . . It wasn't till ten weeks later, on New Year's day, that I understood the trumpet sound. I was crying up at the grave, and started to mimic his moaning, and suddenly understood that what he was doing was calling my name. Nothing in my life or death to come hurts as much as that, him calling me without a voice through a wall he could not pierce.

— Paul Monette, *Borrowed Time: An AIDS Memoir*

This drawing is constructed from hypodermic needles, IV lines, pill capsules, gauze, scalpels, oxygen masks, stitches, catheters, body parts, X-ray devices and the lead markings used for radiation positioning.

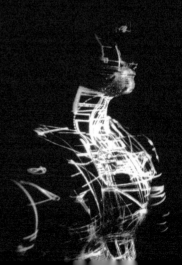

THE UNCONSTRUCTED SUBJECT OF THE CONTEMPORARY CITY

Albert Pope

If there is something comforting—religious, if you want—about paranoia, there is still also antiparanoia, where nothing is connected to anything, a condition not many of us can bear for long. Well right now Slothrop feels himself sliding onto the antiparanoid part of his cycle, feels the whole city around him going back roofless, vulnerable, uncentered as he is . . . Either They have put him here for a reason, or he's just here.

neotraditionalism

In the past decade, the overwhelming reification of neotraditional architecture by aggressive market forces has bankrupted the many apologies for the unmitigated revival of
humanist architectural culture. As vocabularies based on anthropomorphic representation
have been leveled by the reductive terms of commodity production, the naive inscription
of a classical sovereign subject into the contemporary urban environment has moved rapidly
from frustrating to futile to a highly marketable style. It is now clear that even a limited
traditional vocabulary cannot be sustained in the face of escalating volatility in social,
political, and economic relations. The fierce constraints of commodity production, an
increasingly fragmented and brutal urban site, and a fully distracted constituency have all
contributed to a debasement of the traditional architectural vocabulary. In the struggle
against its commodification, the failure of the neotraditionalists to enlist the full authority
of a disciplinary language is decisive; the ramifications of this failed attempt have yet to
be absorbed.

The failure to revive a humane urban environment is not just another shift of trends, or
something to stimulate a new cycle of trade publications and minor cult personalities.
It instead represents the moment in which the collapse of the traditional city must be confronted for what it is. A colossal Faustian bargain must be assessed—the fallout of an
unprecedented postwar economic boom fueled by the consumption of the "life-world" itself.[1]
The present state of contemporary urban development is proof enough that a considerable
portion of the life-world has already been sold off: the simultaneous collapse of public
space and monumental construction has left it impossible to negotiate the economic, political, and cultural identities that have historically constituted civil society. While the market
has thrived, the substance of a recognizably human city has been surrendered. What are
the precise terms of this surrender? By all counts, the terms imply the loss of a city in which
we may perceive ourselves, in which we are literally constituted as subjects in the city's
form and space.

The ancient ambition to recognize the human body as the ultimate measure of the built
world constitutes the subject in the space of the city. This standard has been manifested
in a variety of traditions, ranging from the overt symbolism of the Latin-cross plan to the most
arcane proportioning ratios of classical architecture. Overt analogies to bodies and body
parts as well as more obscure empathetic architectural associations comprise a long history of inscribing anthropocentric signatures onto urban environments. Such inscription has

operated across all scales and statuses of building, from the most significant of public monuments to the most common of urban typologies, from the massing of ideal cities to the vertical proportioning of windows. The overt failure to realize a legible anthropomorphic dimension in the architecture of the contemporary city is thus a historical loss. And while the historical city continues to be reproduced in all forms of contemporary media, it is not reproduced in the city itself; again, the ramifications of this failure have yet to be absorbed.

neomodernism

As the legitimacy of the neotraditional revival has cracked under the pressure of market constraints, modern architecture has been even more fully embraced by the academic and trade presses, by architecture schools, and by cultural institutions as a vital legacy worthy of revival and extension. The result has been an inversion of neotraditional tendencies in the form of neomodern revival. This revival, however, is something more than a seamless resumption of the modern project. Because it follows the collapse of an anthropomorphic renaissance, and the failed attempt to mediate the processes of contemporary production with a humanist vocabulary, modernism is now historically cast as it has never been before: as the operative language of a decidedly post-humanist urban environment. Shorn of its residual utopianism, neomodernism appears as an unapologetic celebration of the collapse of the humanist city. In recent revivals of the modern, the representation of the human figure in the space of the contemporary city has been fully discredited. If neotraditionalism sought to construct an urban subject in historical terms, neomodern ambitions are characterized by an inversion—the inscription of the unconstructed urban subject.

modernism and subject inscription

Modernism grew out of an explicit assault on the anthropomorphic biases of traditional forms of architectural representation. The rejection of these forms sprang from many, and often conflicting, agendas. For some architects, anthropomorphic representation impeded the development of contemporary architectural expression. For others, anthropomorphic representation forestalled the decline of antiquated or regressive political practices. Here the inscription of the body was quite literally a device that subjugated progress by illegitimate

political claims. And for others still, anthropomorphic representation hampered the development of an environment in which the body is no more than a productive instrument.
Put bluntly by Manfredo Tafuri, "the problem was to plan the disappearance of the subject,
to cancel the anguish caused by the pathetic (or ridiculous) resistance of the individual
to the structures of domination that close in upon him, to indicate the voluntary and docile
submission to those structures of domination as the promised land of universal planning."[2]
In this case, the subject is eliminated but the body remains merely as an enabling agent
operating the machines, driving the cars, administering capital, circulating like integers in
an endless industrial cycle.

Whether one desired freedom from repressive classical codes, fixed urban (typological)
forms, regressive architectural hierarchies, cultural pretenses, or bourgeois individualism,
the elimination of the subject from architectural representation cut across all social, political, and cultural fronts. Yet despite all the high-profile crusades to eliminate the subject
from the modern building and city, the effort was never complete. More than a few architects
(often themselves the loudest polemicists) acknowledged the historical limits of modernism
and attempted to inject it with anthropomorphic representation. A series of significant
modern projects sought explicitly to inscribe a subject into the space of the contemporary
city; these inscriptions offer an alternative both to the sovereign subject of neotradition-
ism and to the apparently unconstructed subject of neomodernism.

devices of modern inscription

The representation or inscription of the body into modernist form and space is a complex
topic that goes well beyond the simplistic arguments of orthodoxy. Polemics aside, the
modernist position toward anthropomorphic representation was often ambivalent, equivocal,
and contradictory, claiming a radical rejection of representation while aggressively interpreting and translating it into modern contexts and forms of expression. One need look no
further than Le Corbusier to find the most conspicuous agent of modern tendencies toward
anthropocentric representation. In developing the Modulor, Le Corbusier shifted the conventional trace of movement (the architectural promenade) to the free plan, ubiquitously
expressed the solitary cell, and significantly displaced the classical anthropocentric vocabulary (where vestiges of that figuration survived a certain distortion). Such accommodations
may represent attempts by Le Corbusier (and others) to reinscribe the subject into the

modern project. In contrast to the traditional centering of the singular sovereign subject, modern inscription tended to be decentered, nonhierarchical, and, for the most part, multiple. With regard to these examples, one may argue that modernism's theoretical rejection of the architecturally inscribed figure was by no means total. Within that rejection, there lay a more subtle and far less pervasive project that was concerned with the articulation of alternative subject positions unique to contemporary urban development.

This project of anthropomorphic representation—a form of self-critique lodged within modernism's own orthodoxy—has rarely survived in the ensuing neomodern revivals. Currently prevailing tendencies of the neomodern do not reproduce this ambiguity as they carry forward a relatively transparent revival of the early modern argument, which holds as synonymous the rejection of the sovereign, classically inscribed subject and the rejection of any and all subject inscription. The explicit violation or rejection of the architectural and urban subject has, for the most part, become a defining premise of neomodernism.[3]

In the first blush of their revolution, the early modernists had a more legitimate excuse for their refusal of the subject. The contemporary neomoderns, given their awareness and tendency to subscribe to poststructuralist theory, have far less of an excuse, particularly with regard to the current debate surrounding the construction of the subject. The poststructuralist rejection of the sovereign subject—the conscious and coherent originator of meaning and action—opened the door to various analyses of configurations of power and knowledge, examinations that have subsequently come to preempt that basic sovereignty. Debate over the various and sinister ways in which a subject is now pitilessly constructed— by history, by late capitalism, by information systems, by the invisible arm of so many defining institutions, and especially by language—has rightfully sponsored an intolerance of the overt ways in which architecture has traditionally inscribed the subject. In this light, the poststructuralist critique postdates and decisively challenges a naive revival of modernism.

The rejection of an anthropocentric vocabulary by early modern architects was, at its best, more than a polemical stunt. The received architectural and urban vocabulary was interpreted not as a manifestation of humanist culture, but instead as a coercive, disciplinary technology that humanist culture served only to obscure. In this regard, the inscription of a subject coincided with being "subject to" the exercise of arbitrary political power. Attempts to represent an anthropomorphic measure were made in the service of a predetermined political and ideological subject rather than in the service of a sovereign humanist subject. All differences between, for example, the Pantheon and the Panopticon, break down into a uniform repressive anthropomorphic order of architecture, metaphorically casting into stone the terms of social confinement. Given the potency of such a debate within contemporary theory, it is easy to see how neomodernism gave birth to a contemporary revival of the modern critique.

abandoned sites of power

The dismantling of outward architectural forms of instrumentality does not, however, lead to the dismantling of repressive control; though poststructuralist debate makes this concept clear, it is otherwise lost on contemporary architectural discourse. The disappearance of such outward signs seems to have marked not the disappearance of control, but instead its displacement, its internalization within the self. Long before poststructuralism, psychoanalysis identified the specific agent of this process of internalization. Sigmund Freud likened the displacement of power within the self to a kind of internalized police state sponsored by the superego. Defined at its most basic level, the superego was the device by which society "obtains mastery over the individual's dangerous desire for aggression by weakening or disarming it and by setting up an agency within [the self] to watch over it, like a garrison in a conquered city."[4] Michel Foucault pointed out that traditional architectural forms no longer constitute the essential sites of power (for Foucault, the Panopticon *was* history). In Foucault's view, that power had long since been internalized into a form of "biopower," and to remain fixated on the outward architectural forms was to ignore what now constituted the crucial sites of potential resistance.

As it becomes understood that the instruments of repressive power have not been dismantled, but instead internalized, the elimination of the subject may be interpreted as something other than an attempted liberation. The neomodern rejection of the inscribed subject is by now superfluous to a mechanism of power that has long been displaced. One may argue that by the time the early modernists began to liberate the subject from architectural and institutional inscription, power had already been internalized and architecture had ceased to be a coercive site. Contemporary critique of the outward forms of architectural inscription may now be little more than a regressive smoke screen, the proclamation of a subject liberation that has not, in fact, taken place. Simply put, rejecting an architectural inscription of the subject is work on a false site. These false sites now obscure alternative sites that hold greater potential for resistance. Since World War II, it has become increasingly clear that architecture has been abandoned as a vehicle of political and social inscription. The neomodernist ignores this development (which is precisely why we must speak of a neomodernism rather than modernism or postmodernism) in the attempt to uncritically revive and sustain the fashionable ethos of an architectural avant-garde.

multiple subjects

The outright rejection of the subject in both modernism and neomodernism is shortsighted, unworkable, and politically regressive. In reaction to the naive neotraditional revival of a unified sovereign subject, neomodernism has rejected the articulation of any subject position whatsoever. Caught between a unified sovereign subject and no subject at all, discourse polarizes into extreme and useless positions. Significant alternatives to the present impasse remain, however, and crucial to these alternatives is the idea of a multiple subject—a subject position that is neither entirely constructed nor entirely abandoned.

Multiple subject positions are assumed in order to avoid limiting the subject as singular or exclusively defined. As articulated by Paul Smith, the subject is actually *not* defined, "[n]either in the sense of being entirely submitted to the domination of the ideological, [n]or of being entirely capable of choosing his/her place in the social [domain] . . . of possessing full consciousness or some such version of what can be called sovereign subjectivity." Smith goes on to define an alternative, which is the deliberate cultivation of multiple subject positions:

> the "subject" need no longer be described . . . as the equivalent of the "individual" but rather can be conceived as a set of variable qualities that are taken up as a way of negotiating interpellations and thus of understanding and coping with social relations. Within this more sophisticated and complex view of subjectivity, it would no longer be adequate to posit a social being as "always already" a "subject," capable of recognizing itself as such. It would seem appropriate to talk instead of an overdetermination in the "subject's" process of construction: such an overdetermination is the effect of a continual and continuing series of overlapping subject positions that may or may not be present to consciousness at any given moment, but which in any case constitute a person's history. And a person's lived history cannot be abstracted as subjectivity pure and simple, but must be conceived as a collation of multifarious and multiform subject positions.[5]

The important distinctions between the humanist subject (determined and sovereign) and the neomodernist fully rejected subject will no doubt be played off the alternative of multiple subject positions as articulated by Smith and others. While the idea of a multiple subject may not directly address the impasse wrought by the collapse of traditional anthropomorphic inscription, at the very least it addresses the relevant deficiencies of the neotraditional and neomodern positions and points to an alternative position that already exists within modernism's inadequately understood legacy.

antiparanoia

Having questioned the critical enterprise behind the neomodern rejection of the subject, grappling with the real and continuing consequences of that rejection remains important. A calculated response to the internalized site of power must also be suggested. To that end, it is necessary to identify and define an actual subject—a site for theoretical suppositions. Against the sovereign subject of neotraditional inscription, I would like to posit the existence of an actual but unconstructed urban subject inhabiting the vast stretches of the postanthropomorphic contemporary city.[6] An unconstructed subject would be the consequence of an urban environment in which we could no longer perceive ourselves—our bodies— to be the ultimate measure of the built world. The fantastic residue of the last fifty years of urban construction—the vast parking lots, zones of urban blight, urban expressways, corporate plazas; the *cordon sanitaire* surrounding office parks, theme parks, and shopping malls; the unkempt surroundings of massive slab cities; the endless, ubiquitous extent of corporate housing tracts; the entire collapse of inner-city development—would all serve as a benchmark for what has been termed the postanthropomorphic urban landscape.

Recent discussions of the city have often been diverted from research on and analysis of the actual sites of recent urban construction to aesthetics and linguistics as well as to matters of representation and identifiable urban codes.[7] As discussed, much of neomodernism is based on an open disruption of such established codes as the anthropocentric order of the traditional city and its architecture, yet such theoretical ambitions are inadequate, if not actually laughable, when confronted by the overwhelming results of contemporary urban construction. The contrast between theoretical premises and built urban fact shows that it is much too late to destroy an anthropomorphic urban code in the name of critical theory. Even the most distracted survey of the contemporary urban environment reveals that the present task is not the destruction of codes, but rather a description of their already completed destruction. It is in the contemporary city that the absence of the anthropocentric order is most keenly felt, where a theoretical polemic against humanism and the humanist subject coincides with the brute facts of an inhumane environment. The failure to find alternative means of inscribing the subject into the space of the contemporary city brings to light the full implications of the uninscribed subject of neomodernism.

A detailed survey of the contemporary city is unnecessary here. Apart from the sheer brutality of the urban environment—its complete rejection of the pedestrian subject, its regressive pattern of exclusionary corporate development, its atomization of collective form and neutralization of the political body—the contemporary city represents the complete collapse of the social. Against this backdrop we can read and construct the self that ultimately characterizes the diminished circumstances of the contemporary urban subject. For all the highly paranoid debate concerning the coercive construction of a contemporary subject, there is overwhelming evidence of a far more problematic position, that of an *un*constructed subject, a victim of Thomas Pynchon's antiparanoia in which nothing is connected to anything, "a condition not many of us can bear for long."[8]

The definition of the unconstructed subject as a sometimes liberated but ultimately overexposed citizen suffering from a debilitating antiparanoia may present too absurd or fatalistic a caricature to be useful. Yet the refusal to develop contemporary subject positions does suggest an abandoning relegation of the contemporary urban citizen to a highly doubtful existence. Far from approaching a state of uninscribed liberation, the citizen subject endures subjective free-fall in a void haunted only by ghosts, televangelists, cartoon characters, the successful life-world of prime-time actors and national politicians, and the home-shopping channel. In this poisonous nightmare world of read-only memory, the rejection of a credible subject position amounts to a radical disenfranchisement. Worse still, one could argue that remaining unconstructed—wholly alienated from an environment that has lost its anthropomorphic biases—the urban subject actually becomes *more* vulnerable to the most regressive of contemporary subject positions.

This lack of substantive support from the urban environment suggests that the unconstructed subject of neomodernism is synonymous with the radically disenfranchised inhabitant of contemporary urban development. And it is precisely here, at this nexus of the material and the theoretical, that the priorities and limitations of contemporary neomodern production really do intersect with the depleted reality of contemporary urban development. It is also here that we may begin to address issues of displaced power relations and the long-standing abandonment of externalized architectural forms. Considered in light of displaced and internalized power, what is the consequence of the neomodern abandonment of the subject in architecture and in the city? If architecture no longer plays a substantial role in the social constitution of the subject, is the neomodernist ban on the architecturally inscribed subject really significant? Indeed, is it conceivable that architecture, in its remaining capacity to inscribe the subject, now becomes a potentially liberating agent, a moment of resistance against a debilitating antiparanoia?

Returning to when architecture really was the external, constructed site of power, anthropocentric inscription clearly marked the existence of a repressive social structure. The early modernist ultimately defeated this repressive Panoptic power, rightfully concluding that the humanist subject of the classical tradition had been co-opted by a newly emergent disciplinary technology. The denial of subject inscription was thus advanced by the early modernist and was subsequently consummated by institutional reforms of the immediate post–World War II period. By the time the early modernists had liberated the subject from architectural and institutional inscription, power had already been internalized and architecture had ceased to be a significant relation-defining site. Extending this argument, one may suggest that it was precisely the modernists' elimination of the subject—the elimination of a stable anthropomorphic urban order—that established the preconditions for this internalization of power. No longer depending on a constructed architectural site, power was instead predicated on the opposing condition—the unconstructed subject, a radically exposed and relatively undeveloped ego ready, if not eager, for political, economic, and cultural colonization.

Having based this analysis on the provisional definition of an unstable, antiparanoid, and unconstructed urban subject, it must now be recognized that such a subject is little more than an extrapolated caricature of certain urban circumstances of varying discernibility. It is undoubtedly impossible to locate a position that antecedes subject construction or identity. The subject is "always already" defined; there is no ideologically innocent state. In the end, the unconstructed subject of neomodernism is no more credible than the early modernist ideal, or fantasy, of a fully liberated universal subject that has been architecturally liberated from the repressive forces of history. While we are not wholly defined by the state, by science, by capital, or by history (any more than we are wholly defined by architecture), neither are we entirely innocent of such constructions. The neomodernist refusal of the subject is not so much a return to a liberated, uninscribed state as it is a repeat of modernism's inadvertent preconditioning for the internalization of power. The unconstructed subject is innocent perhaps, but it is also overexposed and vulnerable to the most

Robert Longo. *Untitled*, 1980. From the series *Men in the Cities*.

retrograde cultural and political tendencies. Because the uninscribed state clearly supports these tendencies, the complicit neomodern position must be called into question.

beinahe nichts

While it is clear that we are not sovereign, autonomous subjects inscribed in an idealized anthropomorphic order, neither are we liberated from inscription altogether (two sides of the same utopia). There are clearly claims upon us. But these claims are not universal, nor are they all-encompassing. We are not singularly constructed by outside forces—by state, by science, by capital, by history, by architecture. We are, in fact, structured by *all* of them, negotiating as *agents* in an overdetermined field. Reasserting the outmoded modernist polemic of an unconstructed subject amounts to an abdication of the possibility that architecture can operate in the field of multidetermination, an abdication of the possibility that architecture can support agency and make progressive contributions to heterogeneous identities.

Given this characterization, one might conclude that it is necessary to substantially rethink the subject position advanced by the early modernist. One could speculate that the architectural response might, like the power relation itself, be inverted. As the requisite site for internalized power relations, the unconstructed position of the contemporary urban subject must be resisted. Given the present context, it is not difficult to see how a contemporary inscription of the urban subject becomes a moment of resistance. Simply stated, the visible, concrete, and material components of architecture, in all of its heterogeneous manifestations, are enlisted in the attack against the invisible, immaterial, singular, and internalized site of power.

Such an agenda disregards prevailing neomodern wisdom. In a nostalgic revival of Mies van der Rohe's "beinahe nichts" ("almost nothing"), the visible, concrete, and material aspects of architecture are once again considered suspect, if not entirely sinister, sites of repressive power. Rem Koolhaas, who has articulated one of the most influential contemporary neomodern positions, announces an unabashed prejudice against concrete urban form because it is responsible for the innate "tortures" of daily life:

> Where there is nothing, everything is possible. Where there is architecture, nothing (else) is possible . . . It is a tragedy that planners only plan and architects only design more architecture . . .

Robert Longo. *Untitled*, 1981. From the series *Men in the Cities*.

Only through an evolutionary process of erasure and the establishment of "liberty zones," conceptual Nevadas where all the laws of architecture are suspended, will some of the inherent tortures of urban life—the friction between program and containment—be suspended.[9]

Throughout this century, architecture and urbanism have been driven by a powerful teleological trajectory toward a historical destination that is the complete transparency of form. It is the trajectory of dematerialization—the celebrated "destruction of the box." In response to a number of complex technical, social, and cultural parameters, this trajectory projects the literal dematerialization of architecture and the city. Moving us along on this path is the idea that architectural and urban form inherently functions as an encumbrance to the free play of ideas and actions, institutions and activities, and that the elimination of form will result in the elimination of encumbrance. The belief that buildings and cities are evolving into a state of neutral or transparent instrumentality is so pervasive, so fundamental to what we now understand architecture and urbanism to be, that we rarely stop to question its consequences.

Under the guiding ethos of contemporary neomodernism, less is once again more, and in the nostalgia for urban open space or "liberty zones" we are confronted anew by the false assumption that form constitutes a repressive site, part of an outward disciplinary technology that must be eliminated. Yet who today can actually sustain the faith that social liberation might be bought with a continual stripping-away of form? This stripping-away could be precisely the precondition that repressive social forces now require. As form comes again to be understood as a liability, we are left to contemplate whether its divestment constitutes a liberation or an overexposure. While it is possible to imagine contemporary situations in which there is too much architecture, it is equally possible to imagine situations in which there is not enough. The answer falls between the two extremes—at least Mies declared his ambition for *almost* nothing.

It is important to remember that the space between liberation and overexposure has been negotiated before. The exploration of contemporary subject positions has proceeded along with the development of modernism, albeit in less conspicuous fashion. One cannot look at a building such as Le Corbusier's La Tourette without realizing the various and sophisticated ways in which the subject has been repeatedly inscribed (in the cells, the oratory, the exposed promenade, the side chapels, the organ loft, the visitor's rooms, and so forth), representing a thoroughly contemporary context—a virtual instrument or machine, so to speak—for multiple subject inscription. In contrast to the vagaries of universal space, the

Robert Longo. *Untitled*, 1981. From the series *Men in the Cities.*

multiple and nonhierarchical inscription of subject positions can reintroduce anthropomorphic representation without resorting to the preemptive posturing of neotraditionalism. Following the collapse of the naive anthropomorphism of recent architectural and urban revivals, it is important to explore alternative subject positions available to the contemporary city, but not as gratuitous theoretical positions. This exploration should instead be understood as a project in process, a process set into motion by forces or economies well outside the prerogatives of academic or professional culture.

Le Corbusier. La Tourette, 1957. Eveux-sur-l'Arbresle.

Robert Longo. *Untitled,* 1981. From the series *Men in the Cities.*

Notes

1. The consumption of the life-world by economic imperative is at once both old saw and vital perception. The collapse of the "symbolic representation of the life-world" has been explored by many, including Jürgen Habermas:

> Capitalism was quite a success, at least in the area of material reproduction, and it still is. Granted, it has indulged from the beginning in an enormous plunder of traditional forms of life. But today the imperatives built into the dynamics of capitalist growth can only be fulfilled through a substantial growth in what we call the monetary bureaucratic complex.
>
> As a consequence, we now observe, and feel, and suffer an "overspill," an encroachment by the system on areas no longer at all related to material reproduction. These areas of cultural tradition—social integration through values and norms, education, socialization of coming generations—are, however, ontologically speaking, held together by their very nature through the medium of communicative action. Once the steering media such as money and power penetrate these areas, for instance by redefining relations in terms of consumption, or by bureaucratizing the conditions of life, then it is more than an attack on traditions. The foundations of a life-world that is already rationalized arc under assault. What is at stake is the symbolic representation of the life-world itself. In sum, crises that arise in the area of material reproduction are intercepted at the cost of a pathologizing of the life-world.

Jürgen Habermas, *Autonomy and Solidarity* (New York: Verso Press, 1992), 117.

2. Manfredo Tafuri, *Architecture and Utopia* (Cambridge, Mass.: MIT Press, 1976), 73.

3. See Anthony Vidler's analysis of Coop Himmelblau in "Architecture Dismembered," in *The Architectural Uncanny* (Cambridge, Mass.: MIT Press, 1992), 69. Claiming a return to the body analogy, Vidler states, "As described in architectural form, it seems to be a body in pieces, fragmented, if not deliberately torn apart and mutilated almost beyond recognition." Beyond stating that the reference to the body is "infinitcly ambiguous" (vaguely associated with empathetic responses ranging from Heinrich Wolfflin to Cindy Sherman), it remains to be seen how the body is inscribed as the apparent subject of mutilation. In placing Coop Himmelblau's work within a lineage of anthropomorphic investigation, Vidler seems to lay claim to the very tradition of authority that the work so violently rejects.

4. Sigmund Freud, *Civilization and its Discontents*, trans. James Strachey (New York: Norton, 1961), 71.

5. Paul Smith, *Discerning the Subject* (Minneapolis: University of Minnesota Press, 1985), 24, 32. The present argument concerning the vital distinctions between determined, sovereign, and multiple subject positions versus the absent or unconstructed subject is greatly indebted to this book.

6. For a more detailed analysis of contemporary urban environments in relation to subject inscription, see Albert Pope, *Ladders* (New York: Princeton Architectural Press, 1996), 178–94.

7. The aestheticization of the subject has been commented on extensively:

> The post-modern aestheticization of the subject is simply another way of denying subjectivity as a multidimensional form of agency and praxis, reducing it to a decentered desiring existence. Indeed, post-modern aestheticized subjectivism presents the paradox of a *politics of subjectivity without the subject* [emphasis added] and calls attention to the need for social theory to provide richer accounts of subjectivity. The post-modern repudiation of humanism, without reconstructing its core values, strips the subject of moral responsibility and autonomy.

Steven Best and Douglas Kellner, *Post-Modern Theory: Critical Interrogations* (New York: Guilford, 1991), 290.

8. Thomas Pynchon, *Gravity's Rainbow* (New York: Penguin, 1987), 434.

9. Rem Koolhaas and Bruce Mau, *Small, Medium, Large, Extra-Large* (New York: Monacelli Press, 1995), 199, 201.

Los Angeles

Houston

READINGS OF THE ATTENUATED LANDSCAPE

The desire to see the city preceded the means of satisfying it.

—Michel de Certeau, *The Practice of Everyday Life*

Not only did the year 1945 witness the brink of the American postwar construction explosion and the beginning of a tremendous and pervasive urban transformation that would push the shape of the American city beyond recognition, it also witnessed Jean-Paul Sartre's first visit from Paris to New York. In Manhattan, Sartre found his vision thwarted and his bearings lost by the shock of not being able to locate what he would have considered a "city": "I felt the city was drawing away from me, like a ghost," so much that "for the first few days I was lost . . . I was continually and vainly looking for something to catch my attention for a moment—a detail, a square, perhaps, or a public building."[1] His shock was further aggravated by his encounter, during his westward travels, with a landscape that would supersede New York as a paradigm of the American urban condition: "Frail and temporary, formless and unfinished, [American cities are] haunted by the presence of the immense geographical space surrounding them."[2]

Sartre's confusion did not lead to disdain, however, as he blamed his own "myopic European eyes" for the disorientation.[3] His alienation instead shifted to appreciation, which, not surprisingly, was congruent with his own philosophical prejudices. In addition to what he identified as a "heavy boredom" and vacuity weighing over America—a setting that could accommodate a sort of existential emptiness—Sartre also associated the American urban landscape with a particular sort of freedom, one of a self-determining consciousness made possible from a rejection of surrounding environments and beliefs:

> Here everyone is free—not to criticize or to reform their customs—but to flee them, to leave for the desert or for another city. The cities are open, open to the world, and to the future. This is what gives them their adventurous look and, even in their ugliness and disorder, a touching beauty.[4]

In Sartre's terms, this freedom—one generated independently by the subject in an absence of immutable values, customs, and authority—directly found its spatial correlate in the ephemerality and dilute physicality of the American landscape.[5]

This thinness was only to become more exaggerated as the growth of American cities accelerated. The "immense geographical space" so unfamiliar and unsettling to Sartre was to shift from being a mere exterior to the city, to becoming the constitutive factor of an urban condition characterized by disorder and by the ubiquity of empty lots and interstitial waste spaces. When viewed through the lens of this landscape, however, the Sartrean freedom and

Detroit

its spatial inscription seem to be entrenched in a nostalgic, even romantic utopianisn, as our environments are not as easy to escape, or reject, as Sartre believed in 1945.

The blankness characteristic of contemporary cities forces a reconsideration of Sartre's position. This distended, attenuated, and by now inescapable "American" landscape—now somewhat of an outdated term, as much a European or Asian phenomenon as it is American—remains nonetheless invisible to the most historically refined of European eyes, while its relatively recent nascency lends it a degree of theoretical obscurity. How then might it be possible to approach this attenuated landscape without resorting to the typical responses, which range from a sort of allergic disdain to a euphoric fascination with its apparent freedom?

Preliminary outlines: urban configurations of power

The outlines of a reconsideration of the attenuated landscape can be initially sketched out through Michel Foucault's 1977 statement that "a whole history remains to be written of spaces—which would be at the same time a history of powers."[6] The geographical scope of inquiry shifts toward space itself as one of the primary sites of power relations. As we move within space, domains pregnant with trajectories and deployments of power, both overt and covert, are revealed. This line of inquiry would yield particular interest for geographers and urban theorists because these vectors of power are manifested—whether consciously or not—through urbanism.

In a 1978 lecture at the Collège de France, Foucault presented three models of urban spatial configurations as they corresponded to three models of power: sovereign power, disciplinary power, and bio-power.[7] According to Paul Rabinow, even though these categories may seem distinct, the tripartite division is by no means absolute; all "function in modified ways today."[8]

In the sovereign regime of power, "the basic spatial unit is the territory which must be supervised and given a harmonious order such that all relations of science, the arts, the law, industry, and commerce, as well as agriculture, fall under the benevolent government of the sovereign and serve to increase his glory."[9] In describing the urban manifestation of this model of power, Foucault cited the example of Alexandre Le Maitre's 1682 treatise *La Métropolite*, a utopian scheme that planimetrically configured all the necessary elements of the sovereign regime in direct relationship to the king's hierarchical and centralized position. This organization, directed by the desire to make the sovereign's power absolutely visible, rendered a perfectly ordered, symmetrically and concentrically configured plan.

In the disciplinary model, the trajectories of power rely not so much on an originary source, as in the sovereign model, but on the multiple relations and inscriptions of power. These ultimately aim at the "control and distribution of *bodies* and *individuals* in a spatial ordering whereby they can be made to function in such a manner that efficiency, docility, and hierarchy are simultaneously achieved."[10] In a similar manner as the sovereign, however, this model also relies to a large extent on the *geometric* deployment of spatial relations, albeit to more surreptitious ends, as seen in Foucault's frequently cited Panopticon example.

The deployment of power in the Panopticon is largely reliant on the centralized watch-tower, the locus of the omniscient inspecting gaze, "a gaze which each individual under its weight will end by interiorizing to the point that he is his own overseer, each individual thus exercising this surveillance over, and against, himself. A superb formula: power exercised continuously and for what turns out to be a minimal cost."[11] The simple geometric division into individual cells under the gaze of the inspector is by no means specific to the Panopticon. Jeremy Bentham intended this model to be "applicable to any sort of establishment in which persons of any description are to be kept under inspection."[12] Foucault himself analyzed this adaptability through his interest in the design of schools, madhouses, and hospitals.

In this model, geometry abets surveillance; in other words, "discipline proceeds from an organization of individuals in space, and it therefore requires a specific *enclosure* of space."[13] As Rabinow observed, "Foucault definitely focuses on space as a major aspect of the exercise of power," but "he is not obsessed with buildings per se, as much as he is with cities and how they operate."[14] One can indeed see operating in urban form many of the same spatial techniques for the deployment of disciplinary power.

According to Foucault, this disciplinary mode of power is manifested in the city of Richelieu, a city "conceived as a self-enclosed space within which a hierarchical, visible and functional order could be established."[15] This order literally "plotted onto a graphic space"[16] a direct correlation between the citizen's position in the social hierarchy and the scale, articulation, and location of such elements as streets, houses, and districts. Beyond Richelieu, disciplinary power has been further inscribed into such familiar devices for civic production as the grand axes, monuments, and boulevards deployed in the geometric configurations of Classical urbanism. Even today, the Beaux Arts principles of planning naturalized under the aegis of the "civic" comprise the assumed approach toward urban rehabilitation.

It is interesting to note that not until the eighteenth century did urbanism and architecture acquire specific interest for bodies of authority—most notably the government and the police—as a means of deploying governmental rationality and order. Once this attention was acknowledged, it could be evidenced in such concerns as collective facilities, hygiene, military maneuvering, and the regulation of public gathering. Modern urban planning as a distinct and explicit practice nonetheless did not emerge until the period between 1900 and 1930. Under French colonialism, these new planning efforts were articulated by army engineers in urban planning projects for Morocco, Vietnam, and Madagascar, where, according to Rabinow, "architecture and city planning was sought to demonstrate the cultural superiority of the French." Urban design was seen as providing "one of the means to establish military control, regulate activities, separate populations, and establish a comprehensive order, on both an aesthetic and political level."[17] This strategy was linked to the belief that an individual's behavior was largely connected to social milieu. If the right ingredients could be combined in the urban schema, society would operate with maximized efficiency and order.

This interest in control and maximization is characteristic of Foucault's third model, bio-power. In contrast to sovereign and disciplinary power, bio-power is identified not so much by the correct ordering of the city but by its *regulation,* which is manifested in networks of circulation rather than in hierarchical and differentiated spaces. The goal of bio-power is the maximization and regulation of resources such that their operations and intersections— their flow—will prosper in an orderly, efficient, and coherent manner.[18] Bio-power thus operates through "tabulation and control—the detailed specification of functions, exercised through an ever-expanding complex of social institutions, and thereby in a widening number of building types: hospitals, prisons, workplaces, schools, street plans, housing, and so forth."[19]

In the urban schema, bio-power has to a large extent transcended the sovereign and disciplinary realms of geometric ordering, spatial partitioning, and plan manipulating. Bio-power delineates a domain in which space is "continually analyzed and manipulated as something to be known and used," not through a geometric template, but through flow regulation, empirical data analysis, and the machinations of information technologies.[20] Foucault's urban example of bio-power, eighteenth-century Nantes, was largely determined by the requirements of market exchange and the movements of capital: "Growth, circulation, and trade rather than glory, harmony, or hierarchical order became the central planning concerns of the architects and burghers of Nantes."[21]

In light of these "invisible" infrastructures that configure the city through modes of bio-power, Sartre's formulation—the absence of a visually ordering geometry and the insubstantiality of physical presence in the American landscape equals a sort of freedom from authority—seems more attuned to the visible and physical disciplinary manifestations of power. Sartre's familiar Parisian environment was one in which "the visibility of monuments and sites of rituals such as public squares was extremely calculated"[22] and inescapably present, an urban phenomenon quite absent in the capital-driven environment of the American city. These power trajectories were to become much more devious—much less visible or physical. Foucault recognized this progressive shift:

> But the theme of a spatialising, observing, immobilising, in a word, disciplinary, power was in fact already in Bentham's day being transcended by other and much more subtle mechanisms for the regulation of phenomena of population, controlling their fluctuations and compensating their irregularities.[23]

If power resides not so much in geometric configurations, or in physical presence, but instead in largely invisible, minute, and coercive tactics, then the absence of built fabric and the blankness of the American landscape do little to constitute a Sartrean "freedom." Sartre's position in this context becomes somewhat naive, though more than fifty years later it is one still ascribed to by some contemporary architects and theorists.

Urban effluence: the no-man's-land

The production of the attenuated landscape is propelled by a self-regulating flow of power relations that has mostly transcended the geometric. Operating through networks and regulations, these power relations are excessively prolific in the production not only of intended creations but also of their own effluent remains: residual spaces left in the wake of the rapacious, promiscuous, and efficient pathways of urban production, wasteland spaces that perhaps embody the emptiness so admired by Sartre and that could be termed no-man's-land.[24] The no-man's-land results from the widespread disappearance of a familiar civic identity from the physical urban locus. According to Fredric Jameson, it is an interstitial space "not merely of warfare as such but of all previous traditional forms of boundaries" in which "neither private property nor public law exists." This space "replaces the medieval natural landscape of romance with a fully built and post-urban infinite space, where corporate property has somehow abolished the older individual private property without becoming public."[25] If the space of civil society was constructed as a private, bourgeois realm "separate from the other classes," which therefore created spaces of "radical otherness," then the no-man's-land results from the "wholesale dissolution of civil society." The disappearance of civil society as an arena of public appearance marks "the enfeeblement, if not extinction, of the category of otherness" and the end of any coherent separation between public and private.[26]

This urban wasteland is generated by a complex panoply of factors both mutually supportive and contradictory, including urban and economic decay; rampant development

Houston

speculation characterized by a predatory resilience that renders irrelevant any principles of classical urban design; and the extinction of the commercial need for geographical proximity, which has led to a dissolution of dominant centers and civic image, leaving a landscape of independent islands of activity. The no-man's-land has in fact become so constitutive of the city as to render it simultaneously repugnant to and largely invisible to the classical eye. This new spatiality is symptomatic of a globalized, late-capitalist stage in which capital is no longer locale-based but geographically decentered, leading to a condition Homi Bhabha has described as a "transnational attenuation of local space."[27] This attenuation amounts to a virtual obsolescence of the city as it was once known, effectively confounding any traditional notions of public appearance, any hopes for civic representation, and any attempts at the inscription of a sovereign, classical subject.

Out of this dilution of physical space, the no-man's-land is not only generated as an effluent by-product of urban production and decline but is also a result of the large-scale desuetude of vast areas of the city in response to the perpetually shifting demands and movements of capital. This pattern of disuse is a symptom of a phenomenon described by Jameson as "the moment of the multinational network . . . a moment in which not merely the older city but even the nation-state has ceased to play a central functional and formal role in a process that has, in a quantum leap of capital, prodigiously expanded beyond them, leaving them behind as ruined and archaic remains of earlier stages in the development of this mode of production."[28] What is left, according to Susan S. Fainstein, is a perpetually unstable landscape no longer hinged to the laws of geometry or local identity:

> Changing modes of corporate finance and control, causing and produced by the geographic decentralization of production, globalization of financial and product markets, and the internationalization of the giant corporations, increase the vulnerability of places to disruptions in the markets of commodities on which they are dependent for their economic well-being. Moreover, the instability of foreign exchange levels increases their exposure to uncontrollable outside forces, regardless of their efficiency of production, since it causes the world-market price of their output to vary independently of their production costs.[29]

Whether the ideal of a physically coherent and centralized city can be supported in the late-capitalist economy is rendered highly questionable. In *The Geography of Nowhere*, James Kunstler outlines some of the prevalent reasons behind the dissolution of the fabric of the American city. He uses the specific example of Saratoga Springs, in upstate New York, tracking its transformation and eventual decline into blighted landscape. Some causes derived from planning decisions. The familiar scenario of a building floating within a surrounding parking lot was mostly dictated by zoning laws: a minimum lot size of at least one quarter of an acre for businesses and, in some areas, minimum interior square footage;[30] mandatory deep setbacks from all sides of the property, effectively preempting any possibility of contiguous urban coherence; and a requisite number of parking spaces.[31] The postwar notion that people shouldn't live where businesses are narrowed the range of uses and functions within areas of the city—a belief which reduced the desirability of urban density and fueled suburbanization.[32]

The success of suburbanization and the subsequent obsolescence of the city center was particularly bolstered by the rise of new commercial typologies, most notably the shopping mall, the prime representative of interiorized and decontextualized activity. The shopping mall was to be such a success partly because it served as a laboratory for new profit-making strategies such as the method of "unbundling the rights of real estate," which set up several overlapping tiers of ownership and rental, effectively multiplying profit margins for mall owners and developers.[33]

The city of Detroit provides a clear example of the domino effect of factors leading to such urban deterioration. The federally encouraged development of expressways led to hyperactive real-estate development in the suburbs and the mass exodus of the white middle class from the older sections of the city. This pattern left in its wake a landscape of residual wastelands: freeway on- and off-ramps, zones beneath elevated freeways, and chasms dividing the city into enclaves, with vast areas of the core obsolete and left to decay. Even the decay was federally sponsored—between 1956 and 1967, the city undertook the federally subsidized demolition of 8,000 condemned housing units but built only 758.[34]

The 1967 Detroit riots—one of the worst such disturbances in national history—marked a particularly violent moment in the city's transformation. Factors contributing to the uprising included racial strife, poor living conditions, and high unemployment resulting from the steady decline in the American automobile industry. The scale and violence of the riots further motivated the massive white exodus to the suburbs, a trend that was still being encouraged by federal highway grants and racially biased FHA-subsidized mortgages. As blacks moved into the abandoned, formerly white neighborhoods, many of the areas that had burned down in the riots became unpopulated and were left to deteriorate.[35]

Exodus can be registered not only by racial and economic migrations, but also by substantial architectural transformations. Space as the locus of events and public appearance has mostly withdrawn to the interior, an event signaled by the success of the atrium as found in the shopping mall or hotel. This process has been described by Rem Koolhaas:

195

Since the Romans, the atrium had been a hole in a house or a building that injected light and air—the outside—into the center; in [John] Portman's [the architect credited by Koolhaas to have reinvented the atrium] hands it became the opposite: a container of artificiality that allows its occupants to avoid daylight forever—a hermetic interior, sealed against the real. Actually, the evacuation of the center implied by the atrium, the subsequent covering of the hole, the mostly cellular accommodation of its perimeter—hotel rooms, office cubicles—make it a modern panopticon: the cube hollowed out to create an invasive, all-inclusive, revealing transparency in which everyone becomes everyone else's guard—the architectural equivalent of Sartre's *No Exit*, "Hell is other people."

Downtown becomes an accumulation of voided panopticons inviting their own voluntary prisoners: the center as a prison system.[36]

The success and proliferation of interiorized activity, and the fact that its nodes can be placed anywhere as islands whose connective tissue is a sea of formlessness and nothingness, has left the outside amputated, mostly uninhabitable, and quite often a space of threat. The meeting of the two realms—Portman's atrium and Detroit's vacated no-man's-land—creates a zone that is entirely different from the intertwined and mutually dependent totality of the classical city. This intersection instead spawns a zone of strife, irresolvable difference, and hostility.

The confusion and difficulty of the scenario that dumbfounded Sartre's "European" eyes has only deepened. If in 1945 Sartre could not find familiar objects—such as the continuous Parisian facades and monuments that provide the familiar civic identity of the European city—what then is today left of the exterior, that abandoned battlefield overlooked, ignored, and abandoned by the market economy? Where does the subject reside in this sea of nothingness? What kind of visuality could be developed to confront this space?

Does freedom have a locus?

The absence that characterizes the no-man's-land is a negative version of the architectural presence and disciplinary machinery of the Panopticon; in this negativity resides the Sartrean realm of freedom from the disciplinary. One might think of this as a conceptual inversion: if the no-man's-land is a sign of freedom, waywardness, and deviance, then it signals a subjectivity outside the disciplinary. Recent interest in the physical dissolution of the city echoes this view. Spanish architect Ignasi de Solà-Morales Rubió has referred to this landscape as the "terrain vague" where the connotations of "vague" as "indeterminate, imprecise, blurred, uncertain" are seen to imply a condition in which an "absence of limit

Detroit

Houston

precisely contains the expectations of mobility, vagrant roving, free time, liberty."[37] This romanticism also extends beyond the promise of freedom, to fix upon some concealed but essential urban character. In an existence "devoid of strong forms representing power" that occupies a "position external to the urban system, to power, to activity," asks Solà-Morales, "why does this kind of landscape visualize the urban in some primordial way?"[38] Fredric Jameson also holds some optimism regarding this landscape:

> But such conceptions of the no-man's-land are not altogether to be taken as nightmares; they do not . . . have any of the bleak otherness of the classical dystopian fantasy, and the very freedom from state terror lends the violence of the no-man's-land the value of a distinctive kind of praxis, excitement rather than fear.[39]

It is, however, precisely this assumption of the connection between space and freedom with which Foucault would find contention, not only because such an assumption overlooks the abstract, locus-free trajectories of bio-power, but also because it holds the promise of some primordial meaning underneath the layers of urban constructions.

It is rather presumptuous to identify the blankness that characterizes the no-man's-land as the locus of a condition free from "state terror" and as the marker of a vagrant, mobile subjectivity. This reading is both naive and erroneous, for it assumes the correspondence of space and subjectivity. Modern urbanism represents the desire for the production of a certain kind of efficient subjectivity, precisely the subjectivity to which these spaces are invisible. Power for Foucault is not something to be possessed but exercised—in other words, it is not inherent but relational. It can thus be said that power has no specific locus, that it has as much potential to be exercised through the no-man's-land as through the compartmentalized divisions of a disciplinary architecture. The connection between space and free subjectivity entirely misses the fact that resistance and waywardness, like power, also have no specific loci. They are not so much a question of place as of practice. As articulated by Foucault, resistance is generated *within* the very relations and pathways produced by a pervasive and subtle disciplinarity; waywardness, or freedom, could not automatically claim these spaces. Waywardness and resistance, in other words, happen just as much in the panopticon-building as in the formless no-man's-land. Stated Foucault, "I do not think that there is anything that is functionally—by its very nature—absolutely liberating. Liberty is a *practice*."[40]

Disciplinary slippages

The very assumption that there is an *outside* to the disciplinary would be—given the pervasiveness of the disciplinary grid and the fact that its spatiality is ultimately an effluent product of dominant power relations—an assumption fraught with utopianism. Utopia, according to Foucault, can be identified in those "sites that have a general relation of direct or inverted analogy with the real space of society. They present . . . society turned upside down, but in any case these utopias are fundamentally unreal spaces."[41]

Positing an exterior to power, even when motivated by the hope for an exteriorized freedom, only serves to reconfirm the power systems one is trying to work against. States Rebecca Comay:

> To dream of escaping the system . . . is to long for a point of transcendental privilege (therefore in complicity with what we oppose); to participate in the system is to reconfirm our complicity once again, and so on.[42]

Instead of attempting to inscribe freedom in these spaces, it is perhaps more useful to recall Foucault's notion that "power summons up counter-power at all the pores, all the capillaries, of its reach."[43] Foucault was to himself recognize this resistance from within with regard to the limits of the panoptic model's hegemony: "One of the factors which shifts Bentham into the domain of the unreal" is the "effective resistance of the people."[44] Rem Koolhaas makes a similar observation in his description of the transformation of a modern Panopticon, the Koepel, a prison located in the Netherlands:

> One hundred years later, the Panopticon Principle, with its mechanistic ideal—the naked power exercised by the authority in the center over the subjects in the ring—has become intolerable. In fact, without a single change in the architecture of the Koepel, its principle has been abolished. Guards have abandoned the center and now circulate randomly on the ground and the rings, among prisoners who are often released from their cells . . . the central control post—the former "eye" of the panopticon—has become a canteen for the guards; they now sip coffee there, observed by the prisoners on the rings.[45]

Such practices not operating in tandem with the grip of Panoptic power were explored by Michel de Certeau in "Micro-Techniques and Panoptic Discourse." In criticizing the hegemony of the disciplinary reading, de Certeau noted that it is "impossible to reduce the functioning of a whole society to a single, dominant type of procedure" implied by the disciplinary apparatus.[46] The singularity and coherence of this apparatus are called into doubt by the "existence and survival of a 'polytheism' of concealed or disseminated practices" not registered by the "official" records of history.[47]

Foucault recognized that the benevolent intentions of a supposedly "liberating" space in themselves do not directly influence subject formation; a collusion of social relations and spatial distributions is necessary for that. This confluence also introduces the possibility for divergences:

> Men have dreamed of liberating machines. But there are no machines of freedom, by definition. This is not to say that the exercise of freedom is completely indifferent to spatial distribution, but it can only function when there is a certain convergence; in the case of divergence or distortion it immediately becomes the opposite of that which had been intended.[48]

Similar observations have been made in architectural theory. Koolhaas states that "changes in regime and ideology are more powerful than the most radical architecture—a conclusion both alarming and reassuring for the architect."[49] Manfredo Tafuri expresses skepticism as to whether architecture or space in themselves could claim any definite correspondence to power and subject determination: "It must be clearly understood that between institutions and power systems perfect identity does not exist."[50] Nor should one, according to David Stewart, be deceived by the belief that architecture could lay claim to the "'political' in any simple transparent sense."[51]

The cartography of discontinuity

Space emerges from these considerations as a realm to which one cannot posit fixed subjective correspondence or a familiar iconography. Produced by laws alien to the visual and compositional realm, the no-man's-land is thus cloaked with a certain invisibility that disables subjectivity from comprehending the thoroughly non-geometrical, decentered spatial configurations and trajectories of the late-capitalist production of space. It therefore is no surprise that the processes that constitute urban configurations can no longer be adequately represented by a Cartesian mapping system. The simultaneous invisibility and ubiquity of these spaces is symptomatic of the fact that, according to Fredric Jameson, "mapping has ceased to be achievable by means of maps themselves."[52] New tools would be needed to provide some

Houston

degree of intelligibility or even visibility.

In his 1967 lecture "Of Other Spaces," Foucault detailed his concept of the heterotopia and in so doing revealed the importance of space as an issue central to his thought. In accordance with his suspicion of overarching and unifying concepts, beliefs, orders, and essential depths and truths beyond the manifold surfaces of representations, Foucault's heterotopias are predicated on the idea of discontinuity. If there is to be any discernible order behind the heterotopia, it is to be found in the simultaneity and geographical coexistence or juxtaposition of things:

> The present epoch will perhaps be above all the epoch of space. We are in the epoch of simultaneity; we are in the epoch of juxtaposition, the epoch of the near and far, of the side by side, of the dispersed.[53]

Foucault continues on to note that this spatiality has replaced prior epistemologies of space: the space of emplacement of the Middle Ages, in which space was localized and hierarchically ordered from the sacred to the profane; and the homogenized, "infinitely open space" of extension as represented by Galileo.[54]

Rather than being a two-dimensional model, as in conventional mapping, or even a three-dimensional, Cartesian coordinate system, the spatiality of simultaneity tends towards the topological, consisting of "a network that connects points and intersects with its own skein."[55] Within this network, ruptures, deformations, and dissonances constitute spatiality itself. Physical space thus breaks from the unity of the model of extension—a spatiality manifested in the continuous fabric of the traditional European city—and is instead, according to Jameson, "a multidimensional set of radically discontinuous realities."[56] This discontinuity comes to characterize the composition of the city, which no longer follows, in the words of Manfredo Tafuri, an "ars combinatoria."[57] The homogenizing impulse, no longer located in the geometric formulation of the city, has, it might be claimed, been abstracted into what Jameson refers to as "the unmappable system of late capitalism itself."[58] In other words, the inability of conventional mapping to comprehend this spatiality is symptomatic of the transference of dominant ordering systems from the visible realm of spatial extension and geometric configuration—as in Foucault's Richelieu example—to an abstracted realm no longer comprehensible by the eye alone:

> This latest mutation in space—postmodern hyperspace—has finally succeeded in transcending the capacities of the individual human body to locate itself, to organize its immediate surroundings

perceptually, and cognitively to map its position in a mappable external world . . . [marking] that even sharper dilemma which is the incapacity of our minds, at least at present, to map the great global multinational and decentered communicational network in which we find ourselves as individual subjects.[59]

The configuration of the contemporary city is characterized by a "fragmented space without proportion," to borrow Foucault's description of the work of turn-of-the-century experimental playwright, poet, and novelist Raymond Roussel.[60] This fragmentation is abetted by the fact that capital support for the physical production and maintenance of cities is no longer spatially configured according to locale, but is instead dislodged into globally circulating pathways. In other words, an evacuation of capital from local reinvestment to global affairs heavily contributes to the widespread physical decay of American cities. The lack of a unifying urban fabric has rendered the city a collection of coexisting yet disjointed separate entities. This spatiality parallels "a set of relations that delineates sites which are irreducible to one another and absolutely not superimposable on one another."[61] Foucault reiterates this scenario in another description of Roussel's work:

> There is no privileged point around which the landscape will be organized and with distance vanish little by little; rather, there's a whole series of small spatial cells of similar dimensions placed right next to each other without consideration of reciprocal proportion . . . their position is never defined in relation to the whole but according to a system of directions of proximity passing from one to the other as if following links in a chain.[62]

The heterotopia thus stands in contrast to the familiar methods of spatial comprehension reliant on the extensive Cartesian model; its apparent unmappability renders it a spatiality "rarely seen for it has been obscured by a bifocal vision that traditionally views space as either a mental construct or a physical form."[63] The heterotopia is, in effect, an invisible negativity to a positivistic visuality.

Part of its invisibility to an objectifying visuality rests in the heterotopia's instability. Its order is constituted more by its transient deformations and discontinuities than by its static, formal composition. Models of thermodynamics or of seismic activity would provide better formal cognates than would standard models of composition. According to Jean Baudrillard,

> We could perhaps develop a model of drifting plates, to speak in seismic terms, in the theory of catastrophes. The seismic is our form of the slipping and sliding of the referential . . . Nothing

SLOW SPACE

remains but shifting movements that provoke very powerful rare events. We no longer take events as revolutions or effects of the superstructure, but as underground effects of skidding, fractal zones in which things happen. Between the plates, continents do not quite fit together, they slip under and over each other. There is no more system of reference to tell us what happened to the geography of things. We can only take the geoseismic view.[64]

The market-encouraged production of discontinuous realities produces an interstitial spatiality characterized by slippages, fissures, and lacunae—the sheer magnitude and pervasiveness of which effectively write the obituary of any blanketing, singular, and extensive spatial grid as a means of reading the contemporary city.

Hybridity

The disturbing presence of this cartographic vacuum and the silent blankness of the interstices inevitably prod the imagination as to how one might intervene in these spaces. Rather than positing definitions and correspondences, one might, in light of its inherent instability, imagine this landscape in terms of its unpredictable potential, a position articulated by Koolhaas:

> If there is to be a "new urbanism" it will not be based on the twin fantasies of order and omnipotence; it will be the staging of uncertainty; it will no longer be concerned with the arrangement of more or less permanent objects but with the irrigation of territories with potential; it will no longer aim for stable configurations but for the creation of enabling fields that accommodate processes that refuse to be crystallized into definitive form; it will no longer be about meticulous definition, the imposition of limits, but about expanding notions, denying boundaries, not about separating and identifying entities, but about discovering unnameable hybrids.[65]

It is important to keep in mind that through a semblance of choice and freedom, a strategy of underdetermination is dangerously susceptible to apparently benevolent—yet subtly coercive and sinister—forms of discipline firmly set within principles of limitation. Nevertheless, in positing the unpredictability of "unnameable hybrids," Koolhaas' strategy could open up the no-man's-land as a zone between enclaves, offering a space in which, according to Jameson, "the various groups and separatisms meet and briefly coexist in patterns visible to none of them from the outside." Jameson speculates that "architecture thereby becomes the place of compensatory imagination, where the collective with some deep unconscious logic tries desperately to imagine, to figure, and to project a public space that has ceased to exist in historical reality."[66] The potential of this spatiality could further be manifested as a destabilizing field that might displace and disrupt the resoluteness and stability of urban and cultural identities and essences—in other words, an alchemy based on multivalent interactions.

This is a position quite apparent in Homi Bhabha's involved textuality, which is rife with spatial metaphors: interstices, overlaps, "displacements of domains of difference," borders, edges, horizons, and liminal and interstitial spaces.[67] For Bhabha, the theoretical vehicle for this interstitial condition is hybridity: "The importance of hybridity is not to be able to trace two original moments from which the third emerges, rather hybridity to me is the 'third space' which enables other positions to emerge."[68] In a similar manner as the seismic model, this position, according to Gillian Rose, belies Bhabha's interest in the "fluid epistemological dynamics of negotiation [and] translation."[69]

Implicit in these dynamics is a critique of the fully transparent, enveloping space that Bhabha identifies as a reflection of unified Western subjectivity. Rose characterizes this space as one that

> constructs the external world as a transparent territory laid out before [a unified and conscious] self. The interiority of the Western self is projected onto the exteriority of the world, and the world is understood as a visible territory as vulnerable as the self to the Western gaze of knowledge. It produces a vision of the world which assumes mimetic knowledge is possible: a map of the social. Bhabha argues that this is a regulatory space because it is a space which presumes its own universality of lucid representation. It is a space which cannot therefore acknowledge cultural difference, in the sense of incommensurability; it can only structure cultural diversity. That is, the content of diverse cultures can vary but not the category of "culture" itself.[70]

Because of its distance from the encompassing nature of Western spatiality and culture, Bhabha's "third space" of hybridity, like the attenuated landscape, is also somewhat cloaked with invisibility; it is "a space which, in the eyes of dominant contemporary theorising, must seem obscure indeed."[71] Its obscurity nevertheless does not prevent difference and hybridity from being described with a spatial vocabulary. The plausibility of the claim that a hybrid third space poses a challenge to the dominant, regulatory space of power, however, would rest, to recall Foucault's warning, on the convergence between space and practices. Bhabha describes this possibility as the moment of "the return of the post-colonial peoples to the metropolis":

Their very presence there changes the politics of the metropolis, its cultural ideologies and its intellectual traditions, because they—as a people who have been recipients of a colonial cultural experience—displace some of the great metropolitan narratives of progress and law and order, and question the authority and authenticity of those narratives.[72]

In this sense, according to Bhabha, there is always the possibility of subversion, since the so-called dominant spaces always carry within them their own dissolution: "The power of regulatory space is constantly subverted because its transparency is in fact always stained by the trace of its absent other."[73]

Bhabha's optimistic interest in hybridity, however, tends to suffer from tinges of utopianism. He romanticizes difference and hybridity as potential catalysts for undoing dominant systems: "Cultural difference is not about mapping diversity across the territory of Western space, but rather about moments of opacity when the regulatory surveillance of that space fails."[74] Hybridity is nevertheless useful in reimagining the seemingly benevolent yet subtly sinister concept of community, which has become the trope and vehicle for contemporary urban reconstruction and rehabilitation, because the concept effectively forces a reconsideration of the "profound limitations of a consensual and collusive 'liberal' sense of community."[75] Relying on a palette of traditional urban planning principles not so far removed from those formulated under the terms of disciplinary intentions, the recent phenomenon of New Urbanism has gained a disconcerting amount of momentum and realization throughout the United States. New Urbanism capitalizes precisely on what many accept as being the legible signs of community as they are iconographically inscribed into urban and architectural form, a surreptitious cultural blanketing with an even and naturalized application. Erased from the New Urbanist's equation is any sense of the incommensurability inherent in cultural and spatial difference. According to Bhabha,

People cannot be addressed as colossal, undifferentiated collectivities of class, race, gender or nation. The concept of a people is not "given," as an essential, class-determined, unitary, homogenous part of society *prior to a politics;* "the people" are there as a process of political articulation and political negotiation across a whole range of contradictory social sites.[76]

The narrow concept of "the public" used as a marketing device by the New Urbanists stands exposed as a self-manufactured, singular receptacle for cultural diversity. In a similar manner to Foucault's space of extension, this concept is far removed from the space of simultaneity and the discordant nature of the public sphere today, where, according to Bhabha,

Los Angeles

"We really do need the notion of a politics which is based on unequal, uneven, multiple and *potentially antagonistic,* political identities."[77]

To complicate the situation, however, one must also be aware of a different set of considerations. According to Rebecca Comay, these stem, like the danger of romanticizing the hybrid, from blind fascination:

> What is there to prevent *différence* from sliding into sheer *désagrégation*—into a mere symptom of the fragmentation of our modernity? What prevents pluralism from becoming, willingly or not, one more ideology of late capitalism? The celebrated loss of the subject, for example . . . must be carefully distinguished from the de facto fate of subjectivity under late capitalism.
>
> The dilemma goes back to the '30s. Consider, for example, the early confrontation between Benjamin and Adorno. Adorno warns, already by 1936, to be wary of merely reifying the fragments, to take care that heterotopia is not collusive, to be careful not to fetishize the parts.[78]

Granting visibility and comprehensibility to the spatial discontinuity of both the contemporary city and the incommensurability of cultural difference, then, might not be so desirable, as these spaces might thereby be offered up to the voracity of the system.

Protracted ablation

Out of these confrontations, the no-man's-land stands enveloped in an uneasy silence. Its subject has vanished either because spatial signs and configurations have failed to achieve a possessive, figurative correspondence to subject formation; or because our perceptual and mapping tools have been inadequate to imagine a nongeometric space, thus rendering the space invisible.

What would happen if one *was* to look at this space bereft of a correspondence to subjectivity? In his 1903 essay "The Metropolis and Mental Life," Georg Simmel wrote that the nervous stimulation from the chaos of the metropolis combined with the bewildering modernization of daily life had helped to create a blasé subjectivity in which "the meaning and differing value of things, and thereby the things themselves, are experienced as insubstantial."[79] Massimo Cacciari reiterates this thought by stating that the monetary economy has penetrated into behavior and experience to the point that subjectivity has been reified, "estranged from phenomena and least open to any experience of communication."[80] In 1997, one might say that the attenuated environment of the contemporary city, far from being the realm of chaotic stimulation, has *itself* become blasé and undifferentiated, precluding the possibility of any stimulus for subjective inscription or even reaction.

In addition to the confounding order of the no-man's-land, the absence of a "glue" to hold the city together—a function once fulfilled by simple geometric and compositional laws—further destabilizes any attempts at urban coherence. In this light, the interstitial disorder of the no-man's-land can be compared to Foucault's first definition of heterotopias:

> Heterotopias are disturbing, probably because they secretly undermine language, because they make it impossible to name this and that, because they shatter or tangle common names, because they destroy "syntax" in advance, and not only the syntax with which we construct sentences but also that less apparent syntax which causes words and things (next to and also opposite one another) to "hold together" . . . [H]eterotopias . . . desiccate speech, stop words in their tracks, contest the very possibility of grammar at its source; they dissolve our myths and sterilize the lyricism of our sentences.[81]

Without its own grammar, language, or discernible signs to grant legibility or visibility, this landscape stands as silent reserve—an unwanted yet inevitable product of an abstracted, predatory economy unhinged from the comforts of familiar spatial registers. The no-man's-land writes the unintended yet definitive obituary for the city as it was once known.

Houston

Notes

1. Quoted in Annie Cohen-Solal, *Sartre: A Life* (New York: Pantheon, 1987), 226.

2. Jean-Paul Sartre, "American Cities," in *The City: American Experience*, eds. Alan Trachtenberg, Peter Neill, and Peter C. Bunnell (New York: Oxford University Press, 1971), 205.

3. Quoted in Cohen-Solal, 226.

4. Sartre, 205.

5. The equation between the absence of the urban and freedom, however, is not without precedent: "The threat that cities posed to democracy was articulated most forcefully by Thomas Jefferson. For him, democracy could only flourish where individuals lived freely and worked independently, and this could only take place in the countryside. City people were forced to work for others and thus enter into hierarchical relations that undermined their good judgment. In turn, the city engendered and then juxtaposed inequalities, thereby making individuals susceptible to the crowd." Robert A. Beauregard, "Voices of Decline," in *Readings in Urban Theory*, eds. Susan Fainstein and Scott Campbell, (Cambridge, Eng.: Blackwell, 1996), 374.

6. Michel Foucault, "The Eye of Power," in *Power/Knowledge: Selected Interviews and Other Writings 1972–1977*, ed. Colin Gordon (New York: Pantheon Books, 1980), 149.

7. As summarized in Paul Rabinow, "Ordonnance, Discipline, Regulation: Some Reflections on Urbanism," in *Humanities in Society* 5:3–4 (summer–fall 1982): 267–78.

8. Rabinow, 271.

9. Rabinow, 271.

10. Rabinow, 271.

11. Foucault, "The Eye of Power," 155.

12. Jeremy Bentham, *The Panopticon Writings* (London: Verso, 1995), 29. Written in 1787.

13. Gwendolyn Wright and Paul Rabinow, "Spatialization of Power: A Discussion of the Work of Michel Foucault," in *Skyline* (March 1982): 14. Emphasis provided.

14. Wright and Rabinow, 15.

15. Rabinow, 273.

16. Rabinow, 273.

17. Rabinow, 267.

18. Rabinow, 275.

19. Wright and Rabinow, 14.

20. Rabinow, 275.

21. Rabinow, 274.

22. Wright and Rabinow, 14.

23. Foucault, "The Eye of Power," 159–60.

24. This effluent production was also to be recognized by Manfredo Tafuri, who stated that "the construction of a physical space is certainly the site of a 'battle': a proper urban analysis demonstrates this clearly. That such a battle is not totalizing, that it leaves borders, remains, residues, is also an indisputable fact." Manfredo Tafuri, *The Sphere and the Labyrinth* (Cambridge, Mass.: MIT Press, 1990), 8.

25. Fredric Jameson, "Demographies of the Anonymous," in *Anyone*, ed. Cynthia Davidson, (New York: Rizzoli, 1991), 57.

26. Jameson, "Demographies of the Anonymous," 57.

27. Homi Bhabha, *The Location of Culture* (London: Routledge, 1994), 216.

28. Fredric Jameson, *Postmodernism, or, the Cultural Logic of Late Capitalism* (Durham, N.C.: Duke University Press, 1991), 412.

29. Susan S. Fainstein, "The Changing World Economy and Urban Restructuring," in *Readings in Urban Theory*, eds. Susan Fainstein and Scott Campbell, (Cambridge, Eng.: Blackwell, 1996), 171.

30. James Howard Kunstler, *The Geography of Nowhere* (New York: Simon & Schuster, 1994), 184.

31. Kunstler, 136.

32. Kunstler, 141.

33. Kunstler, 145.

34. Bruno Cartosio, "Detroit, Michigan: The ghost town," in *Casabella* 587 (January–February 1992): 118.

35. Kunstler, 194.

36. Rem Koolhaas, *S, M, L, XL* (New York: Monacelli Press, 1995), 841.

37. Ignasi de Solà-Morales Rubió, "Terrain Vague," in *Anyplace*, ed. Cynthia Davidson (Cambridge, Mass.: MIT Press, 1995), 120.

38. Solà-Morales, 121.

39. Fredric Jameson, *The Seeds of Time* (New York: Columbia University Press, 1994), 159.

40. Michel Foucault, "Space, Knowledge, and Power," interview by Paul Rabinow, in *Skyline* (March 1982): 18.

41. Michel Foucault, "Of Other Spaces," in *Diacritics* 16:1 (spring 1986): 24.

42. Rebecca Comay, "Excavating the Repressive Hypothesis: Aporias of Liberation in Foucault," in *Telos* 67 (spring 1986): 112.

43. Comay, 115.

44. Foucault, "The Eye of Power," 162.

45. Koolhaas, 237.

46. Michel de Certeau, "Micro-techniques and Panoptic Discourse: A Quid Pro Quo," in *Heterologies: Discourse on the Other* (Minneapolis: University of Minnesota Press, 1986), 188.

47. de Certeau, 188.

48. Foucault, "Space, Knowledge, and Power," 18.

49. Koolhaas, 239.

50. Tafuri, 5.

51. David Stewart, "Why Foucault?" in *Architecture and Urbanism* 21 (October 1980): 105.

52. Jameson, *Postmodernism*, 410.

53. Foucault, "Of Other Spaces," 22.

54. Foucault, "Of Other Spaces," 23.

55. Foucault, "Of Other Spaces," 22.

56. Jameson, *Postmodernism*, 413.

57. Tafuri, 40.

58. Jameson, "Demographies of the Anonymous," 57.

59. Jameson, *Postmodernism*, 44.

60. Michel Foucault, *Death and the Labyrinth: The World of Raymond Roussel* (London: Athlone Press, 1986), 109.

61. Foucault, "Of Other Spaces," 23.

62. Foucault, *Death and the Labyrinth*, 107.

63. Edward W. Soja, *Postmodern Geographies* (New York: Verso, 1989), 18.

64. Jean Baudrillard, "Forget Baudrillard: An interview with S. Lotringer," in *Forget Foucault* (New York: Semiotexte, 1987), 125–26. Quoted in C. Philo, "Foucault's Geography," in *Environment and Planning D: Society and Space* 10 (1992), 158.

65. Koolhaas, 969.

66. Jameson, "Demographies of the Anonymous," 60.

67. Bhabha, *The Location of Culture*, 2.

68. Homi Bhabha, "The Third Space: Interview with Homi Bhabha," in *Identity: Community, Culture and Difference*, ed. Jonathan Rutherford (London: Routledge, 1990), 211.

69. Gillian Rose, "The Interstitial Perspective: A Review Essay on Homi Bhabha's *The Location of Culture*," in *Environment and Planning D: Society and Space* 13 (1995), 367.

70. Rose, 369.

71. Rose, 369.

72. Bhabha, "The Third Space," 218.

73. Rose, 370.

74. Rose, 369.

75. Bhabha, "The Third Space," 219.

76. Bhabha, "The Third Space," 220.

77. Bhabha, "The Third Space," 208.

78. Comay, 119.

79. Georg Simmel, "The Metropolis and Mental Life," in *The Sociology of Georg Simmel*, trans. and ed. Kurt H. Wolff (New York 1950), 52.

80. Massimo Cacciari, *Architecture and Nihilism: On the Philosophy of Modern Architecture*, (New Haven: Yale University Press, 1993), 8.

81. Michel Foucault, *The Order of Things* (New York: Vintage Books, 1973), xviii.

Port of Houston
Main Entrance
Clinton Dr.

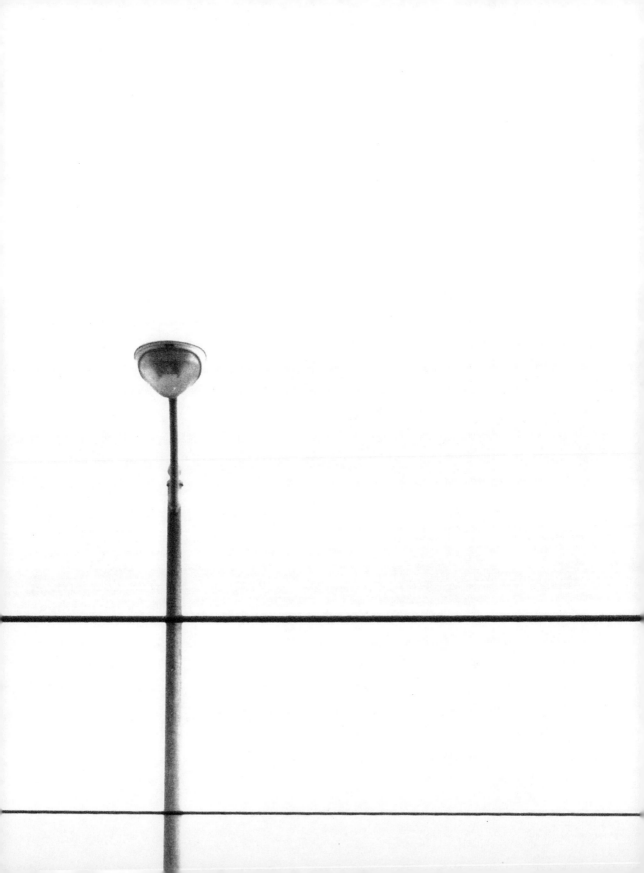

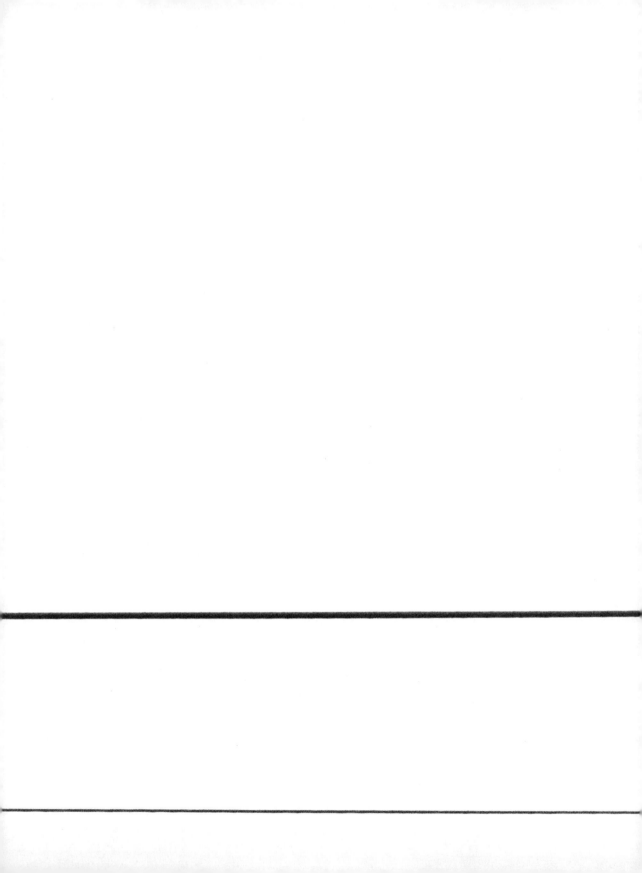

KNEE PLAY

Mark Wamble

I. Architecture is an expression of economic force. That the discipline of architecture exists at all is evidence that potential wealth is in play; always searching for the next, and inevitable, augmentation of its material form. Indeed, no discipline of consequence, and no theory of architecture, is comprehensible outside this base dynamic. Given recent shifts in economic practices, it should be of little surprise that productive strategies that once sustained comprehensive fiscal relationships between *building* and *city* have become reconfigured. Outmoded by its material and human connection to stable markets, the institution of *city* is compromised by a free-market system in transition, a transition defined by promiscuous forms of capital in search of the next play.

In Houston prior to World War II, financial investment in property and in manufacturing and service-related industries focused the city's economic influence locally. Political and economic support for these investments could be found almost exclusively within a single, geographically annexed, collectively imageable center. Cooperation between corporate and civil interests enabled the city to prosper and grow. Indicators of prosperity—productivity, market support, employment, personal buying power, profit, risk management—could be monitored and, if necessary, adjusted through the observation of economic trends within a given region. Throughout American history, cities have evolved in accordance with this localized economic ideal.

Despite the prevalence of this civic model, there has been no such urban ethic in Houston during the postwar period. By tracing the industrial history that follows Houston after World War II, it is easy to detect an eagerness on the part of business leaders to expand and compete in international economic arenas. While this global focus is not unique among late-twentieth-century cities, Houston has experimented notably with the protocol between private and civil interests, especially in cases where new markets could provide significant gain. Investment of public and private capital in interstate commerce combined with the actively encouraged relocation of international corporations to annexed land outside the city center has effected a peculiar economic balance—one of simultaneous business growth and urban disintegration—that has slowly and consistently transformed both the formal and operative character of Houston. The civic economic protocol established during periods of industrial growth, a protocol that afforded other American cities local prosperity and identity, eroded in Houston long before a culture of urbanism could evolve. *City*—the fundamental expression of growth, development, and prosperity—was effectively canceled due to lack of participation.

At the very minimum, the city provides us with an indicative image. The creation of the city is predicated on the migration of rural populations to urban centers, attracted by the employment opportunities of manufacturing industries. This shift set into afferent motion a *city* economy. Both the successes and failures of economic practices could be observed on the street. Today, the civil aspirations of cities such as Houston can offer little to defend against the inevitable *digitization* of urban life. And while corporate management gurus Tom Peters and George Gilder debate the hopes and regrets of contemporary business practices "at warp speed," architecture, as conventionally conceived, struggles to keep up.

The postwar city is best described as the significant disintegration of physical space relationships, a city that is no longer driven by modern industry and the resultant centripetal distribution of capital. The most fundamental precepts of urbanism, attributable to economic principles pioneered in the eighteenth century, are relegated to the status of memory. Information-based industry, job exportation, liberalization of global currencies, and increasing promiscuity of free-market systems have repositioned growth poles that were once situated between urban population centers and agrarian outposts. Undermined are the principles and relative distinctions of the free-standing city. The civil doctrines of Thomas Jefferson and Adam Smith, once the defining factors of a new national ethic, are laughable in the context of global market strategies. If the past stability of the city paradigm provided architecture with its original operative context, is it beyond the scope of architecture to now describe the civilizing forces that have emerged in its place?

WAMBLE

II. Two factors are worth consideration. First is the well-documented shift in the deployment of technology from a centralizing, urbanizing force during periods of industrialization to an instrument of fragmentation so totalizing in its effect that it has transformed the "rites of passage," as Virilio observed, from physical, or "intermittent," to virtual, or "immanent."[1] Units of value are redefined; atoms, as Nicholas Negroponte describes it, merge with bits.[2] Second is the deregulation of currency worldwide, the economic analogue to electronic fragmentation. This deregulation is in part a result of the dismantling of the World Bank and the International Monetary Fund under Richard Nixon. In order to avoid the catastrophic mistakes of the Treaty of Versailles, the International Bank of Reconstruction and Development (the World Bank) was established in 1944, prior to the end of World War II. Along with the International Monetary Fund, the World Bank set aside moneys to assist with the physical development of industry in war-torn nations, as well as to ease the imbalance between import and export costs that is associated with redevelopment. Both the World Bank and the International Monetary Fund were located in Washington, D.C., and from this central location surveillance of the world's economic development could occur. The decentralization of this postwar system combined with the more recent, and more radical, liberating of trade through diplomatic initiatives relegates the internally dynamic ideological distinctions of city, state, and nation, to synonyms for mid-twentieth-century ideals. Technology has evolved geocide, where monetary practices develop more in accordance with the demand for global access than geopolitical allegiance. No longer acting in the interests of the state, virtual corporations and temporary confederations of capital coalesce, propagating an expanding world market that is no longer tethered to sovereign political entities. All previously understood relationships between geography, politics, sovereignty, access, and capital are, as Zbigniew Brzezinski says, out of control.[3]

Capitalism in the twenty-first century will view the cooperative capacity of the public sector as an impediment to economic success rather than as an indispensable source of strength. Not only has the workplace changed, but with it the basic assumptions of Jean-Baptiste Say's law of markets, a central tenet of orthodox economics from the nineteenth century until the Depression. Say's law outlined the fundamental balances between labor, markets, and the ultimate destination of profit, postulating that supply creates its own demand. Today, elected representation defers to corporate policy. Where there was once a city, sinks of globally active yet locally provincial populations evolve. Space, once a pervasive and egalitarian medium, yields to the ephemeral intellectual-property-rights-meet-equity domain of speculation. No longer can we know the "victims of our leisure."[4] As the unimpeded flow of private interest rides the corridors of international finance in a vacuum created by the collapse of forces philosophically opposed to the free-market system, the alliance of architecture with urbanism fails. What lingering significance of civil space, now operating without the armature of *city,* will unleash the intellectual energy of architecture?

III. *History has witnessed what Zbigniew Brzezinski calls the "centrality of the metamyth," pitting the closed ideology of the coercive utopia against the philosophic-scientific ideology of the permissive cornucopia. According to Brzezinski, the former utilized the power of technology to motivate and mobilize an increasingly literate population thus susceptible to pamphleteering and galvanization by utopian social doctrines.[5] The latter, secular materialism, results from disenfranchised interests unable or unwilling to participate in the transcendental arrogance of the metamyth but are nonetheless legitimated by increased access to free-flowing information and multiple centers of decision making. While the destruction effected by coercive utopias in Germany, the Soviet Union, and China, to name the big three, is indisputable as evidenced by loss of life and material assets, destructive forces within the realm of the permissive cornucopia can also be identified, in particular the complete absence of any ethic resilient and cohesive enough to encompass diverse free-market interests and hold them together on pragmatic grounds. As a result, the twenty-first century will witness many new versions of capitalism. While the North American Free Trade Agreement and the General Agreement for Trades and Tariffs attempt to provide a level playing field for global opportunity, qualitative goals are quickly overshadowed by local obstacles impossible to counter or recognize as part of an emerging global milieu.*

IV. "Mediology," according to Regis Debray, is a discipline that studies the way in which abstract ideas are transformed into influential ideas—how "words become flesh." Mediology combines, and in so doing alters, ideology (or what we now call "systems of belief") with electronic mediation. Ideologies become "part and parcel of the material delivery system by which they are transmitted."[6] Mediology affords the permissive cornucopia a functional, but not an ideological, rudder to navigate a vaguely comprehensible mediosphere. Personal ideologies of the philosophical and scientific order are no longer disembodied words but very fast and very seductive mediologies; indeed the next level of abstraction, from writing to printing to computing. Though we can begin to understand the mediosphere, and through it the forms of influence, diverse cultural values remain unresolved, hostile, estranged.

Site plan. Texas Ice House, Houston, Texas. Mark Wamble, Interloop Architects. 1994

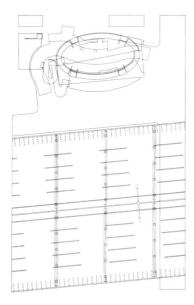

transformation diagram

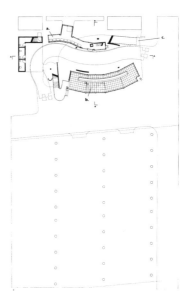

level one plan a. drive-through
b. lunch counter
c. sidewalk

V. The local disintegration of free-market interests (the dispersal of the city economy), combined with the virtual (electronically enhanced) accessibility of new world environments, combined with the ideological vacuum (the emergence of the philosophic-scientific, small beliefs), has displaced the discipline of architecture in three ways: in the relationship of architecture to program; in the relationship of architecture to patronage; and in the relationship of architecture to a recognizable spatio-temporal continuum once provided by peripatetic and automobilized urban networks.

WAMBLE

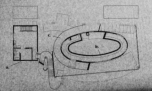

level two plan a. proprietor's flat
b. stock ramp
c. sidewalk

VI. It is particularly true of the Southwest to say that the right to procure land—to claim it, tame it, and defend it—is integral to citizenship. But pastoral notions of more than two centuries ago that placed the individual as private owner also made him caretaker. So improved by his distinctly American condition, he would assume broader responsibilities as landowner, engendering and reflecting the civil spirit of a democratic society. However, this passion for the individual ownership of property stifled any hope for ethos and spawned instead an ethic of territorialism emerging in, and possibly through, a dislike of most things civil. On a Southwestern flood plain, not far from the Mexican border, land was purchased at the confluence of three bayous. Rather than cultivate, the owners sold for a profit. Land was commodity rather than civil currency, and the rest is Houston's history.

VII. The case of the ice house demonstrates the legacy of conforming a bastard brand of civility to the free-market system. In Texas, the ice house was originally a private commercial venture for the purpose of selling refrigeration. Two significant economic factors together elevated it to microeconomy status: the availability of the automobile in a sparsely populated, expansive landscape, and the mobile culture this created; and the unavailability of electricity in the rural outposts and fringe suburbs of the Southwest. Mobility combined with the cessation of domestic modernization sanctioned the ice house. By providing blocks of ice, a civil hybrid emerged that fulfilled both an important egalitarian, social need while instituting a public roadside gathering-place as important to Texans as the town common and city square vernacular of other regions. Although conceived as a private, commercial enterprise, the selling of ice also produced a collective forum, and the commercial elements of the ice house in turn thrived. Purchasing ice, in part, became an excuse for a trip to the ice house. If you forgot to bring home the ice, or if it melted on the floor as you made your civil "purchases," it was justified so long as the conversation was interesting. The unprogrammable aspect of the ice house, though at

North elevation

odds with the more strict parameters of economic performance, today offers an important insight. It is a form of resistance. By relegating commercial and domestic priorities to the perimeter, the ice house mobilized a new and unattributable realm that defied categorization: pastoral or urban, public or private.

Responding over time to changes such as power grids that extended into outlying settlements, affordable home refrigeration, air-conditioning, and the one-stop, self-service grocery store, this resilient transformer endured. Ice houses reinvented themselves, drifting from ice, to ice and groceries, and finally to beer garden, competing in a world of growing economic stakes against progressive combinations of groceries-and-gasoline and air-conditioned restaurant bars. Soon ice houses began selling a narrow line of staple items. For a nickel a day plus penny tips, young boys—"runners"—shuttled items to parked cars while their drivers sat on the hood or stepped into the shade to greet a familiar face. Although the ice house's original consumer purpose was no longer viable, the unspoken reason for its existence remained unchanged by advances in modern living. Regardless of commercial necessity, the ice house had evolved into an essential civil institution.

South elevation

VIII. The paradigm of the embassy provides an adaptable civil concept for private development in its complex model of deputation. This emissarial component is generally applicable to the free-market system and offers the potential for redeeming the civil in the absence of city. As a general program type, the embassy conforms remote interests (political, cultural, capital) with the regional material of site. It does so by using the dual concept of deputation: the cultural attaché who in good faith reasserts the *proprietor* in proprietary ventures; and the embassy, the localized program of the proprietor-as-guest extended into the realm of the host geography. In other words, money gets a face.

Perspective view

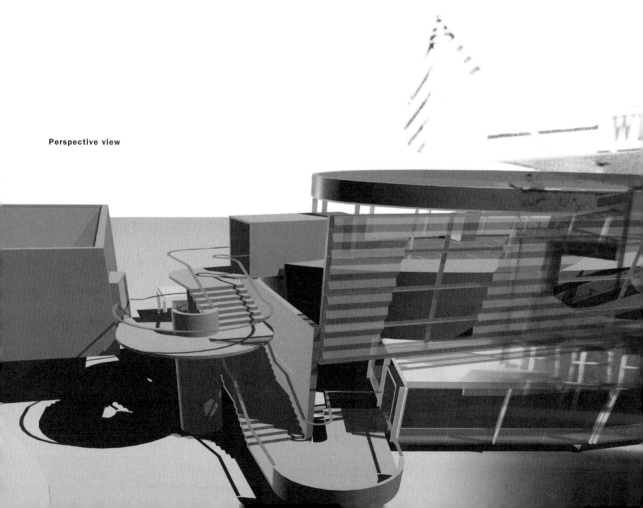

IX. The popular enclave type has produced a new and pervasive disurbanization, more accurately identified as pastoral outposts divided by despondent urban adjacencies. In this milieu, civil space can only be induced through constraints of time, movement, and the bundled program. En route from one enclave to the next, converging intervals of time and task enable listless and otherwise invisible spaces to conform, dissolve, and then reconform as spatio-temporal eddies, the new genetic material of the postwar city. In the eddy, dimensions of the street and degrees of mobility enter the sanctioned territory of the private lot. The tension between enclosure and exposure is exercised along continuous trajectories that seem never to leave the street nor truly enter the building. Threshold is induced but never given over fully to its divisive effect. Edges instead become pliable material, deforming, deflecting, squeezing, and stretching elliptically into the site, pleating the near-private inside with the ubiquitous outside; slowing the laminar flow of the street through its turbulence. The topology of the extended containment of the street combines with the new metabolism of the lot to create a strange attraction. Eddies perpetuate the *en passant* strategy of nomadic life. Dimensions of the interior with its cloaked corporate conventions enter the grit and peril of the street. Interiors augment and merge into a programmatic flux of porous outcroppings. In the end, physical models will help us to explore, but never to explain, the architecture of the drift and its peculiar form of occupation. Just as the pendulum is driven by the spring and damped by friction, the eddy provides for and is activated by the orbital yet nonperiodic flow of corporate, consumer, and leisure modes that comprise urban life. All absorb and perpetuate the temporal surge of space, giving form to time.

Notes

1. Paul Virilio, The *Lost Dimension* (New York: Semiotext[e], 1991), 11.
2. Nicholas Negroponte, *Being Digital* (New York: Alfred A Knopf, 1995), 13.
3. Zbigniew Brzezinski, *Out of Control* (New York: MacMillan Publishing, 1993), 52.
4. D. Boon and Mike Watt (The Minutemen), "Maybe Partying Will Help," from *Double Nickels on the Dime* (Lawndale, California: SST Records, 1989), track 14.
5. Brzezinski, *Out of Control,* 19.
6. Regis Debray, "Revolution in the Revolution" (interview by Andrew Joscelyne), in *Wired,* vol. 3, no. 1 (1995), 116.

Perspective view

project: *Texas Ice House*, Houston, Texas
client: Sawyer Properties
architect: Mark Wamble, Interloop Architects, 1994
design team: Mark Wamble, Mason Wickham

CROTON AQUEDUCT STUDY

RAAUm Group: Jesse Reiser, Stan Allen, Polly Apfelbaum, and Nanako Umemoto

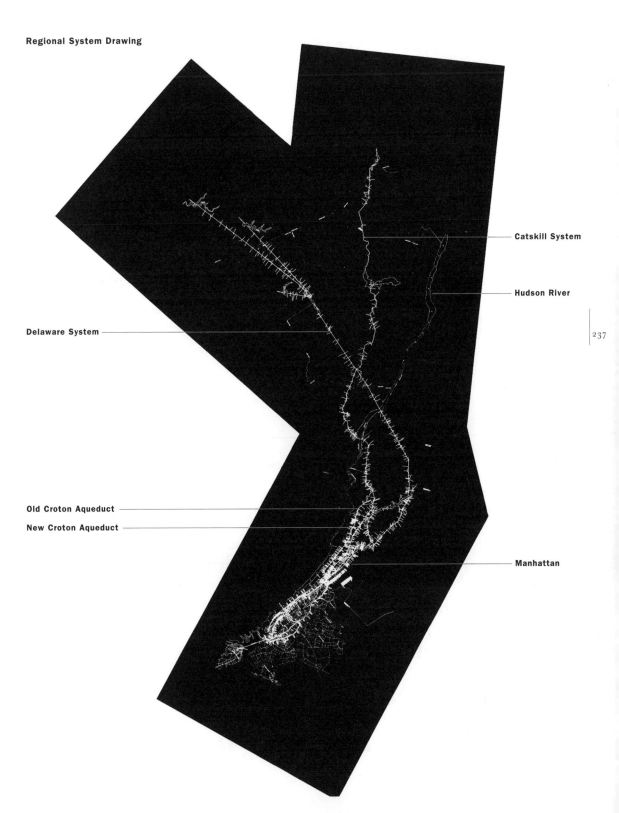

Catskill System

Hudson River

Delaware System

Old Croton Aqueduct

New Croton Aqueduct

Manhattan

The only works of art America has given are her plumbing and her bridges. —Marcel Duchamp, *The Blind Man*, 1917

Central to the Croton Aqueduct Study is the question of negotiating between the dominant linear character of the water-supply system at the local level and the capillary, or rhizomatic, character of the system as a whole, which brings into play rivers and streams, topography, watersheds, and complex natural systems. In order to function, the water supply must regulate and domesticate this wild proliferation; as part of our project, we also wanted to bring something of the complex overall character of the system down to the local level.

By calling attention to the necessary and vast infrastructure that supports the city, architecture can increase awareness of the city as a complex, interrelated system that must be treated with respect. By focusing attention on the Croton Aqueduct system as a whole—a complex that extends throughout much of New York State—we propose new definitions of site based on a systematic integration of political, regional, and natural factors.

Our intention is to use these monumental structures as an architectural occasion. We have endeavored to discover appropriate strategies for making the system more accessible, and to produce a civic expression for this vast public-works system. It is the view of the group members that social, programmatic, and political innovation must not be incompatible with formal innovation. Believing that an interdisciplinary approach can best address new problems of environmental design, our group includes a landscape architect and a sculptor as well as architects. In order that all work be conceived and executed with full group collaboration, we needed to invent new working methods and explore new forms.

RAAUM GROUP

Croton System History

The oldest of the four water systems that serve New York City, the Croton system originally supplied water to the city of New York when it comprised only the borough of Manhattan. The **Old Croton Aqueduct** went into service in 1842, supplying water from a 375-square-mile watershed collected in Croton Lake. The standard section was constructed in a horseshoe shape that lay close to the water's surface and extended across valleys on earth embankments and occasional viaducts. The Harlem River is crossed by Highbridge, a masonry structure with a central arch span of steel that carries a steel pipe 90 inches in diameter. The aqueduct thus continues to the Central Park Reservoir. Although in good condition, the aqueduct is no longer used. The route of the aqueduct through Westchester County is designated as parkland.

The **New Croton Aqueduct** was constructed from 1885 to 1891, when two boroughs, Manhattan and the West Bronx, constructed the city of New York. It draws water from the Croton Reservoir impounded behind the Croton Dam, newly built at the time of the aqueduct's completion. The aqueduct consists mostly of a horseshoe-shaped tunnel that runs from the dam to the Jerome Park Reservoir, as well as a pressure tunnel that continues from the Jerome Park Reservoir to the 135th Street Gatehouse in Manhattan. The delivery capacity of the New Croton Aqueduct is 275 million gallons per day.

Site

The site is located along the New York City water-supply infrastructure, a branching, linear network of reservoirs, aqueducts, and tunnels that stretches from rural upstate New York to the city, where the system becomes a dense web of urban water mains. Our definition of site is both unconventionally broad (encompassing over 250 linear miles) yet extremely precise: a vertical and regional cut united by a single purpose and administered by the city. By taking the entire water-supply system as site, we are given a **regional cross section** encompassing the rural areas of collection reservoirs, control chambers, and holding reservoirs throughout Westchester County (an environment of suburbs and small towns), as well as distribution sites within the city.

Process

The project consists of a series of interventions along the entire system, architectural events that foster new connections between the public and private realms and serve to encourage public awareness and participation through new programs. Design work has progressed through a series of increasingly focused studies. After researching and mapping the entire system, we decided to concentrate on the right-of-way of the Old Croton Aqueduct. Along this route, we chose three sites that exemplified distinct conditions: the Croton Dam in upper Westchester (rural); the Tarrytown Interchange (suburban); and Highgate in East Harlem (urban). We have developed in detail **site 2: the Tarrytown Interchange,** where the aqueduct is interrupted by the New York State Thruway. Finally, armed with our catalog of strategies and kit of architectural parts, we have revisited some of the more remote sites and grafted new programs onto the given terrain of those areas.

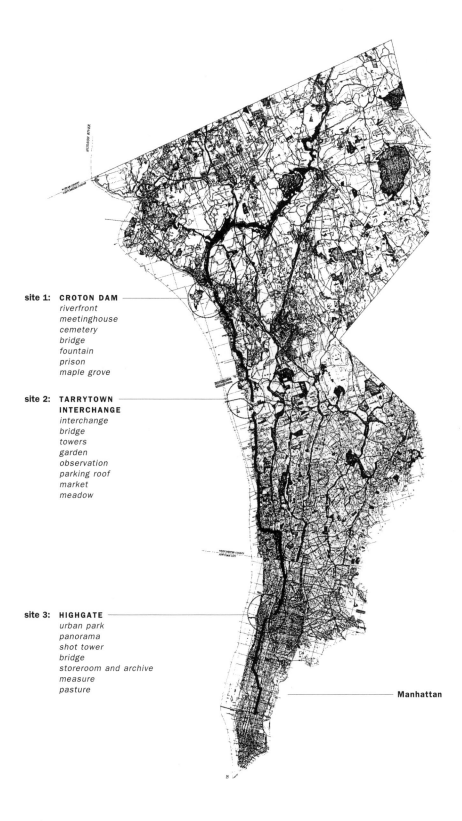

site 1: CROTON DAM
riverfront
meetinghouse
cemetery
bridge
fountain
prison
maple grove

**site 2: TARRYTOWN
INTERCHANGE**
interchange
bridge
towers
garden
observation
parking roof
market
meadow

site 3: HIGHGATE
urban park
panorama
shot tower
bridge
storeroom and archive
measure
pasture

Manhattan

Justification

Taking its inspiration from the civil engineering and public works already in place, the project seeks to establish the **necessity of intervention** in order to create a public presence. Any architect working on a site characterized by extreme dimensions, exceptional demands, and high architectural quality, as is the case with the water-supply infrastructure, must submit to the same criteria and create architecture adequate to what already exists. It is important to give visibility not only to the public dimension of these works but also to the related issues of ecology and conservation. Everything associated with the water-supply system must respond first to necessity as manifested in the double theme of (functional) **imperative** and (aesthetic) **indifference**.

Area rule

The operation devised as a result of detailed design work on specific sites is referred to as the **Area Rule**. Rather than following the strict linearity of the given system to string together a series of isolated, discrete architectural objects, we have developed our interventions in accordance with existing property lines, articulated surfaces, and contiguous areas. Surfaces fold up and form structures, blurring the strict division between architecture and landscape. The notion of the public realm we propose is thus not dependent on monumental objects; instead we suggest a **new condition of surface,** an **open field for active participation,** and a **new network of public programs.**

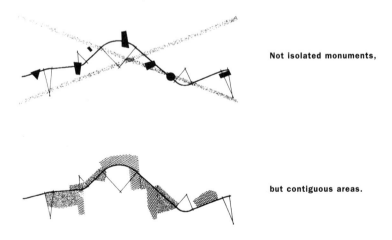

Not isolated monuments,

but contiguous areas.

**Tarrytown Interchange Map: Key for series
of collage plans with program notations on
pages 245, 247, 249, and 251.**

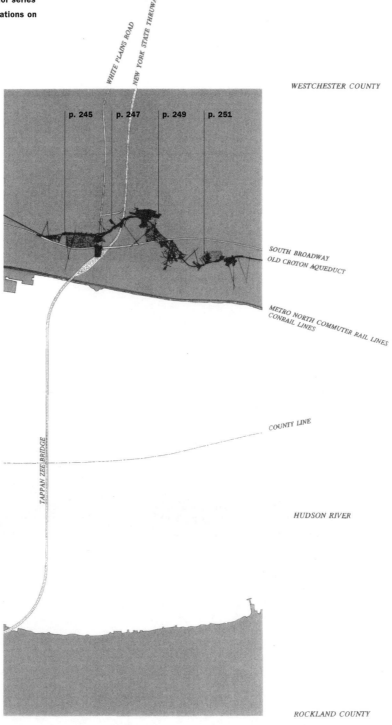

WHITE PLAINS ROAD

NEW YORK STATE THRUWAY

WESTCHESTER COUNTY

p. 245   p. 247   p. 249   p. 251

SOUTH BROADWAY
OLD CROTON AQUEDUCT

METRO NORTH COMMUTER RAIL LINES
CONRAIL LINES

COUNTY LINE

TAPPAN ZEE BRIDGE

HUDSON RIVER

ROCKLAND COUNTY

243

RAAUM GROUP

A sectional transition: garden parking

B oblique transition: marketplace

C bridge abutment

D shopping cells

E open program (convoluted space)

F long-span (event) structure

G garden

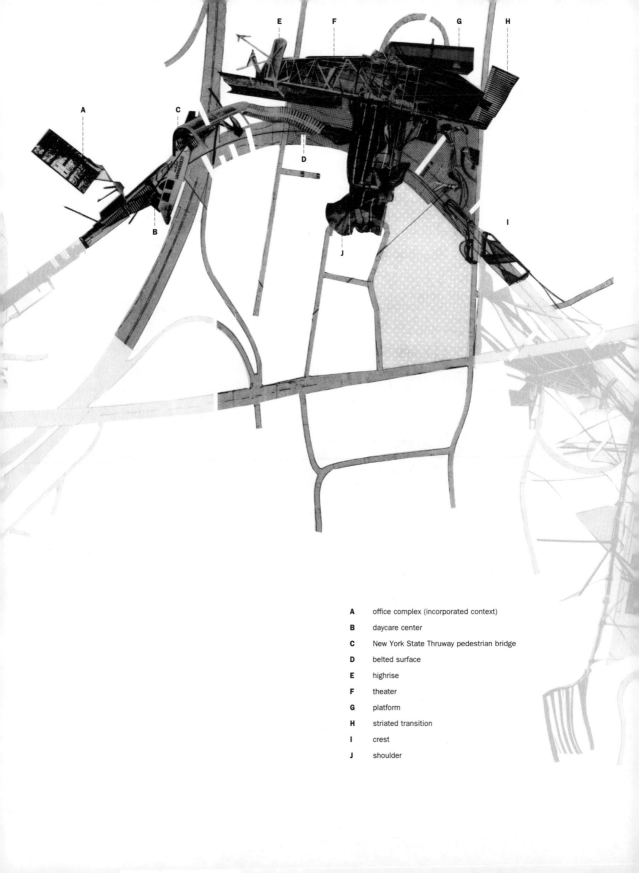

A   office complex (incorporated context)

B   daycare center

C   New York State Thruway pedestrian bridge

D   belted surface

E   highrise

F   theater

G   platform

H   striated transition

I   crest

J   shoulder

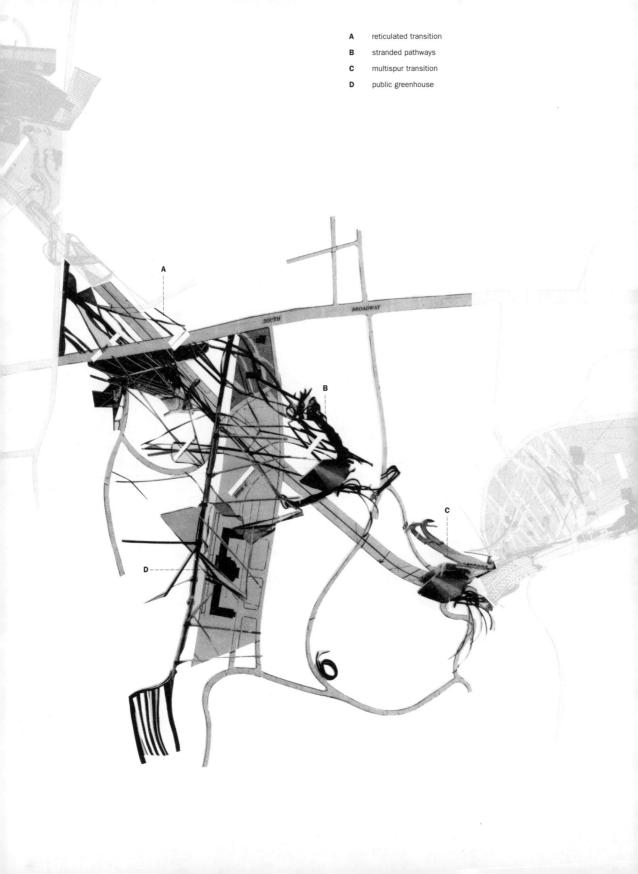

A   reticulated transition
B   stranded pathways
C   multispur transition
D   public greenhouse

A   plexed landscape garden

B   conference extension

C   athletics

D   plaid transition

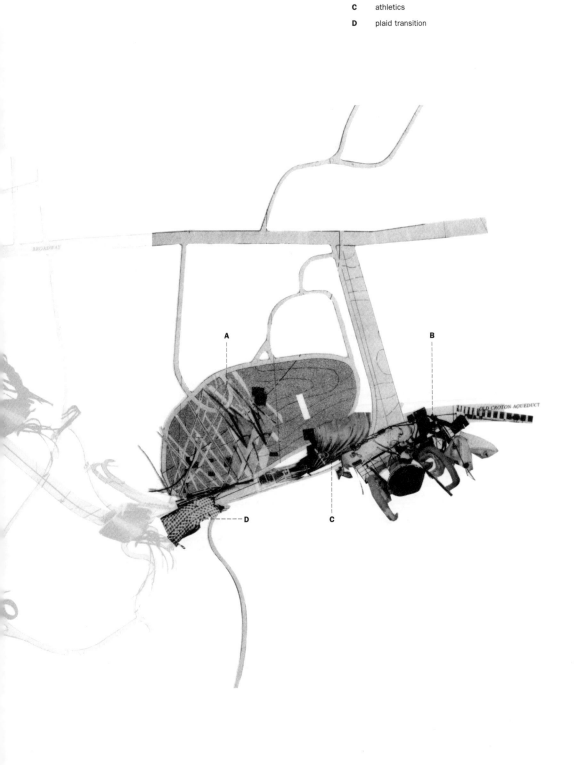

Rural reclamation: habitat corridors.

Program

The project proposes as its primary strategy **programmatic grafts:** readings of the site and its context as developed through a **mapping procedure** that seeks to uncover shifting site histories, patterns of land use, and changing articulations of public and private usage as encoded in place
names and street designations. French social theorist Michel de Certeau has noted the uncanny
persistence of meaning in place names:

> Disposed in constellations that hierarchize and semantically order the surface of the city, operating chrono-
> logical arrangements and historical justifications, these words slowly lose, like worn coins, the value
> engraved on them, but their ability to signify outlives their first definitions . . . A strange toponymy that is
> detached from actual places and flies high over the city like a foggy geography of "meanings" held in sus-
> pension, directing the physical perambulations below.[1]

This "foggy geography of 'meanings'"—a semantic surplus encoded in place names—seemed to
us a productive device to generate programs with distinct connections to the places while maintaining a detachment allowing for invention and critique. De Certeau proposes a specifically political reading of this condition:

> Linking acts and footsteps, opening meanings and directions, these words operate in the name of an emp-
> tying out and wearing away of their primary role. They become liberated spaces that can be occupied. A rich
> indetermination gives them, by means of a semantic rarefaction, the function of articulating a second, poet-
> ic geography on top of the geography of the literal, forbidden or permitted meaning. They insinuate other
> routes into the functionalist and historical order of movement. Walking follows them: "I fill this great empty
> space with a beautiful name."[2]

Kit of props.

Cinematic Grafts

The final steps in the design work consist of returning to the map of the overall site to apply the Area Rule in a consistent manner. Given the detailed vocabularies developed in the design work for the Tarrytown Interchange, we were able to increase the realism of the proposal through the use of aerial photographs (a "sampling" process of typical terrain) and expand the investigation to encompass the full range of sites as originally proposed. Architectural models are not seen as scaled reductions of individual projects, but instead as nomadic props to be used in multiple contexts and interchangeable combinations. Working very directly with the particularities of the site, a field of complex and unexpected exchanges develop as a result of these grafts, suggesting in turn a further reprogramming of the architecture and a redefinition of the site itself. This "putting into play" of multiple possibilities has, we feel, enormous potential, leading to a structure as fluid and suggestive as the water-supply system itself.

Notes

1. Michel de Certeau, *The Practice of Everyday Life,* trans. Steven Rendall (Berkeley: University of California Press, 1984), 104.
2. de Certeau, 105.

The Croton Aqueduct Study, an ongoing project begun in 1992, has been supported by grants from the Design Arts Division of the National Endowment for the Arts, the New York State Council on the Arts, and the Graham Foundation for Advanced Studies in the Fine Arts.

RAAUm was assisted by John Kelleher, Tsuto Sakamoto, Michael Silver, Maki Uchiyama, and Lynn Rice.

THE PARSING EYE

Mark Wamble

ARTISTS' SPACE INSTALLATION

Greg Lynn

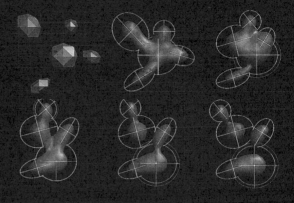

Unlike a conventional geometric primitive such as a sphere, which has its own autonomous organization, a metaball is defined in relation to other objects. Its center, surface area, mass, and organization are determined by other fields of influence. The inner volume defines a zone within which other metaball objects can influence and inflect the surface of the metaball object. The surfaces are surrounded by two halos of relational influence, one defining a zone of fusion, the other defining a zone of inflection. When two or more metaball objects are related to another, given the appropriate proximity of their halos they can either mutually redefine their respective surfaces based on their particular gravitational properties or they can actually fuse into one contiguous surface defined not by the summation or average of their surfaces and gravities, but instead by the interactions of their respective centers and zones of inflection and fusion.[1]

It is perhaps as Greg Lynn would have it that we view his architecture as a preoccupation with form. To view this work as anything other than a selection of stills from a self-generating digital animation would eventually lead us to discover that they are exactly that: images of forms interacting through operations we can only reconstruct in our mind's eye. But as we play the images through, anticipating the folds, twists, and bends, as they slide into what seems to be a complete developmental collapse, an image stasis, another more complex organization appears: the development of an extreme program of occupation that finds an important beginning at the limits of conventional vision.

It would be imprecise, however, to suggest that within the economy of computer animation there lies an essential factor in the success of Lynn's work. While mechanical drawing is too often characterized as inadequate in describing complex geometries, in reality its only disadvantage is that it is slower. Given the right software, hyperrealistic depictions of complex forms—once only possible to represent through the tedium of calculators, compasses, and applied color—can be produced in a fraction of the time. Aspects of light, view, surface, and resolution become a simple matter of preference, conditioned by the desired effect the anticipated object might produce were it to become a material assemblage. There is little reason to believe that any imaging technology alone could provide more than a quantitative leap in productivity without another visual reference. Without such a reference, any use of information technology will simply produce more of the same.

But Lynn's conception of form points to a larger architectural project, one that attempts to bring the conventions of the formal into a new realm of relational influence, which, in the process, relies upon an equally new conception of vision. By coordinating basic neural processes with the operational mode of information technology—something we do each time we sit down in front of a computer—the conventions of vision and the physical limitations of the eye are turned to our

Photographer unknown. Portrait of Marcel Breuer.

advantage. That is to say, the familiarity of technical operations engineered to facilitate a user's intuition compensates for the eye's limited acuity. Our fears of losing something fundamentally human to the invasion of technologies of this kind can be soothed by the understanding that there is also something very natural about it. The parallel processes of the nervous system and the microchip are in many ways compatible. For the eye that sees no further than the modeled surfaces of Lynn's architecture, there will never be a level of sophistication at work beyond what we might appreciate in any other refined object. But these images hold our interest because of their promise of performance, their durability, and their ability to communicate the method of their making, and perhaps most importantly their ability to allow us to occupy a different kind of time and space, however simply. They reveal to us, and induce in us, a response that while inconclusive, does connect to an *operative emblematic*, or perhaps even an *operative gestalt*.

Given the limits of conventional representation—whether aided by advanced imaging technologies or not—any qualitative difference that might promote a new intellectual relationship to form will also require an equally radical conception of vision. While an exhaustive study of such a subject is beyond the scope of this essay, some sense of the argument can be gathered by the following simplification: with architecture, form in the most traditional sense is defined as the sum of a structure's apparent physical characteristics. In this regard, all effects produced by form, as well as those contained within it, operate through that form's ability to sustain external relationships. These relationships are brought about either through semantics, wherein meaning is accommodated by the attribution of signs and symbols or the recognition of a discernible pattern, or through the form's brute qualities—what it produces in the subject that confronts it. In both cases, the primary objective of form, as directed by its author, is to make available to the eye certain fixed,

material characteristics. This particular conception of vision is categorical in that it exploits the mechanical limitations of retinal processing to the exclusion of other aspects of visualization: vision is limited by the instrumentalization of the eye as defined by these formal choices.

Often the limits that we assign to architectural form are also the limits that we accept from a sophisticated product that is grossly underutilized. To access the full potential of any architecture, the eye must envision the extremes of an operational context—a context that avoids the mechanical appropriation of form in favor of an improvisational, in*formation* mode.

In his 1965 article "Vision in the Ganzfeld," Lloyd Avant stated that visual processes are anything but mechanical when exposed to extreme conditions.[2] Avant resumes an earlier investigation from 1930 initiated by Gestalt psychologist Wolfgang Metzger entitled *Optische Untersuchungen am Ganzfeld* wherein Metzger described the disorienting effects of vision in a structureless field. Much of Metzger's work on the Gestalt position is reflected in Koffka's 1935 statement of Gestalt thinking, a principal text of the Gestalt school. Metzger held the position that vision occurred in tridimensional rather than bidimensional space. His research on the Ganzfeld sought to illustrate that primitive vision was more complex than had originally been thought, and that perception was a spatial concern.

Taken literally, the term *Ganzfeld* means "total field," the absence of all inhomogeneities perceivable within an otherwise normal visual mechanism. In the Ganzfeld, the ability to distinguish figure from field is either minimized or eliminated completely due to the flattening of brightness, chromaticity, and contrast variables within the observer's natural field of view. Without this ability, a functional separation occurs between the discerning optical processes of the retina and the visual cortex of the brain, resulting in what later came to be known as clinical "blank-out." Avant

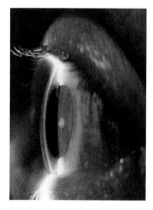

Lennart Nilsson. Light bending as it passes from the cornea toward the retina, marking the moment information undergoes the first of many cerebral processes.

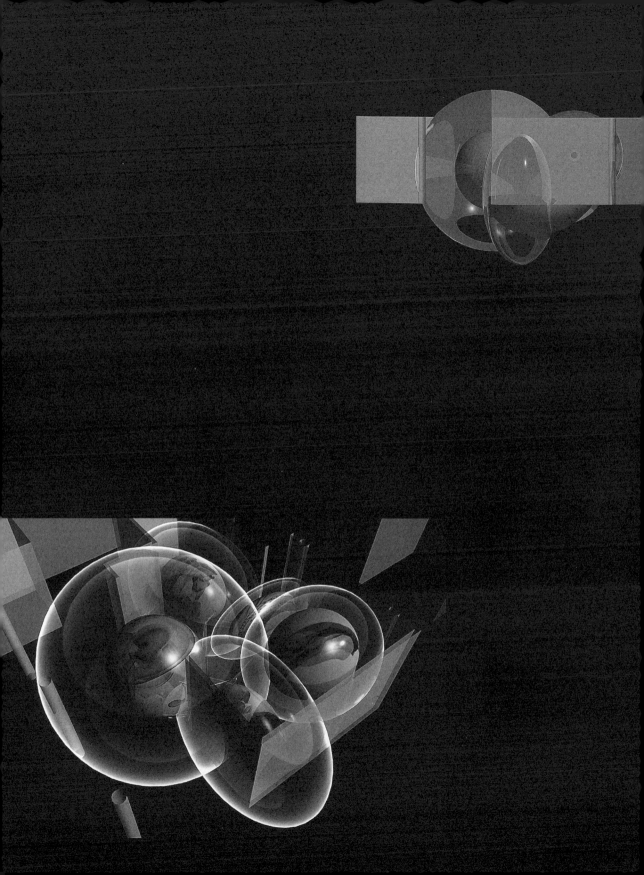

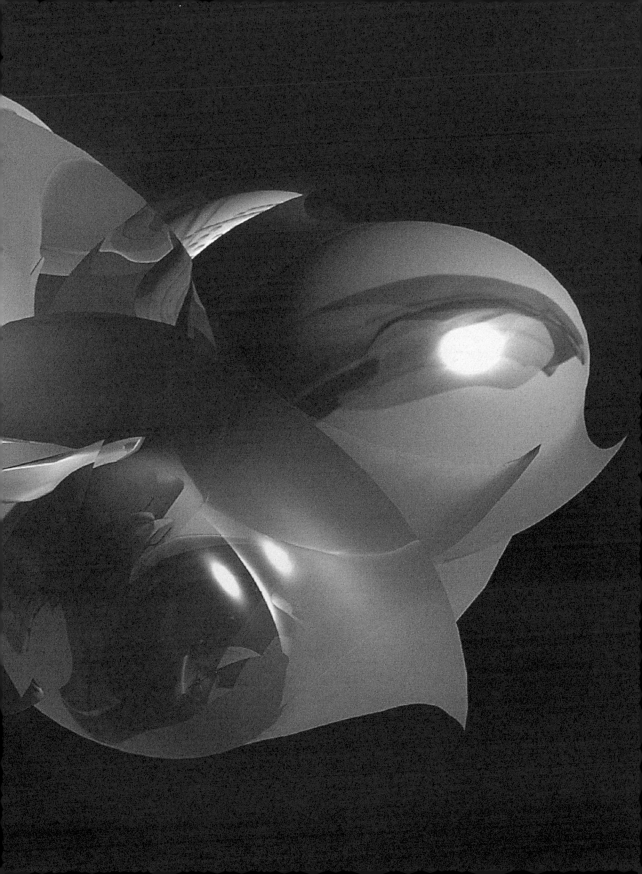

describes how, during the blank-out phase, vision can produce no phenomenal field as a result of the absence of actual visual stimuli. Blank-out is not only the inability to see in the undifferentiated field, but moreover a "complete disappearance of the sense of vision for short periods of time," resulting in the observer's inability to know whether his or her eyes are open, or if they are moving.[3] Subsequent studies during the 1950s and early 1960s observed that immediately following the blank-out phase there also occurred in patients a sharp increase in brain activity, as evidenced by commensurate bursts of alpha activity as recorded in the EEG. Where vision is occluded, the brain searches for an alternative imaging process. Through these early studies, science made the initial determination that the visual *sense*, as guided by the retina, could be isolated to reveal a more complex process of visualization.

During the 1960s, the advent of high-altitude supersonic flight and space travel revived interest in the Ganzfeld. Scientists began to pursue the more practical effects of the Ganzfeld due to similarities found between the recorded findings of Metzger's study and the actual accounts of pilots under extreme flight conditions. Parallels between "empty field" myopia in the Ganzfeld and "sky" myopia in high-altitude flight suggest that the evolution of the eye is not only challenged under certain physical conditions, but the eye-to-brain interface, as recorded under extreme circumstances, will fail to recognize established pathways of neural communication. Both high-altitude supersonic flight and the "ground-rush" phenomenon experienced by skydivers between 500 and 600 feet thwart the eyes' ability to accommodate orientation relative to the stabilizing effects of ground and horizon.

Throughout the twentieth century, the desire to define and alter visual processes has been pervasive, indeed synonymous with modern intellectual development since the Renaissance. There

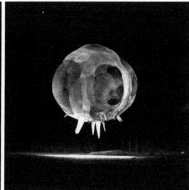

Harold Edgerton and James Killian. Stop-motion photographs of placement kick and atomic bomb explosion.

can be little doubt that photography—from Muybridge, to Moholy-Nagy, to Arbus, to Sherman— has come to be considered a window to worlds otherwise obscured or overlooked. Subsequent advances in digital imaging provide instruments to see what is both faster and slower, larger and smaller, closer and further from what the eye is able to see in its unenhanced plenitude. The operative domain of the eye as characterized by these chemical and digital media is nonetheless relegated to the surveillance of objects and dedicated to the degree to which the observation of physical phenomena might be improved. That some form of chemical or digital truth might be constructed by way of the still image and the camera frame confirms both the belief in, and simultaneous disdain for, technologies so advanced.

The goal of advanced optics is to record and process levels of information that lie beyond the visual acuity of the naked eye. One legacy of technoscopics is the belief that seeing more is equivalent to knowing more, and that the limits of retinal performance are the limits of progress. On the other hand, Metzger's study shows that the limit of retinal performance reveals not only a functional limit of the eye's capability but more importantly a limit to the kind of information the eye occludes. As is the case in the Ganzfeld, the eye automatically shuts down, forcing the patient's perceptions to be guided by alternative neural processes as compensation for an absent retinal image.

Greg Lynn's architecture creates a structure for the *parsing* eye. That is to say, the role of the eye in the visualization process is to maintain a direct interface between the cognitive processes of the brain and external fields of activity. By conceiving of the visual field as behind the eye, where the formal image is downloaded into a processual and operative state of malleable information, rather than in front of the eye, where the conditioning of form is categorical and exclusive, issues

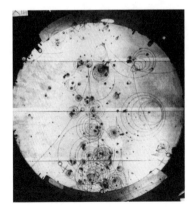

Harold Edgerton and James Killian. Stop-motion photograph of bubble chamber arabesques.

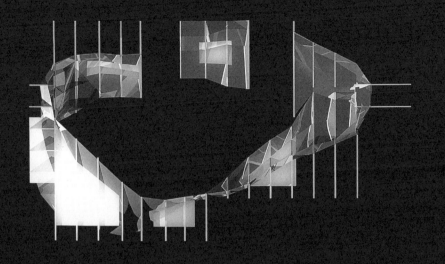
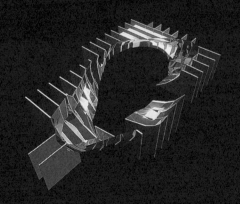

of structure and organization become anticipatory. Occupation precedes realization. By structuring and organizing the center, surface area, and mass of the digital form, and thus making available the influencing parameters of the forms to an external audience, all material evidence of Lynn's architecture becomes the documentation of an operational history. It offers an alternative to conventional vision by integrating the nervous system, as initially accessed through the mechanical functions of the eye, with the processes of computer modeling. If we place these models into the conventional frame of vision, they appear as frozen music—at best, a footnote to the history of radical form. But advances in information technology, and more specifically the proliferation of personal computing, enable the formal aspect of this work to engender something commonplace, almost banal. In a sense, the models become an interactive ploy responding to the demands of external forces, or input data, and internal forces built into the histogram—the retained digital history of the image. As mutable images, they animate a kind of dynamism that attracts and accommodates the operative influences of external forces. Feedback is formalized through the subsequent, ongoing information loop as represented by the image mutation. The topology of the surface carefully plots the interaction of the externally deployed parameters relative to each other and to the internal constitution of the information surface.

What emerges is an operative image that is always one step ahead of the anticipated effect it will produce in the working information model. The eye speeds past the stasis of the flash image to read and factor into a response format the implications of the slightest pattern deflection. The eye's mechanical apparatus is utilized totally to facilitate the maintenance of the parsing process. The operative image is not retinal, but cognitive; it pre-occupies the economy of built form, resisting the saturated optical field and with it the myopia of retinal vision.

Notes

1. Greg Lynn, "Blobs: Or Why Tectonics Is Square and Topology Is Groovy," in *ANY* 14 (1996), 59.
2. Lloyd L. Avant, "Vision in the Ganzfeld," in *Psychological Bulletin* 64, no. 4 (1965), 246–58.
3. Avant, 255.

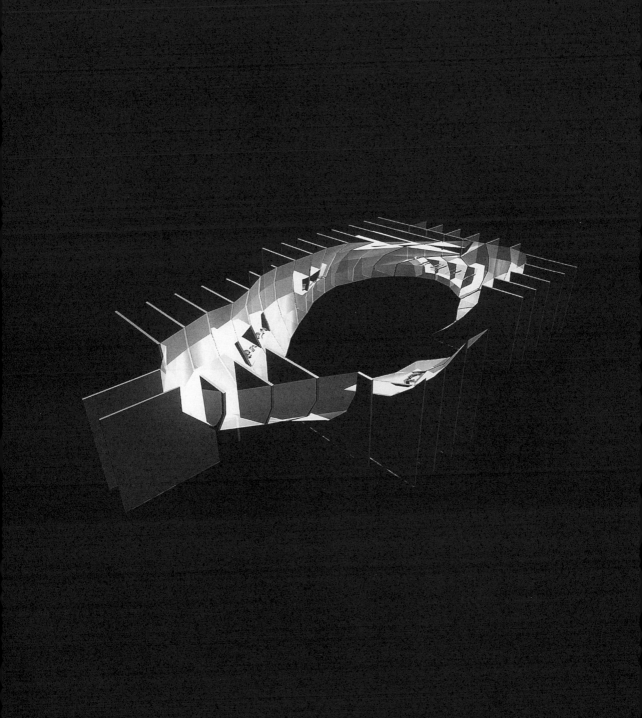

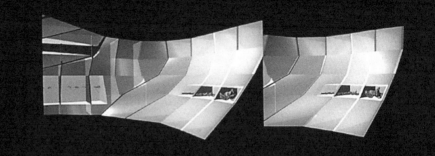

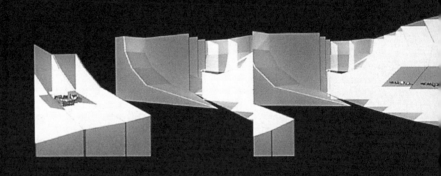

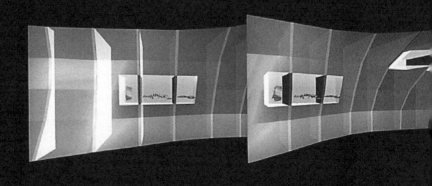

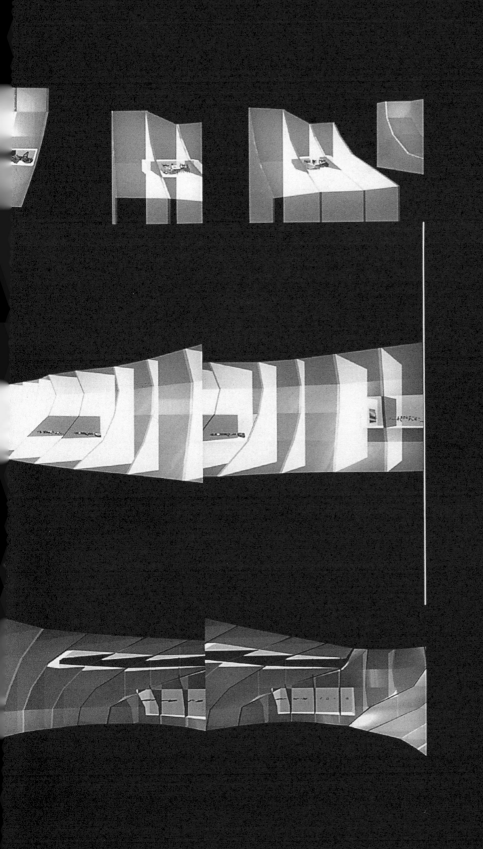

GAINING A FREE RELATION TO TECHNOLOGY

Hubert L. Dreyfus

SLOW SPACE

I. Introduction: What Heidegger is *not* saying:

In *The Question Concerning Technology,* Martin Heidegger described his aim: "We shall be questioning concerning technology, and in so doing we should like to prepare a free relationship to it." He sought to reveal the essence of technology in a manner that "in no way confines us to a stultified compulsion to push on blindly with technology or, what comes to the same thing, to rebel helplessly against it." He claimed that "when we once open ourselves expressly to the *essence* of technology, we find ourselves unexpectedly taken into a freeing claim."[1]

We will need to explain essence, opening, and freeing before we can understand Heidegger here. But already Heidegger's project should alert us to the fact that he was not announcing one more reactionary rebellion against technology, although many respectable philosophers, among them Jürgen Habermas, take him to have done just that. Neither was Heidegger doing what progressive thinkers like Habermas want him to have done—propose a way to get technology under control so that it can serve our rationally chosen ends.

The difficulty in defining Heidegger's stand on technology is no accident. Heidegger was not always clear about what distinguished his approach from a romantic reaction against the domination of nature, and when he did finally arrive at a clear formulation of his original view, it was so radical that everyone has been tempted to translate it into conventional platitudes about the evils of technology. Thus Heidegger's ontological concerns have been mistakenly assimilated into humanistic worries about the devastation of nature.

Those who want to use Heidegger to support contemporary antitechnological banalities can find evidence in his texts. During World War II, he attacked consumerism: "The circularity of consumption for the sake of consumption is the sole procedure which distinctively characterizes the history of a world which has become unworld."[2] As late as 1955 he held that "the world now appears as an object open to the attacks of calculative thought . . . Nature becomes a gigantic gasoline station, an energy source for modern technology and industry."[3] And in this address to the peasants of Schwarzwald, he also lamented the appearance of television antennas on their dwellings:

> Hourly and daily they are chained to radio and television . . . All that with which modern techniques of communication stimulate, assail, and drive man—all that is already much closer to man today than his fields around his farmstead, closer than the sky over the earth, closer than the change from night to day, closer than the conventions and customs of his village, than the tradition of his native world.[4]

Such statements suggest that Heidegger was a Luddite who advocated a retreat from consumerism, mass media, and the exploitation of the earth, a return to the world of the pre-Socratic Greeks or the pretechnology Schwarzwald peasants.

II. Heidegger's ontological approach to technology:

As his thinking developed, however, Heidegger did not deny that the advent of these modernizations posed serious problems, but he came to the surprising and provocative conclusion that focusing on loss and destruction is still technological: "All attempts to reckon with existing reality . . . in terms of decline and loss, in terms of fate, catastrophe, and destruction, are merely technological behavior."[5] Viewing our situation as a problem to be solved by appropriate action also turns out to be technological: "The instrumental conception of technology conditions every attempt to bring man into the right relation to technology . . . The will to mastery becomes all the more urgent the more technology threatens to slip from human control."[6] Heidegger definitively stated that this approach could not work: "No single man, no group of men, no commission of prominent statesmen, scientists, and technicians, no conference of leaders of commerce and industry, can brake or direct the progress of history in the atomic age."[7]

Heidegger's outlook is both darker and more hopeful than it appears. He felt that a more dangerous situation faced modern humans than the technological destruction of nature and civilization, yet characterized the situation as one about which something *could* be done, at least indirectly. The threat was not a problem for which there could be a solution, but an ontological condition from which we could be saved.

Heidegger was concerned about the human distress caused by the *technological understanding of being* rather than about the destruction caused by specific technologies. Heidegger consequently distinguished between the current problems caused by technology (such as ecological destruction, nuclear danger, and consumerism) and the devastation that would result if technology solved all our problems:

> What threatens man in his very nature is the . . . view that man, by the peaceful release, transformation, storage, and channeling of the energies of physical nature, could render the human condition . . . tolerable for everybody and happy in all respects.[8]

The "greatest danger" is that "the approaching tide of technological revolution in the atomic age could so captivate, bewitch, dazzle, and beguile man that calculative thinking may someday come to be accepted and practiced as the only way of thinking."[9] The danger is then a restriction in our way of thinking—a leveling of our understanding of being.

To evaluate this claim we must describe what Heidegger meant by an understanding of being. The modern concept of disposability is a useful illustration. We now look upon things, and even sometimes people, as resources to be used until they are no longer needed, and then we put them aside. A Styrofoam cup is a perfect example. When we want a hot or cold drink, the cup does its job, and when we have finished we throw it away. This understanding of an object differs significantly from what we can suppose to be the everyday Japanese understanding of a delicate teacup. The teacup does not preserve temperature as well as its plastic replacement, and it must further be washed and protected, but it is preserved from generation to generation for its beauty and social meaning. It is difficult to picture a tea ceremony around a Styrofoam cup.

Note that the traditional Japanese understanding of what it is to be human (contented, gentle, social) fits with that culture's understanding of what it is to be a thing (delicate, beautiful, traditional). It would make no sense for active, independent, and aggressive Westerners who constantly strive to cultivate and satisfy immediate desires to relate to things in the way that the Japanese do, nor would it make sense for the Japanese (before their understanding of being was tinged with ours) to invent and prefer Styrofoam teacups. In the same vein, Westerners tend to think of politics as the negotiation of individual desires while the Japanese seek consensus. In sum, social practices contain an understanding of what it is to be a human self, reveal an interpretation of what it is to be a thing, and define society. These social practices fit together and add up to an understanding of being.

Because the shared practices into which we are socialized provide a background understanding of what counts as things, what counts as human beings, and ultimately what counts as real, we can direct our actions towards particular things and people. The understanding of being thus creates what Heidegger called a "clearing" in which things and people can show up for us. We do not produce the clearing; it produces *us* as the kind of human beings that we are. Heidegger described the clearing as follows:

> Beyond what is, not away from it but before it, there is still something else that happens. In the midst of beings as a whole an open place occurs. There is a clearing, a lighting . . . This open center is . . . not surrounded by what is; rather, the lighting center itself encircles all that is . . . Only this clearing grants and guarantees to human beings a passage to those entities that we ourselves are not, and access to the being that we ourselves are.[10]

What, then, is the essence of technology—that is to say the technological understanding of being and the technological clearing—and how does opening ourselves to it give us a free relation to technological devices? To begin, when we ask about the essence of technology we are able to see that Heidegger's question cannot be answered by defining technology. Technology is as old as civilization. Heidegger noted that it could be correctly defined as "a means and a human activity." He called this "the instrumental and anthropological definition of technology."[11] But if we ask about the *essence* of technology (the technological understanding of being) we find that modern technology is "something completely different and . . . new"[12]—and even different from using Styrofoam cups to serve our desires. The essence of modern technology, according to Heidegger, is to seek more and more flexibility and efficiency simply for its own sake: "Expediting is always itself directed from the beginning . . . toward driving on to the maximum yield at the minimum expense."[13] Our only goal is optimization:

> Everywhere everything is ordered to stand by, to be immediately at hand, indeed to stand there
> just so that it may be on call for a further ordering. Whatever is ordered about in this way has its
> own standing. We call it standing-reserve.[14]

No longer are we subjects turning nature into an object of exploitation: "The subject-object relation thus reaches, for the first time, its pure 'relational,' i.e., ordering, character in which both the subject and the object are sucked up as standing-reserves."[15] A modern airliner is not an object at all, but just a flexible and efficient cog in the transportation system. Heidegger concludes, "Whatever stands by in the sense of standing-reserve no longer stands over against us as object."[16]

All ideas of serving God, society, fellow, or even our own callings disappear. In this view, human beings become a resource to be used—but more importantly to be enhanced—like any other: "Man, who no longer conceals his character of being the most important raw material, is also drawn into this process."[17] In the 1968 film *2001: A Space Odyssey*, the robot HAL, when asked if he is happy on the mission, answers, "I'm using all my capacities to the maximum. What more could a rational entity desire?" This is a brilliant expression of our current understanding of being. We pursue the growth or development of our potential simply for its own sake—it is our only goal. The human-potential movement perfectly expresses this technological understanding of being, as does the attempt to better organize the future use of our natural resources. We thus become part of a system directed by no one but moving toward the total mobilization of all beings, even humans. This explains Heidegger's view that a perfectly ordered society dedicated to the welfare of all is not the solution to our problems but rather the culmination of the technological understanding of being.

III. What then can we do?

Even Heidegger, of course, used and depended on modern technological devices. He was no Luddite, and he did not advocate a return to the pretechnological world: "It would be foolish to attack technology blindly. It would be shortsighted to condemn it as the work of the devil. We depend on technical devices; they even challenge us to even greater advances."[18] Heidegger suggested instead a way to keep technology and still remain true to ourselves: "We can affirm the unavoidable use of technical devices, and also deny them the right to dominate us, and so to warp, confuse, and lay waste our nature."[19] To understand this possibility we need to illustrate Heidegger's important distinction between technology and the technological understanding of being. Again, we can turn to Japan. In contemporary Japan a traditional, nontechnological understanding of being coexists with the most high-tech production and consumption. Television sets and household gods share the same shelf—the Styrofoam cup coexists with the porcelain. Just as one can have technology without the technological understanding of being, so can the technological understanding of being be dissociated from technological devices.

Heidegger held that this dissociation entailed rethinking the history of being in the West, which would show that although a technological understanding of being is our destiny, it is not our fate. Our conception of things and ourselves as resources to be ordered, enhanced, and used efficiently has been building since Plato, and indeed dominates our practices, but we are not stuck with it. Rather than the way things must be, this outlook is nothing more nor less than our current cultural clearing.

Only those who think of Heidegger as opposing technology will be surprised at his next point: once we see that technology is our latest understanding of being, we will be grateful for it. We did not make this clearing nor do we control it, but if it were not given to us to encounter things and ourselves as resources, nothing would show up as anything at all and no possibilities for action would make sense. And once we realize—not just in our heads, but also in our practices—that we *receive* our technological understanding of being, we have stepped out of the technological understanding of being. We then see that what is most important in our lives is not subject to efficiency enhancement; indeed, the very tendency to control everything is precisely what we do not control. This transformation in our sense of reality—this overcoming of calculative thinking—is precisely what Heidegger's analyses seek to bring about. Heidegger explained that we must acknowledge and thereby overcome our restricted and willful modern clearing precisely by recognizing our essential receptivity to it:

> Modern man must first and above all find his way back into the full breadth of the space proper to his essence. That essential space of man's essential being receives the dimension that unites it to something beyond itself . . . that is the way in which the safekeeping of being itself is given to belong to the essence of man as the one who is needed and used by being. [20]

This transformation in our understanding of being—unlike the slow process of cleaning up the environment which is, of course, also necessary—would take place in a sudden switch of gestalt: "The turning of the danger comes to pass suddenly. In this turning, the clearing belonging to the essence of being suddenly clears itself and lights up . . . The selfsame danger is, when it is as the danger, the saving power." [21] This remarkable claim gives rise to two opposing ways of understanding Heidegger's response to technology. Both interpretations agree that once one recognizes the technological understanding of being for what it is— a historical understanding—one gains a free relation to it. We neither push forward techno-logical efficiency as our only goal nor always resist it. Free of the technological imperative, we can, in each case, discuss the pros and cons. As Heidegger put it,

> We let technical devices enter our daily life, and at the same time leave them outside . . . as things which are nothing absolute but remain dependent upon something higher. I would call this comportment toward technology which expresses "yes" and at the same time "no" by an old word, releasement toward things. [22]

One interpretation of this proposal holds that once we strike the right relationship with technology (recognize it as a clearing), that clearing is revealed to be just as good as any other. Efficiency—getting the most out of ourselves and everything else—is fine insofar as we do not think that efficiency for its own sake is the *only* end for man, dictated by reality itself, to which all others must be subordinated. Heidegger could be read as supporting this acceptance of the technological understanding of being:

> That which shows itself and at the same time withdraws [the clearing] is the essential trait of what we call the mystery. I call the comportment which enables us to keep open to the meaning hidden in technology, openness to the mystery.

Releasement toward things and openness to the mystery belong together. They grant us the possibility of dwelling in the world in a totally different way. They promise us a new ground and foundation upon which we can stand and endure in the world of technology without being imperiled by it. [23]

But, Heidegger continues, acceptance of the mystery of understandings of being is not the whole story: "Releasement toward things and openness to the mystery give us a vision of a new rootedness which *someday* [emphasis added] might even be fit to recapture the old and now rapidly disappearing rootedness in a changed form."[24] "Releasement" gives only a "possibility" and a "promise" of "dwelling in the world in a totally different way."

Mere openness to technology, it seems, omits much of what Heidegger finds essential to being human: embeddedness in nature, nearness or localness, and shared meaningful differences that have played important roles in our history, such as noble and ignoble, justice and injustice, salvation and damnation, and mature and immature. Releasement, while giving us a free relation to technology and protecting our nature from distortion and distress, cannot give us any of these.

For Heidegger, there then remain two issues: "The issue is the saving of man's essential nature. Therefore, the issue is keeping meditative thinking alive"; and "If releasement toward things and openness to the mystery awaken within us, then we should arrive at a path that will lead to a new ground and foundation."[25] Releasement is only a stage, a kind of holding pattern while awaiting the new understanding of being that would give some content to our openness—what Heidegger calls "a new rootedness." This explains why Heidegger goes on to talk of the divine whenever he discusses releasement and the saving power of understanding technology as a gift:

> Only when man, in the disclosing coming-to-pass of the insight by which he himself is beheld . . . renounces human self-will . . . does he correspond in his essence to the claim of that insight. In thus corresponding man is gathered into his own, that he . . . may, as the mortal, look out toward the divine. [26]

The need for a new centeredness is reflected in Heidegger's famous remark from his last interview: "Only a god can save us now."[27] But what does this mean?

IV. The job of a god:

Merely preserving pretechnological practices, even if we could do it, would not give us what we need. Pretechnological practices no longer constitute a shared sense of reality, and a new understanding of being cannot be legislated. For such practices to give meaning to our lives and unite us in a community, they must be focused and held up to the practitioners. This function, which later Heidegger calls "truth setting itself to work," can be performed by what he calls a work of art. Heidegger took the Greek temple as his illustration of a working artwork. The temple displayed to the Greeks what was important, and so allowed there to be heroes and slaves, victory and disgrace, disaster and blessing. With their practices manifested and focused by the temple, the Greeks had guidelines for leading good lives and avoiding bad ones. The medieval cathedral functioned in the same manner, making it possible to be saint or sinner by revealing the dimensions of salvation and damnation. In either case, one knew where one stood and what one had to do. Heidegger held that "there must always be some being in the open [the clearing], something that *is*, in which the openness takes its stand and attains its constancy."[28] We could describe such special objects as cultural paradigms. A cultural paradigm focuses and collects the scattered practices of a culture, unifies them into coherent possibilities for action, and holds them up to society; people can then act and relate to each other in terms set by the shared exemplar.

For Heidegger, only those practices focused in a paradigm could establish how things can appear and what it makes sense to do. This explains why Heidegger was pessimistic about salvaging aspects of the Enlightenment or reviving past practices. In Heidegger's world view, we can and should try to preserve such practices, but they can only save us if they are radically transformed and integrated into a new understanding of reality. In addition, we must learn to appreciate marginal practices—what Heidegger called the "saving power of insignificant things"—such as friendship, backpacking in the wilderness, and drinking wine with friends. These practices are marginal precisely because they are not efficient. They can be enacted for the sake of health and greater efficiency, but that is precisely the greatest danger. These saving practices could, however, come together in a new cultural paradigm that holds up to us a new way of doing things, focusing a world in which formerly marginal practices were central and efficiency marginal. Such a new object or event that grounds a new understanding of reality Heidegger would call a new god. This is why he maintained that "only another god can save us."[29]

Once we see what is needed, we also see that there is not much we can do to bring it about. A new sense of reality is not something that can be taken as the goal of a crash program such as the Apollo moon mission—a paradigm of modern technological power. The rock-and-roll music of the 1960s offers a hint of what such a new god might look like. The Beatles, Bob Dylan, and others reverberated for many as the articulation of new understanding of what really mattered. This new understanding almost coalesced into a cultural paradigm at the 1969 Woodstock Music Festival where for a few days people actually lived in an altered understanding of being: the mainline contemporary concern with rationality, sobriety, willful activity, and flexible, efficient control was subordinated to such Greek virtues as openness, enjoyment of nature, and Dionysian ecstasy and revelry as well as the neglected Christian values of peace, tolerance, and love for one's neighbor with neither desire nor exclusivity. Technology was not smashed or denigrated; instead, the power of the electronic media was put to the service of the music, which focused the concerns outlined above.

If enough people had found in Woodstock what they most cared about, and realized that others shared this recognition, a new understanding of being might have coalesced and stabilized. In retrospect we can see that the ideals of the Woodstock generation were neither broad nor deep enough to resist technology and to sustain a culture. We have nonetheless been given a hint of how a new cultural paradigm might work, of how we must foster human receptivity and preserve endangered but extant pre-technological practices in the hope that one day they will be pulled together into a new paradigm, rich and resistant enough to give new meaningful directions to our lives.

To many, however, the idea of *a* god that could give us a unified but open community—one set of concerns that everyone shares, if only as a focus of disagreement—sounds either unrealistic or dangerous. Heidegger would probably have agreed that the open, democratic version of this uniformity looks increasingly unobtainable, and that its closed, totalitarian form can certainly be dangerous. But Heidegger held that given our historical essence—what we have become during the history of our culture—such a community is necessary to us. This raises the question of whether our need for one community is dictated by our historical essence, or whether the claim that we cannot live without a centered and rooted culture is simply romantic nostalgia.

Heidegger conveys a message even for those who hold that we should not expect and do not need one all-embracing community in this pluralized modern world. Those who think of communities as local enclaves in an otherwise impersonal society—from Fyodor Dostoyevsky to the hippies to Richard Rorty—still owe us an explanation of what holds these local communities together. If Dostoyevsky and Heidegger were right, each local community still needs its local god—its particular incarnation of what the community is up to. This vision of multiple, local gods leads us back to the belief that releasement is not enough, to a modified Heidegger slogan: only some new *gods* can save us now.

Notes

1. Martin Heidegger, "The Question Concerning Technology," in *The Question Concerning Technology* (New York: Harper, 1977), 25–26.
2. Heidegger, "Overcoming Metaphysics," in *The End of Philosophy* (New York: Harper & Row, 1973), 107.
3. Heidegger, *Discourse On Thinking* (New York: Harper & Row, 1966), 50.
4. Heidegger, *Discourse On Thinking*, 48
5. Heidegger, "The Turning," in *The Question Concerning Technology*, 48.
6. Heidegger, "The Question Concerning Technology," 5.
7. Heidegger, *Discourse On Thinking*, 52.
8. Heidegger, "What Are Poets For?" in *Poetry, Language, Thought* (New York: Harper & Row, 1971), 116.
9. Heidegger, *Discourse On Thinking*, 56.
10. Heidegger, "The Origin of the Work of Art," in *Poetry, Language, Thought,* 53.
11. Heidegger, "The Question Concerning Technology," 5.
12. Heidegger, "The Question Concerning Technology," 5.
13. Heidegger, "The Question Concerning Technology," 15.
14. Heidegger, "The Question Concerning Technology," 17.
15. Heidegger, "Science and Reflection," in *The Question Concerning Technology,* 173.
16. Heidegger, "The Question Concerning Technology," 17.
17. Heidegger, "Overcoming Metaphysics," in *The End of Philosophy*, 104.
18. Heidegger, *Discourse On Thinking,* 53.
19. Heidegger, *Discourse On Thinking,* 54.
20. Heidegger, "The Turning," 39.
21. Heidegger, "The Turning," 39.
22. Heidegger, *Discourse On Thinking,* 54.
23. Heidegger, *Discourse On Thinking,* 55.
24. Heidegger, *Discourse On Thinking,* 55.
25. Heidegger, *Discourse On Thinking,* 56.
26. Heidegger, "The Turning," 47.
27. "Nur noch ein Gott kann uns retten," quoted in *Der Spiegel,* May 31, 1976.
28. Heidegger, "The Origin of the Work of Art," 61.
29. This is an equally possible translation of the famous phrase from *Der Spiegel.*

WE PLAY UNTIL DEATH SHUTS THE DOOR [1]

TOWARD A REDEMPTIVE PRACTICE OF ARCHITECTURE

Elizabeth Burns Gamard

A postmodern artist or writer is in the position of a philosopher: the text he writes, the work he produces is not in principle governed by pre-established rules. (These) rules and categories are what the work of art itself is looking for. The artist or writer, then, is working without rules in order to formulate the rules of what will have been done. Hence, the fact that work and text have the characters of event.
  —Jean-François Lyotard, *The Postmodern Condition: A Report on Knowledge*

A living system is always in process, incomplete, in play, whereas a system without play is functionally dead: doomed to perfectly rational but lifeless exactitude because it has followed to its conclusion the structural impulse to foreclose play . . . the very idea of structure is essentially a rational instrument that has the goal of all putatively rational systems to . . . exclude play as much as possible, to the extent of achieving total rigidity.
  —Elizabeth Deeds Ermarth, *Sequel to History: Postmodernism and the Crisis of Representational Time*

The contemporary city is a process of construction and assemblage entailing contingent associations and juxtapositions. Minor, or supplemental, texts—what might be termed minor architectures—emblematize the myriad possibilities and multiple voices at work in the life-world (*Lebenswelt*) around us. This diverse plenitude has spawned many questions about urbanism in Western culture. With a dissimulating approach to the contemporary city, I attempt to situate what I call, after Walter Benjamin, a redemptive critique of urbanism in architecture. Derived from the Hegelian concept of *Aufhebung* (sublation), Benjamin's redemptive critique implies the simultaneous negation and preservation of the past whereby the contents of tradition are dialectically preserved in a different, "redeemed" form. The critique aims to gain access to the increasingly remote "recesses of past life" so that culture—memory—can be preserved.[2] Formulated as an antidote to cultural oblivion, *Aufhebung* illuminates the remnants of the past precisely at the moment of their disappearance.[3] The momentary apprehension of remnants of cultural production is not a nostalgic enterprise, however, but a search for the underlying connective tissue between the past and the present—the primal continuum that flows through time. The negation of the past does not govern the dialectical process of *Aufhebung,* but rather enables its preservation, for "this fleeting image of truth is not the process of exposure which destroys the secret, but a revelation which does it justice."[4] Moreover, Benjamin's version of *Aufhebung* renounces purely idealist contemplation—along with its habit of illusory remedies—by recognizing that the resolution of problems inherent in the life-world can only be accomplished in the sphere of material life itself.[5] When applied to our urban environment this approach suggests that it is not necessary to reiterate the past in order to rebuild, nor is the promulgation of additional theories (and with them the comprehensive displacement of the past) or the formation of new technologies necessary to recovering the dynamic qualities inherent in the life of the city. The development of a viable urbanism instead necessitates a regard for the practical and immediate conditions—not to mention the effects—that inform the daily life of cities. Even latter-day technological advances portend representative impulses which constitute the essential, vital drives of the human condition. A redemptive practice of urbanism recognizes the flow of human experience as a continual, regenerative process.

The practices of architectural urbanism must address the dense panoply of human experiences and their affects, many of them marginalized as extrinsic or minor. These experiences enable and frame the conditions in which and through which the working mechanisms of the city—political and infrastructural mechanisms—present themselves to the world. A redemptive critique must begin with an understanding of the profound failure of the modern imagination in the West. Two principal concepts have provided the ground upon which modern thought is constructed: totalization and rationalization. The overarching motif of both is the modern project of history, a history which casts an objective, cognitive light on world events and cultural aspirations. Indicative of our primary mode of intellectual and material production in the West, the modern project of history has enormous implications for the built environment. Through excessive theorizing as well as the application of abstract models to the built environment, the tendencies inherent in modern historical thought have presented an exclusive, rather than inclusive, approach to the conditions that inform modern life. The violence of history's project for architecture is a violence that has been inflicted not only on the past but also on the collective vision for the future. Aided and abetted by modernity's embrace of totalization (*Ganzheitlichkeit*) and rationalization (*Rationalisierung;* also, *Vereinfachung*), history's effects on modern urbanism cannot be underestimated or overstated.[6]

In his discussion of Paul Klee's *Angelus Novus* in the essay "Theses on the Philosophy of History," Benjamin recognized the ramifications of the universal project of the West.[7] Benjamin regarded the doctrine of historical progress and its corresponding frame of mind as single-mindedly scientific or causal, and cautioned against its totalizing effects. Benjamin's critique encapsulates a set of issues that have had extraordinary resonance in the development of twentieth-century intellectual thought in general and modern urbanism in particular. These issues may be represented in architectural terms as an overarching project or plan orientation, thus predisposing them to a scientific frame of mind and, as such, resisting contingencies and circumstances.[8] Yet in a critical slippage, universal history—the progressive history that provides the undertext for the apocalyptic visions of Western development—is principally an article of faith.[9] Not without a good deal of irony, this way of formulating history appears to be made up of operational mechanisms largely devoid of human intervention. The imagination of the Christian West is bound up with the sense of an unrelenting trajectory, a pursuit of tragic absolutes. Historical progress in the West, like the ineluctable project of development, relies on a set of fixed constructs that are, at least in this sense, inert to the possibilities of being otherwise.[10] A critique of the modern project of urbanism must subvert the tendency to approach problems in terms of projects or plans, teleology, and linear and prospective unfolding by seeking to construct an urbanism disposed to play, multiply, and diversify. This critique must not be pursued as an overarching prolegomenon (indeed it cannot), but rather as a *practice*. It must be put into play; it must be shown.

Two projects that attempt redemptive critiques of modern urbanism are Kurt Schwitters's conceptual project for the *Merzing* of Berlin, exemplified by his highly personal diagnosis of Germany's pathology in his better known *Merzbau*, and Walter Benjamin's *Passagen-Werk*, also known as the Arcades Project. Both projects were developed during the 1920s and 1930s and, while there is no evidence of an association between Schwitters and Benjamin, the projects could be said to parallel one another. Schwitters's Hannover *Merzbau*, begun as early as 1921 and continuing sporadically up to the point of his forced emigration from Nazi Germany in 1938, constituted a private, highly autobiographical extension of his literary and artistic productions. The work represented a *Carceri*-like phantasmagoria or dream grotto composed of the material detritus of late nineteenth and early twentieth century Hannover.[11] Benjamin's *Passagen-Werk*, begun in 1927 and continued until his suicide in 1940, was, in similar mode, an attempt to apprehend the image-fantasies or collective wish-images that become "harbingers of a new order."[12] Depicting the Parisian arcades as representative of the "phantasmagoria of the nineteenth-century," Benjamin's project was to be a literary exhumation of the rudiments of modernity's prehistory (*Urgeschichte*).[13] As was the case with Schwitters's *Merzbau*, Benjamin's Arcades Project was developed largely in private, though the mention of its undertaking populates his correspondence during the period.[14]

In excavating the ruins of the past in the material of the present, both projects sought to apprehend the underlying consciousness(es) that conditioned the modern psyche, yet neither Schwitters nor Benjamin subscribed to Sigmund Freud's description of latent or unconscious meanings; rather, in the manner of the surrealists, the two men believed in the "manifest content of the dream images themselves."[15] Though thoroughly involved with the various issues that informed more prominent versions of Modern art and architecture, neither man sought to fully incorporate himself into contemporary literary or artistic movements

Kurt Schwitters, *Hanover Merzbau,* c. 1925.

but instead stood outside—even to the side—in their preferences for alternative critiques of modern assimilation. Both men operated against the prevailing *Zeitgeist:* while each could be said to have attended to the literal materials of modern life, neither engaged in what Jürgen Habermas has characterized as the "universalism of the West."[16] Promulgating what may be regarded as redemptive practices, their works did not unfold in a linear, teleological manner; one could not assume either a plan or a clear set of hypothetical premises. Both dealt instead with the temporal contingencies of the urban environment in a highly personal, albeit abstruse, fashion.

Gifted with profound literary imaginations, Schwitters and Benjamin expressed the need for redemption, albeit a redemption without recourse to transcendence.[17] In many ways autobiographically motivated, their works wander episodically through space and time, cultivating melancholic themes of disease, death, and decay. Both individuals were burdened with a saturnine disposition, a somewhat erratic psychological profile that produces a near-sighted tendency to move slowly, indirectly, sideways.[18] The world did not present itself to Schwitters or Benjamin in a clear way, but seemed confounding and opaque. Yet consistent with the melancholic's temperament, neither man saw the need to overcome the situation, but rather sought to negotiate a path through the miasma by means of creative production. This formulation of redemptive (creative) practice implies a parallel recognition of the progenitive forces inherent in nature's tendency to (re)create and recover itself. Schwitters and Benjamin benefited from the legacy of German romanticism, an intellectual and artistic heritage that was remarked on by their contemporaries.[19] While their methods were discursive, they were discursive in the minor sense, comprised of a series of rambling run-ons that densely, paratactically interweave circumstances and contingencies resulting in a tactical rather than transcendent or strategic response to given conditions. As Richard Sieburth remarks in his article "Benjamin the Scrivener":

> By deploying [the] materials [of the Arcades Project] into a rhythm of caesurae it will break the illusion that anything like continuity or causality connects past to present . . . history is not a cumulative, additive narrative in which the uninterrupted syntagm of time flows homogeneously from past to future, but rather a montage where any moment may enter into sudden adjacency with another. History as parataxis—time scattered through space like stars, its course no longer taking the form of progress but leaping forth in the momentary flashes of dialectical constellations.[20]

Denying taxonomic regulation, the men dispensed with subordinate and connective clauses, thereby diffusing the possibility of dictating—or even indicating—an overall plot or plan.

In short, no argument was made, no single story told. Such an approach directly counters the tendency of most intellectual production to "state, qualify, and conclude."[21]

Schwitters and Benjamin developed their respective works during a period of extended crises in Western culture. Both foresaw the inevitable conclusion of a chain of events, "the catastrophe which keeps piling wreckage upon wreckage."[22] By excavating and reassembling the ruins of the past, Schwitters and Benjamin endeavored to grasp the underlying conditions that informed the present, perhaps in order to find a way out of—or around—an inexorable future. Though both possessed prophetic insights, neither sought refuge in idealism or ideological categories, nor did they try to provide answers to the startling and highly conflicted conditions of modern life. In attempting to provide a redemptive critique of Western culture, they immersed themselves in the experience of modernity itself. While their field of inquiry was the modern city and their method one of allegory, their ultimate aim was to propose a redemptive, practical critique of Western culture, however tentative their offerings appear in retrospect.

The modern project of history in architecture

As is manifest of utopian sentiments, the modern project of history in the West is a process of totalization (*Ganzheitlichkeit*). Its "universal sweep" excludes the nonessential so far as to presume that anything outside its ordained contract be understood as nonexistent.[23] Ever encompassing, the modernist conception of time as history represents a projective, teleological unfolding based on "development and stagnation, crisis and cycle, the accumulation of the past, the surplus of the dead."[24] Time is an essentially linear construct that motivates and necessitates a series of successively refined developments (*Entwicklungen*).[25] As the nearly universal sociosymbolic contract of most, if not all, political discourse in the West, the pursuit of absolute perfection requires the marshaling of intellectual, economic, and material resources in its war on excess and want. Multiplicity, diversity, and lack are run down and incorporated into the larger project or plan fueled by rationalizing constructs such as efficiency quotients, logistics, and quantitative prerogatives which provide—and promote—the mechanisms of capitalist corporations and bureaucratic organizations.[26]

This tendency toward totalization, refined during the large-scale conflicts of the late-nineteenth and twentieth centuries, informs not only our notions of time, but also of space. This is the case with the modernist formulation of urbanism, which is reminiscent in both concept and deed of large-scale military projects.[27] Such urban constructs as Le Corbusier's

Plan Voisin, City for Three Million Inhabitants, and Ste. Die proposals; Ludwig Hilberseimer's Hochhausstadt Project; Hannes Meyer's Co-op Vitrine; and Ivan Leonidov's Magnitogorsk proposals as well as such derivative exemplars as Lucio Costa and Oscar Niemeyer's Brasília represent attempts to promote similar measures of totalization.

For the West, temporal (dialectical) history—the history of Hegel and his adherents—organizes and structures (*Aufbau*) our consciousness, not only of the world that surrounds us and of ourselves with respect to this world, but of each other as interrelated subjects. The politics of this project cannot be overemphasized. Traditional approaches to urbanism in architecture substantiate Jürgen Habermas's critique of the "universalism of the West," a hegemonic position whose manifestations have been under attack since the high point of its Enlightenment-Romantic articulation, modernism.[28]

In *The Archaeology of Knowledge*, Michel Foucault argues that modernism is the "highest" ultimate elaboration of the Cartesian-Newtonian world view and all it implies: the supremacy of the sciences and technology as seen in architecture, rules, principles, technology, and the "deification" of method. Yet even science pays homage to a more commanding narrative—or metanarrative—that of History.[29] Motivated by a thinking process disposed to state, qualify, and conclude, the modernist conception of History represents a "universal sweep," a housecleaning of all that is judged extrinsic to its grandiose project. Dialectical notions of progress facilitate the ability to unify and divide simultaneously, eradicating questions of difference. By definition, the historian is an individual who creates the necessary categories and causal diagrams that enable him or her to effectively "keep the world in mind."[30] Theory becomes the governing principle, relegating the contingencies, accidents, and circumstances of the life-world—practice—to a secondary position. Hence, the project of History itself, represented by Hegel as the *Idea, Mind,* or *Spirit (Geist)*—is wholly determined and determining.[31] Hegel's version of dialectical history (further enacted in the Marxist "rule of progress") complicated, or for some simplified, the means and ends, portending ever greater efficiency, economy, and harmony.[32] Hegel's thesis on the philosophy of history states:

> The sole thought which philosophy brings to the treatment of history is the simple concept of Reason—that Reason is the law of the world and that, therefore, in world history, things have come about rationally.[33]

Implicit in this view of history is the presumption of a world separate from the perceiving subject. The subject is no longer immersed in the world of experience, dependent on the whims of an inscrutable God, but hovers above or outside of temporal and spatial experience.

The mind and body are separated into two distinct, if conflicted, realms, with the mind *(res cogitans)* taking precedence. Benefited by the transcendent faculty of reason, the thinking subject has the ability to "keep the world in mind" by projecting him- or herself into the object-world. In so doing, he or she cognitively (theoretically) apprehends, codifies, and rationalizes the work. Part of this apprehension is the ability to grasp (establish a perspective on, represent), an ability that is contingent on *method.*

Rationalization: the eyes have it

> *Turbantibus aequora ventis: pockets of turbulence scattered in flowing liquid, be it air or salt water, breaking up the parallelism of its repetitive waves. The sweet voices of the physics of Venus. How can your heart not rejoice as the flood waters abate* (décliner) *and the primordial waters begin to form, since in the same lofty position you escape from Mars and from his armies that are readying in perfect battle formation? In these lofty heights that have been strengthened by the wisdom of the sages, one must choose between these two sorts of physics.*
>
> —Michel Serres[34]

William Ivins, in the preamble to his book on perspective entitled *The Rationalization of Sight*, states that "science and technology are predicated on the power of invariant pictorial symbolization."[35] Leon Battista Alberti's 1436 work *Della Pittura*, the first complete treatise on perspective method in painting, marked, according to Ivins, perhaps the single most important discovery since the Middle Ages. Heralding the dawn of the modern age, the mechanics of perspective enabled the subject, albeit from an individual point of view, to represent the object-world in a logical, rational, and consistent manner. Even more important, the world could be apprehended absolutely and in its entirety.[36] Nothing could be, nor would be, left outside the frame or in the margins. While privileging sight as the *bon sens* of the rational mind, perspective was also an orientation device by which and through which one could perceive space—and time—as absolute and infinite, yet within the purview of human knowledge.[37] Perspective became a new means of exercising control and may, as such, be regarded as the first space-time machine.

The modernist conception of the city borrows the capacities of perspective: the rationalization of sight *and site.* In selecting, codifying, and authorizing both the divine and profane *telos* rationally and truthfully, the time and space of the city is not experienced in the manner of immersion, but conceptualized as a plan or project manifest in absolute time and space. In this sense, the city constitutes, in Newtonian terms, reality at a distance. It is over there and out there or, in Heideggerian terms, *beyond.* Transmuting Friedrich Nietzsche's critique "On the Advantages and Disadvantages of History for Life," urban conditions are effectively normalized, perceived *on the horizon,* for modern man—that is, historical man. Our perspectively oriented gaze, projected as a plan, is necessarily future oriented, beyond real time and space, directed instead towards infinity.[38] Life—the vital, circumstantial contingencies of human activity—is perpetually deferred elsewhere. Scientifically oriented approaches to urban planning, dependent as they are on quantifiable causes and effects, are predisposed to thoroughly, if not always efficiently, negate chance, excess, and marginalia. According to Elizabeth Deeds Ermarth, the modernist conception of the city, immutable and universal, "transcends particulars and always exceeds them . . . in a convention that extends the rationalizing powers of human attention. No atrocity need remain unexplained, no mystery unsolved, no mistake unrectified."[39]

Homo fabricans

> *Play is the function that distinguishes living systems from dead ones . . . provides possibilities of continuing substitution and improvisation, exists in constant tension with structure that limits play.*
>
> —Elizabeth Deeds Ermarth[40]

Recent scholarship has promoted the "end of modernity."[41] For Foucault, our current staging of critical dispensation, if it may be called that, is also the crisis of the subject, whereby *Homo cogitans* (Claude Lévi-Strauss's engineer) becomes instead *Homo fabricans* (his *bricoleur* or constructor). No longer is there a subject-object dialectic, but rather the topic of discourse (history, all forms of human knowledge) *is the subject* and the subject's activity as he or she exists in a world that is as it is *how it is,* to borrow from Samuel Beckett.[42] The object-world can no longer be rendered in depth, harbored in absolute time and space, and perceived perspectively from an objective point of view. Instead it disappears into arrangement and pattern, fluctuating and fluid. In turn, the crisis of the subject dissolves the basis of and for a totalizing project of space and time.[43] A plurality of discourses replaces the hegemony of the modernist canon. Narratives proliferate, multiplying in accordance with the activities of *Homo fabricans.* Alternately, space and time are redefined as a function of position, a dimension of particular events, always described in terms of language, because in general, "the confinement of language to history (history as linear, language as a linear sequence)

Kurt Schwitters, *Merz-column,* Hanover, c. 1925.

has been *literal* throughout Western discourse."[44] Again, the alternative does not deny the voice of modernism as a legitimate discourse; rather, it questions its totalizing effects—as well as its affects. Whereas the discourse of modernism as we know it promotes "totality, infinity, truth, identity, and exclusion in all its guises," thereby delimiting thinking, voices of a more critical turn of mind suggest that we seek to promote an open work, making allowances for alternative texts, circumnavigations—simply, other kinds of order.[45]

Merzbau

> *Dada was the materialization of my disgust. Before Dada, all modern writers held fast to a discipline, a rule, a unity. After Dada, active indifference, spontaneity, and relativity entered into life . . .*
> *If it is the INTELLECTUAL DRIVE which has always existed and which Apollonaire called the NEW SPIRIT (L'Esprit Nouveau), you wish to speak to me about, I must say that modernism interests me NOT AT ALL. And I believe it is a mistake to say that DADA, CUBISM, and FUTURISM have a common base. The two latter tendencies were based primarily on a principle of intellectual and technical perfectibility while Dada never rested on any theory and has never been anything but a protest. Poetry is a means of communicating a certain amount of humanity, of vital elements that the poet has within himself.*
>
> —Tristan Tzara[46]

The German artist Kurt Schwitters might initially seem an unlikely candidate for participation in a critical debate on architecture and urbanism. Even his position as an artist and architect is difficult to characterize. Yet a number of ideas in his works bear consideration, not the least of which concern modern life and the city.

While Schwitters's work—an extensive panoply of paintings, collages, assemblages, literary works, and performances—appears to run the gamut of the avant-garde, his overall intention remains the same across his media. Aesthetic production provided Schwitters the means for mediating between art and reality, whereby the transparency of art and life could be recognized.[47] Like his compatriot Tristan Tzara, a principle voice of the Dadaists, Kurt Schwitters spoke out against the delimiting and totalizing effects of scientific modernism. Though he is most often associated with the various Dadaist movements, it is important to understand the exceptional nature of Schwitters's artistic and literary productions.[48] His influences—which he both acknowledged and promoted liberally—included Hans Arp, Raoul Hausmann, El Lissitzky, and Theo van Doesburg. At first glance many of his collages

and assemblages mirror the works of these artists and could be critiqued as highly derivative, but Schwitters's tendency to appropriate, while at the same time pay homage to his
colleagues, is actually a deliberate aspect of his overall intentions.[49] To him, the work of art
did not represent an inviolate object but was instead an organic enterprise, one that could
be worked on—or, as he put it, "worked through"—repeatedly. Artistic production represented a dynamic unfolding that was itself ever changing, a part of the same generative
forces that shaped the natural world.

In claiming aesthetic production as an extension of the creative forces of life, Schwitters
resisted the protests of many of his Dada compatriots, some of whom saw his creative work
as deeply nostalgic or, at the least, derivative. He also resisted any consignment to the political ideologies that motivated the works of other avant-garde artists, stating at one point
that art must remain pure of explicit political associations. For this he paid a price. Because
the work of Richard Huelsenbeck provided the nucleus for the Berlin Dadaists, Schwitters's
artistic program was largely marginalized in Berlin due to Schwitters's tendency to repeatedly criticize the political nature of Huelsenbeck's project.[50] Accordingly, Schwitters countered
what he perceived to be Dada's negative tendencies by developing a "third way"—an affir-
mation of art and life through creative means, and in so doing, he fabricated and constructed his own movement. This movement, of which he was the sole member, was called *Merz*.

Merz is an arbitrary and meaningless word fragment culled from the German word
Kommerzbank (bank of commerce) which appeared by chance in one of Schwitters's earlier
collages.[51] Under the umbrella of his own movement, Schwitters stressed not only protest
and revolution, but also what might be regarded as an "aesthetic of redemption."[52] The
words Schwitters used to describe his conceptual apparatus and method for his literary and
visual works were *Entformung* and *Formung*.[53] *Entformung*, a neologism of Schwitters's invention, translates roughly as the "metamorphosis" or "dissociation" of form from its originary
context. *Formung* entails the (re)forming of the work from the artifacts and materials that
had been dissociated.[54] In the terms of his art, *Entformung* and *Formung* meant the transformation or transubstantiation of the old into the new, the "making [of] new art from the
remains of a former culture."[55] Yet the goal was not the radical replacement of the past with
the present—the temporal and modern—but rather the preservation of remnants of the
past in the present. Schwitters's process was similar to the Hegelian concept of *Aufhebung*
(sublation). His poems, collages, and assemblages were fashioned from the material detritus
and fragments, the *Abfall* and *Banalitäten* (banalities), of modern culture. By dissociating
the materials and fragments from their normative context, their *Eigengift* (the specific mark
of use, context, or personality) is effaced. The "esthetic cleansing" of Schwitters's formula

implies that Schwitters felt a need to re-create reality in a way that undermined the chaos and incessant change indigenous to modern culture. Not only was the world made anew, but the context itself was reconstituted in a way that mirrored nature's ability to recover and re-create itself.[56]

John Elderfield has characterized Schwitters's work as an urban art. Indeed, the source of much of his material, like many—if not most—of the Dadaists, was, both literally and figuratively, the city. Schwitters considered becoming an architect, though he completed only two semesters of study at the Technical University in his hometown of Hannover before resuming his artistic career.[57] He nonetheless maintained a significant interest in architecture. Architectural projects and programs for architecture were often featured in his self-published journal *Merz,* and in the mid-1920s, Schwitters examined the possibility of starting a journal that would be devoted exclusively to architecture. Over the course of his career he wrote various critical essays on the work of architects he supported. In the 1926 article "Kunst und Zeiten," he stated his support for Theo van Doesburg, El Lissitzky, Mies van der Rohe, and Ludwig Hilberseimer, among others.[58] In an article published in *Der Sturm* on the Weissenhof Exhibition ("Stuttgart die Wohnung Werkbundausstellung"), he reiterated his support for Mies van der Rohe: "Mies van der Rohe has designed to good effect; instead of varied, the house is straightforward and is sited correctly."[59] He also stated his support for Hilberseimer's work, referring to his Weissenhof projects as "basic, normal, and devoid of daydreams."[60] In the same article, he suggested that Le Corbusier is a "romantic genius" who is not concerned with practical issues—the opposite of Hilberseimer—while the works of architects Peter Behrens and Hans Poelzig were "modern in the prevailing sense"—that is, trendy.[61] Hugo Häring's work is considered singularly functional, while Walter Gropius's house is of interest because of its use of new materials. Other architects Schwitters mentioned include Victor Bourgeois, a French architect he praised highly; the Dutch architects J. J. P. Oud and Willem Marinus Dudok; and the Germans Mart Stam and Bruno Taut.

While it is difficult to understand how Schwitters might align himself with Mies van der Rohe, Ludwig Hilberseimer, and Walter Gropius given his own creative practice, Schwitters saw all of them as being in one way or another under the Dada umbrella. Schwitters understood Dada (to which he did and did not subscribe, since this too was "all part of the game") as a "mirror of the times . . . it reflected not only the old and dead part of tradition but also the new and vital."[62] In this sense, Mies, Hilberseimer, and Gropius were, according to Schwitters, Dadaists. Yet in his search for the ultimate synthesis of nature, spirit, and form, Schwitters dissociated himself from the mainstream Dada organizations, aligning *Merz* with various other avant-garde movements throughout the 1920s. His attempts to formulate his vision for art present a confusing and at times conflicting set of ideas. Yet the inconsistency and complexity of his research is a function of Schwitters's process and is, in this sense, utterly consistent: the seemingly endless array of articles and pieces reflect the constant metamorphosis and growth of his personal development through creative activity. In an article he wrote for the English magazine *Ray* in 1927, Schwitters discusses how the work of art, in being like Nature *(Natur)*, is essentially an organic enterprise, "a new natural(ism)," becoming like nature itself.[63] Comparing a drawing by Lissitzky to a crystal and Mies van der Rohe's skyscraper to the "austere construction of an upper thighbone," Schwitters adjoined the idea of unity in nature with machine-age themes; Elderfield describes this as "an organicist version of Elementarist theory."[64] To Schwitters, form was not an immutable entity, but merely the *Stilstand* of the dialectical process: "Every form is the frozen instantaneous picture of a process. Thus a work of art is a stopping place on the road of becoming and not the fixed goal."[65] The vitality of modern technology depended on the fact that man was ultimately the one who had engendered technological development. To Schwitters, Mies van der Rohe's works from the late teens and early twenties appeared to embrace the organicist principle of dynamic flux—a principle to which not only the Dadaists subscribed, but is found in Lissitzky's formulation of constructivism as well. Schwitters's perception of flow in Mies' works was not only figurative, but in assuming the organic nature of technological processes, provided the conceptual apparatus as well.

Schwitters's first architectonic projects were a series of *Merz* "sculptures." One of these, *Schloss und Kathedrale mit Hofbrunnen* (Castle and Cathedral with Courtyard Well), is clearly an attempt to assert himself as a visionary architect. The sculpture, a photograph of which accompanied an article Schwitters prepared for publication in Bruno Taut's expressionist journal *Frühlicht,* is similar to the visionary projects of the German Expressionist architects Hans Scharoun, Hermann Finsterlin, and Bruno Taut.[66] In the article, also titled "Schloss und Kathedrale mit Hofbrunnen," Schwitters detailed both the concept and method for a *Merz*-architecture. Mirroring the sentiments of many of expressionism's goals, *Merz*-architecture aimed to create and develop new forms *(neue Gestaltung)*.[67] The use of the castle and cathedral as principle themes suggests Schwitters's subscription to the expressionist notion of *Gesamtkunstwerk* (total work of art). In an earlier article entitled "Merz," published in the Munich-based journal *Der Ararat,* Schwitters was even more explicit in this regard:

My aim is the total work of art *(Gesamtkunstwerk),* which combines all branches of art into an artistic unit . . . first I combined individual categories of art. I have pasted poems from words and sentences so as to produce a rhythmic design. I have on the other hand pasted up pictures and draw-

Kurt Schwitters, *Hanover Merzbau*, c. 1925.

BURNS GAMARD

ings so that sentences could be read in them. I have driven nails into pictures so as to produce a plastic relief apart from the pictorial quality of the paintings. I did so as to efface the boundaries between the arts.[68]

While being closely affiliated with van Doesburg, Lissitzky, Hilberseimer, and Mies van der Rohe, Schwitters never actually executed buildings. His only urban proposal, itself an allusion to the possibilities of achieving an urban *Gesamtkunstwerk,* was detailed at some length in the *Frühlicht* article. Conceived as a *Merzkunstwerk* (a *Merz*-artwork) for the city of Berlin, the proposal was an obvious play on the idea of the *Gesamtkunstwerk.* Similar to his collages from the same period, Schwitters's conceptual project for the *"Merzing* of Berlin" entailed the "working through" of both old and new—in this case architecture—in order to form a unified whole. This "working through"—which he referred to as the absorption of both beautiful and ugly buildings, required the appropriation of superior rhythms (*übergeordneten Rhythmus*) in the manner of "correctly distributed accents" or focal points (*richtiges Verteilen der Akzente*) and materials. The city was to be transformed from a set of fragmentary episodes into a continuous, if reconstituted, fabric of light and color, whereby the "important centers" would naturally correspond with the "nodes of circulation." *Merz*-architecture, in clarifying the nature of the city, would add a "significant degree of value to the center of the city."[69]

While formulating his program for a *Merz*-architecture, Schwitters also produced a series of quasi-architectonic assemblages that presage not only the ideas but the methodology he would undertake in the development of his *Merzbau.* These sculptures did not entail the same "working through" that one finds in the collages, but maintain a distinctly figurative quality. Nor are they similar in nature to the fantastical synthesis of his expressionist work *Schloss und Kathedrale mit Hofbrunnen.* The titles themselves—*Die heilige Bekümmernis* (Holy Affliction), *Der Lustgalgen* (the Pleasure Gallows), *Die Kultpumpe* (the Cult Pump), and *Haus Merz* (Merz House)—contain traces of both Expressionism and Dada and are transitional, albeit talismanic, episodes to what would become the literal and figurative center of his existence: the *Merzbau.*

A detailed outline of the contents of the *Merzbau* presents an enigmatic array of material and literary sources. They include "Das Biedermeierzimmer" (the Biedermeier Room), "Das Stijlzimmer" (the de Stijl Room), "Die Goethehöhle" (the Goethe Cave), "Die Nibelungenhöhle" (the Nibelungen Cave), "Die Arphöhle" (the Arp Cave), "Die Goldgrotte" (the Gold Grotto), "Die Mieshöhle" (the Mies Cave), "Die Freundschafthöhlen" (Caves of Friendship), "Das Ruhrgebeit" (a model of the Ruhr valley area of Germany, with "authentic brown coal and glass coke"), "Der Kyffhäuser" (a model of the mythological mountain in the Black Forest region, complete with a "stone table"), and "Die Luthersecke" (Luther's Corner). Also included in the *Merzbau* were a "submerged personal-union city" of Brauns-chweig-Lüneberg with houses from Weimar by Lyonel Feininger, Persil advertisements, Schwitters's design for the official emblem of the city of Karlsrühe, the "Sex-Crime Cavern" with the "mutilated corpse of a young girl painted tomato red with splendid votive offer-ings," a sculpture of Mona Hausmann ("in homage to Raoul Hausmann"), the "10% disabled war veteran," "das Bordell" (the Brothel), "Sodom and Gomorrah," the "Madonna," and the "Cross of the Redeemer." By some accounts there were over forty grottoes in all. Schwitters's materials list included "approximately 100 bags of plaster, an equal quantity of wood and plywood; 70 kilograms of spackle putty; 70 kilograms of paint; and 30 kilograms of varnish."[70]

While the existence of many of these artifacts and "allegorical" units are largely derived from anecdotal evidence, it is possible to assume that Schwitters's project was not merely a formal enterprise, but a compelling cultural, albeit highly personal, assemblage of the time and space of the city—in this case the city of Hannover, Germany.[71] Begun in 1923, the *Merzbau* was left unfinished when Schwitters, pursued by the Gestapo, fled Hannover in 1937.[72] Completely destroyed in the Allied bombing raids of 1943, remaining knowledge of the *Merzbau* constitutes Schwitters's greatest legacy. A vast and complex yet highly concentrated assemblage, it has been described as an odd amalgam of medieval and Piranesian influences, a *Carceri*-like *Kathedrale* containing multiple grottoes (caves), votives, and shrines housing both sacred and profane objects. Its growth was endless and nearly boundless, originating in the corner of Schwitters's atelier with *Der Erste Tag Merz-säule* (The First Day *Merz*-column). Assuming what might be referred to as biblical proportions, the *Merzbau* eventually took over four rooms in Schwitters's apartment (though it has been suggested that the project was even more extensive). The work extended into the apartment on the floor above and finally, in its latter phases, into the attic.[73] Like an unchecked growth, the *Merzbau* eventually made its way out onto the rear balcony and down the side of the house, terminating, if only for the moment, in a cistern in the side yard. Yet despite its role as the center of Schwitters's art and life, he did not publicly admit to its existence until 1931.[74] It was clearly his "private world, idealized and primordial, a diary at a grand scale."[75]

Considered to be a kind of "phantasmagoria and dream grotto," the project, also referred to by Schwitters as *Die Kathedrale des Erotischen Elends* (The Cathedral of Erotic Misery), was made up of layer upon layer of ever increasing density and sculptural effect.[76] Thought to be as many as six layers deep in some areas, its autobiographical nature was undeniable. For some who saw it, the *Merzbau* represented the uncanny. To others it was suggestive of a reli-gious experience, even a holy place. In 1927, Rudolf Jahns, upon visiting Schwitters's atelier, described the *Merzbau* in these terms:

[Upon entering the *Merzbau*, I] experienced a strange, enrapturing feeling. This room had a very special life of its own. The sound of my footsteps faded away and there was absolute silence. There was only the form of the grotto whirling around me, and when I was able to find words to describe it they alluded to the absolute in art. I saw the grotto again soon afterwards, and it had changed once more.[77]

For others, the project was more benign, a three-dimensional representation of the collective process of Schwitters's overarching mission, *Merz*. Alfred Dudelsack described the *Merzbau* as follows:

[It was] a carpentry shop . . . Planks, cigar-chests, wheels for a perambulator for MERZ-sculptures, various carpentry tools for the "nailed-together" pictures (collages), are lying between bundles of newspapers, as are the necessary materials for the ANNA BLUME poems. With loving care, broken light switches, damaged neckties, colored lids from Camembert cheese boxes, colored buttons torn off of clothes, and tram tickets are all stored up to find a grateful use in future creations.[78]

Though the chaotic collection of planks, cigar-chests, and broken light switches in Schwitters's studio might be viewed as merely a series of found objects gathered for "grateful use in future creations," there was a profound motive underlying the materials and works assembled in the *Merzbau*. In his 1931 article "Ich und meine Zeile" (I and my Direction), Schwitters wrote a lengthy explanation of his artistic intentions, an explanation that clearly suggests the religiosity he conferred on the work.

Do not consider this work to be a blaspheme of the concept of divinity, [a concept] which has gathered humanity together for millennia, and which has broken down national and social barriers, and has presented us with beautiful art. *The immersion in art, like the immersion in religious faith,* liberates man from the worries of daily life.[79]

To still others, Schwitters's *Merzbau* represented a deeply troubled psychology, or at the very least, a melancholic's dispensation.[80] For the museum director Alexander Dorner, a supporter of the avant-garde, Schwitters's construction was appalling and unsettling, "the free expression of the socially uncontrolled self who had here bridged the gap between sanity and madness." El Lissitzky and his wife, Sophie Küppers, expressed similar views, stating that they too were unable to "draw the line between originality and madness."[81] According to Käte Traumann Steinitz, the *Merzbau* represented "a hallucinatory confusion of tiny fetish objects displayed like specimens in glass boxes: a miniature theater of the absurd. In each cave was a sediment of impressions and emotions with significant literary and symbolic allusions."[82] Richard Huelsenbeck's eyewitness account refers to Schwitters's own take on the work, albeit according to his usual playful, if ironic, cast.

> This tower or tree or house had apertures, concavities, and hollows in which Schwitters said he kept souvenirs, photos, birth dates, and other respectable and less respectable data. The room was a mixture of hopeless disarray and meticulous accuracy. You could see incipient collages, wooden sculptures, pictures of stone and plaster. Books, whose pages rustled in time to our steps, were lying about. Materials of all kinds, rags, limestone, cufflinks, logs of all sizes, newspaper clippings . . . We asked him for details, but Schwitters shrugged, "It's all crap."[83]

In a 1930 article, Schwitters publicly recounted for the first time the ideas that surrounded the construction of the *Merzbau.* He alluded to the transitional, vital nature of his project:

> As the structure grows bigger and bigger, valleys, hollows, caves appear, and these lead a life of their own within the overall structure. The juxtaposed surfaces give rise to forms twisting in every direction, spiraling upward. An arrangement of the most strictly geometric cubes covers the whole, underneath which shapes are curiously bent or otherwise twisted until their complete dissolution is achieved . . . But the column has been under construction for seven years and has taken on a more and more severely formal character, in keeping with my spiritual development, especially insofar as the outer sculpture is concerned. The overall impression is thus more or less reminiscent of Cubist painting or Gothic architecture (not a bit!).[84]

Like Joseph Cornell, Schwitters was indeed the "modernized Piranesi of the *Carceri,* a connoisseur of fragments and spiritual homelessness."[85] An inveterate collector, he salvaged perishable fragments—the "refuse (*Abfall*) of modernity"—building on them in such a way that may initially have seemed almost disinterested or merely compositional. However, the work was highly charged with residual affects. In a manner not unlike Walter Benjamin's nineteenth-century figures, the collector and the flaneur, Schwitters was obsessed by the transitory existence of the everyday, assembling "a picturesque collection of the used, tawdry, and unnoticed." His special brand of activity, that of a deliberative "melancholy and mystery that is conferred on what is picked out of the flux of time," is profoundly elegiac, motivated by a need to create a world removed from its larger context for personal reasons as well as by a desire to apprehend and possess the world, patterning it anew. Like Georg Simmel's "metropolitan man," Schwitters sought to "summon the utmost uniqueness and particularization in order to preserve his most personal core. He had to exaggerate this personal element in order to remain audible even to himself."[86]

Schwitters's *Merzbau* provides innumerable, intriguing venues for a reconceptualization of the urban environment in terms of the articles and artifacts that constitute what most would regard as garbage or refuse. In his book *Modernism and the Posthumanist Subject*, K. Michael Hays suggests a correlation between Mies' skyscrapers and Schwitters's *Merzbau* (*Merz*-column), detailing a latent critique of the modernist city in Schwitters's work:

> It is in the sense of the artistic object as a cognitive-registration mechanism that Mies' skyscraper project can be identified with Kurt Schwitters's *Merz*-column in Hannover begun around the same time. Both projects share an antagonism toward a priori and reasoned order. Both plunge into the chaos of the metropolis to seek another order within it through a systematic use of the unexpected, the aleatory, the inexplicable. Both are objects in crisis. They attest to the fact that the humanist conception of formal rationality and self-creating subjectivity cannot cope with the irrationality of actual experience. In the modern city, such constructs of rationality fail to function, and the mind, the subject, is consequently unable to perceive a pattern in the chaos. At such a moment, the subject has its one opportunity to escape reification: by thinking through what it is that causes reality to appear to be only a collection of fragmented images; by looking for structures and processes operating in time behind what appears to be a given and objectified modality; by constructing, in an aesthetic modality, a cognitive mechanism understood "as a dialectically entwined and explicatively indecipherable unity of concept and matter."[87]

This cognitive mechanism—constructed, according to Hays, as an aesthetic modality—stresses the unity of concept and matter that lies at the very heart of Schwitters's redemptive critique of modernity. In assembling his fragmentary images, he simultaneously negates and preserves—in the manner of *Aufhebung*—the underlying conditions that flow through time. The life-world is illumined in the instant that the work of art reveals itself. The causal nature with which object-artifacts are arranged not only speak to the fading past, but also embrace the remnants of modern technological society. In repeatedly working through these objects, Schwitters enjoins them and preserves them, albeit in a recontextualized form. Thus he embraces the inherent beauty of modern daily life—a daily life informed by an embrace, rather than a rejection, of modern technological development. To apprehend and work through the technological formations as a natural condition was not only to comprehend them, but to renew them according to the technology of human intervention. Rather than a nostalgic retreat, Schwitters wrests the very conditions of modern life from their moorings, thereby redeeming the past in terms of the present. Raoul Hausmann suggested a confrontation with, if not an embrace of, modern technology in the minor, residual artifacts and processes of modern life:

> Naive anthropomorphism has played out its role. The beauty of our daily life is defined by the mannequins, the wig-making skill of the hairdressers, the exactness of a technological construction. We strive anew towards conformity with the mechanical work process: we will have to get used to the idea of seeing art originating in factories.[88]

The artworks portend the critical nature of an increasingly technological society, yet the conditions in which and by which the material world—and life-world—is formulated cannot be denied, but must be reconstituted in terms of a temporal redemption, that is as part of the continuum of human experience. Schwitters's support of Hilberseimer and Mies suggests an embrace of the naked reality of modern life, a reality that is always in flux. The romantic excesses of stylistically motivated versions of modernism represented a superficial solution, or, in the case of Le Corbusier, an architecture that did not respond to the obvious economic, normative conditions of reality, but instead masked them with formal manipulations and affects, leading to a "dangerous" architecture that modeled dynamism, but did not, indeed could not, directly respond to it.[89]

Despite Schwitters's editorial proclamations, he did not entirely relinquish the romantic ideals of expressionism. The *Merzbau* became the site of his continual reformulation, or working through, of romanticism: love, organic unity, loss, and subjective excess. As K. Michael Hays suggests, the *Merzbau* was the primary locus of his attempts to find "patterns in the chaos." Not unlike a *Wunderkammer* (cabinet of wonders), it was the construction site of reflection, as well as the scene of preservation.[90] Though replete with autobiographical details and sentiments, the project embraced expressionism's faith in art and architecture as a redemptive enterprise, one that could enlist the beneficent capacity of human creativity "in order to overcome the hatred amongst peoples."[91]

Paris, Passage du Grand Cerf, 1824–25.

Die Passagen-Werk

CONSTRUCTION SITE: Pedantic brooding over the production of objects—visual aides, toys, books—that are supposed to be suitable for children is folly. Since the Enlightenment this has been one of the mustiest speculations of the pedagogues. Their infatuation with psychology keeps them from perceiving that the world is full of the most unrivaled objects for childish attention and use. And the most specific. For children are particularly fond of haunting any site where things are being visibly worked upon. They are irresistibly drawn by the detritus generated by building, gardening, housework, tailoring, or carpentry. In waste products they recognize the face that the world of things turns directly and solely to them. In using these things they do not so much imitate the world of adults as bring together, in the artifact produced in play, materials of widely differing kinds in a new, intuitive relationship. Children thus produce their own small world of things within the greater one. The norms of this smaller world must be kept in mind if one wished to create things specifically for children, rather than let one's adult activity, through its requisites and instruments, find its own way to them.

—Walter Benjamin, *Einbahnstrasse*[92]

Previously hidden among Theodor Adorno's papers stored in the British Museum in London are Walter Benjamin's writings on the city. These writings, or notes, constitute a material history based on Benjamin's analysis of consumer culture or, more precisely, on the myriad significant and insignificant artifacts that inhabit and inform daily life. In these notes, the Parisian Arcades, or Passages, as they have come to be known, are understood as a framing device, a site for a field of inquiry in which and through which one might cut a section through modernity. In effect, Benjamin's project posited an approach to a comprehensive, though not totalizing, definition of modern culture. In choosing to assess the Arcades, Benjamin tried to apprehend the *Abfall*—the minor voices—that occupy the margins of daily life. In collecting the secondary excesses of modern culture, he pursued a rather elaborate, even Byzantine, methodology of cataloguing and indexing. Benjamin paratactically placed indexed propositions and bits of information side by side without indicating the connecting clauses. The taxonomic relations between these propositions and bits of information therefore remain open to interpretation. The relationships between the particles, or names, could only "be recognized through the interrelations of experience . . . We live in (or as) a name; it is that which we correspond to, a locus of identity, a configuration of experience, a connecting space—a passage."[93] This cataloguing and indexing—a project that remained incomplete at the time of his suicide—provided the constructive means, the material, for an understanding of the city that was not manifest in the logic of the *logos* (such as

Haussmannization). The project is a metaphysical, but highly complex material arrangement that can be apprehended as a dense, textual weaving of multiple venues. The critical nature of modern material culture, manifest in the architecture of the Passages, was not deemed progressive, nor was it subjected to the criteria of a master narrative. Rather than fixed constructs, it was a web of associations, a spatial allegory made up of the materials and artifacts of daily life that mark events:

> This Arcades project can be construed as an encyclopedic unfolding of the historical potential that lies dormant within the word passage . . . It was Louis Aragon's evocation [in *Le Paysan de Paris*] of the demise and demolition of the Passage de l'Opéra that initially provided Benjamin with the metaphor of the arcade as a figure for the ephemeral, the passing, the out-of-date, a dense emblem of that particular (capitalist) logic whereby the New is fated, at an ever-accelerating rate, to fall out of style and plunge into eternal oblivion.[94]

Benjamin observes the fatedness of architecture in terms of the fatedness of history; that is, both "architectural form and the historical process reveal the mythology of modernity." As architectures, albeit architectures that are not understood to contain the status of architecture in terms of History, the Passages provide the name for the condition, as well as the spatial projection of "bourgeois ideology, technological advance, and as a transparent repository of the collective fantasies of nineteenth-century capitalism," an economic process that relies primarily on the city's development and progress. Accordingly, one might "travel along an itinerary that leads away from the history of metaphysics as the history of Being (as metaphysics is aided and abetted by 'naming'), although not toward any fixed point of arrival: it indicates a direction rather than a destination," a direction or path that remains unresolved.[95] One wanders as a *flaneur* through the artifacts and remainders that exist at the margins of our awareness, artifacts that are the circumstances and contingencies that inform the habits of daily life.

Benjamin's approach to the architecture of the city might be construed as a "redemptive critique," one engaged not only with the subject of urbanism but also with intellectual (critical) production in general. This is what Benjamin refers to when he talks about a dialectics of sight and site—a dialectics of seeing.[96] In short, the pursuit of a "thinking eye"— a project akin to that of Paul Klee's pedagogical project—is averse to the merely cognitive, discursive machinations that inform the determinant clause of philosophical production in the West.[97] The proposition entails a spatial-temporal construct of the city rather than as a plan or mapping that represents two-dimensionally, univalently, the binary conditions of this and that, here and there—what might be regarded as our primary mode of constructing thought in the West.[98] In endeavoring to present Paris as a series of contingencies based on the activity of daily life, economic exchange, and architectonic residue, the dynamic space of the city is recovered, albeit replete with its residual (secondary) affects. A multiplicity of venues are brought back into play, in contradistinction to a museum city of carefully designed monuments to culture, and subtle (and not so subtle) control mechanisms. The city—in this case Paris—is regenerative and dynamic, a living entity, because "play is the function that distinguishes living systems from dead ones . . . provides possibilities of continuing substitution and improvisation, exists in constant tension with structure that limits play."[99] The many ways in which the material of the *Passagen-Werk* can be understood is further testament to the potential of such a project: the structure itself is in flux.

Conclusion

> *A living system is always in process, incomplete, in play, whereas a system without play is functionally dead: doomed to perfectly rational but lifeless exactitude because it has followed to its conclusion the structural impulse to foreclose play . . . the very idea of structure is essentially a rational instrument that has the goal of all putatively rational systems to . . .* exclude *play as much as possible, to the extent of achieving total rigidity.*
>
> —Elizabeth Deeds Ermarth[100]

The works of Kurt Schwitters and Walter Benjamin resist prescriptive measures and stress the mesmerizing nature of human creativity's elusive *mysteria:* creative prolegomenas and momentary insights that might act as stations along a path. It is in this sense that architecture, and more specifically the architecture of the city, might be recognized as vital, generative, and redemptive, akin to Ludwig Wittgenstein's "philosophical investigation" of *forms of life.*[101]

Notes

1. Kurt Schwitters, "Letter to Christof Spengemann, July 24, 1946, in *Wir spielen, bis uns der Tod abholt: Briefe aus fünf Jahrzehnten* (Frankfurt-am-Main: Verlag Ullstein, 1974), 210.

2. Richard Wolin, *Walter Benjamin: An Aesthetic of Redemption* (New York: Columbia University Press, 1980), 273–74.

3. As with many of Hegel's concepts, *Aufhebung* is difficult to translate into English. The word that comes closest to *Aufhebung* is "sublation," meaning "to negate or eliminate (as an element in a dialectic process) but preserve as a partial element in a synthesis." *(Merriam Webster's Collegiate Dictionary, Tenth Edition,* 1996).

4. Walter Benjamin, *Trauerspiel* study I, quoted in Susan Buck-Morss, *The Dialectics of Seeing: Walter Benjamin and the Arcades Project* (Cambridge, Mass: MIT Press, 1989), 146.

5. Wolin, 172–74.

6. While rationalization translates simply as *Rationalisierung*, *Vereinfachung* implies simplification or reduction (the simplification of matters). The belief that the secularization of progress (*die Säkulariserung des Fortschritts*) led to the view that history was a rational process is developed by Gianni Vattimo in his book *The End of Modernity,* trans. Jon R. Snyder (Cambridge, Eng.: Polity Press, 1988).

7. Walter Benjamin, "Theses on the Philosophy of History," in *Illuminations,* trans. Harry Zohn, ed. Hannah Arendt (New York: Schocken Books, 1968), 257. The entire quote is as follows: "A Klee painting named *Angelus Novus* shows an angel looking as though he is about to move away from something he is fixedly contemplating. His eyes are staring, his mouth is open, his wings are spread. This is how one pictures the angel of history. His face is turned towards the past. Where we perceive a chain of events, he sees one single catastrophe which keeps piling wreckage upon wreckage and hurls it in front of his feet. The angel would like to stay, awaken the dead, and make whole what has been smashed. But a storm is blowing from Paradise; it has got caught in his wings with such violence that the angel can no longer close them. This storm irresistibly propels him into the future to which his back is turned, while the pile of debris before him grows skyward. This storm is what we call progress (history)."

8. For example, Kenneth Frampton argues that Le Corbusier was given to a "dialectical habit of mind," or binary thinking.

In the manner of Michel Foucault, this could be seen as a tendency to resort to the simple distinction of "this" versus "that" when propounding arguments. See Kenneth Frampton, *Modern Architecture: A Critical History* (Cambridge, Mass.: MIT Press, 1985), 149. Also see Michel Foucault, *The Order of Things: An Archaeology of the Human Sciences* (New York: Vintage Books, 1973), xv–xxiv.

9. Colin Rowe, in a lecture given to the School of Architecture at Rice University, intoned similar sentiments with regard to the project of Modern architecture. His introductory statement, a reiteration of Le Corbusier's thoughts of around 1930, is indicative of the epistemological-eschatological rejoinders of the period; Rowe quoted Le Corbusier as follows: "Architecture which is the expression of the spirit of an epoch, delivered an ultimatum . . . You think the time is not yet ripe? What terrible sounds, what rendings, what avalanches must assail your ears then, before they will hear? The thunder now rolling around the world fills the heart of the coward with fear and the hearts of the brave with joy . . . And to you, the idlers, the pleasure seekers and the liars, you in your niches, conservatives and robbers, I say: tomorrow will see the necessary task accomplished . . . On the day when contemporary society, at present so sick, has become properly aware that only architecture and city planning can provide the exact prescription for its ills, the time will come for the great machine to be put in motion." Colin Rowe, "Epistemology and Eschatology" (presented at the School of Architecture, Rice University, Houston, Texas, March 1989).

10. A similar critique of the metaphysical connotations of history was put forth by Martin Heidegger in his discussion of projective *Überwindung* (overcoming) versus *Verwindung*, the "getting over" manifest in the process of recovery. While history is generally construed as a universal project in which limits, including the limits of the past, are overcome, the notion of *Verwindung* connotes the prospect of a plethora of possibilities and, consequently, the signaling of convalescence and healing. While Heidegger's critique of the metaphysics of truth and Being (and by implication, historicity) is decidedly well-taken, the underlying claims of *Verwindung* rely on truth and Being, albeit truth and Being as events. Hence, any consignment to *Verwindung* can be regarded as a furtherance of philo-

310

sophical metaphysics in that it necessitates a subscription to structural objectivity, the logic of the *logos*. See Vattimo, xx.

11. John Elderfield, *Kurt Schwitters* (London: Thames and Hudson, 1985), 144–171. Elderfield's art historical elision of Giambattista Piranesi's *Carceri* and Charles Baudelaire's phantasmagoria and dream grotto seek to establish both a genealogy and reference point for Schwitters' project.

12. Wolin, 175. See also Rolf Tiedemann, "Dialectics at a Standstill," in *On Walter Benjamin: Critical Essays and Recollections,* ed. Gary Smith (Cambridge, Mass.: MIT Press, 1988), 260–291.

13. Wolin, 174.

14. In 1935, Benjamin compiled a shortened version of the Arcades Project, entitled the Arcades Exposé, which he submitted to his friend Theodor Adorno for criticism. For an explanation of this particular incarnation of the work, as well as Adorno's criticism of the piece, see Wolin, 173–183.

15. Wolin, 126–127.

16. This statement regarding the "universalism of the West" was made by Jürgen Habermas during a faculty colloquium at Rice University (Houston, Texas) in the spring of 1992.

17. The phrase "metaphysics without transcendence" has been used to describe the essential thrust of André Breton's surrealist project. See Anna Balakian, *Surrealism: The Road to the Absolute* (Chicago: University of Chicago Press, 1986). Owing much to the metaphysical philosophies of nineteenth-century German romanticism, French surrealism was preoccupied with the ideas of Hegel, Nietzsche, and Freud. Both Walter Benjamin and Kurt Schwitters were obviously influenced by their surrealist contemporaries. In the case of Schwitters, many of his Dadaist compatriots were eventually subsumed into the surrealist epitome, while Benjamin wrote appreciative critiques on surrealism in the late 1920s. See Walter Benjamin, *Reflections: Essays, Aphorisms, Autobiographical Writings,* ed. Peter Demetz (New York: Schocken Books, 1978), 177–192.

18. My suggestions regarding the psychological profile of Schwitters and Benjamin owe themselves to Susan Sontag's penetrating observations of Benjamin's character. See Susan Sontag, "Under the Sign of Saturn," in her collection of essays *Under the Sign of Saturn* (New York: Doubleday, 1980), 109–136. See also Julia Kristeva, *Black Sun: Melancholy and Depression* (New York: Columbia University Press, 1989). Kurt Schwitters

mentioned his "melancholic disposition" in the autobiographical essay "Grundzug meines Wesens Melancholie" he wrote for the *Sturm-Bilderbuch* IV in 1920. Reprinted in Kurt Schwitters, *Das literarische Werk* (Cologne: DuMont Buchverlag, 1981) as "Kurt Schwitters Herkunft, Werden und Entfaltung." See also Werner Schmalenbach, *Kurt Schwitters* (Munich: Prestal-Verlag, 1984), 28.

19. Benjamin's doctoral dissertation, entitled *Der Begriff der Kunstkritik in der deutschen Romantik* (1919), examined the aesthetic theories of Friedrich Schlegel and Novalis (Friedrich von Hardenberg), both principal figures in the development of German romanticism. See Wolin, 43.

20. Richard Sieburth, "Benjamin the Scrivener," in *Assemblage* 6 (Cambridge, Mass.: MIT Press, 1985), 14.

21. In her analysis of the twentieth-century novel, Elizabeth Deeds Ermath examines the works of Alain Robbe-Grillet, Julio Cortázar, and Vladimir Nabokov, highlighting literature that has openly critiqued the tendency of most intellectual production to "state, qualify, and conclude." Elizabeth Deeds Ermarth, *Sequel to History: Postmodernism and the Crisis of Representational Time* (Princeton: Princeton University Press, 1992). See also Alain Robbe-Grillet, *For a New Novel* (Evanston, Ill.: Northwestern University Press, 1989). Jennifer Bloomer, *Architecture and the Text: The (S)crypts of Joyce and Piranesi* (New Haven: Yale University Press, 1993), elucidates the impact of modern scientific discourse on theories and practice of architecture.

22. Benjamin, "Theses on the Philosophy of History."

23. Elizabeth Deeds Ermarth attributes the phrase "universal sweep" to Meyer Shapiro. See Ermarth, 5. This tendency towards totalization (*Ganzheitlichkeit*) is imminent in Hegel's pronouncement of "reason in history," whereby the "universal sweep" is accomplished according to an ongoing process of dialectical development (*Dialektikerentwicklung*). See Georg Wilhelm Friedrich Hegel, *Introduction to Philosophy of History,* trans. Leo Rauch (Indianapolis: Hackett Publishing Company, 1988).

24. Michel Foucault, "Other Spaces: The Principles of Heterotopias." The entire quote is as follows: "As is well known, the great and obsessive dread of the nineteenth century was history, with its themes of development and stagnation,

crisis and cycle, the accumulation of the past, the surplus of the dead . . . The nineteenth-century found the quintessence of its mythological resources in the second law of thermodynamics. Our own era, on the other hand, seems to be that of space. We are in the age of the simultaneous, of juxtaposition, the near and the far, the side by side and the scattered. A period in which . . . the world is putting itself to the test, not so much as a great way of life destined to grow in time, but as a net that links points together and creates its own muddle. It might be said that certain ideological conflicts which underlie the controversies of our day take place between pious descendants of time and tenacious inhabitants of space."

25. In her essay "Woman's Time," Julia Kristeva comments on the dissociative effects of temporal history with respect to the intuiting subject's recognition of multiple temporalities, such as those manifest in the regeneration of natural conditions: "Female subjectivity, as it gives itself up to intuition becomes a problem with respect to a certain conception of time: time as project, teleology, linear and prospective unfolding: time as departure, progression and arrival—in other words, the time of history. It has already been abundantly demonstrated that this kind of temporality is inherent in the logical and ontological values of any given civilization, that the temporality renders explicit a rupture, an expectation or an anguish which other temporalities work to conceal. It might also be added that this linear time is that of language considered as the enunciation of sentences (noun and verb; topic-comment; beginning-ending), and that this time rests on its own stumbling block, which is also the stumbling block of that enunciation—death." Julia Kristeva, "Woman's Time," in *The Kristeva Reader,* ed. Toril Moi (New York: Columbia University Press, 1986), 190–193.

26. Ermarth, 5. Contemporary discussions of political questions surrounding the "wars" on poverty, crime, and drugs are indicative of the way in which political and social problems are likened to military conflicts.

27. Paul Virilio's various writings on this subject have contributed greatly to our understanding of the complex relationships between war, architecture, and urbanism.

28. The questions surrounding the "universalism of the West" find their origin in antiquity, specifically in the form of Roman imperial conquest. The universal project continues throughout the Middle Ages, with the Roman Church at the helm, specifically during Charlemagne's reign. The Renaissance, in seeking to found Humanism as a universal construct, continued the promotion of an "imperialist project" from a cultural standpoint. Further developments regarding the universalism of the West are central to the Napoleonic conquest of Southern and Eastern Europe. Architecture and urban planning become primary to national recognition and cultural dissemination during the Napoleonic age. In architecture, the romantic classicism of Friedrich Gilly and Karl Friedrich Schinkel, among others, provides examples of this trend. In general, classical tenets in architecture have come to represent the pursuit of a universal program for architecture and culture—that is, until modernism effectively provided an alternative scheme. There are numerous texts to consult with respect to this issue. See Joseph Rykwert, *The First Moderns: The Architects of the Eighteenth Century* (Cambridge, Mass.: MIT Press, 1987), 80–95. Walter Gropius's "Scope of Total Architecture" is indicative of the carry-over of these ideas into twentieth-century architecture.

29. Friedrich Nietzsche actually suggested the opposite, that history was beholden to science. See Friedrich Nietzsche, "The Advantages and Disadvantages of History for Life," in *Unmodern Observations,* trans. William Arrowsmith (New Haven: Yale University Press, 1990).

30. Ermarth, 5.

31. Hegel, *Introduction to the Philosophy of History.* The work *geistig* in German means intellectual, spiritual, and self-absorbed. All three of these meanings shade Hegel's philosophical interpretation of the project of universal (dialectical) *Geschichte* (history).

32. This is perhaps most true of the Jena School (Johann Gottlieb Fichte, and others) and the Post-Hegelians. See Harald Höffding, *History of Modern Philosophy,* vol. 2 (New York: Dover Publications, 1955). Also see Hegel's later work, particularly *The Philosophy of Right.*

33. G. W. F. Hegel, *Reason in History,* trans. Robert S. Hartman, (New York: Library of Liberal Arts, 1953), 11.

34. Michel Serres, "Representation and Bifurcation: Borges' Garden of Chaos Dynamics," in *Chaos and Order,* ed. N.

Katherine Hayles, (Chicago: University of Chicago Press, 1991), 223. Current discourse asks that we acknowledge the differences between what Jacques Derrida refers to as "the structurality of structure," a worldview conditioned by and dependent on the Cartesian/Newtonian (classical) *episteme*, and another *episteme*—if indeed it may be called that—described by Luce Irigaray (*This Sex Which Is Not One*) and David Farrell Krell (*Of Memory, Reminiscence, and Writing: On the Verge*), among others, as involving, in short, "the mechanics of fluids." Both venues propose extremely divergent "models" for space and time. They are not opposites, however, but orders of a different kind. In either case, initial assumptions differ greatly, resultant biases radically. See Jacques Derrida, "Structure, Sign, and Play in the Discourse of the Human Sciences," in *Writing and Difference,* (Chicago: University of Chicago Press, 1987), 278; Luce Irigaray, *This Sex Which is not One,* trans. Catherine Porter (Ithaca, N. Y.: Cornell University Press, 1985), 106–118; Luce Irigaray, *The Speculum of the Other Woman,* trans. Gillian C. Gill (Ithaca, N. Y.: Cornell University Press, 1985), 227–242; and David Farrell Krell, *Of Memory, Reminiscence, and Writing: On the Verge* (Bloomington, Indiana: Indiana University Press, 1990).

35. William Mills Ivins, *The Rationalization of Sight* (New York: Metropolitan Museum of Art, 1938), 13.

36. Ivins, 10.

37. Stephen A. Tyler, *The Unspeakable: Discourse, Dialogue, and Rhetoric in the Postmodern World* (Madison, Wisc.: University of Wisconsin Press, 1987). Tyler provides a critical explanation of the privileging of sight in the Judeo-Christian universe. Of particular note is the section entitled "The Vision Quest in the West, or What the Mind's Eye Sees," 149–170.

38. It should be noted that the title of Nietzsche's treatise on the problem of history has been alternately translated as "The Use and Abuse of History," thereby leading to a confusion of references.

39. Ermarth, 28.

40. Ermarth, 147–148.

41. Michel de Certeau, Gianni Vattimo, and German theorist Arnold Gehlen have all recognized this condition, though it should be noted that the phenomenon of postmodernism is viewed as "positive" by de Certeau and Vattimo, while Gehlen

sees such a development in a largely negative light. For a comprehensive outline of the debate concerning "post-history" see Vattimo, i–lv.

42. Samuel Beckett, *How It Is* (New York: Grove Press, 1964). Beckett's protracted soliloquy is exemplary of the elision between the subject's perception and the activities recorded by and through the subject's experiences.

43. Michel Foucault, "The Discourse on Language," in *The Archaeology of Knowledge*, trans. A. M. Sheridan Smith (New York: Pantheon Books, 1972), 221–22.

44. Ermarth, 116.

45. In their work on chaos theory, scientists Ilya Prigogine and Isabelle Stengers figure prominently in this discourse, particularly with respect to the idea of regeneration. According to Prigogine and Stengers, chaos theory represents a "probability process," which, in their words, effectively ordains a *"new conception of matter* that introduces us to a *new conception of order* that is independent of the closures and finalities of classical dynamics and that permits us to see how non-equilibrium brings order out of chaos." Ilya Prigogine and Isabelle Stengers, *Order out of Chaos: Man's New Dialogue with Nature* (New York: Bantam Books, 1984), 286–87. Such a conception of matter—dependent as it is on *process*—supports the view that the life process is itself borne out of multiple, generative phases where a "particular phase has to end in order for the life process to continue" and that this "sustaining translation" depends seemingly on *chance* (though its conditions may in fact be nested within the given condition), a correlate of Stephen Jay Gould's *Burgess Shale* thesis. The more traditional determinist views of history, evolution, and generation, empowered as they are by fixed rules, principles, and laws, appear limited "the more open the universe is to fluctuation and innovation." A particular, yet significant effect of this is the view that individual behavior is decisive; small fluctuations may grow and change the overall structure. In *Sequel to History: Postmodernism and the Crisis of Representational Time,* Elizabeth Ermarth proposes the revisionary tactic of supplanting—or addending to—Alberti's treatise *Della Pittura.* This supplement would provisionally be entitled *Della Figura*, in which *figura* (figure), finding opportunity in what is accidental, surprising, and contingent, presents something living

313

and dynamic. This proposition can also be formulated with regard to Benjamin's redemptive critique of history. So-called minor voices exhibit significant characteristics, thereby motivating flexibility as in adaptability, change, and growth—in short, exhibiting the force of life found in natural organisms. See Ermarth, 63 and 178. See also Stephen Jay Gould, *Wonderful Life: The Burgess Shale and the Nature of History* (London: Hutchinson Radius, 1989), 289.

46. Robert Motherwell, ed., *The Dada Painters and Poets* (Cambridge, Mass.: Harvard University Press, 1981), 154–155. This quote was first published in Kurt Schwitters's journal, *MERZ* (Holland issue). A facsimile reproduction of *Die Merzheften* was published by Friedhelm Lach in 1980.

47. K. Michael Hays, *Modernism and the Posthumanist Subject: The Architecture of Hannes Meyer and Ludwig Hilberseimer* (Cambridge, Mass.: MIT Press, 1992), 253.

48. Unlike many of the more unified avant-garde movements, Dada was fragmented according to urban contexts. Hence there is Hannover Dada (Schwitters), Cologne Dada (Johannes Baargeld, Max Ernst), Zurich Dada (Hans Arp, Hugo Ball, Tristan Tzara), Paris Dada (André Breton, Paul Eluard, Francis Picabia, Guillaume Apollinaire, Arthur Rimbaud, Alfred Jarry), New York Dada (Marcel Duchamp, Man Ray), and Berlin Dada, (Richard Huelsenbeck, Johannes Baader, John Heartfield [Herzfelde], Raoul Hausmann, George Grosz, Hannah Hoch), among others. Dada movements also existed in Magdeburg, Amsterdam, Antwerp, and Karlsruhe. See Motherwell.

49. Schwitters's earliest work actually extends the project of prewar German Expressionism. See John Elderfield, *Kurt Schwitters* (London: Thames and Hudson), 30–48.

50. In point of fact, Schwitters was specifically singled out for repudiation by Huelsenbeck in his introduction to the *Dada Almanach* (1920): "Dada rejects emphatically and as a matter of principle works like the famous 'Anna Blume' of Kurt Schwitters." While Schwitters was told that he was allowed to remain a member of the group "without commitments," it was clear that he was being marginalized. Later on he coined the phrase "husk-Dadaists" to describe the Berlin faction, referring to the Zurich group as the "kernel-" or "core-Dadaists." The contrast between the two groups was clear in Schwitters's differentiation between the two groups. To him, Zurich Dada was more truly Dada; the Berlin group, under the administration of Huelsenbeck, had corrupted the original Dadaist program with political incursions. Schwitters was also likely put off by the incendiary negativity of Huelsenbeck's project. For an account of the strained relationship between Huelsenbeck and Schwitters, see Elderfield, 40–41. See also Käte Steinitz, *Kurt Schwitters: A Portrait from Life* (Berkeley: University of California Press, 1968), 6.

51. While the word fragment *Merz* was initially construed as meaningless and arbitrary, Schwitters proceeded to mine the word for associations. Words that he aligned with *Merz* included the nouns *Scherz* (joke, witticism), *Herz* (heart), and *Schmerz* (pain, suffering), and the verb *ausmerzen* (destroy, eliminate, cut out). Moreover, *Merz* was not the only pseudonym Schwitters used: "Kuh Witter," "Ku Wi" (or "KuWi"), "Ku. Witt, Er," and "Kwit" were only a few of the ways in which he signed his works and correspondence. See Marc Dachy, *Kurt Schwitters: Merz écrits* (Paris: Editions Gérard Lebovici, 1990), 7–8.

52. I owe this phrase to Richard Wolin's *Walter Benjamin: An Aesthetic of Redemption.* Walter Benjamin's "redemptive critique" of social history provides the title for Wolin's overview of Benjamin's philosophical-critical project.

53. Elderfield, 43, 45, 235, and 237.

54. Annegreth Nill, "Decoding Merz: An Interpretive Study of Kurt Schwitters' Early Work, 1918–1922" (Ph. D. diss., University of Texas at Austin, 1990), 12–18. In an attempt to apprehend the meaning of Schwitters's early collages, Nill discusses the development components of Schwitters's process at length.

55. Dietrich, 46.

56. Underlying Schwitters's artistic ethic is a tradition in German philosophy which depends on the mystical correlation between nature, spirit, and form: the artist, in recognizing the *Urphänomen* of the human condition, exhibits a spiritual intuition which mirrors the unconscious poetry of nature. The concept is found in Goethe's philosophical writings.

57. Elderfield, 12.

58. Schwitters, "Kunst und Zeiten," in *Das literarische Werk, Band 5,* ed. Friedhelm Lach (Cologne: DuMont Buchverlag, 1981), 236–239.

59. Kurt Schwitters, "Stuttgart die Wohnung Werkbundausstell-

ung," in *Das literarische Werk, Band 5,* 286.

60. Schwitters, "Stuttgart," 284–285.

61. Schwitters published short pieces on Mies van der Rohe's sky-scraper projects in his *MERZheften.* One of the *MERZhefte* featured Hilberseimer's "Grosstadtarchitektur." See *"MERZ 18–19,"* in Lach. Hilberseimer's "Grosstadtarchitektur" was also published in *Der Sturm* 15, no. 4 (1924). Michael Hays discusses Schwitters's affiliation with Hilberseimer in *Modernism and the Posthumanist Subject,* 225–227.

62. In *Merz* 7 (January 1924), Schwitters explicitly aligns Mies van der Rohe with Dada, while also explaining that artists as varied as El Lissitzky, László Moholy-Nagy, Walter Gropius, and Hans Richter are all "helped by Dada." See Elderfield, 133.

63. Schwitters' issue of *Merz* 8/9 entitled "Natur von Lat. Nasci" (Nature from the Latin Nasci), published in 1924, stresses similar ideas. See "Art and the Times," *Ray* 1 (1927), 4–8. The piece is a partial translation of "Kunst und Zeiten," 1926.

64. Elderfield, 137–38. Much of the comparative analysis of art and nature as "a mere cut made by thought in universal becoming" derives from German romanticism. The Dadaists subscribed to Henri Bergson's idea that "reality is flux." Friedrich Schelling's *Naturphilosophie,* developed in his *System des transcendentalien Idealismus* (1800), addresses the relationship between art and nature. Harald Höffding encapsulates Schelling's thesis as follows: "The absolute principle (the original ground) which underlies all things contains the absolute unity of subject and object . . . Schelling regarded artistic intuition as the highest form of spiritual life. Art is the only true and eternal organon and at the same time document of philosophy. It is ever-authenticating that which philosophy cannot exhibit externally, i.e. the unconscious in action and production, and its original identity with the conscious. It is precisely on this account that the philosopher regards art as the highest, for it reveals to him . . . the holy of holies, where, in eternal and original union, burns . . . in one flame, that which is sundered in Nature and history, and which in life and action, as in thought must eternally flee one another. To him . . . everything is is reality poetry—the process of Nature is an unconscious poetry which bursts into consciousness in and from man . . . the creative activity of Nature or the absolute, of which experience can only show us the products, not itself,

can only obtain development by means of a series of forms. Each particular form originates in the infinite process of production, not in other forms." Harald Höffding, *A History of Modern Philosophy* (New York: Dover Publications, 1955), 167–69. See also Jean-Christophe Bailly, *Kurt Schwitters* (Paris: Editions Hazan, 1993), 25.

65. Schwitters, in the issue of *Merz* entitled *Nasci* (1924).

66. Dietmar Elger, "L'oeuvre d'une vie: les Merzbau," in *Kurt Schwitters* (Paris: Editions du Centre Pompidou, 1994), 145. *Frühlicht* was the principle organ for Die Gläserne Kette (The Glass Chain), a "secret society" of architects and artists. Initiated in 1919, the principle mission of Die Gläserne Kette entailed the revision of society according to expressionist ideals. These ideals were represented in terms of utopian (fantastic) architecture. Members of Die Gläserne Kette, many of whom had code names, included Walter Gropius, Carl Krayl, Hans Scharoun, Max Taut, Hermann Finsterlin, Wassily Luckhardt, and Hans Luckhardt.

67. Kurt Schwitters, "Schloss und Kathedrale mit Hofbrunnen," in *Das literarische Werk* 5, 95–96. The relevant section of the text is as follows: "the principles for the formation of a Merz-architecture: a Merz 'sketch' (*Merzentwurf*) for architecture and the transformative effect of Merz on new architectural forms." Though considered an intellectual model, Schloss mit Kathedrale mit Hofbrunnen was in actuality no more "fantastic" than other architectural proposals Taut presented in his journals. These proposals included works by Wassily Luckhardt, Taut's own sketches for an "alpine architecture" (Die Alpiner Architektur) and Wenzel Hablik's Fliegender Siedlung (Flying Settlement). In fact, some of the utopian-romantic architects promoted by Taut did build. Some of these projects included Bruno Taut's own Glaseisenhaus (House of Glass and Steel, or Glass House) from the 1914 Cologne Werkbund; Hugo Häring's Luckenwalde Hat Factory; Hans Poelzig's Opera; and Erich Mendelsohn's Einstein Tower. All these projects, theoretical and built, bore some relationship to the notion of an architectural *Gesamtkunstwerk.* See Elger, 145.

68. Kurt Schwitters, "Merz," in *Das literarishe Werk* 5, 78. This section of the article is an obvious allusion to Walter Gropius's "First Proclamation of the Weimar Bauhaus."

315

69. Elger, 145. See Schwitters, "Schloss und Kathedrale mit Hofbrunnen," 95.

70. An accounting of the materials and labor necessary to reconstitute the original *Merzbau* appeared in a grant proposal to Museum of Modern Art director Alfred Barr Sr. The labor schedule included "for a column, 5–6 weeks, for a niche, 2–3 months, for an interior, about 3/4 of a year . . . (as well as the services of a carpenter, glassworker, electrician)." Elderfield, 155.

71. The problem of verifying the contents of the *Merzbau* is exaggerated by the number of accounts. Käte Steinitz, a close acquaintance of Schwitters during the 1920s and 1930s, recounts the visual and material aspects, as well as the literary (historical) designations contained in the *Merzbau* project. However, it is likely that numerous components have been left out, lost from the memory of those who partook of Schwitters's work and its themes. See Elderfield, 144–171. Also see Steinitz, *Kurt Schwitters*.

72. The actual date on which Schwitters commenced construction of the *Merzbau* is open to some debate. There are eyewitness accounts that put the beginning of construction as early as 1920, though the actual formulation of the project as a coherent entity probably occurred a bit later. In a 1931 article detailing the contents and method of the *Die Kathedrale des Erotischen Elends* entitled "Ich und meine Ziele," Schwitters dated the project from 1923 (*Das literarische Werk* 5, 340–348). He did not refer to the project as the *Merzbau* until 1933 article "Le Merzbau" (*Das literarische Werk* 5, 354). He alludes to the developmental aspects of the *Merzbau* in his essays and statements regarding his *Merz-bühne* (Merz-stage). See "Die normale Bühne Merz," "Normalbühne Merz 1925," and "Einige praktishe Anregungen zur Normalbühne" in *Das literarische Werk* 5, 204–213.

73. The extent of the *Merzbau* has been the subject of some debate. Elderfield claims that the extent of the project has been highly exaggerated, and was really localized to four rooms with extensions onto the balcony (Elderfield, 156). However, other accounts—including an account by Schwitters' son Ernst—indicate that the *Merzbau* did fill numerous rooms, extending into the attic, down the side of the house, and into the cistern in the side yard.

74. "Ich und meine Ziele (I and my direction)" explicates the *Merzbau*, which Schwitters refers to as "Die Kathedrale des Erotischen Elends" (The Cathedral of Erotic Misery) at some length. See Kurt Schwitters, *Das literarishe Werk* 5, 340–348. Photographs of aspects of the project had been published in previous years, though not with any note explaining their context as part of a larger whole. See also Elderfield, 148.

75. Elderfield, 165.

76. Elderfield uses the historian Thomas Carlyle's phrase for the title of his chapter on the *Merzbau*. See Elderfield, 171.

77. Rudolf Jahns, *Künstlerisches Tagebuch*, as cited by Dietmar Elger, *Der Merzbau, Eine Werkmonographie* (Cologne: Verlag der Buchhandlung Walter König, 1984), 113.

78. Alfred Dudelsack, *Beilage zur Braunschweiger Illustrierten Woche* (Braunschweig, 1920), as cited in Elderfield, 144; and Dietmar Elger, *Der Merzbau: Eine Werkmonographie*, 28. This particular quote begins with the following allusion to the uncanny (expressionist) nature of the work: "The visitor to this most holy place . . . is struck by a holy shudder, and only then dares raise his eyes when he has found a little spot for himself, but where he cannot stay because there is not enough room to stand." Schwitters's own paintings from this period are replete with religious themes that characterize German romantic painting, in particular the works of Caspar David Friedrich and Zumthor. Of particular note is Schwitters's painting *Hochgebirgsfriedhof* (Mountain Graveyard) of 1919. Later works, including a variety of pieces from the *Merzbau*, continued to delve into religious themes.

79. Schwitters, "Ich und meine Ziele," 95–96. Original emphasis.

80. Schwitters himself, in recounting his life, spoke of his melancholic disposition. See Schmalenbach.

81. Elderfield, 162.

82. Steinitz's account of "tiny fetish objects displayed like glass boxes" is probably an allusion to an aspect of the *Merzbau* entitled "die Goldgrotte" (Gold Grotto). See Steinitz, 90.

83. Richard Huelsenbeck, *Memoirs of a Dada Drummer*, ed. Hans J. Kleinschmidt (New York, 1974), 66. Quoted in Elderfield, 145.

84. Schwitters, "Ich und meine Zeile," in *Das literarishe werke*, 344–345.

85. See Carter Ratcliff, in Kynaston McShine, ed., *Joseph Cornell* (New York, 1980), 60. Quoted in Elderfield, 168.

316

86. Georg Simmel, "The Metropolis and Mental Life," in *Man Alone: Alienation in Modern Society,* eds. Eric and Mary Johnson (New York: Laurel Editions), 164. Overt melancholy in response to the difficulties with modern society is also present in the works of Adolf Loos, Max Brod, Franz Kafka, and much other art and literature of the period.

87. Hays, 193–94. In this section, Hays quotes Theodor Adorno's "Thesen über die Sprache des Philosophen" (*Gessamelte Schriften,* 1:369)

88. Quoted in Hays, 227. This quote by Raoul Hausmann was originally published as the "Presentist" manifesto in *De Stijl* 4, no. 9.

89. See Hays. See also Schwitters, "Stuttgart die Wohnung Werkbundausstellung," 283–284.

90. Popular in nineteenth century Germany, a *Wunderkammer* was a piece of furniture that contained souvenirs and memorabilia representative of travels, exotica, and professional and domestic events. Made up of numerous small drawers, it was often used as both an encyclopedic record of a family's history and a cabinet in which various fetishes were stored, some personal and some of historical or cultural significance. Unlike scientific classification, these items were not usually classified in a rigorous manner, but rather as a colorful assemblage of highly diverse and discrete artifacts.

91. Elger, 146.

92. Walter Benjamin, *Reflections,* ed. Peter Demetz (New York: Schocken Books, 1968), 68–69.

93. Richard Sieburth, quoted in Irving Wohlfarth, *Revue d'esthé-tique,* 9.

94. Sieburth, 9.

95. Vattimo, lv.

96. For a complete rendering of Benjamin's project, see Buck-Morss.

97. Paul Klee's work on the dialectics of sight was undertaken during the same period as Benjamin's Arcades project. Perhaps the impulse—the critique of deterministic-positivist modes of history and science in art and architecture—was the same. See Paul Klee, *Notebooks, Volume 1: The Thinking Eye,* originally *Das bildernische Denken,* trans. Ralph Mannheim (London: Lund-Humphries, 1961).

98. The question of Hegel's diagram for history is a much-debated subject. For the most part, it was the post-Hegelians who defined the project of history as a linear unfolding "plan" or "project." In contrast, Hegel's dialectic was more akin to an ever-enveloping mushroom cloud or spiral in which all things were enfolded and made subject to historical processes over time. In this sense, *Reason in History* might be viewed as a form of calculus in which all things are accounted for and subject to the larger (determining) function of the historical project. In effect, the language of mathematical calculus is itself a universal language. Nietzsche's critique of the impact of science on our understanding of history, that is the scientization of history in its embrace of scientific method, is well taken here.

99. Ermarth, 147.

100. Ermarth, 147–148.

101. Ludwig Wittgenstein, *Philosophical Investigations,* trans. G. E. M. Anscombe (New York: MacMillan Press, 1953), 8e (19), 11e (23), 88e (241). The discussion of "forms of life" represents a difficult and much-debated aspect of Wittgenstein's later philosophy. Two passages, 19 and 24, are significant here. In these passages, Wittgenstein describes language—and the production of meaning in language, or "language-games"—as dependent on the activity in which it is engaged. The first of these passages (19) is—somewhat ironically in this context—a discourse on the process of building. The second passage (24) describes a more fundamental definition, linking developments in language to developments in mathematics: "But how many kinds of sentences are there? Say assertion, question, and command?—There are countless kinds: doubtless different kinds of use of what we call 'symbols,' 'words,' 'sentences.' And this multiplicity is not something fixed, given once for all; but new types of language, new language-games, as we may say, come into existence, and others become obsolete and get forgotten. (We can get a *rough picture* of this from the changes in mathematics) . . . Here the term 'language-game' is meant to bring into prominence the fact that the speaking of language is part of an activity, or form of life."

THE RAPTURE

Adi Shamir Zion

The Sagrada Familia Cathedral in Barcelona was not finished during Antonio Gaudí's lifetime and, in spite—or perhaps in light—of recent building progress, stands almost less finished today than in the years immediately following his 1926 death. The portions that were built— the crypt in which Gaudí is buried and the remarkable Portal of Nativity—seem complete nonetheless, and the intended edifice is whole. The Annunciation, the Flight into Egypt, the Birth of Christ, and other biblical events are presented in the three doorways—De la Esperanza, Del Amor, and De la Fe—that comprise the Portal of Nativity. The portal's surface is swollen and wet with breath, teeming with flowers, birds in flight, and animals: donkeys, hens, roosters, lotuses, papyrus, palms, ducks, tortoises, fruits, skylarks, sparrows, and owls. These figures, however, do not simply emerge from the stone as in relief, and do not simply break from the surface as though entreated into the dimensional realm. Rather, fauna, flora, and saint alike struggle to resist becoming fixed in stone. Entwined fronds, feathers, locks, and limbs seem caught somewhere in the moment just before petrification. Animated by the fight against death, and even in death, the figures attest to the life of the symbolic rendering and to the corporeal properties of the myth. It is therefore not, as is generally believed, the building's structural or tectonic language that is organic, but it is instead the symbolic material—the narrative content—itself that possesses an organic and viscous morphology not purely mimetic or representational but with a durational reality of its own. The scripture's somatic identity evolves from the tedious and exacting, though at all times subjective, portrayal of nature. But the subjectification of nature manifested in Gaudí's architecture involves a further complexity: the collusion of two apparently discordant methods, a delirious "medieval" conveyance, and its supposed antithesis, the process of a modern systematic analysis. This very collusion, the impossible union, is achieved in the Sagrada Familia Cathedral and may grant us entry into the whole of Gaudí's work.

319

Left: Caravaggio, *The Magdalena in Ecstasy,* 1606. Rome private collection.

Right: Gaudi's workshop, Barcelona.

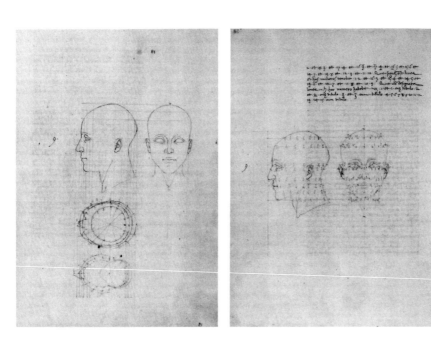

Piero della Francesca. Topographic procedure performed on the human head, subdividing its complex volume into strata. From *On Perspective in Painting*, c. 1470.

For sixteenth-century theorist Benedetto Varchi, the artist's creation was "an artificial imitation of nature"[1] in service of the singular purpose of perfection. The imitative process necessitated that artifice be idealized apart from nature, and that creation be estranged from its source. Renaissance philosophers conceived of themselves as detached from nature, observing the necessary distance from their subjects of study in the application of a metaphorical language for the description of natural phenomena. Their metaphors—the principles of harmonic perfection in the geometric scheme—were distilled from nature and, through the strict application of critical and analytical procedures, left the temporality, fluidity, and spontaneity of nature "vigorously tamed." Their systemic studies introduced the mimetic technique, which preempted and then confirmed the empirical method. These studies became the primary documents of a confident age and the foundation of modern Western culture's faith in the incorruptibility of the analytical procedure.

When Leon Battista Alberti prescribed a theory of painting based on "the basic principles of nature,"[2] he was describing a new (or renewed) naturalized art tempered by mathematical order, wherein beauty was the expression of the immutable laws of an ordered universe. In his treatises on painting and optics, Alberti rationalized vision through mathematics, ascribing absolute value to objects in the natural world while denying the significance of transitory or subjective perception. His perspectival formulas did not account for the movement of the painter's head, the presence of shadows in the composition, or the unpredictable conditions that arise when one is painting "from nature." Art and science were thus bound in an epistemology that avoided the inherent conflict between reality and appearance.

Alberti's broad textual work and the built works with which he is associated prescribed a transformed language of architecture as well. Within this humanist framework, interpretations of the abstract language of Pythagorean metric law were by necessity grafted onto the liturgical specifications of the church. The Latin-cross church plan with its elongated nave and choir was rejected in favor of the more centralized Greek-cross plan. In choosing the ideal geometry of the circle as the image for the church, the "restorers" of Classicism displaced the single most important figure of the Middle Ages, the crucified Christ. This transposition of the material body of Christ with an intangible geometry of the ideal person and cosmos marked perhaps the most significant manifestation of the modern objectification and abstraction of nature as expressed in architecture.

For the medieval West, the Latin cross had been more than a formal or even purely iconic element. It was evidence of a cultivated symbolic syntax in which things were not filtered through an empirical or "optically correct" matrix but believed to be actually true. Illuminated images were neither realistic drawings from life nor were their scriptural subjects dimensionally robust. They were instead phenomenologically literal, their dimensionless physiognomy imbued with reality.

The philosophical foundations for this world view were well established in the writings of scholars such as Saint Augustine, the bishop of Hippo in the fifth century. In describing the rays of light or *acies* traveling between the eye and an object, Augustine was not simply investigating the problems of optical transmission as had Euclid or Ptolemy; rather, he likened the eye to the mind and vision to knowledge. His preoccupation was with images as "the things in themselves," and he located their point of origin along the mobius path of a ray sent out from the mind/eye which receives the very form of the object of its cognition.

But when I hear that there are three kinds of questions—Does a certain thing exist? What is it? What are its properties?—I retain the images of the sounds out of which these words have been fashioned, and I know that they passed with ordered sound through the air, and that they no longer exist. But as to the things themselves which are signified by these sounds, I neither attained to them by any bodily sense nor did I descry them anywhere except in my mind. Yet I stored away in my memory not their images but the things themselves. Let such things tell how they entered into me if they can. For I check over all the portals of my flesh, and I do not discover any through which they have entered.

— Saint Augustine, *Confessiones*[3]

Even as late as the twelfth century, the Realists, led by William of Champeaux, bishop of Châlons-sur-Marne and Peter Abelard's chief rival, believed in the *actual* existence, beyond mere awareness, of the imago, and were unwilling to distinguish between ideas exterior to perception and their corresponding verbal description.

Absent from this epistemological framework are the nuances of abstraction. Perhaps because there was no recognition of reality as polarized, "things themselves" did not exist apart from their ideation and therefore did not require an "other" or suspended interpretation. It has been assumed that the artists of the Middle Ages suffered from a memory lapse in which the Classical schemata for the illustration of depth was forgotten. But if we consider the possibility that abstract thought and the conception of "systematic" space, which it makes possible, were not part of their representational syntax, then we must call this traditional assumption into question. Saint Isidore of Seville, who is known to have catalogued ancient terms in his *Etymologiae*, described many "things," including the cylinder, which was characterized as "a square figure having a semicircle above" [cylindrus est figura quadrata, habens superius semicirculum].[4] Are we to learn from this description

322

Giovanni Cimabue. Detail from *Crucifix*, late thirteenth century. Church of San Domenico in Arezzo.

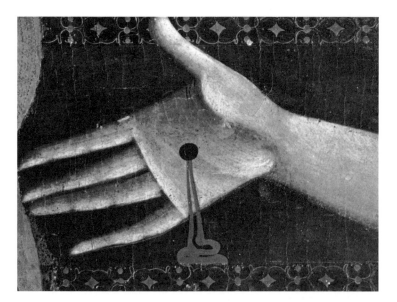

that Isidore did not fully comprehend the volume of the cylinder? While it is true that his cylinder is neither the result nor the suggestion of a staged composition of an illusionistic scene containing an optically documented object (as in the case of Alberti's model), it seems wholly inconceivable that Isidore's symptom was amnesia or an inability to depict three-dimensional space. Rather, in his case, the optical "reality" appears to have been intentionally suppressed. The scribe may have been asking his readers not to visualize or reason, but to *imagine* and *believe* in the figural properties of the object as expressed by his articulate though disembodied rendering. It seems most probable, then, that the scribes and their audience participated in a conscious strategy intended to fortify belief in that which one could literally know but not quite see.

Literalism and materialism are, of course, essential to discussions of the Resurrection. The physical experience of the risen spirit cannot be excised from the incarnation myth, whose central tenet is the "enfleshing of God." Without it how might we, as Walker Bynum asks, understand the passage in Luke in which the resurrected Christ eats boiled fish and honeycomb with his disciples?[5] But we cannot possibly comprehend this image as it might have been understood in the medieval context. The chasm between the modern application of abstraction (which by its very nature distinguishes between factual reality and imaginary portrayal) and medieval literalism (where the absence of metaphor permits the real and the imaginary to share an identity) is difficult to bridge. It therefore becomes particularly awkward today to understand and to critically discuss liturgical material in art and architecture because for us the biblical story is only that: an undisciplined narrative that must at all times remain outside of reality.

In Gaudí's work we are faced with an even greater challenge. From within a rational matrix, it is hard for us to fully accept the reality of Gaudí's iconography, let alone imagine that his uniquely medieval understanding could be enmeshed with our thoroughly modern analytical methodology.

Antonio Gaudí. Sagrada Familia Cathedral, Barcelona. Detail of portal.

La Salvación de humanidad entera está pues, en el nacimiento de Jesus y en su Pasión. Por ello, el Templo tiene una puerta del Nacimiento y otra de la Pasión. El simbolismo de este templo se fundamenta en el "Apocalipsis," cuando dice que la Iglesia es un árbol frondoso, bajo el cual corren fuentes. Los muchos pinaculos de que constrará tendrán una forma tal que pondrán interpretarse fácilmente como copas de árboles.

—Cesar Martinell, "Conversaciones con Gaudí"[6]

For Gaudí, the church and the tree are linked by much more than poetic association: both are corporeal symbols of Christ. His architecture in turn is more than an abstract representation of cosmic alignments—it is the embodiment of Holy Scripture, a perspective of the Apocalypse framed spatially by the supernatural world and temporally by the promise of eschatological judgment. His interpretations of ecclesiastic mythology have been described as ecstatic or even hallucinatory; from within the framework of each of his highly allusive compositions, it is often difficult to know whether the work has been "received" through ecstatic visions or "created" by an enlightened artist from whose individual will arose original material.

Gaudí was unquestionably a devoutly religious man. With his declaration that "the history of Architecture is the history of the Church,"[7] he acknowledged that he would imbue his devotions into his architectural work. While there exist complex canonical arrangements in Gaudí's cathedral, however, it is neither the liturgical structure nor the iconographic content of the edifice that grants his architecture its visionary qualities. *Apokalypsis*—a first-century Greek term meaning revelation—occurred for Gaudí within his architectural laboratory. A workshop on the premises of the church, which in later years also housed Gaudí's single bed, was the site of his labor and search. It is within this sanctuary that rapture—the act of being carried away by force of seizure or conveyance—would take place.

Although only the crypt was completed, the Colonia Guell Chapel in Santa Coloma de Cervello remains a testament to Gaudí's rigorous methodology and to his ethic. It further reiterates a standard of authenticity that the discipline of architecture necessitates and yet cannot prescribe. "The tree is my master" delineated the scope for a task that could only be achieved through the analytical method. Gaudí endeavored to manifest physically what he knew intuitively: a force is never exerted altogether vertically, and vaults and piers are inseparably linked in dynamic unity. He conceived of methods appropriate to the investigation of presupposed physical realities. Over the course of ten years, a funicular skeleton was loaded with weights forming a complex network of lines of force; when inverted, these would operate in pure compression as a parabolic curve. With this method, Gaudí was able

Model for the Virgin (a spinster).

Gutierrez the goatherd.

to approximate the structurally equilibrated posture of his organic paradigm, and these experiments would inform the rhythm of the oblique columns and deep vaults supporting the nave of the crypt. Alberto Pérez-Gómez notes that Galileo Galilei believed the "real incarnated the mathematical, [and] was incapable of recognizing the distance between geometrical theories and experience."[8] Gaudí, who suffered a similar fate in his own studies of statics, willed the transformation of the physical condition into symbolic reality. Gaudí's mystical faith in the vital energy of the parabolic structure as it guided the gaze toward God propelled his unrelenting analytical studies of oblique and inclined orders. His empirical studies, though three centuries after Galileo's, remained "pre-scientific."

Analytical research measured, drafted, and located Gaudí's architecture. Observation yielded for Gaudí the realization that sight must go beyond the blindness of familiarity, yet achieving naturalistic representation was not the objective of his detailed examinations. The statuary that would be integrated into the Sagrada Familia building was to possess the vitality of natural movement—but what are the natural movements of angels or saints? Ordinary and not-so-ordinary people from the neighborhood were recruited as models. Robert Descharnes recounts that the live models were selected to "resemble" their subjects. The model for Christ on the cross was thirty-three years old, while the one for the Virgin was a pious spinster. Descharnes states:

> Gutierrez, a goatherd in the "poblet" district, [was] known as the herder with the huge belly. In 1902 he became a model for the Pontius Pilate of the Passion facade. Opisso recounts that he was also called "they're-not-your-onions," an expression meaning "it's none of your business," because he repeated the expression incessantly and for no reason and it was thought to be equivalent to the words of Pilate before Christ, "I wash my hands of it" . . . A waiter from a tavern was cast as a Roman soldier. He was Tarragonese and according to Gaudí the inhabitants of that ancient Roman colony were similar in type to the Roman emperors and patricians.[9]

Just as Gaudí had consulted the form of actual trees in the process of inventing the parabolic vault, so here did living/live models with their peculiar idiosyncracies lend their forms to their mythical counterparts. The model for Gaudí did not exist in lieu of the symbolic, but rather manifested the symbol's reality. In an ontological transformation, the metaphor was made actual. Resemblance was established on the basis of nonvisual likenesses and correspondences.

Gaudí had been thoroughly educated in perspective rendering. In his day, steel and glass were the new building materials, and the infinite space of the Cubist landscape along

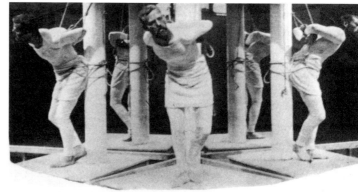

Model for an angel.

Model for Christ.

328

with the hymn of the *Internationale* proposed a new theology for the modern age. Though Gaudí without question belonged to this age, his works are not examples of Modernism in any standard sense. And while it has often been noted that John Ruskin's writings on the endorsement of ornament (which were published in Barcelona in 1903) served as a source of inspiration for Gaudí, it must be clear that Gaudí—unlike A. W. N. Pugin or G. E. Street, both of whom joined Ruskin in advocating a return to the spirit and forms of the Middle Ages—was not a Gothic Revivalist. His work is devoid of the sentimental gesture that the revivalist, even while attempting to simulate the coarse medieval hand, could not avoid. Nor was Gaudí a true Structural Rationalist, though he seems to have read the treatises of Viollet-le-Duc. In his use of traditional Catalan vault techniques to form corbeled arches from laminated layers of tile, Gaudí would rarely explicitly expose the structural logic of the building for the sake of material "authenticity."

Perhaps Gaudí was not only drawn to what Ruskin perceived, but also to the thoroughly modern way in which he did so. In his beautiful musing on the works of Ruskin, Jay Fellows explicates Ruskin's "optical self" and the "biped" nature of his "desiring eyes." On the one hand, Ruskin speaks of sight as the dispassionate precision of the "camera lucida," an optical instrument that projects the image of an external object onto a flat surface for purposes of tracing. On the other hand, Ruskin describes the passionate "optical equipment dependent upon the intellectual lens of the 'Moral Retina,' an entirely spiritual consciousness accurately and absolutely proportioned to the purity of the moral nature and to the force of its natural and wise affections." In embarking upon his optical travels, Ruskin would be aided by "the lens faithfully and far collecting, the retina faithfully and inwardly receiving."[10]

Might Gaudí have recognized in these his own "optical self" when he employed the camera and the photograph to record the recruited models in their various postures? Or did he simply wish to fix the memory of the bodies in motion, images that might otherwise have escaped time? Gaudí arranged his models in front of two mirrors placed vertically and another suspended horizontally above, yielding five images in a single exposure. This was not *nature morte* or a slavish copy of physical reality. These portraits do not wear a melancholic countenance. Unlike the immodest frontality of a typical portrait, here the model turns his or her back to the mirror, causing the very soul of the image to become trapped within the five identities of the single image. As in the case of the inverted weighted funicular, the laws of gravity are at once confirmed and defied; the very real figure recorded in its multiple reflections is spectral and disembodied—as much spirit as it is matter. Thus the medieval insistence on bodily resurrection finds new meaning in Gaudí's practice of transformation which grants the body power to reveal the presence of the divine.[11]

Ruskin referred to the fifteenth-century Humanists' deliberate revival of ideas and practices of Classical antiquity as plagiarism. Humanism's historicist longings were, in fact, mistakenly lavished on the Roman examples that were known to them, because the Classical Greek sites would not be excavated until the eighteenth century. Once again, Gaudí did not exactly follow the Gothic Revivalists' stylistic lead when he claimed that the Sagrada Familia was derived from the purest Hellenic traditions and that his work followed the true ancient methods legitimately passed from the ancients to the Gothic builder. After the renascence of Euclidean geometry, Gothic master builders would draw the basic figures of the square, circle, or triangle on a "tracing floor" in the portion of the building above which the elevation would rise. François Bucher explains that by rotating a square inside a square so that the corners of the inner figure always bisected the sides of the outer, these builders would generate cords and arcs of proportionate lengths that would define the heights of piers, walls, and finials. They would then transfer the measurements from the tracing-floor module to the wall or ceiling by means of strings or templates.[12] The development of Gaudí's work at the building site approximated this type of architectural drafting in which nonillusionistic and nonperspectival projections of three-dimensional elevations were drawn from geometric figures. Much like the master builders whose on-site calculations were an integral part of the construction, Gaudí attended to the unfinished statuary for the Sagrada Familia as adjustments were needed to accommodate for perspectival distortion before the art was mounted along the height of the cathedral towers. He would correct the sculptural figures first by photographing the cast and carved figures, rephotographing the original prints at an angle, and then gradually adjusting the proportions of the actual sculpture, lengthening and shortening parts of the figure at its joints until it looked balanced to the eye from below.

In light of Gaudí's comprehensive studies and extensive experiments these final adjustments might seem somehow imprecise, even crude. However, it is precisely these acts of alteration and distortion that make evident the great pragmatism Gaudí shared with the ancient Greeks. Distortion, as Erwin Panofsky demonstrates, was an essential element of the medieval "optical impression," which, unlike Renaissance linear perspective, accounted for the curvature of the retina, determining apparent magnitudes not in simple measures of length but in degrees of angles or arcs. The "spherical distortions" as seen in the tapered column, the gentle rise of a floor, the increased thickness of corner columns, and variations in column spacing in the Doric temple, rendered reality with much greater precision than the unambiguous spatial structure of the Renaissance proportional grid.[13] "Transparent unity"—in other words, the Platonic ideal—was formed by the merging of disparate beings when their "partial determinate aspects were 'raised up' and placed in the light of disconcealment,"[14] existing at the instant of distortion or conversion. The creation strives not for likeness but for renewal and origination. Like an anamorphic projection whose primacy exists in the distorted appearance of a recognizable image, the translation does not obscure the translated. The original comes into being from within the translation, and its hermeneutical birth attests to the analytical experiment as well as to the artisan's craft.

Gaudí tried to put into effect each day what the Virgin Mary revealed to him the night before.
— Eugenio d'Ors[15]

In the last years of Gaudí's life, work on the Sagrada Familia became all consuming, and although its construction would involve the labors of generations of masons and journeymen, the edifice emerged from Gaudí's singular, ever-present vision. In this sense Gaudí might be compared to Filippo Brunelleschi, the first builder to be identified as the master architect for a project of immense urban significance produced by a community of makers over the span of several centuries. Gothic builder and Renaissance architect, Brunelleschi truly straddled the cusp of two eras. The will to solve the centuries-old problem of completing the dome of the Florence Cathedral inspired his inventions in statics and mechanics. The solutions, however, evolved from within the practice of medieval building technology—the full-scale construction of hoist engines and loading machines—as well as from the practical, pre-Humanist study of the paradigmatic domed structure, the Pantheon. In the end, and in the fact of the built Duomo, the two traditions had merged and the distinction between their roles in the birth of the great double-shelled, ribbed frame had diminished.

331

Gaudí's linguistic and tectonic systems were—as Manfredo Tafuri described Brunelleschi's—"based on *super*historical comparison with the great example of antiquity."[16] Neither architect imitatively transferred or applied externally derived forms; rather each proceeded from precise theoretical premises, *re*discovering a coincidence of construction and representational principles, and thereby transcended their historical limits. Unwilling to abandon the work, Gaudí and Brunelleschi both directed their projects on the building sites, where they would develop models whose scales and cultural implications in a sense surpassed those of the buildings themselves. Like Gaudí, Brunelleschi used the mirror to verify the phenomenon of linear perspective. By looking into a mirror held in his outstretched hand, Brunelleschi could view a reflected depiction of the Baptistry at the Piazza del Duomo painted on a panel the back of which was held directly in front of his face, and which had a viewing hole punctured at the painting's vanishing point. The Baptistry could in this way be charted and accurately reconstructed. As had been the case in Gaudí's experiments, unquantifiable phenomena would be captured nonetheless and rendered alongside empirically gathered data. The clouds in Brunelleschi's painting of the Baptistry which could not be plotted geometrically were instead rendered through the reflections of real clouds on silver leaf which acted as the "sky" of the painting. As Hubert Damisch writes in *Théorie du /nuage/*,

> The process to which Brunelleschi had recourse for 'showing' the sky, this way of mirroring that he inserted into the pictorial field like a piece of marquetry and onto which the sky and its clouds were captured, this mirror is thus much more than a subterfuge. It has the value of an epistemological emblem . . . to the extent that it reveals the limitations of the perspective code, for which the demonstration furnishes the complete theory. It makes perspective appear as a structure of exclusions, whose coherence is founded on a series of refusals that nonetheless must make a place, as the background onto which it is printed, for the very thing it excludes from its order.

The mirror allowed both Brunelleschi and Gaudí to glimpse the essence of an idea and its form simultaneously, to affirm the belief in the truth of the image and belief in the truth of the thing itself. But while the cathedral in Florence was initiated long before Brunelleschi's day, built from the ground up with the expectation of the final crowning and the ultimate roof, it is significant and fortunate that the Sagrada Familia was not developed in plan. Had its footprint been erected floor by floor, Gaudí's life would have ended, and he would have left behind only an immense foundation. Instead, Gaudí built the East Portal as a profile of what it would become—a true Gate. While he may have envisioned the rest of the cathedral, as the model by Juan Matamala certainly indicates, Gaudí admitted at points along the way that he "did not know" what would follow. He was never able to objectify the cathedral. Would it have stood severed and apart from his faith? His impossible ruin remembers not what was, but what would be. It is fitting that the Portal of Nativity, a sublime expression of eternal immanence, looms in silhouette within the skyline of Gaudí's city—the ineffable manifestation of his rapturous devotion.

Gaudí's funeral, Sagrada Familia, 1926.

Notes

1. Michael Levey, *High Renaissance* (London: Penguin, 1975), 38.

2. Cecil Grayson, *Leon Battista Alberti: On Painting and On Sculpture, the Latin Texts of "De Pictura" and "De Statua"* (New York: Phaidon Press, 1972). For a discussion of the uses of the term "nature," see Ivan Galantic, "The Sources of Alberti's Theory of Painting" (Ph.D. dissertation, Harvard University, 1969). For a close reading of Alberti's optical studies, see James S. Ackerman, "Alberti's Light," in *Distance Points: Essays in Theory and Renaissance Art and Architecture* (Cambridge, Mass.: MIT Press, 1991).

3. Saint Augustine, *The Confessions of Saint Augustine*, trans. John K. Ryan (New York: Doubleday, 1960), 239.

4. Saint Isidore of Seville, *Isidori Hispalensis Episcopi Etymologiarum Sive Originum; Libri XX*, ed. William Lindsay (Oxford: Clarendon, 1985), vol. 1, III, xxi. Quoted in Samuel Y. Edgerton, Jr., *The Heritage of Giotto's Geometry: Art and Science on the Eve of the Scientific Revolution* (Ithaca, N.Y.: Cornell University Press, 1993). Edgerton, in attempting to prove the "atrophied" three-dimensional perception of the people of the Middle Ages, cites the example of Saint Isidore of Seville.

5. Caroline Walker Bynum, *Fragmentation and Redemption* (New York: Zone Books, 1991), 243.

6. "The redemption of the whole of humanity lies in the birth of Jesus and in his Passion. The temple therefore has a Nativity door and a Passion door. The symbolism of this temple is based on the Apocalypse, which says that the church is a verdant tree under which streams flow. The many contrasting pinnacles will have forms that could easily be interpreted as treetops." Cesar Martinell, *Conversaciones con Gaudí* (Barcelona: Ediciones Punto Fijo, 1969), 30.

7. Robert Descharnes and C. Prevost, *Gaudí the Visionary* (New York: Viking Press, 1971), 62.

8. Alberto Pérez-Gómez, *Architecture and the Crisis of Modern Science* (Cambridge, Mass.: MIT Press, 1983), 167.

9. Descharnes, 134.

10. Jay Fellows, *The Failing Distance* (Palo Alto, Calif.: Stanford University Press, 1991), 10–17.

11. Refer to Walker Bynum's discussion on medieval debates concerning "material continuity," in "Material Continuity, Personal Survival and the Resurrection of the Body: A Scholastic Discussion in its Medieval and Modern Contexts," in *Fragmentation and Redemption*.

12. François Bucher, "Design in Gothic Architecture: A Preliminary Assessment," in *Journal of the Society of Architectural Historians* 27 (1968): 49–71.

13. Erwin Panofsky, *Perspective as Symbolic Form*, trans. Christopher S. Wood (New York: Zone Books, 1991), 37–45.

14. Here I am borrowing from Hans-Georg Gadamer's analysis of the dialectic and the problem of the "one and the many" as aspects of human discourse and insight. See Gadamer, "Dialectic and Sophism in Plato's Seventh Letter," in *Dialogue and Dialectic*, trans. Christopher Smith (New Haven: Yale University Press, 1980), 120.

15. Descharnes, 55.

16. Manfredo Tafuri, *Theories and History of Architecture* (New York: Harper & Row, 1976), 14.

17. Hubert Damisch, *Théorie du /nuage/* (Paris: Editions du Seuil, 1972), 170–171. Quoted and translated in Rosalind Krauss, "The Grid, the /Cloud/, and the Detail," in Detlef Mertins, ed., *The Presence of Mies* (New York: Princeton Architectural Press, 1994), 142.

HADRIAN'S VILLA

Robert Mangurian and Mary-Ann Ray

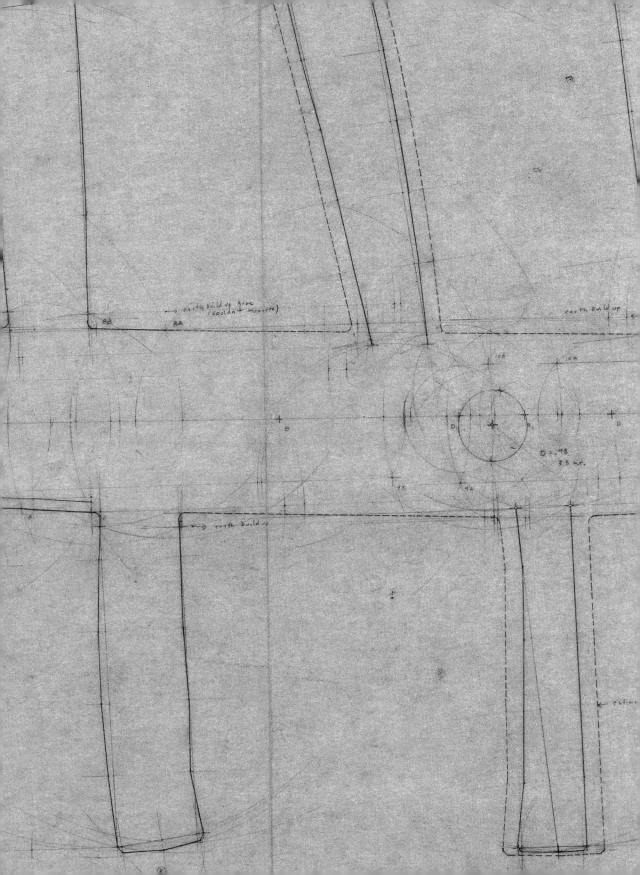

Snow Storage: On the Old Count Centini Land

July 21, 1990

The underground ice house was cleared by Team Mercury. This was our first really clear look at it. The southernmost length was opened up by shoving to both sides rubble from the collapsed skylight overhead, and after inching through on our sides, we found that this stretch did not have side legs like the northern stretch did. The acoustics were incredible, and we made use of the almost endless reverberation by performing our version of a Gregorian chant with a chorus of atonal drones under candlelight. In the time-consuming preparations for measuring, a stand line—an arbitrary but straight line established between two clear corners of the room—was pulled through the entire length of the space, and points were plumbed and marked on the ceiling with delicate graphite cross hairs. In

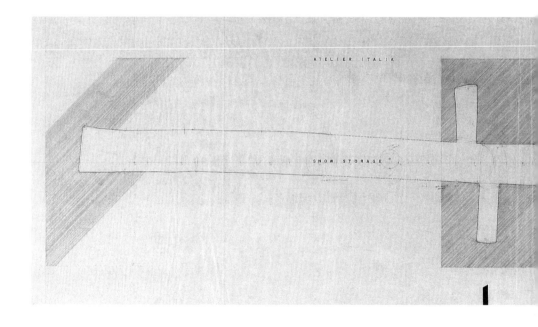

other parts of the villa we used red and blue lumber crayons, but the flawless and intact caseinlike skin—waterproofed with an animal protein such as egg or milk—seemed too sacred for marking. Corrections were made to Salza Prina Ricotti's plan: sixteen side-leg rooms rather than twenty-one, and the southern length without any rooms at all. Judging from the stand line, the plan is nearly straight—not as serpentine as depicted by her and Piranesi. We also saw a small rectangular room just to the north of the ice rooms. It may have been the big, gashed opening where excavated earth could have been pulled out easily, since its ceiling—unlike the entirely carved-out space of the storage itself—consisted of a concrete vault.

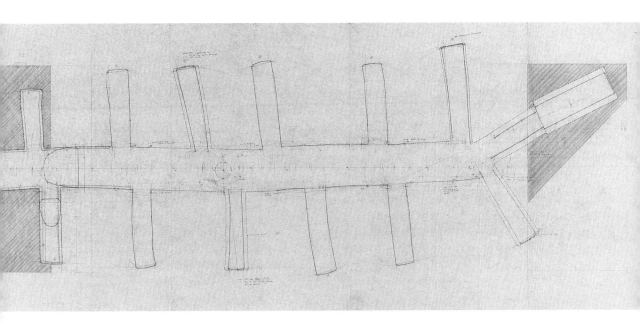

Triclinio: The First Measuring
Summer 1985

For some reason, this was the first space to attract us when we visited the villa. Our intention was to quickly construct a plan over the next few weeks, as a kind of sideline to the studio we were teaching in Ronciglione. We naively surveyed half the space with a series of linear measurements, then doubled the plan to plot the symmetry, and recorded the patterns of the black-and-white floor mosaic and some of the details of the column bases. We also measured a few other spaces that same day. Making the drawings back in our studio was satisfying as we discovered the geometries and proportions built into the space. The central room of the Triclinio was proportioned using a square root of two rectangles, and the diagonal lines of the mosaic inscribed onto the floor the diagonal of the base square and the arc of the surveyor's cord. The following autumn in Los Angeles, we met Bill MacDonald, who was on a Getty fellowship. He pointed us to the Piranesi plan and advised us to take diagonals—to triangulate the spaces we measured and carefully record all of the subtle features and details we saw. His work with Michael Boyle at the villa's small baths was our first example of good archaeological measuring, and we studied it closely. The Piranesi impressed us, and we knew we were following in big footsteps. We were hooked. Eventually we returned to triangulate the rooms.

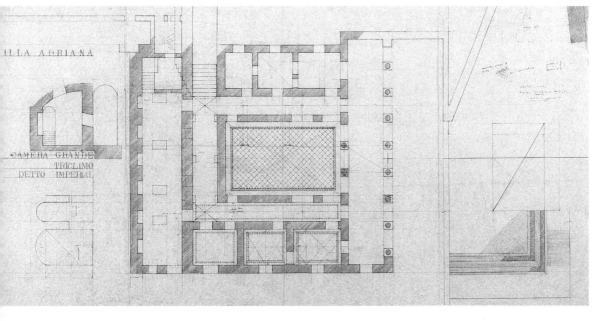

ILLA ADRIANA

CAMERA GRANDE
TRICLINIO
DETTO IMPERIAL

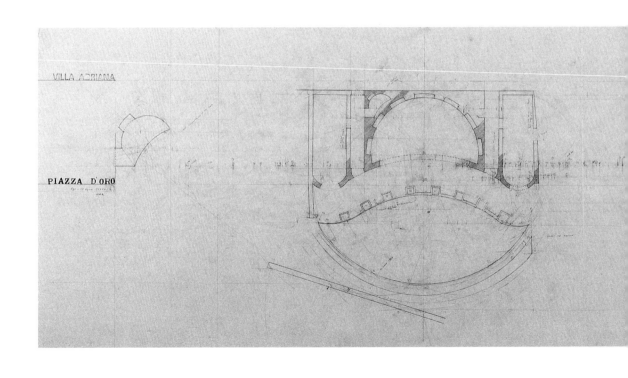

Piazza d'Oro: The Eye-Shaped Terrace

August 20, 1987

We decided that the series of lumps along the serpentine edge of the eye-shaped pool must be foundations or footings for the sub-bases of the missing columns. After inspecting them more closely, however, we saw that the lumps were the cemented infill between the missing sub-bases, of which they bore sharp impressions. The real configuration was a figure-ground reversal of what we had first seen. The intricate curvature of the space was measured from a stand line. Because the architecture of the pool stood lower, we used bubble levels to project points for measurements up to the apse. At the end of the day, looking east, Janet noticed that the shape of the dry and empty pool was a reflection of the contour of the Aniene Mountains in the distance.

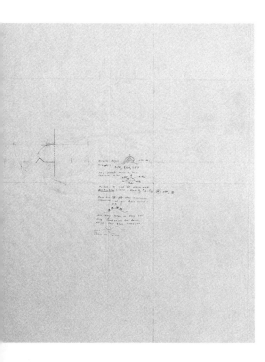

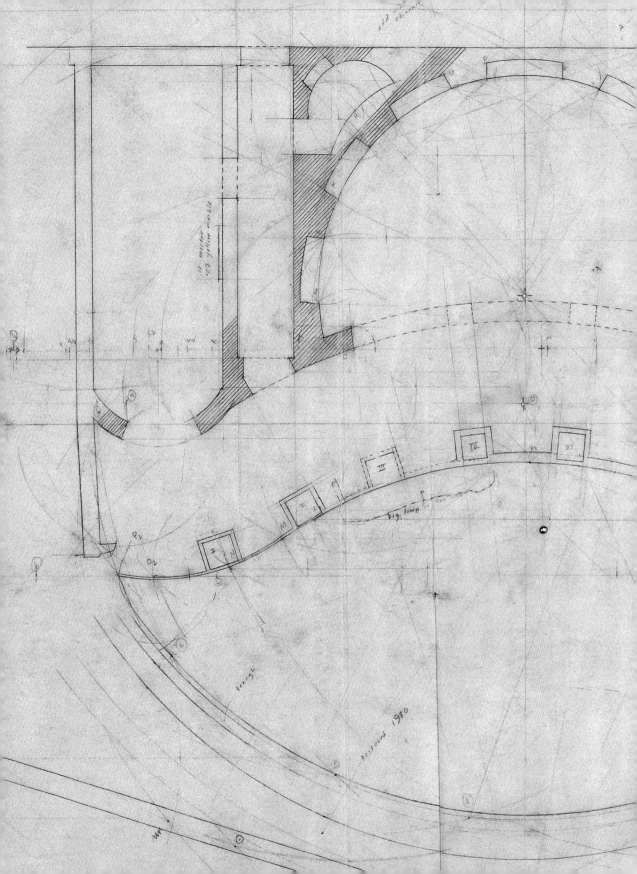

Grande Terme: The Western Sequence

July 9, 1987

Our first big project of the summer was measuring the Palazzo Imperiale, and our second
was the large baths. We split the baths lengthwise along the north-south wall of the
west side of the big frigidarium hall. Robert went east with his team while Mary-Ann and
George took on the western line of rooms with Chris Aykanian, Kathy Lindstrom, and
Connie Wechsler.

   The Eastern rooms consisted of the entry frigidarium and its surrounding large volumes
fronting onto the palestra, or exercise yard. The deeper rooms to the west housed the real
workings of the baths. The spaces and details we measured were sun rooms, tepid and hot
pools, ovens, service corridors, raised hypocaust floors, waterproofed cement, and hollow
walls. We had not done our research into the workings of Roman baths, nor had we seen
much of this before. We learned later that what we were noting as "layers of concrete with
big chunks of red brick" was really *opus signeum,* a waterproof surface that was made using
ceramic-firing techniques, resulting in a material that was as strong as good Roman concrete.

344

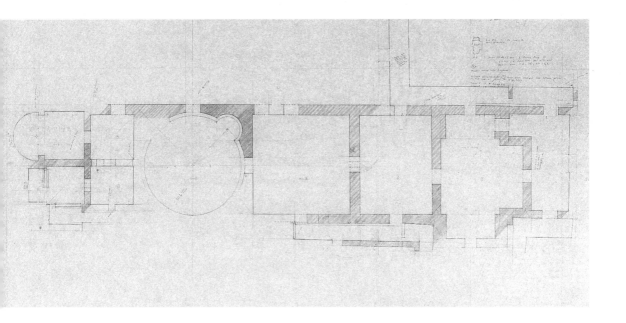

July 10, 1987

While drawing the baths in the studio—one of us on the west, the other on the east—each became independently concerned with a trend developing in the drawings: the triangulations pulled perpendicular walls noticeably off of square by about two degrees. We were subsequently elated, however, to find after comparing separate drawings that the angle coincided perfectly. Our instrument survey later confirmed and refined the angle, and we saw that the building of the large baths mediated the angle between the topography in front of it and a previous construction beside it.

YUAN

Yung-Ho Chang

Recorded here is an attempt to decipher the Chinese conception of enclosure by way of three operations: one, through the dissection of two Chinese ideograms, 园 *(yuán)*, meaning "garden," and 院 *(yuàn)*, meaning simultaneously "yard" and "dwelling"; two, by analyzing of the quintessential Beijing dwelling, 四合院 *(sì hé yuàn)*; and three, by examining the design of a kindergarten, 幼儿园 *(yòu ér yuán)* in Zheng Zhou. This may be seen as an architectural plot in which these four *yuans* have been intertwined players. Through the operations, one discovers that the physical form of 园 and the spatial implications of 院 are compatible through a notion of enclosure that is so simple as to be absolutely complete. This in turn allows the layered voids of the traditional house, 四合院, to structure the imported program of the kindergarten, 幼儿园. Eventually, the 院 of 四合院 substitutes 园 in 幼儿园, and an architecture of Chinese space arises from the catachresis 幼儿院.

347

园 *YUÁN*

With "garden" being its standard English translation, 园 seems innocently simple and clear. Because Chinese is a hieroglyphic language in which meanings are inscribed in visual forms, however, one cannot help but wonder what message is built into the character. Classical lexicons offer a rather clinical reading of 园 by disassembling its composition into two distinctive components: 元 *(yuán)* for sound and 口* for meaning.

Without difficulty, one can discern the implication of the rectangular form 口 —it is an enclosure. A silent fragment in modern Chinese, 口 was at one time a self-sufficient ideogram signifying enclosure and pronounced *wéi*. 园's spatial condition of being enclosed with walls or fences seems to be more important than what it keeps, vegetation and/or animals. Thus the character 园 does not suggest a garden in general, but specifically a walled garden.

There are other garden types. 苑 *(yuàn)* is almost identical in definition and pronunciation to 园, but its form differs. The lower portion, 夗, describes the pronunciation, while the grassy top, 艹, symbolizes the garden's floral content. Unlike 园, the ideogram 苑 has no clearly defined boundaries, which is consistent with an historic open country garden.

348

---

* Most basic structural components of Chinese ideograms do not have pronunciation and thus cannot be read.

Another garden, 囿 *(yòu)*, also possesses the 囗 form but illustrates a different territorial property—the frame in 囿 represents a two-dimensional space. 囿 derives from the ancient pictograph 𡦠 *(yòu)*, a diagram of four trees, 木 *(mù)*, in the flats of farmlands or fields, 田 *(tián)*. 𡦠 exemplifies a linguistic period in China when drawing and writing had not yet been distinguished. The evolution of the language brought the calligraphic simplification of 田 to 囗; meanwhile, the purely phonetic 有 *(you)* isolated and abstracted the picturesque woods. Like 苑, 囿 also belongs to the city outskirts.

The physical conditions of the various gardens must have initially dictated their respective ideograms. To decode the original pictographic patterns of these words yields fairly accurate spatial observations. After comparing the three gardens, one can make one more extrapolation: the enveloped 园 is urban. 园 descended from 園 *(yuán)*, wherein 袁 *(yuán)* functions as the sound giver. Yet the garden wall 囗 persisted.

The following is an attempt to restructure the pictorial design of the ideograms 园 and 園 to reveal certain otherwise obscured spatial relationships and perhaps to generate new ones. The results depart from proper Chinese, and even produce nonwords:

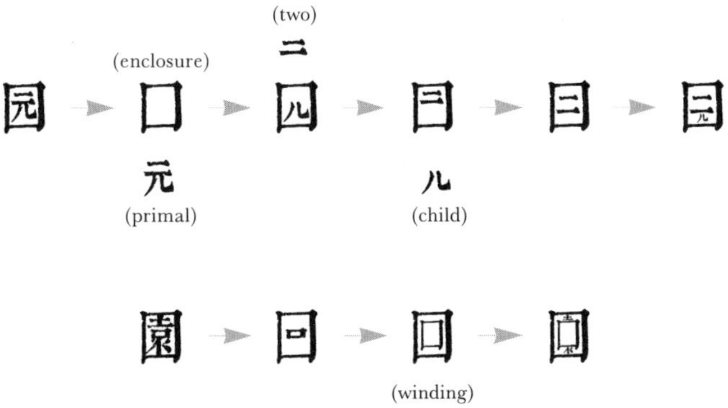

349

园 ▸ 囗 ▸ 㐅 ▸ 彐 ▸ 彐 ▸ 彐
(enclosure) (two) 二
元
(primal) 儿
(child)

園 ▸ 曰 ▸ 回 ▸ 回
(winding)

YUÀN

院's standard translation is "yard," with "dwelling" as a secondary meaning. As accurate as these definitions might be, they fail to reflect the inclusive nature of the character: 院 simultaneously signifies the physical enclosure, the void created, and the combined entirety of all voids and solids (buildings and walls) within such enclosures.

One can quickly isolate the 元 in 院 to confirm its phonetic similarity to 园. To visually identify the spatial characteristics of 院 proves to be far more complex, as this modern ideogram contains no significant enclosures. One must again search the classical lexicons for clues to help unravel the pictographically reductive process of the evolution of Chinese characters.

The earlier versions of 阝 and 宀 thus reappear. 阝 (nicknamed "ear" because of its appearance) turns out to have two origins: the 阝 on the right side of a character comes from 邑 *(yì)*, meaning town or city, while 阝 on the left side, as in the case of 院, is derived from 阜 *(fù)*, a rare word that has undergone many transformations in appearance while maintaining certain forms of repetitive enclosures—more precisely, a group of two or three rectilinear spaces organized in a parallel fashion. The proportion of the rectangular boxes

350

curiously resembles the footprint of a typical room-building in a 院 dwelling, and their lay-ered order echoes the house's north-south building arrangement. While a more definitive architectural implication of these forms is not known, it is of interest to notice that the earliest retrievable meaning of 阜 is "earth mound," and "earth" always connotes construction and building in Chinese.

If the previous spatial analysis is primarily planar, 宀 can only be perceived as a sectional image. Although the modern 宀 may simulate a roof form, the ancient 宀 assimilates the diagram of a building skeleton—posts and truss, or a building shell of roof and walls. Under the shelter of 宀, "home" 家 (jia) is made and "house" 宅 (zhái) built. 宀 not only defines space but also renders it domestic.

When one cross-references the spatial implications of the characters 园 and 院, it becomes possible to construct a more comprehensive model of the Chinese concept of enclosure. However, the fact that the English words "garden" and "yard" originated from the Old High German *gart*—meaning no other than enclosure—makes one wonder if a universal desire to define space governs the regional formation of corresponding words.

四合院 *SÌ HÉ YUÀN*

The blank wall.

One of the oldest pictographs for "house" is literally a drawing of a house: ⊕ *(gong)*. At the center of the image lies a square courtyard plan, with surrounding building elevations on the four sides. Today this ancient pictograph assumes a completely different appearance— 宫 *(gong)*—and signifies only the residences or palaces of emperors. The courtyard house referred to by the ancient pictograph is now written as 四合院.

四 means "four"; 合 "closed"; and 院 "courtyard," "dwelling," and all of the spatial conditions described above. After five millenia of development, 四合院 has itself distilled certain Chinese notions of enclosure and space. 四合院 is about:

1. *An introverted void.* With a blank perimeter wall defining a complete enclosure, 四合院 has no exterior. The only opening in the wall is the front door, which is uncompromisingly blocked from the inside by a screen to prevent any spatial leakage. On the interior, the house is widely open toward its center—the 院 per se—with wood-paneled doors and rice-papered windows barely separating the indoor from the outdoor.

2. *A miniature universe.* As a symbolic empty nucleus, 院 organizes the house into a cosmos where life unfolds between heaven and earth. Simulating the introverted nature of the Chinese universe, the center of this void also establishes a conceptual infinity, from which physical density is pushed out toward the edge. In the dense periphery, meaning multiplies: the four surrounding structures interpret the cardinal directions as seasons, life

35²

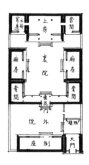

**A four-closed-yard/dwelling (四合院)
in Beijing.**

Courtyard defined by its own walls.

cycles, and totems, and translate family relationships into social hierarchy. The orthogonality of the dwelling is a cosmic necessity.

3. *An autonomous courtyard.* 院 is not a by-product of a building arrangement, but is a primary space preceding the buildings. 院 owes its autonomy to its rural origin, 場 *(chang,* meaning "field") 院, a walled open-air hall for farming and domestic work. The courtyard in 四合院 extends the rooms and accommodates both daily activities and special events. Since no distinction is made between outdoor and indoor conditions, there is no residual space.

4. *Room-buildings.* In 四合院, a room is a building and a building a room. The timber-frame structure produces a basic architectural element that may vary in size but not in form. The prototypical unit promotes repetition and subtlety without leaving any room for isolated dramas, narrowing the design task to the determination of relationships between ready-made components.

These qualities of 四合院 construct a cultural background for domestic scenes but do not prescribe any particulars to a house. There is nothing to forbid 院 from becoming a public institution. As a matter of fact, "public institution" is 院's third definition.

院 is the building typology of ancient China; it welcomes an infinite programmatic variety within its hollowed enclosures.

幼儿园 *YÒU ÉR YUÁN*

The Western idea of the kindergarten arrived in China to find no local precedent. The recently coined Chinese phrase 幼儿园 provides a literal translation of the German term: 幼儿, meaning "child" or "children," and 园, "garden"—thus *children's garden*.

    This is a garden without typical garden attributes. Vegetation gives way to enclosures for playing and for learning. The emptied garden looks suspiciously close to a yard. At this very moment, 院 takes over 园.

    I shall let the following drawings describe 幼儿院.

354

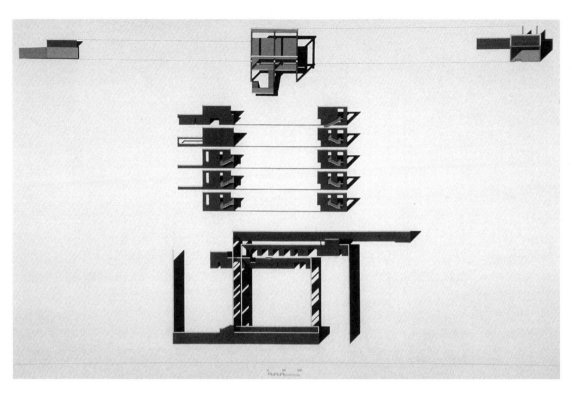

Anatomical axonometric

Roof plan

W

S 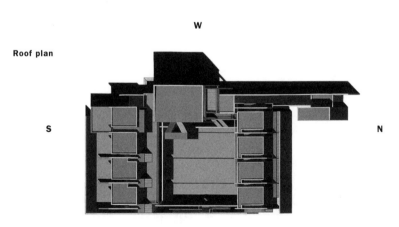 N

E

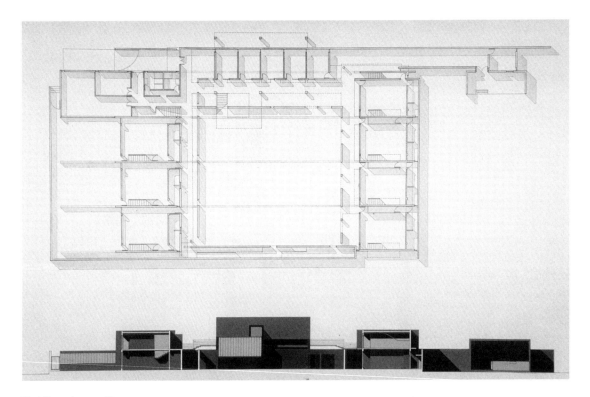

First-floor plan, section

East elevation

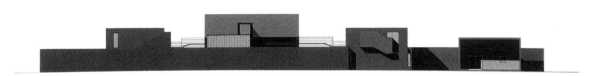

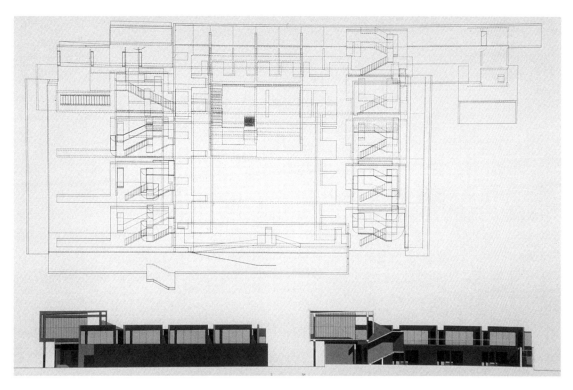

Experimental analysis, south elevation, section

Gliding section / perspective

CHANG

Gliding 360° perspective

CHANG

MILL RACE PARK STRUCTURES

Stanley Saitowitz

The quality of the city of Columbus, Indiana, should reflect in the park. In the way that a tree inhabits the city, remembering nature . . . the structures inhabit the park, remembering the city.

The group of nine buildings in the park is conceived as a family, each with the same genes, derived from the same geometry, speaking a common language. The family is divided into two groups, one having the characteristics of use specificity, where program informs the form, the other having the characteristics of site specificity, where amplifying the site is the formal generator.

SAITOWITZ

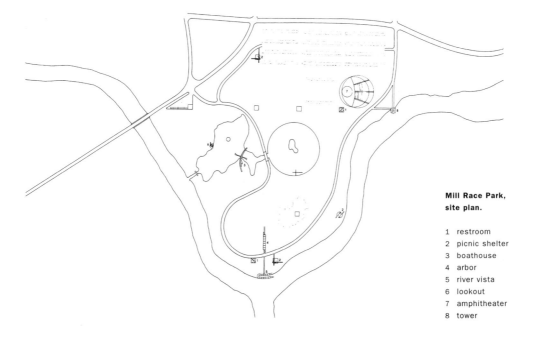

**Mill Race Park,
site plan.**

1 restroom
2 picnic shelter
3 boathouse
4 arbor
5 river vista
6 lookout
7 amphitheater
8 tower

The genetic structure of the buildings is synoptic of formal explorations which revolve around an architecture of roofs both as primal elements in shelter-making, and as fragments of the dome of the sky, cut by forms which emerge as plans on the ground. Each structure presents a gesture of singularity which aims to create an object of definite ambiguity. All structures arise from similar geometries—squares intersecting with circles—interpreted specifically in relation to site or to program. All are made of concrete ground structures with steel roofs—some corrugated, some perforated—supported by steel tube structures.

The nine park structures concretize their situational reality. They amplify the site, and proclaim their functions publicly.

362

Restroom

The Restrooms have W- and M-shaped roofs, with interlocking glass block screens. The walls float above the ground, allowing flood waters to wash through. The roofs float above the screen walls, allowing smells to escape. They facilitate ablution in an atmosphere of openness.

364

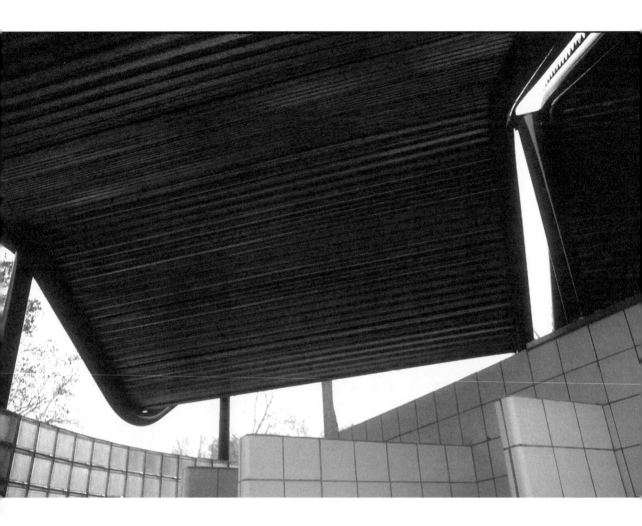

SLOW SPACE

Arbor

The Arbor is a tunnel to the River Vista, a lens which focuses on the river ahead which divides and forms the boundaries of the park. Its woven wire skin supports creepers which drip into the tunnel, which is lined with benches.

368

River vista

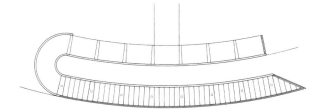

The River Vista weaves ground and water. It is a curled pier for viewing down the river, reached by crossing over the water to a piece of detached land.

370

Picnic shelters

The Picnic Shelters consist of a roof draped over a table, with fragments of a room establishing their space.

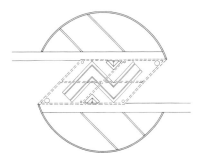

Lookout

The Lookout is a chaise-formed bank for sunbathing, with a shady fishing pier above.

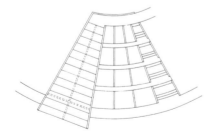

Boathouse

The Boathouse connects land and water. Its roof is an upturned hull. Two jetties
connect to two bodies of water of varying heights—one man-made and constant, the
other natural and varying.

Amphitheater

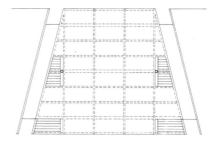

The Amphitheater is a sculpted berm. The earth heaves to form a crater, a dish of seating which transforms into a structure consisting of a scaffold above a circular stage. The stage has two fronts. One faces the berm; the other, for large audiences, faces the tree-lined field.

378

SLOW SPACE

Tower

The Tower is a primal version of the tower of Saarinen's First Christian Church, the building which inspired the Cummins Foundation Program which turned the city of Columbus into a museum of architecture. The park tower is stripped to basic elements: a wall, a stair, an elevator, a clock, and a viewing platform. The wall establishes a dialectic between city and park. On the side facing the city, an elevator and a clock climb the wall; on the side facing the park is a stair. The ascent up the tower denies the view to the city that is revealed only when one reaches the viewing platform, which displays a map showing the architecture of Columbus. From this position, a synoptic view of the city and its architecture is provided.

MUSEUM OF CONTEMPORARY ART, HELSINKI

Steven Holl

OVER DILATION / OVER SOUL:
STEVEN HOLL'S "LINE OF CULTURE"

Michael Bell

The psychic core of a room is a reverie. —Steven Holl

With his Helsinki Museum of Contemporary Art (1992), Steven Holl has not only matured to fulfill the promise of his early experimental urban works, but has also been able to incorporate the Emersonian themes of "direct experience" and nature that have engaged Holl over the course of his career. At Helsinki, Holl has intertwined ideas of matter via Ralph Waldo Emerson and Henri Bergson with those of urbanism and the politics of urban life in an era of the late-capitalist city. Holl's now fully mature urban works confront the political and economic history of the city with a sophisticated and troubling chiasmatic coupling of nature and history, a joining that threatens the segregate stability of both by now disparate but organic enterprises. With the Museum of Contemporary Art, Holl has mastered a provision of access to the natural and to direct experience, a career-long effort, in the most meaningful confrontation of city as deterritorialized artifice and nature as organic site that he has ever confronted. Even Holl's refined work in Japan has not been able to offer such a calibrated scrutiny of the city as a governing mechanism. At Helsinki, Holl has achieved the evolutionary promise of his interest in matter with a building that promises to calibrate the durational attributes of Emersonian nature with those of the productive city. The project requires that Holl's work be appraised as Theodor Adorno would have it, as a form of "natural-history," a chiasmatic conflation of nature and city as lived experience. Holl's building dilates the city and filters nature.

I. Matter

Photography is a thermodynamic process; negatives and prints are the recording surfaces upon which scenarios of industrial capital are played out in the guise of latent images: memories, records, news, history. Photography delivers to the chemical industry a consuming audience—figuration provides the means to sustain an industry of immense economic proportion. Nature and organic life are subsumed within the inorganic machinations of a technological industrial economy. In his first monograph, *Anchoring*, Steven Holl recalls being warned as a student that "photographs cannot be trusted."[1] A professor of Holl's had cautioned that one must travel in order to have a "direct experience of architecture." In his introduction to *Anchoring*, Holl offers similar advice and actually seems reluctant to offer the written word in place of experience: "Writing's relation to architecture affords only an uncertain mirror to be held up to evidence."[2] Holl does allow, however, that words can "present a premise," and in *Anchoring* they are tendered in a manner that seems to give a sense of the architect's ideas in the literal presence of the words themselves.

Holl not only struggles to offer the written word as a descriptive device, but also to present it as something real in itself, and to an extent he has succeeded. His descriptive texts often have had the resonance of Lawrence Wiener's physical linguistics. Like Wiener, Holl's words give a sense of weight, and even tonality, to his proposed spaces—they are at times metallurgical. Holl's phrases ascertain the timbre of architectural space and materials and his abstractions are palpable and of the present. *Anchoring* is in this manner not so much a text or even a monograph, but instead it functions as a kind of lab manual and catalog of materialized thoughts. Even as Holl's ambitions tended toward the inferable, he still offered explicit diagrams of his methods and of the mechanics of his techniques. At its release *Anchoring* was a useful book; one was asked to engage in it and to experience it directly. But what then can be said of Holl's distrust of photography, particularly in light of his own admonitions of its limits and the proliferation of photographs of his own work? The answer is perhaps best sought in the design and layout of both *Anchoring* and its sequel, *Intertwining*.[3]

In *Anchoring* and *Intertwining*, Holl relies upon black and white photographs to serve as both representation and experience of his works. These photographs offer something real in themselves, however, and as such they have correlative value to the space of Holl's architecture. In other words, Holl may not represent the proposed spaces of his works in these books, but offers the reader the ability to recreate them instead. Holl's architecture—and especially the models of his recent projects—often have made use of innovations in glass fabrication. His design experiments have included poured, etched, bent, tempered, and colored glass, often in some relation to program and sometimes in relation to construction methods. Early on, Holl's notes, sketches, and diagrams indicated an espousal of artisan craft and a reterritorialization of building components in an era of standardized production. While Holl's projects often attempt to record the presence of the fabricating hand, the photographs of these projects offer critical insight into Holl's incantations that architecture be experienced first, *even* in the photographs. Within the realm of the photograph, Holl has used glass in its varying degrees of translucency and reflectivity to prompt and to thwart the camera's ability to reveal something of material and of experience beyond the monocular figuration of form. By exposing materials in a certain light, Holl has consistently overexposed the eye (as camera) in a manner similar to the optic dilations seen in the films of László Moholy-Nagy's Light-Space Modulator (1921–30), and the blinding whiteout screens in Martin Scorsese's *Raging Bull*.

With the Giada Showroom (1987), Holl entered a phase of his work in which he began to use material as it responds to light in order to dismantle the quantitative and relative focus of the camera lens. At Giada the photographs that were published of the poured-glass corner detail appeared to be overexposed and were cropped to prevent any sense of foreground or background.

387

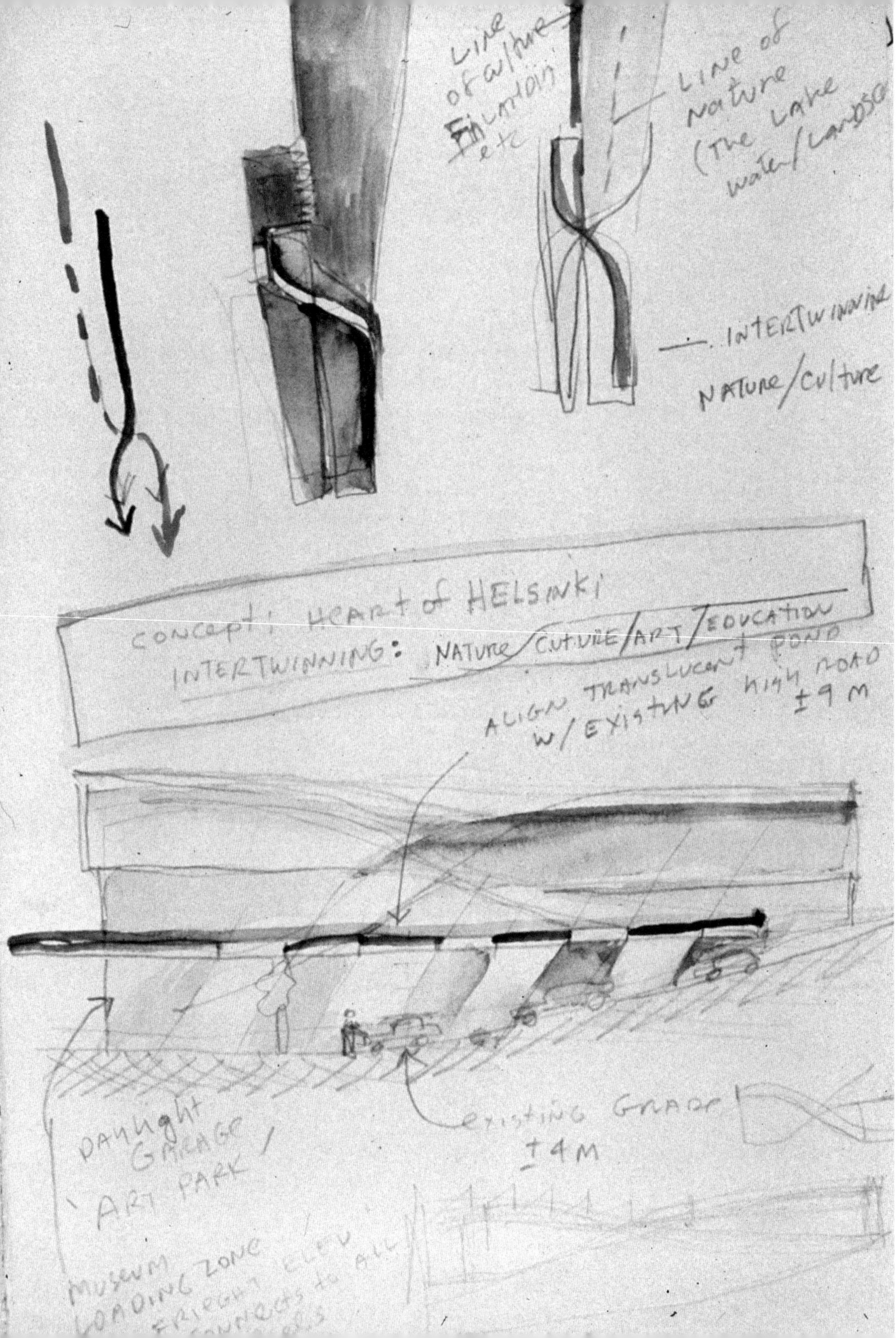

Line of culture Fountain etc

Line of nature (the lake water/landsc

—·— INTERTWINING
NATURE/Culture

CONCEPT: HEART of HELSINKI
INTERTWINNING: NATURE/CULTURE/ART/EDUCATION

ALIGN TRANSLUCENT POND
W/EXISTING HIGH ROAD
±9M

DAYLIGHT
GARAGE/
ART PARK

EXISTING GRADE
±4M

MUSEUM
LOADING ZONE
FRIEGHT ELEV
CONNECTS TO ALL

In these and subsequent photographs, Holl seemed to be suggesting that a dissolution of the quantitative focus of lens mechanics was required to partake in the space of his architecture. This dilation transforms the photograph into an actual site; the quantitative and segregate relativity of the eye in pictorial space is replaced with the durational attributes of filmic thermodynamics. The photograph is not a representation but a chemical process whose surface congeals in a uni-lateral development process. Space in Holl's photographs is flattened, but the Cartesian surface becomes four-dimensional as an entropic mode of chemical time. Even as Holl's works have required and even at times nourished the standing subject and relative perceiving I/eye, one is drawn to believe that Holl has always wanted the viewer to see much more than the outline of form and the shape of space or material. The Fukuoka Housing Project (1989), the Van Zandt House (1982), the House at Leucadia, California (1984), and the Porta Vittoria Project (1986) are each explicit both in locating and dislocating the standing subject. In these projects, Holl situated the feet but led the eye onward. Each project broke from the quantitative dimension of perspecti-val time and focused the eye on an emergent event. At Porta Vittoria, Holl went so far as to give some drawings multiple vanishing points in the manner of an El Lissitzky *proun*. The Porta Vittoria designs were pictorially nothing short of willfully and outrageously deliberate. One could claim that these premises are the prognoses of form and space in Holl's early architecture.

Chiasma

At the Helsinki Museum of Contemporary Art, Holl has extended a segment of the adjacent Töölo Bay toward the building site and woven it within the museum's entrance. Holl calls this inter-twining of landscape and city a "chiasma." He indicates that a "line of nature" (the bay) and a "line of culture" (the city) are modulated within a new relationship accorded by the building. The Museum of Contemporary Art, according to Holl, is a "synthesis of building and landscape . . . a chiasma" that links the segregate worlds of nature and history.[4] Holl strives for a building that could open a connection between nature and city—he has done so throughout his career—but at Helsinki, in this truly public and urban context, Holl's intentions take on a new proportion. Here the intertwining ceases to operate in the context of Emersonian man and instead engages in a dimension of economic and political criticism that Holl's work has never directly confronted. At

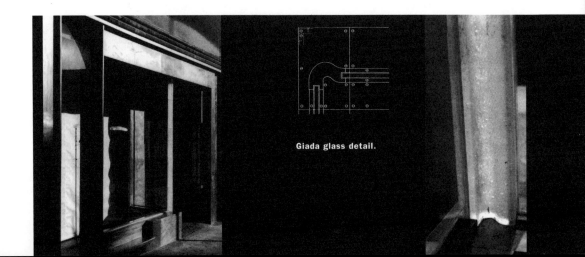

Giada glass detail.

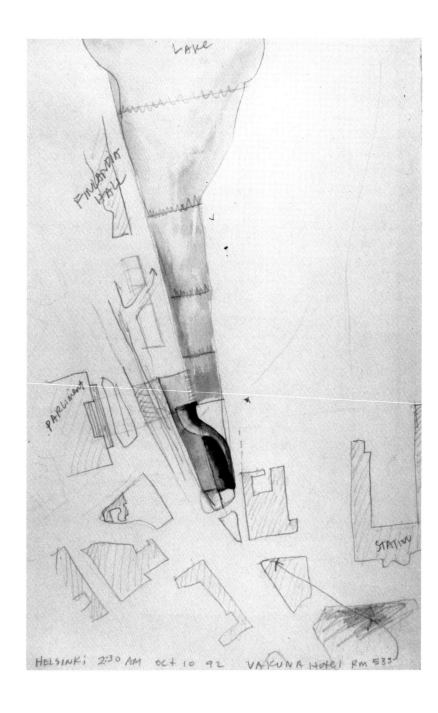

LAKE

FINLANDIA HALL

PARLIAMENT

STATION

HELSINKI 2:30 AM OCT 10 92 VAKUNA Hotel RM 533

Helsinki, Holl's use of the word *kiasma* (a Finnish spelling of chiasma) can be understood in the context of the philosophy of Theodor Adorno, whose use of the phrase coupled nature and history into a "chiasmatic couplet" as "natural/history."[5] While Holl has often alluded to Emerson to clarify an ideal of man's relation to nature, his use of the word "kiasma," if seen in Adorno's context, acknowledges the evolution of capitalism in the shaping of social relations and the mechanized exclusion of nature from its industrial/economic techniques. Helsinki finds Holl on new ground in an architectural realm of evolved political dimension, yet Holl's mentor Ralph Waldo Emerson still seems to provide the fundamental ideals in Holl's invocation of the natural.

Nature

For Emerson, "every property of matter" was "a school for . . . understanding" and the comprehension of matter was the comprehension of nature itself.[6] "The Supreme Being," wrote Emerson, does "not build up nature around us, but puts it forth through us."[7] Emerson's man and woman partake in nature; they are "dilated" by it and they "conspire" with it. The distinctions that Henri Bergson makes in how we may have knowledge of matter's essence (nature's essence) find particular resonance in this context: Bergson warned that to know something from without is to be relegated to a relativistic and limited vantage of representation; to know something in the full would require taking up that entity's essence in ourselves.[8] For Emerson, the constraints of space and time that constitute the relativity of Bergson's formulation of lesser knowledge are vanquished in man's reciprocity with the natural—man is nature, and has no need to "represent" it. In place of the representational and relative lie the durational attributes of matter *as* time rather than *in* time. Emerson offers a caveat, however, that depicts the struggle of the architect (and artist) who seeks to account for the organicism of nature. In a statement given almost in passing, Emerson wrote that the architect necessarily seeks to "concentrate the radiance of the world on one point." Emerson seems generous in the seemingly open manner in which he allows that nature in this way is not represented, but allowed to flow through art: "Thus is Art a nature that passes through the alembic of man."[9] Does Holl attempt to concentrate the "radiance" of the natural in "one point," and if so how does this attempt avoid the relativism of the represented? Is Holl's process alembic?

In the case of the Giada showroom, the (seemingly) overexposed photos of the glass corner detail reveal a singularity of form as well as some sense of latent unsprung energy. At Giada the viewer is urged to realize not only how sublime this stacked corner of poured-glass bars is, but also how trivial and odd it looked in the ink plan and oblique drawings that accompanied its publication. Were these drawings warnings that representation "cannot be trusted" and that we should move on to experience? Did the overexposure of the photo subvert the camera's relative

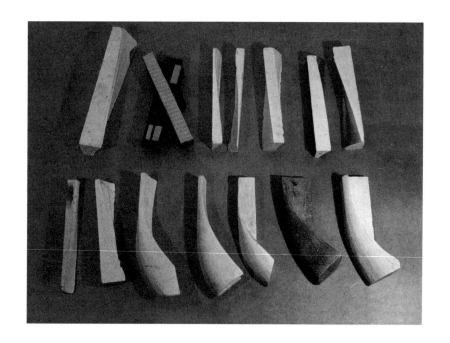

and singular monocularity? The stacking seems essential in this regard because it reveals Holl's frequent reliance on the generative possibilities of gravity, and the stacking allows gravity to become operative in our visual comprehension of space and form. The spatial aspects of weight were also put to effect in abetting a comprehension of matter's duration. At Giada, the haptic qualities of matter emerge in a postvisual field of optic dissolve. Form's quantitative outline is undermined by the immanence of a structural failure induced by gravity's incessant pull. Within a chasm of a postvisual comprehension, Holl mechanically disallows the simple visual description of form and begins a process played out in almost every project that chronologically follows.

For Holl, the experience of architecture is often the intuited experience of matter, and this intuition is achieved through a dismantling of quantitative vision. At Giada, Holl set poured-glass bars end upon end, and the stacking instigated an unnerving vertical instability. A simple lateral push of the slightest magnitude would disable the design; while such a force was not forthcoming, one had the sense that one was expected to wait for it. The stacking, composed of sequentially repetitive dimensions, held the linear sequence on the verge of dissolve as well: the bars have a formal immanence toward toppling. The effect is not unlike the kind of immanence Rosalind Krauss identifies in the sculpture of Auguste Rodin and Robert Smithson, an immanence she characterizes as that of an "immobile cyclone."[10] Holl's architecture has been involved in the same kind of systemic production of energy held in repose, a kind of *work* that keeps form on the verge of unpredictable and presumably instantaneous transformation. This transformation, should it occur, threatens the loss of its generative origins; in other words, Holl indicates the potential of an uncharted domain whose origin is unretrievable, a glimpse of matter on the verge of losing its expected distribution of energy and force. These are systems on the verge of entropic disorder— of energy dissipation.

Despite the question of relativism and fixity, Holl has also consistently allowed a figural and formal dimension not only to remain in his work but indeed sometimes to drive it. Holl has always been preoccupied with the formless, but his work has played on a dangerous edge skirting both figuration and form. Much of Holl's work has been advanced in a taunting manner—as if the architect is daring us to relinquish certain cognitive skills and almost, but not quite, providing a view to the spatial aftermath if we did. Again, experience should prevail, and Holl withholds the represented spaces. If Holl's work does taunt and dare, it also leaves its subject in the wake of revision. Holl moves freely, sometimes prosaically, within the syntactic structures of formal histories while at times abandoning the political progenesis of those formal histories. Why, one critic has asked, does a new museum in Helsinki, in 1996, have a curtain wall derivative of Walter Gropius and Peter Behrens, especially if this new building is the work of an architect whose project has often seemed to be very much one of reterritorialization?

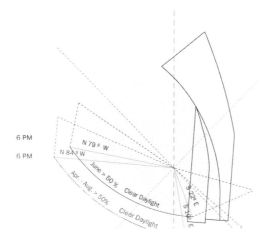

N 79 ° W

N 84 ° W

June > 50 % Clear Daylight

Apr. - Aug. > 50% Clear Daylight

S 22° E

S 16° E

LINE OF NATURE

Töölo Bay

LINE OF CULTURE

LINE OF THE CITY

II. Ghosts

Steven Holl's Helsinki Museum of Contemporary Art is a building rife with ghosts. Holl's masterwork picks up evolutionary threads of the formal history of architecture and in transposition plies and extends them into a renewed cultural task. At Helsinki and in much of his earlier work, Steven Holl reestablishes certain architectural histories. The Metz House and the Bridge of Houses in New York City's Chelsea, for example, have a marked relation to Adolf Loos's *raumplan*. Like Loos, Holl has often internalized his subject's horizon and in doing so has turned his back on the metropolis (although it is not clear that we today live in the metropolis). At times Holl's works defer the horizon's closure in trying to alleviate its quantitative dimension. Holl's architecture both positions its occupant and simultaneously reveals other potential positions. With the soon-to-be-completed Helsinki Museum of Contemporary Art, however, the architect has moved more fully into an urban terrain, a terrain in which Holl has now completely relinquished the discrete basin of the house and its private subject/citizen. Holl must now allow for a civic person and has thus moved into the role of providing an architecture of the city. At this juncture his work can no longer offer the deferment of the solitary figure, of Emerson's person, but must instead put forward a form of association; Holl's architecture must posit a civic relation among men and women. The reciprocity of house/subject and city that characterized the urban intentions of the Hybrid Building at Seaside, Florida (though Seaside hardly qualifies as urban), is at Helsinki challenged by more advanced and contemporary demands for collective metropolitan synthesis. Holl's architecture moves confidently into this realm and in doing so has become emboldened by a topological complexity at which his early work only hinted.

The museum is bolstered by much of Holl's early work, but the research that composed his Edge of a City projects is of particular importance here. For Holl, the Edge of a City is a "philosophic region" where city and natural landscape meet.[11] These edge sites attract endless attention as we foreclose on the twentieth-century city, as indeed they attract Holl, but it is Holl's characterization of these sites as "existing without choice or expectation" that sets his premises apart from almost anyone else's.[12] One must ask if the spaces Holl offered at these crucibles are to be understood as provisional: do Holl's Edge of a City projects portend a life without expectations? Has the architect scrutinized what politics were kept at bay in those scenarios—what economic passions are to dissolve in the topologies of the urban spaces he proposed? In response, Holl offered the phenomenology of experience, and if built the projects surely would have offered a renewed ideal of collective space. The projects themselves offered an aggressively modeled plastic space not seen in urban work since Le Corbusier. Holl's political intentions, however, seemed vague at best and recall issues raised by Rafael Moneo's analysis of Aldo Rossi's Modena

Cemetery.[13] Moneo suspected that Rossi's urban intentions could be understood to be a form of "delay," and asked whether such a mode of operation could be successful in light of the pervasive nature of technology's economic demands and popular vernacular's taste. Moneo pointed to the architecture of Archigram as of technology, and that of Robert Venturi as of "vulgar" popular taste. While the Edge of a City projects could clearly alter the trajectory of Rossi's thoughts, they seem to refrain from overt political or economic commentary. A direct critique of New Urbanism's complicity with market forces, Holl's urbanism sustains a revised social space. Perhaps Helsinki can reinvigorate the contemporary significance of the Edge of a City projects.

The masterful inventiveness of the Helsinki Museum of Contemporary Art provides some semblance of an answer to the question of politics and space, and if the formal invention of Holl's urban works provide for social invention as well, then certainly Holl's urban spaces do critique the political and economic. What did Holl anticipate in the vacancy of the delayed perspectives of the Edge of a City projects and the urbanism of Porta Vittoria, which expands inward rather than out? Surely Holl was not only suggesting urban redensification; was he projecting an equipoise of inward and outward growth as an existential inability to choose? The formal virtuosity of the Edge of a City projects and the desperation of their American sites (edge of Phoenix . . .) surely promised more than the phenomenological.

Holl's involvement with architectural history shows that his formalizations do convincingly offer genuine social invention. His spaces can be understood as a ground for new ideals of culture if inhabited to their full potential. The still and quiet vortex at Helsinki's center that intertwines bay and building—culture, city, and nature—is haunted by the voided entry of Le Corbusier's Carpenter Center. Helsinki also vaguely recalls the section of Ronchamp, and Frank Lloyd Wright's Guggenheim asks for consideration as well. But these are the overt references—for a more refined correlation, we should consider Le Corbusier's unbuilt Firminy Church, perhaps the most poignant allusion, especially if one is willing to see Le Corbusier's unfinished work as the moment that marked his final move away from the dialectics of figure/field and inside/outside (city/nature). The Firminy Church challenges Ronchamp as Le Corbusier's final composition. Firminy and Helsinki are united in questioning more than formal dialectics; they also offer an unfolding of the historical hierarchies of body and spirit, or nature and artifice. In his frequent references to Emerson, Holl communicates that his premise may be to offer an unfolding of space that accords to occupants a sense of the city as nature. Does the architect intend for us to understand the spiritual as nature or, at Helsinki, does he intend to identify both the city and nature as spiritual and as organic? Firminy was commissioned as theological architecture, and the distinctions it erases between the corporeal and the divine cohere with its program. Holl's building is a museum—a secular institution of cultural patronage—yet Holl's Emersonian incantations of nature

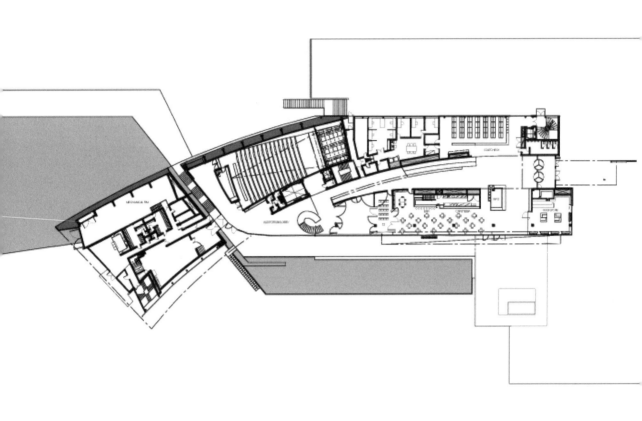

situate Helsinki as a theological building also—of sorts. At Firminy the floor plate unrolls and extrapolates itself into a smooth section (actually, section and plan are one in Firminy, and the historically received distinctions between altar, sacristy, and apse—between corporeal and divine—are swept into a new contiguous relationship). If the basilica is an inversion of the temple—the colonnade moves inside as the cella moves out—then Firminy is the relinquishment of all such binary inversions or classicized originary states.[14] Firminy is a threaded knot—undone. Holl's Helsinki Museum of Contemporary Art takes part in similar topological and political transfigurations. At Helsinki formal inversions transform political states: walls become roofs, floors arc to form ramps, and the hierarchical origins of unaccounted regimes (art historical, patronage . . .) are made dissolute as the leading hand of the promenade turns back on itself.[15] The topology of processual space at Firminy delivers what the Villa Savoye's cubist but linear promenade portrays, yet withholds. The complete formalization of Firminy might have been presaged in the stair of Savoye—Firminy is the surface of Savoye's stair without Savoye's Cartesian basin. It is as if Le Corbusier simply willed the space of Firminy, defiantly daring to design it. What does an architect stare down to accomplish such a feat? Can space constitute defiance?

Can Helsinki be directly compared to Firminy when viewed through the lens of Holl's inspiration in Emerson? At the least, such a comparison reveals more about Holl's intentions than would a comparison of Helsinki to another museum, even the Guggenheim. At Firminy, formal origins are themselves under the duress of a topological process that eradicates the quantitative regulation of position and movement. Firminy is neither figure nor ground; in this sense Helsinki is indebted to Firminy, but Helsinki as a contemporary building must account for different kinds of unseen forces and processes. Helsinki's perceived task—indeed, the one that presumably drives Holl's relentless inventiveness—is to stave off the seemingly inevitable dichotomy between the cultural and the natural. Holl enunciates a "line of culture," a "line of nature," and a "line of the city" in the description of this project; these dimensions take on literal geometries in the executed building. This is surely a standoff in which architecture is expected to

Le Corbusier. Model of the Church at Firminy-Vert, 1960–65.

 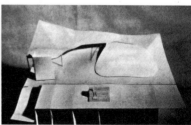

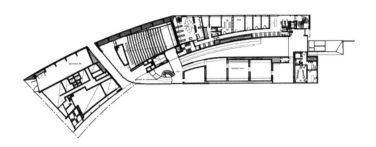

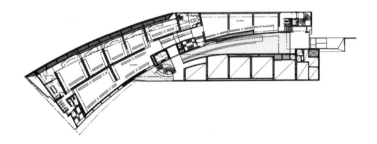

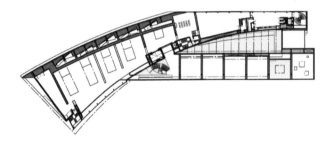

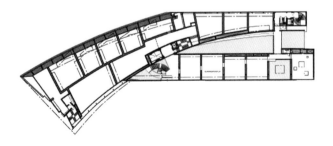

provide not only relief but repose as well; like Firminy, Holl's design accomplishes its task in the eradication of simple figure/ground dialectics.

Helsinki must move between culture—some form of metropolitan political economics—and nature, as understood through Holl's references to Emerson. In the passage Holl uses to introduce his Edge of a City projects; he quotes Emerson: "The health of the eye seems to demand a horizon. We are never tired so long as we can see far enough."[16] In Holl's early works, he internalized the horizon; at Porta Vittoria, in 1988, he offered multiple horizons; but as Holl's urban work is increasingly realized in difficult urban sites—that is, situated in actual practice—he has become more urgent and inventive in his search for an *urban horizon*. To this end he has resorted to literally topological forms that, if understood in time, could be thought to provide an unending delay and an infinite yet still finite formalization. In purely mathematic terms, only three such topological forms exist: the plane, the catenoid, and the helicoid all offer infinite extension without self intersection—they are known as boundaryless surfaces.[17] Helsinki is an approximation of a boundaryless surface. These forms are in fact unbuildable, yet within occupation and experience, and in relation to the sun and weather, Helsinki's mathematic limits are asymptotically approached.

For Holl, Emerson's person speaks from experience and rejects the representation of experience delivered from without: "Life is not dialectics!" wrote Emerson in his essay "Nature."[18] In this light Le Corbusier's Firminy offers a more direct reorganization of man's relation to the spiritual—even, it seems, of man's worthiness of the spiritual. But Helsinki has a murkier task that is particularly important and also of its architect's accord. Helsinki coerces the deterritorializing techniques of the metropolitan into a formally orchestrated abyss—a silent intertwining. The city is brought into the ring with nature (the bay) in a scenario that seems to give the occupant the omniscience to choose a victor. The juncture is one of great duress held in repose: Helsinki enzymatically dilates the city—its site.

The Museum of Contemporary Art requires innovative detailing to resolutely settle into place the mass-produced construction items upon which it must rely. As the instrumentalized remnants of capitalized production, these pieces must rest upon the camber of the building's curvilinear form.[19] Helsinki is really a protest: it is a curvilinear building made in a era of standardized rectilinear parts. Le Corbusier and Wright would have been able to work in a less refined fashion; they would not have had to fit their buildings together so well. The legal ramifications of their sites would have allowed for a degree of finish that one might think of as prelitigious. Holl has had to settle his topological ambitions within an era of invasive and pervasive legal mechanisms. This alone marks Helsinki as a masterwork of significant political and economic enterprise.

At Helsinki, in the fading light of the north, Holl may be understood ultimately to offer only the scrutinization of things in themselves. The city, the bay, the building, the wall, and the art

401

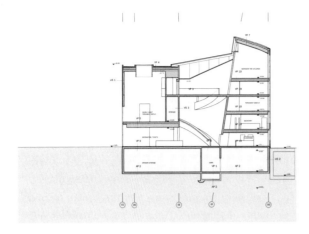

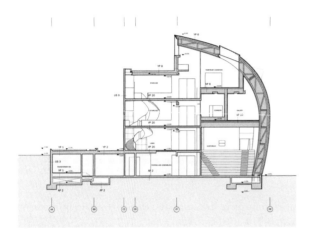

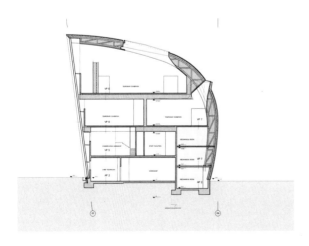

SLOW SPACE

are all held out of time.[20] It is an approximation, an existence of both the inert and the organic defined on the margins of the *almost* natural and the *almost* urban. It is an existence that is perhaps at a distance from either apparent totality—it does not accept the objectification of the formal, yet it allows the natural bay to be filtered, shaped, and held within a basin. Holl's "bay" is delivered to the building's entry, a strategy of integrating water and architecture that the architect has used frequently. This is not the magnificent unanchored river of Thomas Wolfe's novels; we do not perceive ourselves upon this river, but perhaps instead momentarily reflected in its surface. Holl, like John Hejduk, seems to have always wanted to separate time and space—to dislodge his inhabitants from their a priori positions of relativity and to provide access to the mathematics of time. Helsinki must historically be linked with Hejduk in this way, and Hejduk obviously to Le Corbusier. But in some way it seems that Holl has linked himself to Wright, for Holl's prose has never relinquished a sense of landscape and expanse, or some ideal of a subject nourished by the organic. The degree to which he appears to be succeeding in achieving these conditions is startling: his work in solar orientation in Japan and at Helsinki alone offers a depth of connectivity to primordial cycles that is almost unheard of in contemporary architecture and constitutes the sole subject of a paper in itself.

Thoughts of the Guggenheim return, and one wonders if Holl's work hasn't always been critical of the vicarious metropolis—if the architect is intent on keeping the cultural, the learned, the nonexperienced, and the unoriginated at a distance. It seems inevitable that Holl's urban thoughts would lead to this sort of delay—Toyo Ito suspected this and appeared to chasten the architect in the introduction to the *GA* folio of Holl's works.[21] But Holl has support in Massimo Cacciari as evidenced by Cacciari's writings—particularly in Cacciari's interpretation of the works of Adolf Loos. Loos, says Cacciari, opened up a period of not waiting—a period of collecting without accumulation.[22] It is, in the end, Cacciari's only reconciliation with the metropolis—and it seems to be Holl's too. Yet it seems incongruous to believe that Holl's pretheoretical ground is a delay; how could it be if it is prior? Given the degree to which he has truly succeeded in integrating the urban and natural, Holl parts company with Cacciari: Holl's work cannot be understood within Cacciari's "unfulfilled nihilism." While it may be a delay of the formal it is also the anticipation of experience. One wonders what form Holl's work would take if its production relinquished the phenomenological; in other words, is there work that Holl might achieve if he experienced the space of his buildings? In the aftermath of experience, what *work* rather than *works* would follow?

At Helsinki, Holl has simultaneously insisted on the discrete nature of architectural practice, yet retained an undelineated induction of the formless. Holl's urban subject is left to experience the duration of the city and, it seems, to experience something that cannot be modeled or anticipated. Authentic experience on Holl's ground in 1998 is no longer the loosely defined phenome-

nology of his earlier works, but something more immense in scope and challenge. Holl's space anticipates a form of life and presumably even organic governance; his vacant spaces both hold the center and relinquish its dominance. Perhaps these are models for other practices as well, and Holl seeks the center that could resist the dissipation of things yet allow for their free mobility.

Ultimately, we must rely on Holl's own sources and return to Emerson, where we find the representation of at least a century of queries into the traits and characteristics of the modern human being on an American ground as it transforms from agrarian territorialized field to mercantile abstraction. The reconciliation of this transformation required an understanding of human ethics; presumably virtue would assure that the metropolis would not evolve into the enslaving mechanism predicted by history. Experience, however, tells that this is not what happens—then or now—and from Karl Marx to Georg Simmel to Massimo Cacciari to Guy Debord to Félix Guattari the incantations of alienation have prevailed. So in this pause or delay of Holl's urban works, what subject are we to read? What human social ability is possible—a spiritual person who comprehends the city as nature, an unfulfilled subject at a distance and upon an existential cartography of grief, or some new ground of virtue and clarity?

Coda: Experimentation?

Steven Holl's practice of architecture has entered its twentieth year and the works produced during this transformative phase mark a peculiar moment in any architect's oeuvre. An architect of Holl's professional stature must realize that a certain amount of control is now out of his hands. Holl, Stanley Saitowitz, and others of their generation have all entered complex and dangerous realms of cultural progress and building process. The patronage that gives their works new dimension and size as well as possibility is institutional; the irony is that in many ways this marks the most experimental phase of an architect's career. Holl's early works, such as the Pool House and Metz House, were surely experiments, but their scale allowed the architect complete dominion and control over the work. Holl's current practice must coerce and conspire with a level of bureaucracy that offers the work social potential while constituting a vicarious ground in itself. Given the scale at which Holl now works—as do Thom Mayne, Stanley Saitowitz, Tod Williams and Billie Tsien, to name just a few—one has to presume that this represents the most experimental work these architects will ever complete. Surely much is at stake for both architect and city—now is the time to engage these architects critically.

405

Notes

1. Steven Holl, *Anchoring* (New York: Princeton Architectural Press, 1989), 1.

2. Holl, *Anchoring*, 9.

3. Steven Holl, *Intertwining* (New York: Princeton Architectural Press, 1996).

4. Steven Holl, *Kiasma: Working Process* (New York: The Architectural League of New York, 1995), 4.

5. For reference to Adorno see Martin Jay, *Fin-de-Siécle Socialism* (New York: Routledge, Chapman and Hall, 1988), 5.

6. Ralph Waldo Emerson, "Nature," in *Ralph Waldo Emerson: Selected Essays, Lectures and Poems*, ed. Robert D. Richardson Jr. (New York: Bantam Books, 1990), 33.

7. Emerson, 48.

8. Henri Bergson, *An Introduction to Metaphysics* (New York: Knickerbocker Press, 1912), 23.

9. Emerson, 26.

10. Rosalind Krauss on *Spiral Jetty*: "As I looked at the site, it reverberated out to the horizons only to suggest an immobile cyclone while flickering light made the entire landscape appear to quake . . . No idea, no concepts, no systems, no abstractions could hold themselves together in the actuality of that phenomenological evidence." Rosalind Krauss, *Passages in Modern Sculpture* (Cambridge, Mass.: MIT Press, 1990), 282.

11. Ken Kaplan, in his introduction to Holl's *Edge of a City*, warned that "probably the most politically dangerous area of investigation in architecture is imagining new cities." In Steven Holl, *Pamphlet Architecture 13: Edge of a City* (New York: Princeton Architectural Press), 9.

12. Holl, *Edge of a City*, 11.

13. Rafael Moneo, "Aldo Rossi: The Idea of Architecture and the Modena Cemetery," in *Oppositions* (Summer 1976): 21.

14. This logic applies to the Berkowitz House (1984) on Martha's Vineyard, Massachusetts as well.

15. See Lars Lerup, "At the End of the Architectural Promenade," in *Architecture and Body*, ed. Scott Marble (New York: Columbia University, 1989).

16. Holl, *Edge of a City*, 9.

17. Paraphrased from Ivars Peterson, *The Mathematical Tourist: Snapshots of Modern Mathematics* (New York: W. H. Freeman, 1988), 57.

18. Ralph Waldo Emerson, "Experience," in *Ralph Waldo Emerson: Selected Essays, Lectures and Poems,* 232.

19. I use the word camber in reference to Holl's description of the *Edge of a City* projects: "On the fringes of today's modern city, displaced fragments sprout without intrinsic relationships to existing organization, other than the camber and loops of curvilinear freeway." Holl, *Intertwinings*, 51.

20. John Hejduk, "Out of Time and into Space," in *Mask of Medusa* (New York: Rizzoli, 1985), 71.

21. From Toyo Ito's introduction to Holl's *GA* monograph: "Your architecture is adrift in a condition of gentleness, but that cannot continue indefinitely." Toyo Ito, "An Architecture Adrift in Time: A Message to Steven Holl," in *GA Architect 11: Steven Holl*, ed. Yukio Futagawa (Tokyo: A.D.A. Edita, 1993), 11.

22. Massimo Cacciari, "The Chain of Glass," in *Architecture and Nihilism: On the Philosophy of Modern Architecture*, trans. Stephen Sartarelli (New Haven: Yale University Press, 1993), 190 .

LATENT PARALLELEPIPEDS

THE FIRST POSTWAR EXHIBITION AT THE BEIRUT NATIONAL MUSEUM

Farès el-Dahdah

War, however tragic, is often a source of architectural invention. Citadels, ramparts, turrets, and bunkers provide a rich repository of defensive, if not offensive, design strategies, just as spontaneous protective measures transform ordinary objects into machines of war. Beirut's recent civil warfare produced many such inventions. Black drapes, eight stories high and hung across urban interstices shielded pedestrians from the deadly trajectory of a sniper's view so as to veil one fighting camp from another. Shipping containers were filled with sand and arranged as divisive labyrinths along frontlines. Stair landings became to apartment buildings what communal courtyards had been to houses. Entering a building became an oblique experience as one was forced to slither sideways behind oil barrels filled with concrete. War is inevitably linked with architectural experience and does reveal latent meaning in certain building features, be it the social nature of stairwells, the protective obscurity of bathrooms, or the sniping and panoptical violence of a skyscraper. So it is about one building particularly transformed by war that this essay speaks—or more precisely, about the ruins of a building and the temporary exhibition mounted within during Beirut's first postwar year.[1]

The Beirut National Museum closed its doors in 1975 when civil war broke out in Lebanon. Demarcating lines drawn soon after made the museum's location more famous than its collection. What was once a prominent civic building became no more than a stoic sentinel guarding one of the checkpoints that separated the city's east from its west. Until the war's end in 1992, the location's military importance led armies and militias to use the museum building for shelter and strategy, consequently transforming halls and galleries into barracks and bunkers. For almost two decades, the museum walls provided relative protection from the caustic effects of war as they were slowly disfigured into morbid bas-reliefs sculpted by shrapnel, bullets, and a great deal of madness. Within these walls soldiers slept, fought, and died. A sniper even bore a hole for his deadly aim through a hung mosaic. After so much atrocity, one might have expected that the museum would be empty from looting. A few transportable objects from the collection were indeed stolen after having been moved to a so-called safe place, or were simply destroyed because war had moved too swiftly. What remains of the collection, however, never left the building—it had been hidden by a curator who had the instincts of an Egyptian high priest at the drawing of death. Maurice Chéhab, then Director General of Antiquities, systematically sealed off—all in the name of posterity and under tons of concrete— what in effect had been a collection of sepulchral objects. In 1993, when military battles were no longer being waged in Beirut, the museum, now a ruin, propped open its broken doors for a brief period of ten days on the occasion of the Lebanese Republic's fiftieth anniversary of relative independence. The exhibition provoked a flood of curiosity to pour into the galleries only to be insulted by graffiti soldiers had left behind, only to be reminded of the ravages of war.

Beirut National Museum, Interior view, 1940s.

Detail of front elevation.

Graffiti of the word *Beasts* in Arabic over a separated cross and crescent.

EL-DAHDAH

Concrete parallelepipeds and exhibition wall made of corrugated aluminum.

Before proceeding with the actual design project of temporarily refitting the National Museum for exhibition purposes, it is necessary to digress in the domains of archaeology and art history in order to articulate a few observations upon which the inaugural exhibition is theoretically based. These observations are about two rather archetypal, if not ordinary, objects in architecture: the antique sarcophagus, a kind of proto-architectural form, and the parallelepiped, a geometric solid made of six parallelograms.

The Beirut National Museum is known, or rather was known, for its collection of Phoenician, Greek, and Roman sarcophagi. One must imagine that it was once a hall of antiquities strewn with funerary artifacts. Standing in this museum therefore induced one to look at coffins of various types, which is not something one generally does simply, without connotations of architecture, art, or death. The meaning of a sarcophagus inevitably exceeds what one actually sees as it alludes to something that extends beyond its physical and geographical reality: the sentiment of mourning, for example. As Georges Didi-Huberman has pointed out, looking at a container of death no doubt brings about the anguish that stems from being confronted with a decaying body—both whisper in one's ear a fate identical to one's own.[2]

In order to appease such anguish, one can shift back and forth between two conflicting notions of what one sees. On one hand, the box can be viewed tautologically: what is seen is no more than what is seen. It is a funerary box six feet in length, full stop. There is nothing latent about this volume. It has no aura, it does not participate in time, and there are no recognizable signs of decay. Should one persist in keeping this rather cynical posture, one can remain relatively indifferent as to what one sees: nothing more than a body in a coffin that is simply hidden, present and recumbent (this is in fact no more than a flat truth). By relying on the obvious and finding satisfaction in what is evident, this approach in fact refuses any latency to the object and thus consoles the possibility of being anguished. If one were able to view the Sarcophagus of Ahiram, for example, one might automatically refer to its provenance, influences, history, style, not to mention the prototypical alphabet on one of its sides.[3] Had one been able to see the now buried collection of Anthropoid Sarcophagi, one might have focused on issues of art—the beauty of a face or the minimalism of an expression—rather than at death.[4] A marble object six feet in length can therefore be frozen in the present so that one can remain relatively indifferent to its past despite the knowledge that it once ate a body.[5]

Sentiments of mourning can also be allayed through an approach that is the exact opposite of exacerbating the nonlatent object value of the sarcophagus. This second attitude consists of relying on a kind of fiction that exceeds the object by allowing the dead body to exist (or live) elsewhere. The act of seeing is transformed into an ecstatic belief that life, if no longer breathing in a tomb, at least exists in some other dreamed-up place where it can con-

413

Front portico, before and after the war.

tinue living forever. (This is not exactly a flat truth, but it does have some authority, albeit of the religious kind.) That which is invisible takes over that which is visible and one can, in this way, empty the contents of a sarcophagus in an attempt to create a meaningful void.

These two ways of looking at a coffin may well be diametrically opposed—the first is specific and tautological, the second is symbolic and connotative—yet they both serve the same purpose. Neither condition, however, provides absolute satisfaction in neutralizing such sentiments of death, and one must shift back and forth to construct an affective easement. According to Didi-Huberman, it is a kind of paradox that divides the act of seeing in two halves:

> On one side, there is what I see of the tomb, that is to say the evidence of a volume . . . a stone mass, more or less geometric, more or less figurative, more or less covered with inscriptions . . . On the other side . . . there is what looks back at me: and does so in a way that is no longer evident . . . the fate of a body similar to my own, emptied of its life, of its speech, of its movements, emptied of its power to open its eyes even if in some sense it does look back at me.[6]

The same object can thus be at once religious, symbolic, and connotative as well as material, dimensional, and self-referential. We not only look at the simple dimension of things, but also idealize bodies by turning them into stone. The inability to restrict one's thoughts to pure dimensions—providing obvious measures to distinct volumes—when confronted with sarcophagi parallels the temptation to empty a funerary box of its rotting flesh and replace it with ideal images of a body made sublime.

Yet there are objects that can supposedly resist such an affective reception: objects that prefer one rather than both of the two postures just described. Strictly geometric objects that indicate nothing but themselves refuse to look back at the viewing subject by revealing no symptoms, no imagery. These objects are the parallelepiped made radical, which of course is a reference to the sculptures of Donald Judd, Robert Morris, or Tony Smith. The minimalist parallelepiped is an object without aura that supposedly refers to nothing—no illusion, no content—but its own dimensions. It is without symptoms or latency and carries neither imagery nor any special system of beliefs. According to Judd and Morris, it is an object voluntarily reduced to no more than what one sees. Judd rejected illusion altogether—for example, he considered even Rothko paintings to be "almost traditionally illusionistic."[7] Morris resisted an iconographic discourse in which sculpture betrays the object's real or specific parameters.[8] Any discourse generated by the minimalist object had been meant to contend with physical dimensions and refer to no mystery, to no body. Cubes, boxes, or parallelepipeds

414

Concrete parallelepiped.

Beirut National Museum, central stair.

Broken statuary.   **Sniper's lair and hole in Roman mosaic.**   **Debris left behind by soldiers.**

are reduced to their minimal specificity. Nothing about them exceeds the spaces they occupy. They are what they are: simple parallelepipeds, nonrelational, nonillusionistic, nonexpressionistic, nonsymbolic, noniconographic, nonanthropomorphic, non-non, et cetera.

It takes very little, however, for a minimalist object to exceed its own specificity. Physical stability is automatically counteracted by semantic instability as the object drifts into the temporal, the experiential, and even into the anthropomorphic. A parallelepiped's paradox is not merely that it can fall yet stay erect, but also that its reception can neither be exclusively optic (dimensional) nor entirely figurative (symbolic). The act of seeing is a messy and unsettling experience when eyes are not pure or without affect; other senses are attached to them, and so they cannot be satisfied by optics alone. A minimalist sculpture, therefore, must by definition be just as paradoxical as an object like a sarcophagus that can be understood both specifically and connotatively. The discussion on the nature of specificity in minimalism has for that matter been sufficiently treated in the history of art yet one can approach it from an entirely different and funerary perspective, by going first through the first postwar exhibit of the Beirut National Museum.

The sarcophagus and the parallelepiped had in fact been conflated inside the museum due to circumstances of war: the sarcophagi of the Beirut National Museum were literally entombed in protective parallelepipeds made of reinforced concrete. These bunkerlike structures had been built at the rhythm of cease-fires as the sandbags with which the sarcophagi were first covered slowly turned into stone. The rest of the collection was either buried in the basement or simply hidden in secret passages and double walls. The hostile climate of war had induced the curator to "encrypt" an antiquities collection that for the most part had itself come from funerary crypts.

Reburying the collection may have been a protective wartime measure, but it was also an act very much in keeping with archaic notions of death by which one recedes beneath the ground's surface in order to precede eventual resurrection. The collection was wrapped in sheets of reinforced concrete just as bodies were once mummified in order to prolong their afterlives. War had in effect returned the museum to its archetypal origin: the mausoleum, in which bodies and collections are preserved hidden from public view. With such funereal notions in mind, the National Museum's literal reference to an Egyptian edifice might be thought of as uncanny. The museum's original architect, Antoine Nahas, could not have foreseen how his choice of a neo-Egyptian style would someday correspond with the activities of those who were ultimately in charge of the collection's safeguard. The building had been designed in the 1920s during a renewed vogue of Egyptian architecture—Egyptomania—following the discovery of Tutankhamen's tomb in 1922.[9] In light of the more recent events,

Concrete parallelepipeds with tags.

Nahas's original choice of exterior lotiform columns with closed buds seems to have been prescient of a day when the museum would become the mausoleum of a culture that no longer builds any such tombs. Lotus capitals usually "bloom" when hit by the sun and are usually reserved to a building's exterior. The National Museum's closed buds might otherwise suggest that the building was once the inner chamber of a much bigger structure. This semantic slippage could be interpreted as an academic mistake or as a fictional allusion hinting that these columns may once have guarded the interior crypt of a colossal edifice. These columns hint at an evidence that was to be further amplified by a state of siege or by a war that served to heighten what in a museum seems latent: a process of entombment. It is a theoretical process that began with the building's architectural references to ancient Egypt— which was later literalized by a zealously protective curator—and was finally revealed, or perhaps completed, with the temporary reopening of a ruined museum. The reference to ancient Egyptian architecture seemed to approximate two distant institutions that suddenly have a great deal in common—museums and mausoleums are both depositories of images, with secrets guarded in their crypts and artifacts isolated within the civic space of their grand architecture.[10]

Latent or apparent, entombment became the paradigm for understanding the meaning of a destroyed museum temporarily reopened after seventeen years of war. In lieu of a sarcophagus collection that was once exhibited within the same halls, the public was invited to see a series of concrete volumes stricken with an element of mourning that Phoenician, Greek, and Roman sarcophagi had themselves lost the moment they were put on display. Such an event presented a daunting design task due to the difficulty in having to manage the violence recorded on every cubic inch of the ruined building. It took three months for a group of archaeologists and architects to conceive, convince, and execute an exhibition of concrete parallelepipeds that were both objects and subjects within a destroyed museum, all in the hopes of generating enough momentum to launch the process of the museum's eventual reconstruction.

It is not difficult to imagine how eerie it was to linger among large concrete volumes that stood as if they were already on exhibit within a museum's forgotten galleries. One of the galleries is called the Galerie du colosse. Though derived from a giant statue of uncertain origin, the plural form of the gallery's name might have referred to the present state of the museum as a *gallery of colossi*. For just as the building's Egyptomaniac style had become complicit with the fate of the collection it contained, so had the concrete parallelepipeds acquired the funerary properties of that which they protected. They had become the body doubles for the sarcophagi that could no longer be seen. In the archaic sense of the word, a

418

Beirut National Museum, front portico.

colossi function was not to represent someone's image but instead acted as a double for a body that had not been buried and whose spirit remained fleeting; the word *kolossos* in ancient Greek refers to a kind of stone that had little to do with grand dimensions, it simply provided fixity for an absent body. The concrete parallelepipeds were thus true colossi in the archaic sense and very much like a minimalist sculpture—pure presence without being figurative or representational.[11] Colossi appear present, however, only to fix an inaccessible elsewhere just as concrete parallelepipeds become substitute objects of mourning standing in for what they contained, the sarcophagi that had been stripped of condolences and rendered invisible due to the causticity of war.

Although concrete parallelepipeds had been erected solely to protect the cultural heritage of a young republic, they somehow recovered an affective charge with which they were now laden and which a sarcophagus on display had once lost. Attributing titles to these concrete volumes was the only alteration required to transform them into a series of minimalist "Untitleds," seemingly forgotten by the history of modern art. The concrete parallelepipeds literally stood where people had died but had not yet been buried. They were tombs of tombs whose minimalist specificity could no longer resist an affective reception. These giant concrete solids were thus both laden and void. They were strict geometry that indicated nothing but themselves while protecting a famous collection of antique sarcophagi that had once been emptied for exhibition purposes. They stood as minimal volumes that were to be exhibited as if they were a series of minimalist sculptures, as if they were the plural of *Die*.

Die is a six-by-six-by-six-foot black cube produced by Tony Smith in 1962 and is an obvious precedent for the National Museum's parallelepipeds. Smith's sculpture is a tautology *par excellence* and is as specific as a minimalist cube can get. One sees a black volume that refers to its own stability, to its nonfiguration and lack of illusion. It is proposed as a flat, unidimensional truth when it is otherwise semantically rippled. It is quite true, for instance, that *Die* is the imperative tense of the verb *to die* just as it is the singular form of *dice*. The title may thus refer to the expression "to dice with death" while its dimensions, six-by-six-by-six, may inspire some people to think of the Devil.[12] Smith himself already provided all these interpretations with a cryptic phrase in an exhibition catalog: "Six feet has a suggestion of being cooked. Six foot box. Six feet under."[13] Six feet high is just about the size of a man, which might inspire one's arms and legs to stretch against four of *Die*'s faces as if one were Vitruvian in design. Six feet deep is deep enough for a body to lie inside. So *Die* may be more than a cube. It is the black outside of a dark inside. It is a tomb, a room, a bed, in which one can lie and be buried six feet under. *Die* had in fact preempted associations between the concrete and the illusory, the archaic and the modern, the specific and the referential. *Die* could

Exhibition walls made of corrugated metal.

indeed be seen in shadows cast by the concrete blocks inside an antiquities museum just as Smith had, in fact, given his cube an ancient Egyptian precedent: the oracle at the temple of Leto that Herodotus described as a colossal cubic monolith.[14]

Bridging the millennia that separate the mausoleum from the museum did indeed nurture a suspicion that minimal art stands on some sort of archaic foundation. Yet it would be futile to conclude that such an art is inadvertently figurative, subject-centered, symbolically funereal, relational, illusionistic, and so forth. *Die* makes death quite clear and so might Robert Morris's ironic *I-Box* (also of 1962) which renders the anthropocentricity and subject-hood of minimalist art quite evident. Seemingly referenceless minimalist art is in fact riddled with references to tombs, and antiquity's own monolithic volumes are not altogether void of semantic latency. The twelve-hundred-ton megalith cut as a temple base in Baalbek, for example, is curiously enough colloquially named "stone of the pregnant woman" (*hajar el hibla* in Arabic).

Archaic forms of sacrifice are indeed inscribed in the National Museum's Egyptianizing architecture, in its sarcophagi contained within concrete, and in the atrocities of a civil war that the building itself had hosted. Architecture's own origin can also be inscribed in the outcome of such sacrificial rituals as lapidation, for instance, which resulted in a mound of stone covering a dead body.[15] So it is on the basis of the archaism of such violence, implied both by architecture and bellicose circumstances, that an affective charge was produced and upon which the exhibition was designed. The initial design instinct was simply to open the museum as it was. The instinct went so far as to suggest that the museum should never be restored; the civil war had built its own memorial. The argument was that the museum had already become a vivid mnemonic monument capable of triggering affects with no more than the minimalist cube, that which is supposedly lacking in affective charge. This would mean, however, that the sarcophagi would never again be seen. Considering the imperatives of postwar reconstruction, such a proposal was out of the question; the practice of memorializing civil wars is something one usually wisely prefers to defer. Nonetheless, the colossal parallelepipeds for the exhibition were left bare, at their minimal, since they were already redolent with the smell of melancholia, anguish, if not with death itself. After all, they held within and outside them the memory of those who died in their proximity (militia warriors and ancient monarchs).

The concrete parallelepipeds were simply tagged with the title of what they contained. Construction for the exhibition consisted simply of a series of temporary walls made of corrugated galvanized metal as well as a large mirrored box that occupied a prominent position in the main hall. As a surface, the wall's corrugation alluded to shipping containers that had

President Elias Hraoui viewing the tag of a concrete parallelepiped.

been used during the war for all sorts of military purposes. The walls were built not only as a background for the concrete parallelepipeds but also as shields that could be used, abused, and later replaced, much like the many protective architectural inventions of war. The slanted mirrored box served prismatically as the final tomb, the tomb in which the museum itself could be entombed. It contained, if only allegorically, the building's interior blurring for once and for all the distinction between the museum and its funerary precedent, the mausoleum. The mirrored box completed the process of entombment that began literally in the sarcophagi themselves; was represented symbolically in the museum as mausoleum; became latent in the building's egyptomaniac style; and was later made real when the collection itself was entombed and sarcophagi transformed into latent parallelepipeds.

Notes

1. The exhibition called *Uprooted Heritage* lasted ten days and was the National Museum's first event after seventeen years of war. It was curated in situ and was a collaboration of architecture, archaeology, and a great deal of benevolence. Anne-Marie Afeich, Amaly Beyhum, Claude Doumet-Serhal, Suzy Hakimian, Carole Sabbag, Helen Sader, Helga Seeden, Mona Yazbeck, and myself comprised the curatorial/design team.

2. Georges Didi-Huberman, *Ce que nous voyons, ce qui nous regarde* (Paris: Les Editions de Minuit, 1992).

3. The Sarcophagus of Ahiram was excavated in Byblos (Phoenician, eighth century B.C.).

4. The collection of twenty-six anthropoidal sarcophagi was excavated in Sidon (Phoenician, fifth and fourth centuries B.C.).

5. Sarcophagus comes from the Greek word *sarkophagos*, which literally means flesh-eating stone.

6. Didi-Huberman, 17.

7. Donald Judd, "Specific Objects," in *Qu'est-ce que la sculpture moderne?* (Paris: Centre Pompidou, 1986), 385.

8. Robert Morris, "Notes on Sculpture," in *Minimal Art*, ed. Gregory Battcock (New York: E. P. Dutton, 1968), 222.

9. Examples of such a neo-Egyptian style are abundant in the decorative arts of the 1920s and 1930s as well as in the architecture of motion pictures, movie theaters, and

even in that of steamship interiors, especially those launched by the French in 1926, the most famous of which was the *Champollion*, which ran aground on the coast of Beirut during a storm in 1952.

10. Régis Debray compares the museum and the tomb as equal depositories of images in *Vie et mort de l'image* (Paris: Gallimard, 1992), 17–23.

11. Jean-Pierre Vernant, "Figuration de l'invisible et catégorie psychologique du double: le colossos," in *Mythe et pensée chez les grecs* (Paris: Maspero, 1966), 252.

12. The expression "to dice with death" in relation to *Die* is noted by J. P. Criqui, "Trictrac pour Tony Smith," *Artstudio* 6 (1987): 43.

13. Tony Smith, *Two Exhibitions of Sculpture* (Hartford: Wadsworth Atheneum, 1967), unpaginated.

14. Smith, unpaginated. The description of the Temple of Leto occurs in Herodotus, *The Histories*, Book II, 155.

15. On the subject of architecture and sacrifice, see Renée Girard, *Des choses cachées depuis la fondation du monde* (Paris: Grasset, 1978).

A first version of this essay was presented as the Caudill Lecture on Architecture at Rice University on March 18, 1994.

423

Mirrored box.

BURN

Karen Bermann, Jeanine Centuori, and Julieanna Preston

Three people were required to make these photographs of burn sites in Detroit. We were all afraid. One hid behind the camera, one wore the mask of a mirror, and one watched the street. It was necessary to maintain a distance, to keep from physically transgressing the boundary that had been violated by fire. Entering the buildings was a spiritual trespass we did not want to commit.

The mirror and the camera are tools of attraction and repulsion. It is believed that the photograph entraps the soul and that the mirror wards off evil or is a threshold of spirit passage. We used these soul-catching devices to steal sights for us, to lure the black interior out through the orifices of the envelope, and at the same time to ward them off, to blind ourselves to them. We committed the trespass of distance.

430

Most of these buildings were abandoned before being burned. The city administration maintains a policy toward abandoned buildings. A Detroit planning report states: "Presently vacant buildings and land are great detractors from the streetscape image." The report proposes the following strategy: "Cover the windows of vacant buildings with plywood on at least the street level and paint graphics on the covers. This will show a concern for possible reuse at a future time, while providing visual interest."

Fire destroys the mask. It reveals the horror of space beyond, private space thrown into the public domain. These facades no longer shield their interiors. We wore these facades on our faces, porous and weak, filled with sorrow: death masks. The photograph was the moment of not-looking, a moment of empathy and distance.

The photographic method used here was partially developed during a collaboration between Jeanine Centuori and James Cathcart.

You shall keep my statutes. You shall not let your cattle breed with a different kind; you shall not sow your field with two kinds of seed; nor shall there come upon you a garment of cloth made of two kinds of stuff.

—Leviticus 19:19.

GESTATION

Rebeca Méndez

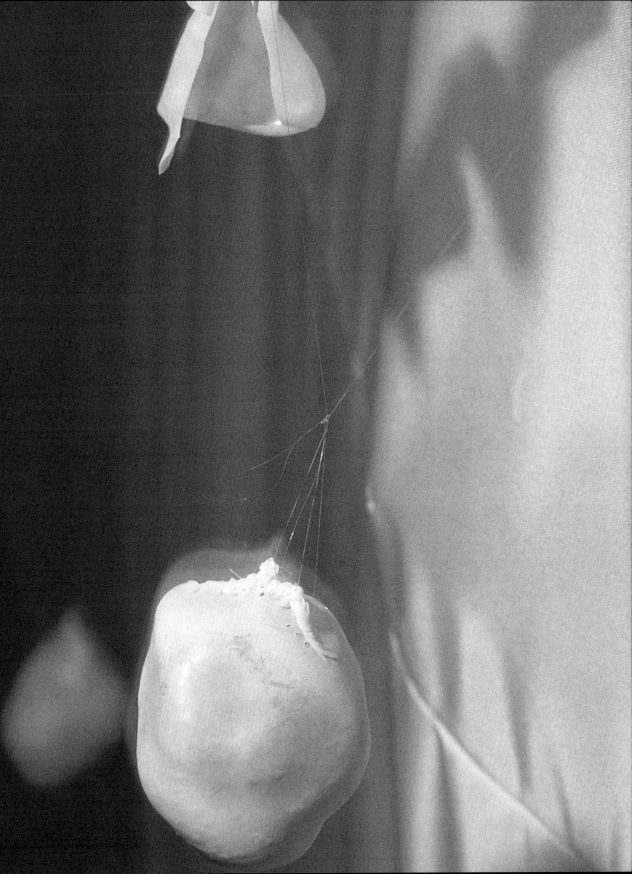

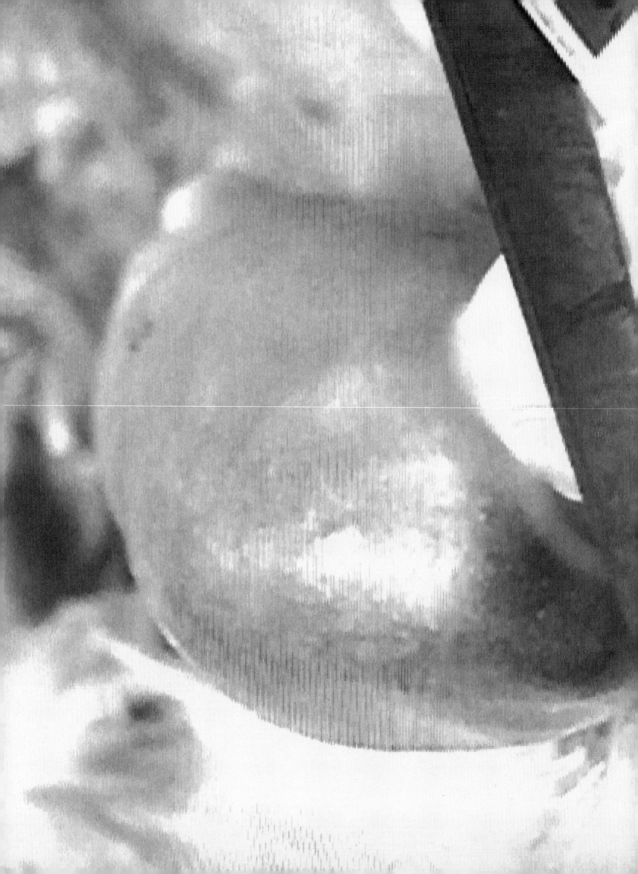

It is not lack of cleanliness or health that causes abjection but what disturbs identity, system, order. What does not respect borders, positions, rules. The in-between, the ambiguous, the composite.

—Julia Kristeva, *Powers of Horror*

Separating, purifying, demarcating, and punishing transgression have as their main function to impose system on an inherently untidy experience. It is only by exaggerating the difference between within and without, above and below, male and female, with and against, that a semblance of order is created.

—Mary Douglas, *Purity and Danger*

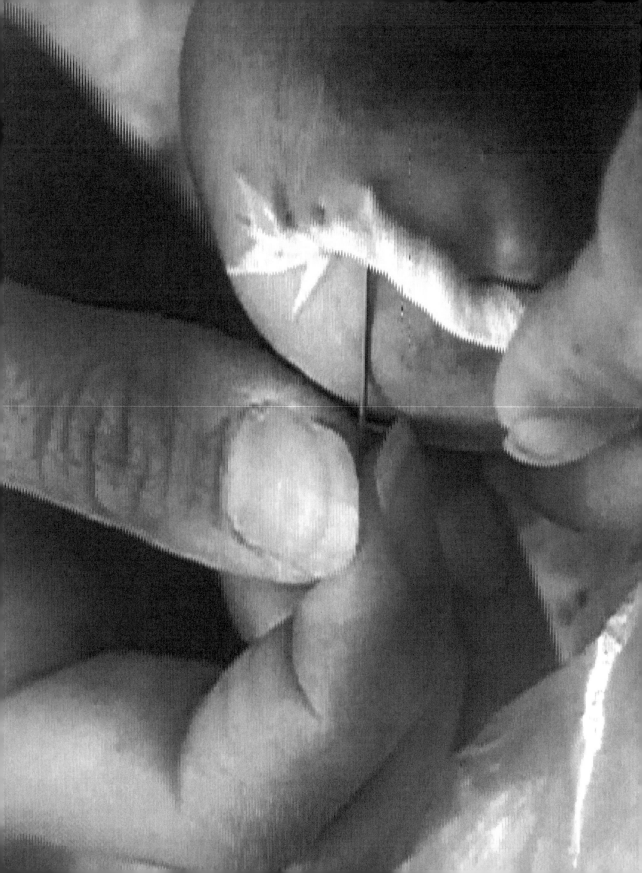

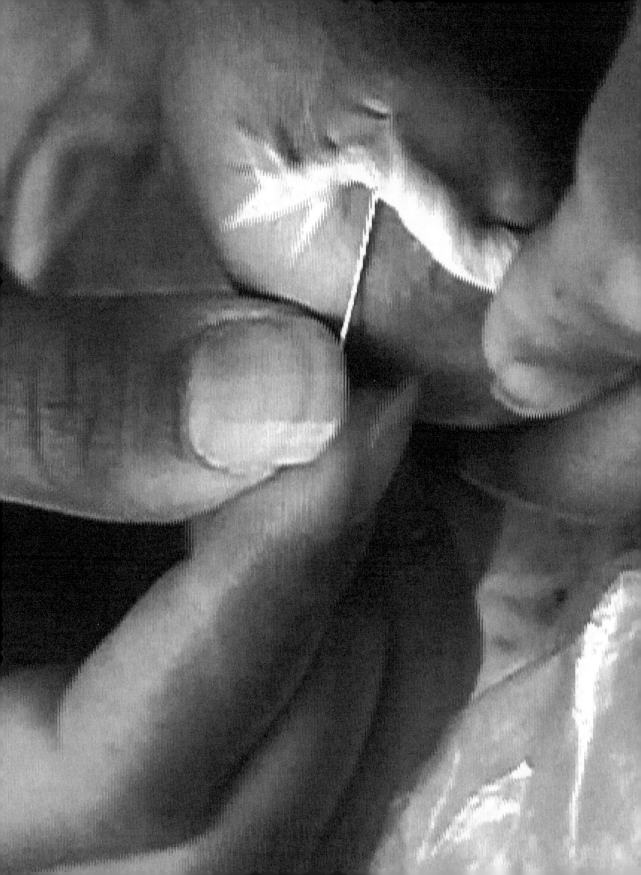

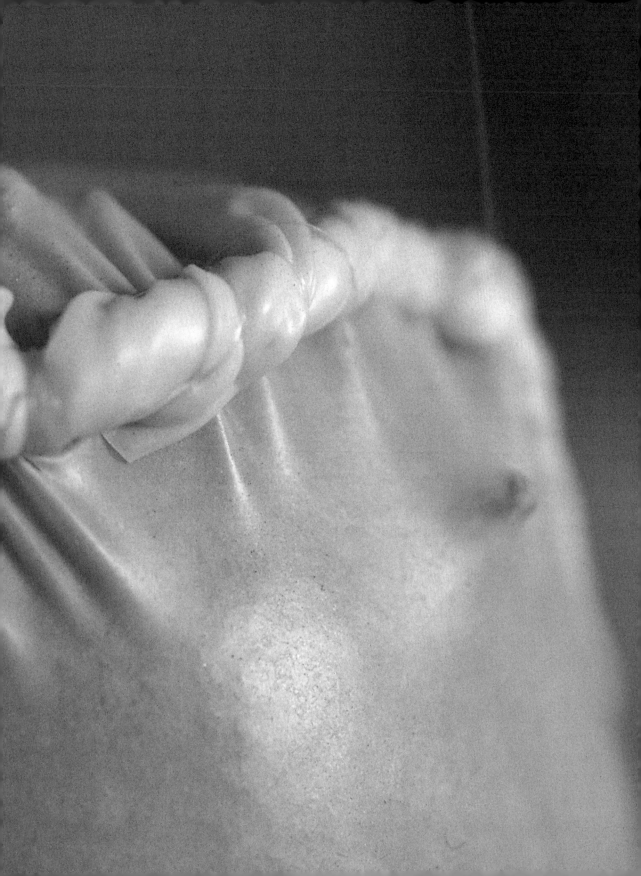

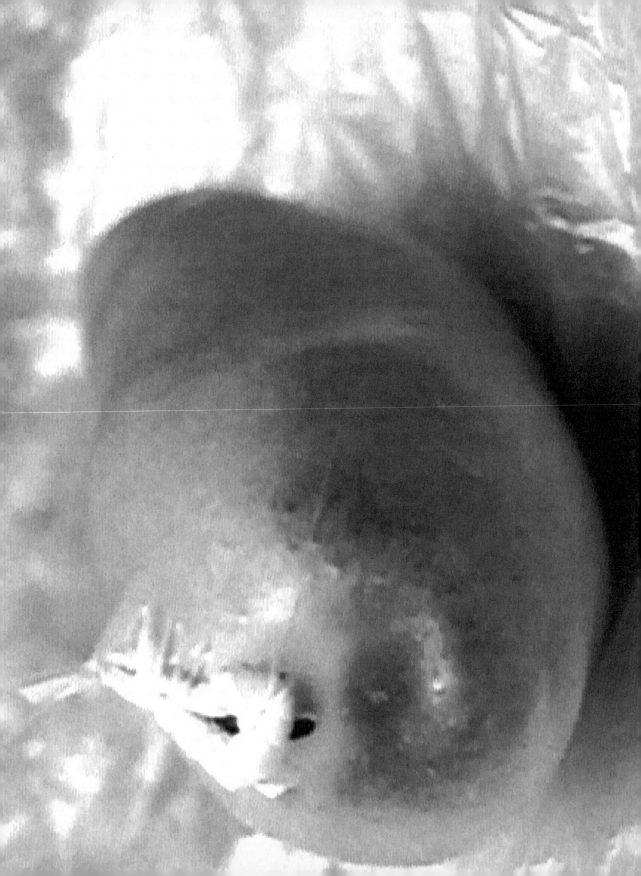

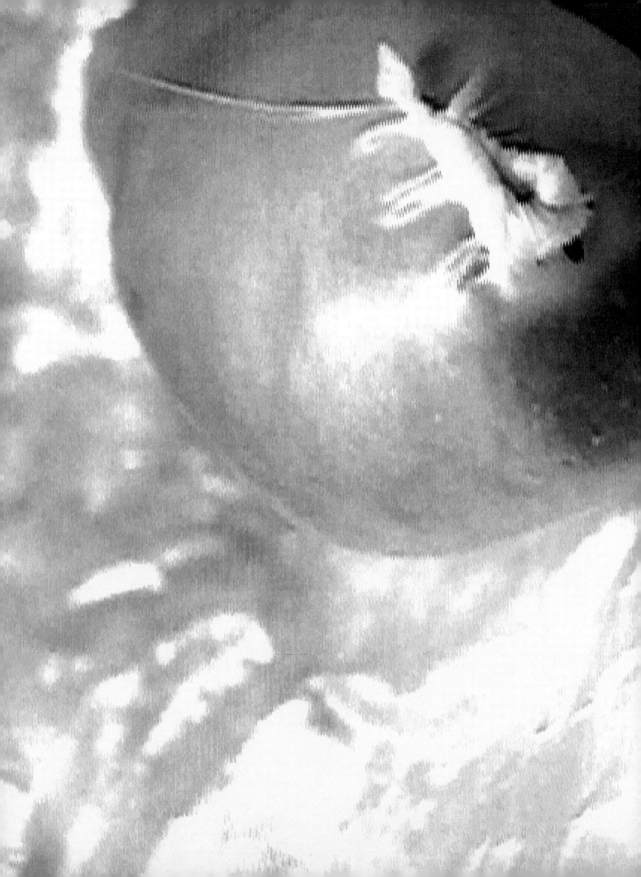

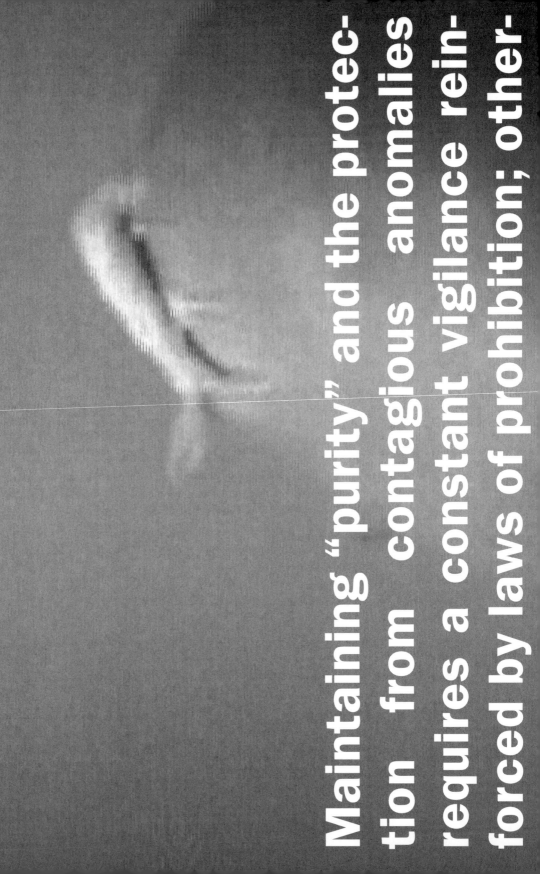

Maintaining "purity" and the protection from contagious anomalies requires a constant vigilance reinforced by laws of prohibition; otherwise systems of classification reveal themselves as fertile incubators of the anomalous.

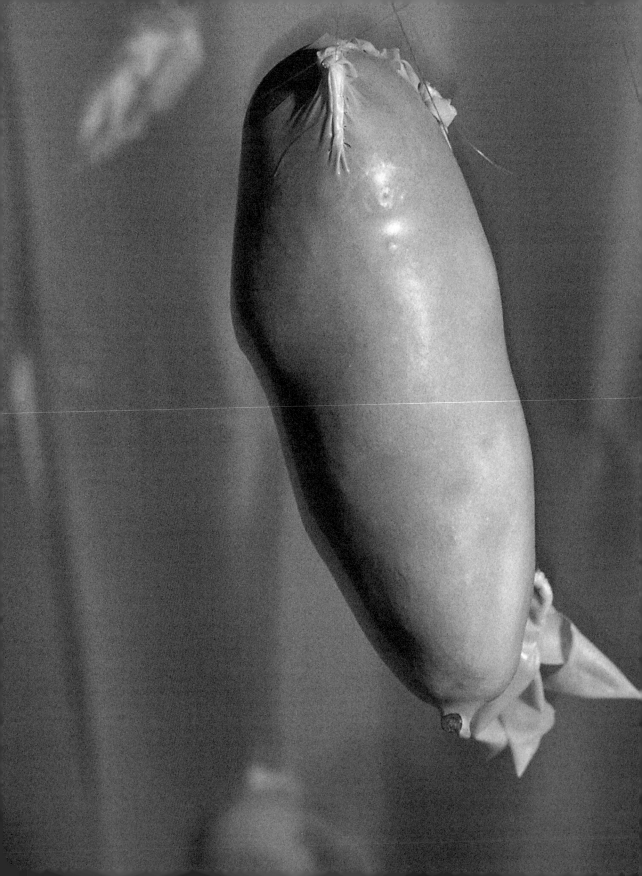

My installation "Gestation" explores the tensions that are implicit in social contracts between individuals and institutions, and how these "agreements" form our identity.

Only a fine line separates nurture and control. I see the potato as a metaphor for the human being for several reasons: one, the potato is the lowest common denominator of vegetables; two, as a basic staple food, its consumption transcends social boundaries; three, the potato holds energy within, enough to power a radio; and four, its form resembles that of an organ.

When I wrap the potato in latex, I ward off the germs, as would a surgeon when exposing the interior of a human body. I hold the object as I sew the protective pouch and I feel like I'm nurturing it, but at the same time I'm confining the object within this simulation of skin. When the potato hangs suspended from a thread, and with the passing of time, disturbances in the clinical begin to germinate. As the latex either melts with the potato skin as it rots within the pouch, or is stretched and punctured by the roots of a growing potato, the latex sheath becomes an index of the often indistinguishable gradations between artifice and nature, decay and life.

NOTHING BUT FLOWERS: AGAINST PUBLIC SPACE

Aaron Betsky

We live in fear of the shapeless, the void, the violence that threatens our ability to stake a claim on a small plot of space. Most people identify the sprawl of American cities as formless—a contributing factor to the inconvenience, environmental irresponsibility, all too easily manipulated reality, and lack of controlling representation of everyday life.[1] Living in California especially, one is constantly confronted with demands for a return to public space and public order. Motivated by a desire to reintroduce a sense of order into the city, a search is on for form that can shape and signify by means akin to traditional modes of urban organization. This desire for order, largely functioning to combat a sense of hopelessness, is generated out of a city that has grown far beyond the bounds of traditional metropolitan agglomerations. The desire appears in the political sphere as demands for greater police protection and as immense growth in security and control systems in the economic sphere. In its most concrete embodiment, desire for order exists as massive prisons and secured compounds for exurban living. Both have become primary growth industries for formerly agricultural communities. Such places of forceful framing represent nostalgia for imposed forms of civic control. Both religious and secular centers have provided the physical context for the exercise of this power, which always has been mirrored by architecture.

These developments ironically result in the further dissolution of clear urban form in their isolation of compounds, regardless of whether those developments are prisons, anonymous tilt-up concrete districts of commerce, isolated office-tower complexes, or gated residential communities. In between such concentrated structures, space sprawls formlessly, while the determination of these objects by requirements—security, economy (value engineering), and seduction (sales)—elides all corners, removes any sense of materiality, and dissolves space into evocations of the continually curving and evenly lit worlds of science fiction. Monuments that give form to such space are not places of worship or culture, but are instead airports (such as the new Denver International Airport), stadiums, and convention centers, acting as economic and physical anchors for most developing American cities. These large voids are activated only by temporary inhabitation and celebrate a simulation of the contest for space.

The most sophisticated security systems are invisible, as are the contemporary ways in which we locate ourselves in the world, by connecting to others with shared interests, and as are the ways in which we construct a collective identity, by surrounding ourselves with familiar images and sounds. Contained in wires, microwave transmissions, or service contracts with local police or security forces, these systems further dissolve a sense of physical location and boundary, rendering real space even more difficult to experience.

This increasingly incoherent and unarticulable urban form has forced theorists who argue for "village formation" to propose a pastiche of isolated moments of coherence.[2] Their arguments are buttressed by an expectation for community organization that seems impractical except, as we are

Los Angeles

now seeing, as defensive measures. The prevalence of self-protective neighborhood activism leads one to imagine a world of science fiction "claves" of warring factions taking care of their own and fending off others.[3] The contemporary prototype of this model has been established by Disney's Celebration Community, newly built and complete with its own experimental school. Although these New Urbanists insist on the return of a "legible city" and a formed void called "public space," the quest for legibility and clarity destroys what we historically have considered urban public space to be. A readable city is a city reduced to a script that we must follow. Architectural theoreticians confuse Hannah Arendt's idea of public space with the Greek notion of the agora, the place of public gathering. They forget that the real action took place in the stoa where deals were made and the state was run in sheltering shadows.[4] Public space is a place where many activities overlap: rich confusion, commerce, seduction, and filth. Public space works not as a designed element, but is instead carved out by wheeling and dealing, crossroads, and the chance at freedom, where a person emerges from shadows into light that grows into the ever-extending space of public gathering and demonstration, and seeps into every open pore of the city.

Along with this truly public space comes meaning: the physical context of actions itself signifies. This meaning does not exist in the silence of an empty square or grand avenue, but emerges in urban form, in all aspects of social life, as well as in the narrative richness of the everyday, and is crystallized into dense form by those we call artists. It is the ability of useful form—whether a skyscraper, bus stop, or pair of blue jeans—to take on the host of shared associations, dreams, and fears that make the forms and spaces of our collective experience cohere.[5] Paradoxically, we need dense spaces of layers, fractures, and confusion to find order.

The most logical place to find order in the city is on the street, since it is the street that created the great urban spaces of places such as California. The public square always had an ambivalent purpose in American urbanism: centralized nodes of power declined to express their means through a symbolic forecourt; the gridded economy, aimed to use every inch of available space for productive means, seldom guided urban strategy; and there has long been a sense that the meaning of civic life should be integrated into daily life rather than segregated into plazas.

Americans turn instead to the open road to find meaning. The cities of California are, after all, the result of the great push into the West, the end of the American road leading toward manifest destiny. The conversion of lines of division into roads activates nature into a Jeffersonian grid pregnant with democratic activities. The road is the American society made real.[6] In California, the road is also the engine of growth, the place that allows the logic of this particular concatenation of economic forces to work its miracles; not only do freeways, strips, and cul-de-sacs make the place visible, as Reyner Banham well understood, but so do its spine, nerves, and overall structure.[7] The road is clearly the place to look for an order that might cohere and elaborate, rather than restrict,

our sense of our place. The more intelligent urban theorists do in fact look for order in the street. The one physical element proposed by writers such as Doug Suisman is the boulevard, which Suisman envisions as an imageable spine and appropriate connective network for a city as expansive as Los Angeles.[8]

Yet even this image, which would seem to hold the promise of a place of authentic alternative urban form, is made up of highly biased models. The grand metropolitan boulevard has become a trope in the description of the modern city. Ever since Baudelaire sang the praises of the new spaces of Paris, we have imagined that these homogenized and rationalized voids, cutting through the complexity of the urban corpus, form the true face (facade) of the city. These road voids are where the modern city performs its most important function—namely to appear.[9] They are also the visible embodiment of the vast system of infrastructural connections (mass transit, traffic, water and sewage distribution, and later, telecommunications) that constitutes the bourgeois body of the city—the skeleton of rationality on which the spectacle of self-definition can appear. The metropolitan boulevard is thus the embodiment not of the city, but of the modern city as it was built and used by the middle class. It is the place where the logic of economics carves out a space that is neither functional (of labor) nor controlling, but communicative and relational. It is the middle realm that mediates between productive citizens and the seductions of consumer society by providing a supposedly neutral scaffolding for development. The boulevard represents the most refined appearance of middle-class social space. This characterization is not meant as an indictment, but rather as a reminder of the programs that gave form to the spaces we regard today as models of public spheres.[10]

The boulevard finds its most perfect embodiment, perhaps ironically, in the American city, where it becomes a part of the omnivalent grid: it is merely the first among equals, the place where the middle class can display itself in a freedom guaranteed and framed by, but also limited to, the rational conceits of the modern city.[11] The boulevard is also the American vector of expansion, the embodiment of the principle of growth that justifies the cycle of production and consumption via the continual subjugation of reality.[12] Yet in cities like Los Angeles, the boulevard, in the process of marching across the countryside, has disintegrated. Its movement function has been taken over by the freeway system, whose speed and isolation remove it from the body politic. What is left of the boulevard is a formless void, its edges eaten out by parking lots, its presence marked by signs, and its rhythms so attenuated that it is difficult to see the boulevard as belonging to, or making sense out of, any particular community. The boulevard has become the strip.

This transformation is not unexplainable or natural. It is the direct result of an economic system allergic to the static and unproductive accumulation of capital, a system that instead seeks

capital mobility at all costs—a system that effectively prevents the formal configuration of the city because it must be continually redeveloped. The new spaces of the boulevards emerge as mere speculative fissures in the accumulated real worth of the city to be found in new neighborhoods, subdivisions, and suburban landscapes beyond urban confines. Capitalism destroys the space of labor—real space—as much as it destroys the individual. Human beings and their locations in space and time are, after all, resistant to the smooth flow of money and to the accumulation of capital. The perfect human being would be a neutral screen that would only consume; the perfect space would function only as storage for memory or for the utopia of the frictionless world that only money can buy.[13]

Thus the boulevard has become the strip whose formlessness, despite Robert Venturi and Denise Scott Brown's valiant efforts in the late 1960s, still defies description.[14] The strip has all the grandeur of the boulevard in terms of its scale and economic importance, but it has no true edge or border. Confined to a car, one is always physically removed from the experience of the strip, one experiences it solely as a spectacle. It is not only removed from any sense of the body (the real), but also escapes from most attempts to control it. The strip is empty because activities shrink behind parking lots and large signs, collapsing the actual space of the strip into those signs, whether of commerce or its lubrication (traffic signs). The strip is the place where the middle class disintegrates as it tries to look at itself from within a bubble of curved glass moving between forty-five and sixty miles per hour.

The real action, meanwhile, takes place within isolated interiors. The business of spectacle (or vice versa) now occurs inside the shopping mall. In its disconnection from both the infrastructure and the body politic, the mall makes it evident that the middle-class (or consumer) sphere is not the same as the open space of cognition, the public sphere. In the shopping mall, the public space is ersatz, appearing as the stage for such commercialized rituals as yearly visits to Santa Claus, or as the gathering place of teenagers and elderly people, who gravitate here by default because there is no true public space.[15]

Bourgeois critics are understandably upset by the demise of the boulevard as the prime locale for urban growth and self-display. To them, the replacement of the metropolitan street by both the high-speed highway and the enclosed shopping mall—way stations toward electronic connectivity, the complete dissolution of what we think of as public space—signals the withering away of community.[16] Yet when they cry for a return of public space—viewed as having been destroyed by an alien element, whether unbridled capitalism or uncontrolled and attenuating growth—all they are lamenting is the loss of the space that had represented and thus defined *them*. Again, the public space of the boulevard or its predecessor, the rationalized square of the late eighteenth century, is not a place where society as whole defines itself, but is instead where the middle class glorifies in consumption. This consumption is made possible by a rational spatial structure that promises an undefined and developable future rather than the closure of monumental structures. Whether behind barricades or in the sensuous caverns carved out behind their facades, such disenfranchised groups as the working class and women carved out spaces of resistance in opposition to the aggressive, grand assertions of the boulevard. By theorizing such spaces, critics created a space, an art, and a literature that justified them and in some ways made them.[17]

What bothers reactionary critics most is the emergence of a new kind of spatiality that defies traditional attempts to define it. This space is not only typified by suburban and exurban expansion, but also by the electronic sphere. It is quite simply the space that is left over: the space that is not. An emptying out implies the growth of a void, but voids are invisible and, by their very nature, formless. I speak here not of the defined spatiality that is made by and makes possible the rational structure of the bourgeois city, nor of the preexisting void that theorists of planned voids tend to postulate as the original and thus authentic condition, but the void that appears out of neglect or lack of focus.

This space is the opposite of the will to form. It is an inevitable result of the systematic attempt to create closure, since any such system sows the seeds of its own self-destruction. This space is created when the self-refining logic of production and consumption reduces physical barriers to ephemera that serve as informational switching stations—facades become signs, signs become systems of zeros and ones, and digits are turned into icons of symbolic logic that float through a placeless void.

One is ultimately reminded that space is no more than a socially determined form of measurement that, like time, allows us to locate ourselves in the world according to commonly recognized criteria. It is, in other words, an artificial interpretation of a particular relationship our body has to the physical world we experience as other. This interpretation is conditioned by social relations and, in turn, determines those relations.[18] Thus, it is not surprising that the transformation of a late-capitalist system into something we can only vaguely define—still—as "postmodern" involves the emergence of new forms of spatiality that feel as alien and formless to us as the metropolitan environment felt to those who first faced it from the feudal space of the fields.[19] Our notions of humanity, morality, and ethics are as bound up with the capitalist metropolitan environment as feudal categories were with the agricultural environment.[20] The disappearance of a space bounded by solid walls and defined by specific and static activities may be as revolutionary as the death of the humanist subject.[21] This is not meant to imply we are approaching Armageddon or will experience some kind of reverse big bang; rather, a socialized spatiality is emerging whose main characteristics are completely alien and incomprehensible to us, but which we, ironically, inhabit with great ease.[22]

The germ of a post-urban and post-Fordist world is thus located in the peculiar spaces created not by design, but by constraints that have emerged out of both the ruthless logic of our economic system and our attempts to form that logic. It is the space made by front lawns, driveways, turning radiuses, security perimeters, lines of sight (for both signs and advertisements), landing patterns, noise abatement programs, concentrations of economic energy into competitive arenas (speculative office parks), and setback requirements. It is the unfenced front yard and the zone lit by the television. It is the space of the parking lot that bleeds into the space of the highway. It is the space of the corner mini-mall or gas station. It is the uncertain depth of the screen. It is the space between edge cities, the space we "fill" with developable lots, potential communities, and service roads. It is the space of potential, speculation, and fantasy, not of rational reality. It is the space of the shopping mall, where all traditional elements of spatial control through structure— whether they are columns, corners, or staircases—elide into endless planes of glass and chrome, highlighted by the stage sets of postmodern recall. It is the space of the car interior, which falls somewhere in between a body suit, a prosthetic device, and the barrierless flow of high modernism. It is the antiseptic space of the airport or the hospital, where the reality of the body must be drowned by Muzak. It is the space of MTV, sliding away in imperceptible jumps from image to image.

This space does have certain characteristics, though not in the sense of a signature. It is profoundly modern in a simple, stylistic sense: it is planar and not volumetric; it is based on a divorce between its context, girded in by machined materials, and the artificial space it opens up; and it is extensive in its tendencies. Its planarity is predominantly horizontal and gridded, and dissolves at the edges. This space is quite close to the Miesian *beinahe nichts*.

This space is, therefore, highly anonymous and abstract, and difficult to picture. Invisible to the naked eye, this space only appears as if in the shadows—implied between two fast-food franchises, seeping out where servants wait for the bus in the shadow of the walled compound where they work, emerging as the space around one's seat in an airplane, or appearing when one turns on the electronic device that loads pixels on a screen. In other cases, this space is highly unstable, emerging *with* those same shadows or appearing only at night as the space created in the pools of security lighting in empty parking lots. It is the space of the empty lot waiting to be developed that now transforms into a garden, revealing the original vegetation of California before green grass was rolled over its rocky soil. It also appears in the abandoned building as a new kind of porous, unstable community where the homeless are not so much at home as they are, to use a telling phrase, hanging (out). It is also the place of illicit activity and the geography of cruising, as mapped by John Rechy and many perversely eager urban geographers: the space of the crack house, for cruising in cars, and once again the space lurking in the shadows.[23] Finally, it is the space of the edge, where urban form disintegrates and the desert or the space of the nomad dominates.[24]

Many other such spaces exist, sharing at least one other characteristic: almost all are universally derided by urban theorists as the detritus of modern society.[25] These spaces do not answer to any traditional notions of beauty, and serve no particular function; they are ungovernable, perhaps because they are unknowable.[26] They are supposed to be the very emblem of the dissolution of civic authority. They mark the extreme threats that now face a political system based on middle class values as it attempts to adapt itself to a post-Fordist, fluid world economy that is the economic equivalent or engenderer of postmodern culture. These are not pretty places or real places, only background noise that threatens to drown out the polite forms of a built polity.

In a sense, the emergence of these spaces justifies itself. It argues for the acceptance of the rhizomatic sprawl of a city like Los Angeles, which implies an acceptance of its essential formlessness. One can never really know or control this city, but can only participate in its continual transformation in a thoughtful manner. Rather than attempting to impose form on Los Angeles, one must discover the inherent relational networks and coherent markers or vectors within the sprawl and go, so to speak, with the flow.

Unfortunately, this statement does not seem to lead to concrete embodiment or action. It might lend itself to the *liebestod* of a novel like *Crash* or the morphing of Michael Jackson, but it does not seem to provide an architectural program.[27] Yet I would argue that there are three elements here that hold promise for engaging this postmodern spatiality: position, state change, and resistance. The first is the *hic stans* of modernist dogma. The second is the uncertain constitution of the postmodern persona. The third is the acceptance of the unformed, ugly void as a means of liberating oneself to a provisional awareness that might constitute one's essence.

Notions of position or pose have recently reemerged in the work of theorists as diverse as Richard Sennett, Félix Guattari and Donna Haraway.[28] It is interesting to note, however, that such thoughts go back at least as far as Siegfried Giedion, with his call for "man in equipoise," and thus lie at the very heart of the modernist enterprise of creating a free and open space in which we may reveal ourselves to be whatever it is we are becoming.[29] All believe in a subjectivity that is embodied in the body in motion, and in the process of taking a certain position that articulates itself into either artistic or socially measured coordinates. This body defines itself in action, creating a space for itself in the act of appropriation. It cannot use frames, only the focal point of the stage, whose edges bleed out beyond the spotlight. It dreams of continual extension.

Whether the models for such a spatial positioning are the dancer on the stage, the political *persona* acting, or the woman who places her body in question, they all make an argument for positioning one's own reality in the here and now. It is as a pose, by posing one's self, that one exists.[30] For architecture, this implies a building practice that is composite, contrapuntal, and provisional. This practice must refuse to solidify into a leaden-footed realization of one particular attitude, which inevitably becomes a tomb of the individual's position as soon as it is finished. It is as much a living thing as any part of our environment may be, rather than that to which we ascribe the function of object. This may be an architecture of the "event space."[31]

This position also implies the impossibility of architecture as a product to be delivered by one creator to a client, and instead sees it as a collaborative and continual effort.[32] This contentious and evolving position is not an easy thing to imagine within the traditional urban environment, where buildings must both have functions and contribute to the overall context of the community. It may imply that we engage in a process of change, unbuilding, and reconstruction, rather than creating recognizable objects.[33]

The notion of state change comes from the world of fluid dynamics: one can imagine the properties of an object most clearly at the moment when it is about to change state. Critics such as Manuel De Landa and Sanford Kwinter have looked to the epigenetic landscape—complete with its moments of crisis and nested unfolding of forms—as the paradigm for the formal unfolding of reality.[34] Despite the strangely deterministic flavor of some of their writing, their application of "high" science to aesthetics and philosophy implies an argument for an understanding of space as a fluid and nomadic phenomenon, and thus for a focus on that which has not (yet) formed over the solidified detritus of the process. Writers as diverse as Gilles Deleuze and Bruce Chatwin have explored the theoretical significance of nomadic cultures existing in a smooth and therefore idyllic space.[35] Fluid space, coupled with nomadic space, foregrounds qualities of mutability, unhierarchical organization, collage, allegory, palimpsest, and once again, lack of definition.[36] The combination argues for the kind of urban nomad William Gibson imagines inhabiting the deserts (or seas) of cyberspace.[37] This is not altogether a utopian vision. One can understand architecture as a moment of crisis that engenders an epigenetic landscape, and thus neither the act nor the inconceivable result will be heuristic.

One is left with a spatiality that exists only as the chance intersection of different positions, a spatiality that disappears as soon as it is defined, and a space that has so many guises it becomes uncatchable. Yet such a space is also liberating: it is the romantic wide-open road that American culture built as an escape clause into its myth of manifest destiny. It is a place of polymorphous perversity where one can wallow in orgiastic self-realization. But it is also the space of the shopping mall, the tract development, and the screen. I am not saying that these spaces are beautiful, meaningful, or desirable. Indeed, I am saying the exact opposite: they are anarchic spaces of self-presentation that cannot be judged, at least within the hierarchy of values we have created for architecture and urbanism. These spaces are the wide-open plains once thought to be this country's destiny where a new kind of man (not woman) could define himself in a new relationship to space and, according to Thomas Jefferson, to others.[38] The latter, however, turned

466

into the bloodstained field of ethnic and ecological massacre.

The destruction of the urban boulevard, the square, and the bounded environment actually may be a good thing because it dissolves the boundaries of thingness—but it also may lead to its own peculiar forms of violence. One cannot help but feel a sense of loss at the disappearance of good city form, just as the dissolution of the civic entity it embodies is profoundly frightening. I do not wish to comment on the desirability of this horror, but instead I offer a bit of translucent cover.

One can, *pace* Gottfried Semper, conceptualize architecture as a texture, a woven connective tissue that creates a communal image.[39] While cloth might cover and even shade, it neither completely buries nor keeps out nor has its own form. It is only a layer, a palimpsest, a weaving together of the many threads of life. One can think of urban form as connective tissue made up of the sinuous threads that weave our lives together every day. These threads, paradoxically, are voids: the streets, the data lines, the open spaces that allow us to use the city and see ourselves in that urban environment.[40] These voids cannot be made, but they can be woven together by carving them out of objects. We do not need to build a connective structure. Instead we need to weave our structures together by burrowing into them, destroying the false separations between inside and outside, reality and appearance, function and form, and between places by turning them into an amorphous web or landscape that may not look like anything itself, but is a space of appearance.[41]

There are different ways of creating such a space of liberation and uncertainty. This space would surely be Lars Lerup's "doublespace," where the mask of appearance or control and the mold of the body brush past each other, leaving something untold, unseen, and unknowable, but certainly worth appearing. It might also be, as outlined in the editorial scope of this book, the "slow space" that puts the fast moves of capitalist development into limbo. It is also the space of myths such as those invented by Lebbeus Woods, Neil Denari, and Diller + Scofidio, a reenacted space that traces normal life, but represents it as something warped, deformed and wonderful.[42]

Most profoundly, this might be a modernist space in which we loosen ourselves from the clothes of civilization, from its walls and its morality, in order to nakedly go wandering as new nomads. Of course, it is not empty space, but something that slides out between dense layers of economic, social, and physical determination as if restaged by a film director. To design this space means to direct the self-organizing systems of the city, as Sanford Kwinter has pointed out, and to wander through the real city along its real spaces—the formless blobs of streets and parking lots.[43] To be an architect in such a space might mean telling stories, having sex, or cutting holes in the fabric of the acceptable.

Certain artists (Richard Serra, Robert Irwin, Gordon Matta-Clark, James Turrell, and Robert Ryman come to mind) have perhaps been here already, providing us with markers as ephemeral as those elusive and illusive street spaces. The wizards at the Visual Language Workshop at MIT are mapping out blurred and soft-focus spaces of a profound modernism, spaces in which pieces of information, the building blocks of our reality, careen in and out of one's consciousness.

The most important characteristic of this space is that one cannot focus on it: the appropriated parking lot becomes a functional place, the building lot becomes a building, the sign reveals its limits. This space objectifies by subjecting us to the primacy of its preexisting rules or by absorbing us into a certain position. It is only seen in the rearview mirror and out of the corner of our eyes as the space of distraction, in which we constitute our selves as thinking subjects.[44] It is perhaps a space that is not a locus, not a foundation for the exercise of power or understanding, but is only what is left over after those actions have failed.

We need a cartography of this unknown and unknowable new continent of continual slippage, this sea of liquid movement that shapes so many of our experiences and sets us free in the modern world while continually drowning us. We must invent a language for Orange County, Orlando, Houston, and White Plains. We have no terms to judge, evaluate, or even describe these spaces or our behavior in them; thus we cannot behave. Some of the most interesting work currently occurring at the fringes of architectural theory is a drifting cataloging of exurban phenomena, or the telling of stories about these spaces.[45] Geography, geology, climate, economic statistics, the periodic rhythms of freeways, and the vestiges of forms are all part of the boundaries of such spaces.[46] It is only through an integrated, mythological narrative that we can even hope to find them.

The brightness of public space has been bleached out of the California landscape, replaced by the reflective glare of the strip. The corrosive space of the strip is everywhere, spreading even as we try to hem it in with such descriptions. This is not a dark vision, but one tinged with irony, regret, and hope. This mythic, in between, unstable, ephemeral, becoming, and pregnant space is, in the words of David Byrne, filled with "nothing but flowers." It is an Edenic vision of urban decay in which our attempt to bury the world under all the artifices of culture has disintegrated. Only the delight in the absence of good form rather than the solace of its presence can fill this modernist romance with all the joy of spatial experience.

This used to be real estate
Now it's only fields and trees
Where, where is the town
Now it's nothing but flowers.
　　　　　　　　　—David Byrne[47]

Notes

1. See Robert Fogelson, *The Fragmented Metropolis: Los Angeles 1850–1930* (Cambridge, Mass.: Harvard University Press, 1967).

2. In *City of Quartz* (London: Verso, 1991), Mike Davis has proven to be the most acute critic of this development, chronicling the transformation of Anglo power from a centralizing force to neighborhood politics. See also Steve Flusty, *Building Paranoia: The Proliferation of Interdictory Space and the Erosion of Spatial Justice* (Los Angeles: Los Angeles Forum for Architecture and Urban Design, 1994). For a historical perspective on the emergence of such spaces, see Evan McKenzie, *Privatopia: Homeowner Associations and the Rise of Residential Private Government* (New Haven: Yale University Press, 1994).

3. Neil Stephenson, *Snow Crash* (New York: Bantam Books, 1992), offers a compelling tale of the future of Los Angeles. Stephenson develops his outlook on a global scale in *The Diamond Age, or, A Young Lady's Illustrated Primer* (New York: Bantam Books, 1995). He conceptualizes "claves" as a revival of tribal communities in which dress, architecture, and custom create a coherent, but not place-specific, reality that seems independent of the actual structures of security. This sense is expanded in the second book by the notion that whole realities can be created in a microwave-like object, or by merely reading a book, so that many possible realities unfold in layers of dreams, expectations, interpretations, and experiences. Just as William Gibson predicted the Web, so did Stephenson seem to presage a confluence of nanotechnology and dispersed economics that will lead to a more fluid notion of our physical landscape.

4. The New Urbanists' writings reflect a certain blindness to the exclusionary nature of Greek politics, which restricted political decisions to male citizens.

5. See David Nye, *American Technological Sublime* (Cambridge, Mass.: MIT Press, 1996). Nye points out that such shared spaces evolved from the space of traditional festivals. These festivals, in which participatory events celebrated collective achievements, have been replaced by permanent yet electronic spectacles in which we are all just passive observers to a formless display.

6. The most brilliant chronicler of the influence of the road is John Brinckerhoff Jackson, whose essays on the subject are collected in *A Sense of Place, A Sense of Time* (New Haven: Yale University Press, 1994). I relied heavily on his work in my essay "Emptiness on the Range: Western Spaces," in *Crossing the Frontier: Images of the Developing West* (San Francisco: San Francisco Museum of Modern Art, 1996), 54–65.

7. Reyner Banham, *Los Angeles: The Architecture of Four Ecologies* (New York: Penguin Books, 1971), 75.

8. Douglas R. Suisman, *Los Angeles Boulevards: Eight X-Rays of the Body Public* (Los Angeles: Los Angeles Forum for Architecture and Urban Design, 1989).

9. The city of appearance has been chronicled by Mark Girouard in *Cities & People: A Social and Architectural History* (New Haven: Yale University Press, 1985). Walter Benjamin analyzed the importance of urban form in the construction of the middle-class personality in his "Passagen" fragments and especially "Paris, Capital of the Nineteenth Century," both in *Reflections: Essays, Aphorisms, Autobiographical Writings*, trans. Edmund Jephcott (New York: Schocken Books, 1978), 146–162. The notion of a clearly defined urban space that would help to create a more rational construction of the (middle-class) self, and therefore the ideal overall polity has of course been central to the urban theories of most modern masters, most importantly Le Corbusier in his calls for a "cité d'affaires." This notion continued beyond modernist styles into Edmund Bacon's exhortations for legible cities at a vast scale in *Design of Cities* (New York: Viking Press, 1967); and into Oscar Newman's idea that we need to create a safer environment by creating empty spaces, in *Defensible Space: Crime Prevention through Urban Design* (New York: Macmillan, 1972). Only recently have urban theorists, starting with Kevin Lynch and continuing with Colin Rowe and Peter Rowe, started to propose models in which a degree of illegibility, enigma, or monumentality has a place. See especially Peter G. Rowe, *Making a Middle Landscape* (Cambridge, Mass.: MIT Press, 1991).

10. Paris has been used as a model for all urban growth in the theories of most theoreticians, from Spiro Kostof to

Manfredo Tafuri. It remains a model for recent critiques of modernist traditions such as those mentioned in the note above. Perhaps only Lewis Mumford, in his *The City in History* (New York: Harcourt, Brace, 1961), has offered a counter to such fixations by focusing on industrial and exurban growth phenomena. Feminist critics are also beginning to look towards antimonumental, accretional spaces as alternatives to the "slash and burn" clarity of the boulevard.

11. For an exploration of the role the boulevard has played in the image of the sanitized and "progressive" American city, see William H. Wilson, *The City Beautiful Movement* (Baltimore: Johns Hopkins University Press, 1989). Even though this book concentrates mainly on the formal achievements of the movement, Wilson traces the attempt by the middle class to bring order to an environment under threat from different urban models, both imported by immigrants and emerging as the result of changing technologies.

12. See especially Mario Manieri-Ella, "Toward an 'Imperial City': Daniel H. Burnham and the City Beautiful Movement," in Giorgio Ciucci, Francesco Dal Co, Mario Manieri-Elia, and Manfredo Tafuri, *The American City from the Civil War to the New Deal*, trans. Barbara Luigia La Penta (London: Granada, 1979).

13. David Harvey, *The Urban Experience* (Baltimore: Johns Hopkins University Press, 1989), provides the best synopsis of these theories, which find philosophical counterpoints in the works of Jean-François Lyotard and Jean Baudrillard, though Harvey remains equally rooted in Marxist theory. One could argue that such notions of an economically transparent spatiality are implied by Marx's famous proclamation that "all that is solid melts into air." "Being the external, common medium and faculty for turning an image into reality and reality into a mere image (a faculty not springing from man as man or from human society as society), money transforms the real essential powers of man and nature into what are merely abstract conceits and therefore imperfections—into tormenting chimeras—just as it transforms real imperfections and chimeras—essential powers which are really impotent, which exist only in the imagination of the individual—into real powers and faculties." *The Economic and Philosophic Manuscripts of 1844*, ed. Dirk J. Struik,

trans. Martin Milligan (New York: International Publishers, 1977), 168–169.

14. Robert Venturi, Denise Scott Brown, "Learning from Pop," in *Casabella* (December 1971), 15–23; and *Signs of Life: Symbols in the American City* (New York: Aperture, 1976).

15. See Michael Sorkin, ed., *Variations on a Theme Park* (London: Verso, 1992).

16. See Andres Duany and Elizabeth Plater-Zyberk, *Towns and Town Planning Principles* (New York: Rizzoli, 1991); and Peter Calthorpe, *The Next American Metropolis: Ecology, Community, and the American Dream* (New York: Princeton Architectural Press, 1993).

17. See Aaron Betsky, *Building Sex: Men, Women, Architecture, and the Construction of Sexuality* (New York: William Morrow, 1995).

18. See Henri Lefebvre, *The Production of Space*, trans. Donald Nicholson-Smith (Oxford: Blackwell Publishers, 1991).

19. Notions of "late" or "post" modernity continue to battle for recognition as the most adequate description of our current social, cultural, and economic condition. Questions about whether we are witnessing a fundamental shift in our situation, or only a future development of capitalism, guide these deliberations. For purposes of this essay, I have arbitrarily chosen the term "postmodern," though I do not believe that we are by definition able to have a current perspective on the absolute nature of these developments.

20. See Michel Foucault, *The Order of Things: An Archaeology of the Human Sciences* (New York: Vintage Books, 1973).

21. This position is argued persuasively by Donna Haraway in *Simians, Cyborgs and Women: The Reinvention of Nature* (New York: Routledge, 1991), though several other critics have followed Foucault's questioning of the notion of humanity as an absolute. More recently, Anthony Vidler has picked up on Haraway's images and grounded them in the history of architectural modernism in his book *The Architectural Uncanny: Essays in the Modern Unhomely* (Cambridge, Mass.: MIT Press, 1992). Certainly the emergence of artificial life, as well as the realization that traditional notions of humanity and its freedom are both culturally conditioned and sometimes destructive, forces us to reappraise what makes us human.

470

22. For critics such as William Mitchell, these spaces might liberate us into a kind of plugged-in posthumanism: "Once you break the bounds of your bag of skin in this way, you will also begin to blend into the architecture. In other words, some of your electronic organs may be built into your surroundings. There is no great difference, after all, between a laptop computer and a desktop model, between a wristwatch and a clock on the wall, or between a hearing aid fitted into your ear and a special public telephone for the hard-of-hearing in its little booth. It is just a matter of what the organ is physically attached to, and that is of little importance in a wireless world where every electronic device has some built-in computation and telecommunications capacity. So 'inhabitation' will take on a new meaning—one that has less to do with parking your bones in architecturally defined space and more with connecting your nervous system to nearby electronic organs. Your room and your home will become part of you, and you will become part of them." William J. Mitchell, *City of Bits: Space, Place, and the Infobahn* (Cambridge, Mass.: MIT Press, 1995), 30.

23. John Rechy, *City of Night* (New York: Grove Weidenfeld, 1988), and *The Sexual Outlaw: A Documentary* (New York: Grove Weidenfeld, 1977). See also Edward William Delph, *The Silent Community: Public Homosexual Encounters* (Beverly Hills, Calif.: Sage Publications, 1978); or David Woodhead, "'Surveillant Gays': HIV, Space, and the Constitution of Identities," in David Bell and Gill Valentine eds., *Mapping Desire: Geographies of Sexualities* (London: Routledge, 1995), 231–244. The first study of sexual cruising, however, is Laud Humphreys, *Tearoom Trade: Impersonal Sex in Public Spaces* (Chicago: Aldine Publishing Company, 1970). For a perhaps more evocative text, see John Greyson, *Urinal and Other Stories* (Toronto: Art Metropole and the Power Plant, 1993).

24. Joe Deal, *Joe Deal: Southern California Photographs, 1976–86* (Albuquerque: Univ. of New Mexico Press, 1992).

25. Though some recognize its inevitability, especially David Harvey, in *The Urban Experience* (Baltimore: Johns Hopkins University Press, 1985).

26. These spaces are unknowable if one assumes, as most urbanists do, that knowledge is only possible through direct sensory experience—what Hannah Arendt calls "knowledge" versus "understanding." Hannah Arendt, *The Life of the Mind: Thinking* (New York: Harcourt Brace Jovanovich, 1971).

27. J. G. Ballard, *Crash* (New York: Random House, 1985).

28. Richard Sennett, *The Conscience of the Eye: The Design and Social Life of Cities* (New York: Knopf, 1990); Donna Haraway, *Simians, Cyborgs and Women: The Reinvention of Nature* (New York: Routledge, 1991); Félix Guattari, "Deterritorialized," in *Semiotext(e): Architecture* (New York: Semiotext(e), 1992), 116–154.

29. Siegfried Giedion, *Mechanization Takes Command: A Contribution to Anonymous History* (New York: W. W. Norton, 1969), 714–723.

30. This is a notion that I further explore in *Queer Space: The Spaces of Same Sex Desire* (New York: William Morrow, 1997).

31. The best description of such theories is to be found in Bernard Tschumi's "Six Concepts" in *Architecture and Disjunction* (Cambridge, Mass.: MIT Press, 1994), 226–259, as well as in his *Event Cities* (Cambridge, Mass.: MIT Press, 1994).

32. See Dana Cuff, *Architecture: The Story of Practice* (Cambridge, Mass.: MIT Press, 1991).

33. It thus implies the death of the architectural profession as we know it today.

34. Manuel De Landa, "Nonorganic Life," in *Zone 6: Incorporations*, eds. Jonathan Crary and Sanford Kwinter (New York: Zone Books, 1992), 129–167.

35. Gilles Deleuze and Félix Guattari, *A Thousand Plateaus: Capitalism and Schizophrenia,* trans. Brian Massumi (Minneapolis: University of Minnesota Press, 1987); Bruce Chatwin, *The Songlines* (New York: Penguin Books, 1987).

36. This is certainly a Derridean position. See Gregory Ulmer, "The Object of Post-Criticism," in *The Anti-Aesthetic : Essays on Postmodern Culture,* ed. Hal Foster (Seattle: Bay Press, 1983), 83–110.

37. William Gibson, *Neuromancer* (New York: Ace Books, 1984), *Count Zero* (New York: Ace Books, 1987), and *Mona Lisa Overdrive* (New York: Bantam Books, 1989). In more recent books, such as *Virtual Light* (New York: Bantam Books,

471

1993), Gibson has translated this nomadic life into a rein-
habitation of existing urban structures.

38. Thomas Jefferson, *Notes on the State of Virginia* [1787], in
Merrill D. Peterson, ed., *The Portable Thomas Jefferson*
(New York: Penguin Books, 1975), 23–232.

39. Gottfried Semper, *The Four Elements of Architecture*, trans.
Harry Francis Mallgrave and Wolfgang Hermann (New York:
Cambridge University Press, 1989).

40. This position has been most eloquently and romantically
phrased by Aldo Rossi in *Scientific Autobiography*, trans.
Lawrence Venuti (Cambridge, Mass.: MIT Press, 1981).

41. I am aware of the Heideggerian uses of this term, especial-
ly in his *Early Greek Thinking: The Dawn of Western
Philosophy*, trans. David Farrell Krell and Frank A. Capuzzi
(San Francisco: Harper & Row, 1984).

42. Myth is understood here as a story about a world that may
have once existed, may come to exist at some point in the
future, or may currently exist in a place or form that one cannot experience. What matters is that the story is possible
and feasible, but not identical to the world one experiences.

43. Sanford Kwinter, conversation with author, April 23, 1995.

44. This notion derives from Walter Benjamin's "The Work of Art
in the Age of Mechanical Reproduction" [1932] in
Illuminations, trans. Harry Zohn (New York: Harcourt Brace
Jovanovich, Inc, 1969), 217–251, 236–237. The space of
distraction is the space Benjamin claims for architecture
and, by implication, for an antifascist art.

45. Much of this work is occurring at the Southern California
Institute of Architecture, where professors Margaret
Crawford and John Kaliski are directing studios that adapt
Situationist International tactics of drift or "derive" to create
interpretations and intensifications of found fragments of
urban fabric. For a more prosaic, but evocative cataloging of
such spaces, see also Grady Clay, *Real Places: An
Unconventional Guide to America's Generic Landscape*
(Chicago: University of Chicago Press, 1994).

46. See Lars Lerup, "Stim & Dross: Rethinking the Metropolis,"
in *Assemblage* 25 (1994), 82–101.

47. Talking Heads, *(Nothing But) Flowers* (Warner Brothers, 1988).

BETSKY

Houston

About the Contributors

Stan Allen is an architect and Assistant Professor at the Columbia University Graduate School of Architecture, Planning, and Preservation. He holds degrees from Brown University, the Cooper Union, and Princeton University.

Polly Apfelbaum is a sculptor and installation artist. Her work was recently featured at the Museum of Modern Art, New York, in "Sense and Sensibility: Women and Minimalism in the Nineties."

Michael Bell teaches at the Rice School of Architecture, Houston, Texas. His work has been recognized in the *Progressive Architecture* Design Awards Program and has been exhibited at the San Francisco Museum of Modern Art and at the University Art Museum, Berkeley. He is a graduate of the University of California at Berkeley where he taught between 1987 and 1993.

Karen Bermann is Assistant Professor of architecture at Iowa State University. She has also taught at the University of California at Berkeley and at the University of Kentucky. Her work has been published in *Art Forum* and received one of four awards for a design that commemorated an African American gravesite in Lower Manhattan. She received an M.F.A. from the San Francisco Art Institute and a B.Arch from Cooper Union.

Aaron Betsky is curator of architecture and design at the San Francisco Museum of Modern Art. He has written several books, including *Violated Perfection: Architecture and the Fragmentation of the Modern, James Gamble Rogers and the Architecture of Pragmatism, Building Sex: Men, Women, and the Construction of Sexuality,* and *Queer Space.* He holds a Masters degree in architecture from Yale University.

Jeanine Centuori is a licensed architect and Professor in the architecture department at Kent State University, Ohio. She has a design practice with projects for communities, memorials, buildings, and landscape.

Yung-Ho Chang is the principal architect of Atelier Feichang Jianzhu in Beijing and an Assistant Professor of architecture at Rice University in Houston. He is currently working on the definition of three Chinese spaces: the traditional, the revolutionary, and the post-revolutionary.

Durham Crout practices architecture in Atlanta, Georgia and is a Ph.D. candidate at the University of Pennsylvania.

Dana Cuff is Professor of Architecture and Urban Design at the University of California at Los Angeles. Her writings focus primarily on the social production of the built environment, particularly architectural practice and professionalism. She also consults on community planning and affordable housing.

Hubert L. Dreyfus is Professor of Philosophy at the University of California, Berkeley. His books include *Michel Foucault: Beyond Structuralism and Hermeneutics* (with Paul Rabinow) and *Being-in-the-World.*

Farès el-Dahdah is Assistant Professor of architecture at the Rice School of Architecture. He is currently involved in the restoration of the Beirut National Museum. He holds a Doctor of Design degree from Harvard University.

Elizabeth Burns Gamard is Adjunct Associate Professor of architecture at Tulane University. She is the author of the forthcoming book on Kurt Schwitters entitled *Die Kathedrale des Erotischen Elends* (The Cathedral of Erotic Misery).

Steven Holl is Professor of architecture at Columbia University. He established Steven Holl Architects in New York City in 1976. Among his many buildings are the Stretto House, Dallas; Void Space/Hinged Space Housing, Fukuoka, Japan; the Berkowitz-Odgis House, Martha's Vineyard; and the soon-to-be-completed Museum of Contemporary Art, Helsinki. His first monograph, *Anchoring,* was published in 1989. His work has been exhibited and published widely.

476

Sze Tsung Leong is currently at the Harvard University Graduate School of Design where he is involved in research with the Harvard Project on the City. He is also assembling *The Charged Void: The Complete Works of Alison and Peter Smithson*, to be published by The Monacelli Press.

Lars Lerup is the Dean and the Harry K. and Albert K. Smith Chair at the Rice School of Architecture in Houston. He has written several books, most recently *Planned Assaults* (1987), and is one of the principals of LMNOP. He is a fellow of the Rice Center for Urbanism.

Greg Lynn teaches at Columbia University in New York and at the University of California at Los Angeles. He is the principal of Greg Lynn FORM, in Hoboken, New Jersey. He edited *Folding in Architecture* (Academy Editions) and is a frequent contributor to *ANY* magazine. He is a graduate of Princeton University.

Robert Mangurian is one of the principals of Studio Works along with Mary-Ann Ray, founded in 1969 along with Keith Godard, Craig Hodgetts, and Lester Walker. He is also Director of the graduate program in architecture at the Southern California Institute of Architecture. He holds degrees from Stanford University and from the University of California at Berkeley.

Rebeca Méndez is an artist and the principal of Rebeca Méndez Design in Los Angeles. Her work includes projects for the Getty Museum in Los Angeles and the Whitney Museum in New York, and is included in the permanent collection at the Cooper-Hewitt Design Museum in New York. From 1991 to 1996 she was Design Director at Art Center College of Design in Pasadena.

Albert Pope is an architect in Houston, Texas. He is the author of *Ladders* and is Wortham Professor at the Rice School of Architecture. He holds degrees from the Southern California Institute of Architecture and Princeton University.

Julieanna Preston teaches architectural design and construction technology at Victoria University in Wellington, New Zealand. Her research is best identified as the practice of the building arts, including ongoing investigations of the relations between architecture and sewing.

Mary-Ann Ray is a principal of Studio Works in Los Angeles along with Robert Mangurian. She holds degrees from the University of Washington and Princeton University, is the recipient of the Rome Prize of 1987–88, and currently teaches at the Southern California Institute of Architecture.

Jesse Reiser is an architect practicing in New York and educated at the Cooper Union and Cranbrook Academy. He is presently Assistant Professor at the Columbia University Graduate School of Architecture, Planning and Preservation.

Stanley Saitowitz practices in San Francisco. He has built extensively, including nine structures at Mill Race Park, Columbus, Indiana, the Boston Holocaust Memorial, and the San Francisco Embarcadero Promenade. He is Professor of architecture at U.C. Berkeley. His work was the subject of the exhibition "Geological Architecture," curated by the Walker Art Center, and shown in the San Francisco Museum of Modern Art and at the Harvard Graduate School of Design.

Álvaro Siza is an architect in Oporto, Portugal. He has built in France, Germany, Holland, Italy, Portugal, and Spain. Among his many buildings and projects are the Malagueira Residential District, Évora, and the reconstruction of the Chiado District, Lisbon. Siza has received numerous awards for his works including the Gold Medal of the Alvar Aalto Foundation, the European Prize for Architecture from the Mies van der Rohe Foundation, and the Pritzker Prize.

Adi Shamir Zion is principal of Eurydice, a San Francisco–based design company. She is also a New York Foundation of the Arts Fellow, Adjunct Professor of architecture at the California College of Arts and Crafts, and has taught at the

University of California at Berkeley, the Cooper Union School of Architecture, College of Marin, and Rice School of Architecture. She is a graduate of the Cooper Union School of Architecture.

Robert Smithson (1938–1973) was one of the most important and influential artists of his generation. His most famous work is *Spiral Jetty*, built in the Great Salt Lake in Utah.

Peter Testa is an architect practicing in New York and Los Angeles. He has collaborated since 1984 with Álvaro Siza on buildings and projects in Europe and the United States. His work and writings have appeared in international journals and he is the author of *Álvaro Siza* published by Birkhäuser Verlag in 1996. He is Associate Professor in the Graduate School of Architecture, Planning and Preservation, Columbia University.

Nanako Umemoto studied urban design and landscape architecture in Osaka, Japan, before coming to New York, where she received an architecture degree at the Cooper Union. She is presently in private practice in New York.

Mark Wamble is an architect and an Assistant Professor at the Rice School of Architecture. He formed Interloop Architects in the spring of 1993. He received degrees from Texas A&M and Harvard University.

"Doublespace": pages 26, 43, Chris Marker, *La Jetée* (New York: Zone Books, 1992). **"Still Architecture"**: page 47, José M. Rodrigues; 48, 54, 56, 57, 58, 61, 62, 65, Hisao Suzuki; 50, 53, Luis Ferreira Alves; 66, Richard Bryant. **"Having Heard Mathematics: The Topologies of Boxing"**: page 79, Ivars Peterson, *The Mathematical Tourist: Snapshots of Modern Mathematics* (New York: W. H. Freeman, 1988), 56–59; 80, 82 top, 84 bottom, Guy Vinson; 83, Milton Van Dyke, *An Album of Fluid Motion* (Stanford, Calif: The Parabolic Press, 1982), 134; 94, R. C. Dove, *Experimental Stress Analysis and Motion Measurement* (Columbus, Ohio: Charles E. Merrill, 1964); 96 right, *Discretization Methods in Structural Mechanics*, ed. G. Kuhn and H. Mang; 104 top, J. E. Gordon, *The New Science of Strong Materials* (London: Penguin, 1968); 109, Hans C. Ohanian, *Physics* (New York: W. W. Norton, 1985). 118–9, City of Houston. **"Community Property: Enter the Architect, or, The Politics of Form"**: pages 120, 127, 141–4, Sze Tsung Leong; 125, John W. Reps, *The Making of Urban America* (Princeton: Princeton University Press, 1965), 217. **"The Unconstructed Subject of the Contemporary City"**: page 160, Bill Owens, *Suburbia* (San Francisco: Straight Arrow, 1973); 171, 173, 175, 177, Robert Longo, *Men in the Cities* (New York: Harry N. Abrams, 1986); 179, 184–5, Sze Tsung Leong. **"Readings of the Attenuated Landscape"**: pages 186, 197, Douglas Aikenhead, reprinted from John J. Bukowczyk and Douglas Aikenhead with Peter Slavcheff, eds., *Detroit Images: Photographs of the Renaissance City* (Detroit: Wayne State University Press, 1989) by permission of the Wayne State University Press; 192–3, 198, 202, 211, 214–9, Sze Tsung Leong; 208–9, Mark Takeuchi. **"Knee Play"**: all images by Mark Wamble. **"Croton Aqueduct Study"**: all images by RAAUm. **"Artists' Space Installation / The Parsing Eye"**: page 256, Hans Maria Wingler, *The Bauhaus* (Cambridge, Mass.: MIT Press, 1969); 260, David H. Hubel, *Eye Brain, and Vision* (Scientific American Library, 1988); 264, 266, Harold Edgerton, *Moments of Vision* (Cambridge, Mass.: MIT Press, 1979). All other images by Greg Lynn. **"Gaining a Free Relation to Technology"**: page 272, Range/Bettmann/ UPI. **"We Play until Death Shuts the Door"**: page 306, Meyer-Veden, Hamburg. **"The Rapture"**: page 318, From John Gash, *Caravaggio* (London: Jupiter Books, 1980), 106; 319, Ferran, Barcelona, from Robert Descharnes, *Gaudi The Visionary* (New York: Viking Press, 1982), 137; 320, from C. Bertelli, *Piero della Francesca* (New York: Viking Press, 1992), pl. 1.151; 325, from Eugenio Battisti, *Cimabue* (Philadelphia: Pennsylvania State University Press, 1967); 324, Sze Tsung Leong; 326 left, Juan Matamala, Barcelona, from Descharnes, 135; 326 right, 330, Alfonso Opisso, Mataro, from Descharnes, 134–5; 332, from Rainer Zerbst, *Antonio Gaudí* (Germany: Benedikt & Taschen Verlag, 1989), 234. **"Mill Race Park"**: photographs by Richard Barnes and Stanley Saitowitz. **"Museum of Contemporary Art, Helsinki / Over Dilation, Over Soul"**: page 399, Le Corbusier, *Oeuvre Complète 1957–65* (Zurich: Artemis, 1965), 136, 139. All other images: Steven Holl. **"Latent Parallelepipeds"**: photographs were provided by the Lebanese General Directorate of Antiquities. **"Nothing but Flowers: Against Public Space"**: pages 456, 460, 464, 473–5, Sze Tsung Leong; 479–80, city of Houston.

Houston